WEBSTER'S
FAMILY
ENCYCLOPEDIA

WEBSTER'S FAMILY ENCYCLOPEDIA

VOLUME 3

1995 Edition

Exclusively distributed by
Archer Worldwide, Inc.
Great Neck, New York, USA

Abbreviations Used in Webster's Family Encyclopedia

AD	After Christ	ht	height	N.M.	New Mexico
Adm.	Admiral	i.e.	that is	NNE	north-northeast
Ala.	Alabama	in	inches	NNW	north-northwest
Apr	April	Ind.	Indiana	Nov	November
AR	Autonomous Republic	Ill.	Illinois	NW	northwest
		Jan	January	N.Y.	New York
at no	atomic number	K	Kelvin	OAS	Organization of American States
at wt	atomic weight	Kans.	Kansas		
Aug	August	kg	kilograms	Oct	October
b.	born	km	kilometers	Okla.	Oklahoma
BC	Before Christ	kph	kilometers per hour	OPEC	Organization of Petroleum Exporting Countries
bp	boiling point				
C	Celsius, Centigrade	kW	kilowatts		
		lb	pounds	Pa.	Pennsylvania
c.	circa	Lt.	Lieutenant	PLO	Palestine Liberation Organization
Calif.	California	Lt. Gen.	Lieutenant General		
Capt.	Captain			Pres.	President
CIS	Commonwealth of Independent States	m	meters	R.I.	Rhode Island
		M. Sgt.	Master Sergeant	S	south, southern
		Mar	March	S.C.	South Carolina
cm	centimeters	Mass.	Massachusetts	SE	southeast
Co.	Company	Md.	Maryland	Sen.	Senator
Col.	Colonel	mi	miles	Sept	September
Conn.	Connecticut	Mich.	Michigan	Sgt.	Sergeant
d.	died	Minn.	Minnesota	sq mi	square miles
Dec	December	Miss.	Mississippi	SSE	south-southeast
Del.	Delaware	mm	millimeters	SSW	south-southwest
E	east, eastern	Mo.	Missouri	SW	southwest
EC	European Community	MP	Member of Parliament	Tenn.	Tennessee
				Tex.	Texas
e.g.	for example	mp	melting point	UN	United Nations
est	estimated	mph	miles per hour	US	United States
F	Fahrenheit	N	north, northern	USSR	Union of Soviet Socialist Republics
Feb	February	NATO	North Atlantic Treaty Organization		
Fl. Lt.	Flight Lieutenant				
Fla.	Florida			Va.	Virginia
ft	feet	NE	northeast	Vt.	Vermont
Ga.	Georgia	Neb.	Nebraska	W	west, western
Gen.	General	N.H.	New Hampshire	wt	weight
Gov.	Governor	N.J.	New Jersey		

Choiseul, Étienne François, Duc de (1719–85) French statesman; foreign minister (1758–70). As ambassador to Vienna in 1757 he began negotiations for the marriage of Marie Antoinette to the future Louis XVI. He secured good terms for France in the Treaty of *Paris at the close of the Seven Years' War (1763). The influence of Louis XV's mistress, Mme *Du Barry, undermined his position at court and he was exiled in 1770.

cholera An acute infection of the intestine caused by the bacterium *Vibrio cholerae*, which is transmitted in drinking water contaminated by feces of a patient. Epidemics of cholera occur in regions where sanitation is poor. After an incubation period of 1–5 days, cholera causes severe vomiting and diarrhea, which—untreated—leads to dehydration that can be fatal. Treatment consists of replacement of fluid and salts by intravenous injections. Vaccinations against cholera provide only temporary immunity.

cholesterol A compound derived from steroids and found in many animal tissues. Cholesterol is manufactured by the liver and other tissues and its derivatives form constituents of cell membranes, bile, blood, and gallstones. High levels of cholesterol in the blood have been associated with an increased risk of heart disease, as a result of fatty deposits in the walls of arteries. *See also* atherosclerosis.

Cholon 10 45N 106 39E A port in S Vietnam, a part since 1932 of present-day *Ho Chi Minh City. It is the city's Chinese quarter (founded c. 1778). A trading center for rice and fish, it has rice-milling, timber, and pottery industries. It suffered badly during the Vietnam War.

Cholula (*or* Cholula de Rivadabia) 19 05N 98 20W A town in central Mexico. A major religious center dedicated to the god Quetzalcoatl before the Spanish conquest, it is the site of a pyramid 177 ft (53 m) high, which was begun in the Teotihuacán period and subsequently enlarged.

Chomsky, Noam (1928–) US linguist, under whose influence the aims and methods of general linguistic theory and especially of *grammar were radically revised. His writings on the subject include *Syntactic Structures* (1957) and *Aspects of the Theory of Syntax* (1965). Chomsky's work draws on and develops that of his teacher Zellig *Harris. Chomsky has also undertaken controversial studies of the theory of speech sounds and of semantic structures.

Ch'ŏngjin 41 50N 129 55E A city and seaport in North Korea, on the NE coast. Originally a small fishing village, it developed rapidly under Japanese occupation (1910–45). It is an important center for the manufacture of iron and steel; other industries include shipbuilding, chemicals, and textiles. Population (1987 est): 520,000.

Chongqing (Ch'ung ch'ing *or* Chungking) 29 32N 106 45E A port in central China, in Sichuan province at the confluence of the Yangtze and Jialing (*or* Chia-ling) Rivers. A major commercial and industrial center, it is a former capital of China (1937–46). Population (1990): 2,266,772.

Chopin, Frédéric (François) (1810–49) Polish composer and pianist of French descent. He studied in Warsaw but later settled in Paris and never returned to Poland. He lived with the novelist George *Sand from 1838 to 1847, but never married her. A fervent nationalist, he was a student of Polish culture and much of his music was influenced by Polish folk music. He developed a highly characteristic style of writing for the piano, for which he composed 2 concertos, 3 sonatas, 24 preludes, and many waltzes, nocturnes, polonaises, and studies. He also wrote a cello sonata, a piano trio, and songs.

Chordata A phylum of animals that comprises the primitive *protochordates and the vertebrates (*see* Vertebrata). They are distinguished from other animals by three features: a hollow dorsal nerve cord; a rodlike *notochord that forms the basis of the internal skeleton; and paired gill slits in the wall of the pharynx behind the head, although in higher chordates these are apparent only in early embryonic stages.

chorea Involuntary jerky movements, particularly of the hips, shoulders, and face, caused by disease of the part of the brain controlling voluntary movement. Sydenham's chorea—formerly known as *St Vitus's dance—is often associated with rheumatic fever in children. It causes no permanent damage and responds to sedatives.

choreography The art of composing *ballet and other theatrical dances. Choreography originally referred only to a dance notation, the lack of which has made precise reconstruction of many ballets difficult. The most comprehensive system for recording dance steps is that devised by the Hungarian dancer Rudolph Laban (1829–1958), known as Labanotation. The choreographer is usually a professional dancer, who selects, arranges into sequences, and teaches the dancers each step of the dance. Often he works in close collaboration with composers, notable partnerships being between *Tchaikovsky and *Petipa and *Stravinsky and *Fokine. Famous contemporary choreographers include *Robbins, *Béjart, *Ashton, and *Balanchine.

chorus **1.** In Greek drama, a group of actors who described and commented on the dramatic action through dance, song, and chanting. Greek tragedy originated in songs and dances performed by a chorus in honor of Dionysus. The dramas of Aeschylus were performed by a chorus and only two actors, but its dramatic role declined in the plays of Sophocles (who introduced a third actor) and Euripides. The chorus, not directly involved in the actions of the main protagonists, represented the responses and judgments of average humanity. Its role has been revived in certain plays by *Brecht, Eugene *O'Neill, and T. S. *Eliot. **2.** A body of singers or dancers who perform together (in contrast to soloists) as in opera or ballet.

Chorzów 50 19N 18 56E A city in SW Poland. One of Silesia's first coal mining centers (1790), it remains a major mining and metallurgical town. Population (1992 est): 132,000.

Chota Nagpur. *See* Bihar.

Chou. *See* Zhou.

Chouans Peasants in W France, including dealers in contraband salt, who revolted in 1793 against the government established by the French Revolution. They were provoked by such measures as the abolition of the salt tax (which ruined the contraband trade) and the enforcement of conscription. The revolt, ultimately unsuccessful, is the subject of Balzac's *Les Chouans* (1829).

Chou En-lai (*or* Zhou En Lai; 1898–1976) Chinese communist statesman; prime minister (1949–76) and foreign minister (1949–58). Chou studied in Japan, France, and Germany. In 1924 he became a political instructor at the Whampoa Military Academy and secretary of the Canton provincial Communist Party. He led workers in the 1927 general strike in Shanghai, after which he escaped *Guomindang (Nationalist) assassins and fled to Nanchang, where he helped to organize an uprising. In 1932 he became political commissar to the Red Army and during the *Sino-Japanese War (1937–45) his reputation as a negotiator grew. After the establishment in 1949 of the People's Republic of China, he gained worldwide prominence as a diplomat and at home was largely responsible for establishing communist China's bureaucracy. Regarded as a moderate he exercised a stabilizing influence on his extremist colleagues.

CHOU EN-LAI *A communist from his student days in France, the Chinese statesman played a prominent part in the establishment (1949) of the People's Republic of China, exerting a moderating influence on policy until his death.*

chough A large black songbird, *Pyrrhocorax pyrrhocorax*, about 14 in (37 cm) long, with red legs and a long red down-curved bill. It occurs in the Alps, Spain, and a few sea cliffs around Britain where it can be seen giving displays of aerial acrobatics. The yellow-billed Alpine chough (*P. graculus*) occurs at high altitudes in European mountains. Family: *Corvidae* (crows).

Chou Shu-jen. *See* Lu Xun.

Chouteau, (René) Auguste (1749–1829) US pioneer and fur trader. Born in New Orleans, he worked for fur trading companies on the Mississippi and Missouri rivers. He helped to build the city of St Louis, Mo. and, when Missouri became part of the US, he served the city and federal government in several capacities. With his half-brother **(Jean) Pierre Chouteau** (1758–1849) he controlled trade with the Osage Indians. By 1804 Pierre was the agent for all the Indian tribes west of the Mississippi and in 1809 founded the St Louis Missouri Fur Company.

chow chow A breed of □dog originating in China more than 200 years ago. The chow has a compact body and—unusually—a blue-black tongue. The thick coat forms a mane around the neck and shoulders and the tail is held well over the back. Height: 18–20 in (46–51 cm).

Chretien, Jean Jacques (1934–) Canadian political leader and prime minister (1993–). A lawyer and Quebec native who opposed Quebec separatism, he was elected to the House of Commons in 1963 and held numerous cabinet posts under prime ministers Lester *Pearson and Pierre *Trudeau. In 1990 he won the party leadership, becoming prime minister in November 1993 after the Liberals defeated the Progressive Conservatives led by Kim *Campbell in a landslide. His initial concern was to revive Canada's economy, and he supported the *NAFTA (North American Free Trade Agreement) pact.

Chrétien de Troyes (12th century AD) French poet, author of the earliest romances dealing with the *Arthurian legend. His octosyllabic verse introduced a psychological subtlety in the treatment of *courtly love and chivalry that contrasts strongly with the heroic themes of the *chansons de geste.

Christchurch 43 33S 172 40E A city in New Zealand, on E South Island. Founded in 1850, it has a gothic-style cathedral (completed in 1901) and fine parks. The University of Canterbury was established in 1873. Industries are primarily agricultural and include meat processing, tanning, chemicals, and flour milling. Population (1991): 292,537.

Christian I (1426–81) King of Denmark and Norway (1450–81) and Sweden (1457–64), who founded the Oldenburg ruling dynasty of Denmark (1450–1863). His claim to the Swedish crown, which was disputed by Charles VIII of Sweden (d. 1470; reigned 1448–57, 1464–65, 1467–70), was finally ended by Christian's defeat at Brunkeberg (1471). In 1460 he gained Schleswig and Holstein but in 1469 the Norwegian islands of Orkney and Shetland were mortgaged to Scotland as part of his daughter Margaret's dowry on her marriage to the Scottish king James III.

Christian (II) the Cruel (1481–1559) King of Denmark and Norway (1513–23) and of Sweden (1520–23). He acquired his nickname for his massacre of Swedish nobles in his conquest of Sweden. He was subsequently deposed and, following an attempt to regain Norway, imprisoned (1532–59).

Christian III (1503–59) King of Denmark and Norway (1534–59), who established the state Lutheran Church in Denmark (1536) after the *Count's War (1533–36). His administrative reforms laid the foundation for 17th-century Danish absolutism.

Christian IV (1577–1648) King of Denmark and Norway (1588–1648). He entered the *Thirty Years' War in 1624 to defend the Protestant cause and Danish interests in the Baltic but was defeated by the Catholic League and withdrew (1629). At war with Sweden (1643–45), he suffered a crushing defeat (1645) with considerable loss of territory and domestic authority. He founded many new towns, including Christiania (now Oslo).

Christian IX (1818–1906) King of Denmark (1863–1906), who fought unsuccessfully with Germany over *Schleswig-Holstein. He succeeded to the throne through his marriage to the cousin of the childless Frederick VII of Denmark (1808–63; reigned 1848–63). He supported minority conservative governments until 1901, when he was forced to accept a liberal ministry.

Christian X (1870–1947) King of Denmark (1912–47), whose courage and dignity during the German occupation of his country (1940–45) won him international respect; rejecting Nazi anti-Semitic legislation in 1942, he was imprisoned from 1943 to 1945.

Christian Democrats Political parties having programs based on Christian principles and generally of a conservative nature. In West Germany the **Christlich-Demokratische Union** (Christian Democratic Union; CDU), founded in 1945 held power, in alliance with the Christlich-Soziale Union (Christian Social Union; CSU), from 1948 to 1969 under Konrad *Adenauer. In Italy the **Democrazia Cristiana** (Christian Democratic Party; DC), founded in 1943 as the successor to the Partito Popolare Italiano (Italian Popular Party), has dominated government since 1945. In 1963 Aldo *Moro brought the Italian Socialist Party into a coalition government with the DC, which has depended on the support of the Communist Party. Other Christian Democratic parties are found in Austria, Belgium, France, Norway, and Spain.

Christianity The religious faith based on the teachings of *Jesus Christ, which had its origin in *Judaism. Its believers hold that Jesus is the Messiah prophesied in the Old Testament. It began as a movement within Judaism, and one of the first disputes among the early Christians was the right of the Gentiles to be admitted to the faith. Chiefly through the missionary activities of St Paul, the Apostle of the Gentiles, Christianity spread rapidly through the Roman Empire, despite persecutions under Nero and later emperors. Christian belief was at first taught by the Apostles by word of mouth; however, the need for a written record of Jesus' life and teaching was soon fulfilled by the *Gospels. The definition of Christian belief and the authority of bishops and scriptures was well developed when Constantine became emperor (312). A series of general councils, the first held in 325 at *Nicaea, defined orthodox Christian belief. Constantine's establishment of his new capital, Constantinople, led to a growing polarization between the Eastern *Orthodox Church and the Western *Roman Catholic Church. Despite the collapse of the Western Empire, Western Christianity, under the Bishop of Rome who claimed authority as St Peter's successor, spread vigorously. The Orthodox Church, not so rigorously centralized, became increasingly isolated, and with the development of doctrinal differences the two Churches drifted apart. The date of the formal separation is generally regarded as 1054. The Orthodox Church, under pressure from Islam to the E and often hostile Christians to the W, nevertheless established itself among the Slavs. The Western Church by the end of the first millennium was rapidly gaining power, the papacy reaching the zenith of its influence in the 13th century under Pope *Innocent III. In the later Middle Ages increasing nationalism and the assertion of power by temporal rulers weakened the united structure of the papacy and *Holy Roman Empire. With the attack on central authority came a greater boldness in dissident criticism of the Church, such as that of John *Wycliffe in England.

By the 16th century the Church no longer had the power to override national interests; in this weakened state it was unable to resist the inevitable fragmentation caused by the *Reformation. Some reformers, such as the followers of Martin *Luther and the English Church, were comparatively conservative, while the *Calvinists, centered in Geneva, were considerably more radical. Coinciding with the exploration of the globe, the Reformation and the Roman Catholic response to it, the *Counter-Reformation, in fact stimulated the spread of Christianity throughout the world, giving rise to the many different Christian denominations and communions of the modern world.

Challenged in the 19th and 20th centuries by materialism, atheism, and agnosticism, the Christian Churches have come under severe pressure in many parts of the world. The ecumenical movement of the 20th century has sought to unite Christendom and after centuries of hostility has had some success in healing its various schisms. The belief of Christianity is based on the New Testament and for most Christians is summarized in the traditional *creeds of the Church. The doctrines of the *Trinity, the *Incarnation of Christ, and the Resurrection are central, as is Christ's role as the redeemer of mankind. The total number of Christians has been estimated at more than 944 million, or approximately 24% of the world population.

Christian Science A religious movement founded by Mary Baker *Eddy in 1866. After being healed of various illnesses by the well-known mesmerist and faith healer Phineas Parkhurst Quimby (1802–66), Eddy formulated a set of principles for curing physical and moral disorders through the use of prayer. This method of universal faith healing, based on the healing powers of Jesus Christ, which Eddy called the "Divine Mind," was expounded fully in her book *Science and Health with Key to the Scriptures* (1875). This work has become one of the central texts of the Christian Science movement, which teaches the denial of the reality of the material world and healing through spiritual control. The form of service is simple, including hymns, Bible readings, and relevant commentary from Eddy's works. The First Church of Christ, Scientist opened in Boston, Massachusetts in 1879. The movement spread to Europe, and since Eddy's death in 1910 it has been regulated by a board of five directors. Among the most well-known publications of the Christian Science movement, which operates public reading rooms throughout the world, is the *Christian Science Monitor,* a daily newspaper founded by Eddy in 1908.

Christian Social Union (German name: Christlich-Soziale Union; CSU) A West German and German political party, the affiliate of the Christian Democratic Union (*see* Christian Democrats). The two parties held power from 1948 to 1969. In 1976, while in opposition, the CSU, led by Franz Josef Strauss (1915–88), staged a walkout on the Christian Democrats. Both parties stood to lose from a split, and after a month the coalition had reformed and is now led by Strauss. Despite its name, the CSU forms the conservative wing in German politics.

Christians of St Thomas The Christians of the Malabar Coast, in SW India. According to tradition, St Thomas the Apostle brought Christianity to the area. Their Church used a Syriac liturgy and originally held *Nestorian beliefs, but since the 16th century the Roman Catholic Church has played a prominent role in its development.

Christie, Dame Agatha (1891–1975) British author of detective fiction and playwright. She introduced her most famous character, the Belgian detective Hercule Poirot, in *The Mysterious Affair at Styles* (1920); he met his end in *Curtain* (1975). Later detective novels include *The Murder of Roger Ackroyd* (1926), *Murder on the Orient Express* (1934), and *Death on the Nile* (1937). She wrote over 50 popular detective stories, creating other well-known fictional detectives, including Miss Jane Marple. A number of her stories have been filmed and her play *The Mousetrap* has had an unparalleled long run in London since its opening in 1952.

Christina (1626–89) Queen of Sweden (1632–54). After reaching her majority (1644), she clashed repeatedly with her former regent *Oxenstierna. Her secret conversion to Roman Catholicism (then illegal in Sweden) led to her abdication, after which she lived in Rome. There, she became an outstanding patron of the arts, sponsoring the composers Scarlatti and Corelli and the architect and sculptor Bernini.

Christmas The Feast of the Nativity of Christ. In the West it has been celebrated on Dec 25 since 336 AD, partly in order to replace the pagan sun worship on the same date. In the East, both the Nativity and Epiphany were originally celebrated on Jan 6, but by the end of the 4th century Dec 25 was almost universally accepted, although the Armenian Church still celebrates Christmas on Jan 6. Many of the popular customs associated with Christmas can be traced back to pagan origins.

Christmas Island An island in the Indian Ocean, SW of Java. It became a territory of the Commonwealth of Australia in 1958. The only commercial activity is phosphate mining. Area: 52 sq mi (135 sq km). Population (1986): 2000.

Christmas Island A large coral atoll in the W central Pacific Ocean, in Kiribati in the Line Islands. British and US nuclear tests were held here between 1957 and 1962. It has coconut plantations. Area: 139 sq mi (359 sq km). Population (1980 est): 1265.

Christmas rose A perennial herbaceous plant, *Helleborus niger,* about 14 in (35 cm) tall, native to central and S Europe and Asia Minor. Grown in gardens for its attractive white or pink winter-flowering blossoms, it prefers rich moist shady sites. The poisonous rhizomes are an irritant to the skin when fresh. Dried, they have been used medicinally. Family: **Ranunculaceae.*

Christoff, Boris (1919–   ) Bulgarian singer. His powerful bass voice and skillful characterization have made him a world-famous opera singer. He is particularly well known in the title role of Mussorgsky's opera *Boris Godunov.*

Christophe, Henri (1767–1820) Haitian ruler. An ex-slave, Christophe served with *Toussaint L'Ouverture against the French and then joined *Dessalines's revolt. After Dessalines's assassination, in which Christophe took part, he ruled N Haiti (1808–20; as king from 1811). His cruelty caused a revolt and he shot himself.

Christopher, St (3rd century AD) Christian martyr of Syria. According to legend, he carried a child across a river where he was working as a ferryman. The child grew heavier and he learned that it was in fact Christ and he was thus carrying the weight of the world. He is the patron saint of travelers. Feast day: July 25.

Christopher, Warren (1925–   ) US lawyer and government official, secretary of state (1993–   ). He served in subcabinet posts under Democratic presidents Lyndon Johnson and Jimmy Carter, helping to negotiate the release of US hostages in Iran for Carter. After playing a leading role in Bill Clinton's 1992 campaign, Christopher was selected as secretary of state, a role that required him to deal with the US presence in Somalia, civil war in the Balkans, and Israeli-Palestinian peace efforts.

chromaticism The use in music of notes that are not part of the normal diatonic *scale: the word comes from the Greek *chroma,* color. Under the system of equal *temperament the octave is split into 12 equal parts, containing 7 diatonic and 5 chromatic notes. The practice of "coloring" music by the use of these chromatic notes dates from the 16th century and was widely used by Liszt and Wagner to effect frequent modulations from one key to another. In the early music of Schoenberg chromaticism became so heavy that the concept of key became meaningless and *atonality resulted.

chromatography A method of chemical analysis in which a mixture to be analyzed constitutes a mobile phase, which moves in contact with an absorbent stationary phase. In **gas chromatography** (*or* gas-liquid chromatography) the mobile phase is a mixture of volatile substances diluted with an inert gas (e.g. argon). The stationary phase consists of a non-volatile liquid supported on an inert material of uniform particles (e.g. diatomaceous earth) in a tall column. The components of the mobile phase are selectively absorbed by the stationary phase. A detector measures the conductivity (or some other property) of the gas leaving the column, the resulting peaks on a strip chart of the detector output indicating the presence and concentration of the various components of the mixture. When the mobile phase is a liquid it can be introduced into a column of the solid stationary phase. The components of the mixture are selectively absorbed and form colored bands down the length of the column. This method is known as **column chromatography**. In column chromatography, the stationary phase is an absorbent material such as alumina. **Thin-layer chromatography** is a similar technique used for analysis. The stationary phase is a thin layer of alumina on a glass plate, and a spot of sample is separated into spots of the constituents. More commonly, **paper chromatography** is used, in which the stationary phase is a sheet of absorbent paper. The solvent soaks along the paper carrying the constituents with it at different rates. Colorless compounds can be made visible by ultraviolet light or chemical developers. The rate at which a constituent moves relative to movement of the solvent can be used to identify it.

chromatophore A granular cell containing pigment, found in great numbers in the skin of many animals. The distribution of the chromatophores accounts for the distinctive colors of these animals. Some animals (e.g. chameleons) have the ability to change the concentration and dispersion of pigment within the chromatophore very rapidly, effecting a change of skin color that is of value in camouflage.

chrome dyes Pigments consisting of chromium salts. **Chrome yellow** and **chrome orange** contain lead chromate ($PbCrO_4$), lead sulfate ($PbSO_4$), and lead monoxide (PbO). They display a range of shades, depending on the composition, and are used in paints. **Chrome green** contains chromic oxide (Cr_2O_3) and, unlike chrome yellow, is resistant to light and heat.

chromium (Cr) A hard gray transition metal, discovered in 1798 by Louis Nicolas Vauquelin (1763–1829). It occurs in nature principally as chromite ($FeCr_2O_4$), which is mined in the Soviet Union, Zimbabwe, and elsewhere. The metal is extracted by reducing the oxide (Cr_2O_3) with aluminum. The principal uses of chromium are in electroplating steel and in making alloys with iron. All chromium compounds are colored and the most widely used, other than the oxide, are chromates (for example K_2CrO_4) and dichromates ($K_2Cr_2O_7$), which are used as oxidizing agents and in the dyeing industry. Lead chromate ($PbCrO_4$) is bright yellow and is used as a pigment. At no 24; at wt 51.996; mp $3378 \pm 35°F$ ($1857 \pm 20°C$); bp 4504°F (2482°C).

chromophore A group of atoms, generally in an organic compound, that absorbs light of characteristic wavelengths, thus imparting color to the compound. Typical examples are the *azo (–N=N–) and nitroso (–N=O) groups. In dyes, groups called auxochromes (color enhancers) help to modify the color conferred by the chromophore, as well as the solubility and related properties of the dye molecule. A group derived from sulfonic acid ($-SO_3H$) is a typical auxochrome.

chromosome One of the threadlike structures that carry the genetic information (*see* gene) of living organisms and are found in the nuclei of their cells. Chromosomes consist of a central axis of *DNA with associated *RNA and proteins. Before cell division, the long filamentous threads contract and thicken and each chromosome can be seen as two identical threads (chromatids) joined at the centromere. The chromatids later separate to become the daughter chromosomes (*see* mitosis)

Chromosome number is characteristic of a species. For example, a normal human body cell has 46 chromosomes comprising 22 matched pairs (called autosomes) and two *sex chromosomes. A human sperm or egg cell has half this number of chromosomes (*see* meiosis). Abnormal numbers or parts of chromosomes often lead to abnormalities in the individual concerned. *Down's syndrome (mongolism) in man is caused by the presence of an extra number 21 chromosome.

chromosphere The layer of the *sun's atmosphere, a few thousand kilometers thick, that lies between the visible surface (the *photosphere) and the *corona. The temperature increases rapidly from about 2250°F (4000°C) near the photosphere to about 278,000°F (500,000°C) at the base of the corona, with the atmosphere becoming increasingly rarified with height. The chromosphere cannot be seen without special equipment, except at a total solar *eclipse.

chronicle plays Plays that dramatize historical events in order to convey general moral lessons. The successors to the medieval *morality plays, they were popular in England during the Elizabethan era. Examples are Marlowe's *Edward*

II (first produced in 1592) and Shakespeare's *King John* (c. 1596). Many of the plots were taken from Holinshed's *Chronicles* (1578).

Chronicles, Books of Two Old Testament books covering the history of Judah from the Creation to the end of the *Babylonian exile (538 BC). They were probably written in the 4th century BC and originally formed a continuous history with the books of Ezra and Nehemiah. After opening with genealogies from Adam, they describe the reigns of David and Solomon and the succeeding Kings of Judah. Special emphasis is given to the building of the Temple at Jerusalem.

chronometer. *See* clock.

chrysalis The *pupa of most insects of the order Lepidoptera. *See also* butterflies and moths.

Chrysanthemum A genus of herbaceous plants and shrubs (about 200 species) native to Eurasia, Africa, and North America. The wild ancestors of the horticultural chrysanthemums are not known, but probably more than one species—almost certainly of Japanese and Chinese origin—was involved. The showy forms are widely and easily cultivated, having colorful single or double long-lasting flower heads. The different varieties may bloom at any time from early spring to autumn. Family: *Compositae. See also* pyrethrum.

Chrysler, Walter Percy (1875–1940) US businessman. A machinist by trade, he joined the Buick Motor Company in 1912 and became its president in 1916. In 1921 he took over Willys-Overland Company and Maxwell Motor Company, reorganized them and combined them to form the Chrysler Corporation. Dodge, DeSoto, and Plymouth cars joined the Chrysler line in 1928. He was responsible for the construction of the Chrysler building (1929) in New York City.

Chrysoloras, Manuel (c. 1365–1415) Greek scholar and envoy. Chrysoloras was sent on several diplomatic missions by the Byzantine Emperor Manuel Paleologus. In Florence, Chrysoloras taught the humanists Bruni, Poggio, and Guarino. His work on grammar, *Erotemata,* introduced Greek to the West.

chrysoprase An apple-green variety of *chalcedony, used as a gem.

Chrysostom, St John (c. 347–407 AD) Bishop of Constantinople and Doctor of the Church. After a period as a hermit, he was ordained in 386 in Antioch and preached extensively there, soon gaining the epithet Chrysostom (Greek: gold-enmouthed). As Patriarch of Constantinople from 398, he was a zealous reformer but alienated the Empress Eudoxia (d. 404) and other powerful persons. In 403 he was unjustifiably condemned on a number of charges, deposed from his see, and banished. He died while journeying to the Black Sea. His *Homilies* are important expositions of various biblical books. The liturgy in general use in the Orthodox Churches is attributed to him, although in its present form it dates from a much later period. Feast day: Jan 27.

Chuang-tzu. *See* Zhuangzi.

chub One of several freshwater fish related to *carp, found in Europe and North America and used as food, game, or bait fish. The European chub (*Leucixus cephalus*) has a plump elongated body, usually 12–16 in (30–40 cm) long, and is dark blue or green above and silvery below. Certain unrelated freshwater fish of the genus *Leucichthys* (order: *Salmoniformes*) are also called chub.

Chu Chiang. *See* Zhu Jiang.

Ch'ü Ch'iu-pai. *See* Qu Qiu Bai.

chuckwalla A North American lizard, *Sauromalus obesus,* occurring in SW arid and rocky regions; 20 in (50 cm) long, it is dark gray with a red-banded and blotched tail. It feeds on vegetation, storing water in sacs beneath the skin, and shelters in rock crevices; if molested it inflates its lungs to increase its body size making it difficult to dislodge. Family: *Iguanidae.*

Chukchi A people of the Chukchi peninsula in extreme NE Siberia. One branch consists of nomadic reindeer herders; the other is a maritime fishing people whose members also hunt whale, walrus, and seal, and live in fixed villages. Their language is of Paleo-Siberian type.

Chukchi Sea 69 00N 171 00W A part of the Arctic Ocean between NW Alaska and NE Siberia, just above the Bering Strait. Icebound for most of the year, it is navigable only from mid-summer until early fall.

Chulalongkorn (1853–1910) King of Siam (now Thailand) from 1868 to 1910. He built roads and railroads, improved education, abolished slavery, and remodeled Siam's administration on western lines. His diplomatic handling of France and Britain ensured Siam's continued independence.

Chungking. *See* Chongqing.

Chur (French name: Coire; Romansh name: Cuera) 46 52N 9 32E A city in E Switzerland. A tourist center, it also trades in Valtelline wines. Population: 31,193.

Churchill, Lord Randolph Henry Spencer (1849–95) British Conservative politician; father of Sir Winston *Churchill. He entered parliament in 1874. After serving as secretary for India (1885–86), he was briefly chancellor of the exchequer, when his budget was not accepted by the prime minister, Lord *Salisbury, because Churchill wished to reduce funds allocated to the armed forces. He married (1874) Jeanette (Jennie) Jerome (1854–1921), an American.

Churchill, Sir Winston (Leonard Spencer) (1874–1965) British statesman and author. The son of Lord Randolph *Churchill, he was a direct descendant of the 1st Duke of Marlborough. Churchill served in the army and as a war correspondent in the second Boer War before becoming a Conservative member of Parliament in 1900. In 1904 he joined the Liberals and subsequently served as president of the Board of Trade (1908–10), home secretary (1910–11), and first lord of the admiralty (1911–15). In 1915, during World War I, he rejoined the army and served in France. In 1917 he became minister of munitions, supporting the development of the *tank. Churchill lost his parliamentary seat in 1922 but was reelected as a constitutionalist in 1924, becoming chancellor of the exchequer in Baldwin's government. From 1929 he was out of office until the outbreak of World War II, when he became first lord of the admiralty and then, in 1940, prime minister of a coalition government. During *World War II, his remarkable oratory and outstanding qualities as a leader made him a symbol of British resistance to tyranny throughout the free world. He was largely responsible for Britain's victorious alliance with the Soviet Union and the US (1941) but came to view Soviet communism as a future threat, speaking later of an "iron curtain" drawn across Europe. Churchill's coalition government was defeated in 1945 but he returned as Conservative prime minister in 1951, serving until his resignation in 1955.

His writings include *The Second World War* (1948–54) and *A History of the English-Speaking Peoples* (1956–58); he won the 1953 Nobel Prize for Literature.

Churchill, Winston (1871–1947) US novelist. He served in the New Hampshire legislature (1903–05) and ran for governor in 1912. From these experiences he drew material for *Coniston* (1906) and *The Dwelling Place of Light* (1917). His earlier novels covered the American Revolution (*Richard Carvel;* 1899), the Civil War (*The Crisis;* 1901), and pioneer days (*The Crossing;* 1904).

SIR WINSTON CHURCHILL *Touring the London docks with his wife following an air raid in World War II.*

Churchill Falls A waterfall in E Canada in W Labrador on the Churchill River. In 1967 work began on a hugh hydroelectricity project expected to generate 5,222,000 kW. Height: 245 ft (75 m); 1038 ft (316 m) including rapids.

Churchill River (formerly Hamilton River) A river in Canada that rises in Ashuanipi Lake in SW Labrador. It loops N and then SE before turning NE to empty into Lake Melville near Goose Bay. Along its course, just below Lobstick Lake, is Churchill Falls, a drop of over 300 ft (90 m). It is the site of a large hydroelectric power plant. From its headwaters to Churchill Falls, it is known as the Ashuanijai River. Length: 450 mi (725 km).

Church of England The established church in England, which embodies Protestant elements but also claims continuity with the English Church as established by St *Augustine, the first Archbishop of Canterbury. Christianity was probably introduced in Britain during the Roman occupation in the 2nd century AD. Conflicts between the indigenous Celtic Church and Rome were resolved in favor of Roman usage at the Synod of *Whitby (664), and thereafter the English Church remained under papal authority until the *Reformation. Under *Henry VIII, papal supremacy was rejected and the king was acknowledged Supreme Head of the Church, but there were otherwise no doctrinal changes. The two bases of Anglican doctrine and worship were formulated in the succeeding reigns: the Book of *Common Prayer, introduced in the reign of *Edward VI, and the *Thirty-Nine Articles, published under Elizabeth I, whose excommunication (1570) by the pope completed the break with Rome. The two provinces of the Church are the archbishoprics of Canterbury (*see* Canterbury, Archbishop of) and York, each of which is further divided into bishoprics. Ecclesiastical affairs are supervised by the General Synod (established 1970 to replace the Church Assembly), composed of bishops, clergy, and laity; its decisions are subject to parliamentary approval.

Church of Scotland The established church in Scotland. The Scottish Church's secession from Rome was effected in 1560, largely under the influence of John *Knox. The argument over Church government between Episcopalians and Presbyterians continued until the reign of William of Orange, who established the Presbyterian Church in 1690.

church year The organization of the Christian churches' calendar around the great festivals of Christianity. In the Western Churches, the beginning of Advent (the Sunday nearest to the Feast of St Andrew, Nov 30) marks the opening of the year. The Sundays of Advent are numbered one to four, leading to Christmas (Dec 25). Epiphany (Jan 6) follows after one or two intervening Sundays. The other major festivals are linked to the date of Easter, itself associated with the Jewish Passover. There are six Sundays in Lent and eight from Easter to Pentecost. The dates of Ash Wednesday, Good Friday and Ascension Day are dependent on Easter. The Eastern Churches' year begins with Easter and ends with Lent.

Churriguera A Spanish family of architects consisting of three brothers, José (1665–1725), Joaquín (1674–1724), and Alberto (1676–1750). The Churrigueras evolved a distinctive, highly decorative form of the *baroque later dubbed "Churrigueresque." This can be seen in all their work, notably in José's church of S Estéban, Salamanca (1693). It stimulated many imitators all over Spain and Mexico.

Chu Teh. *See* Zhu De.

Chuvash Autonomous Republic An administrative division in W central Russia. The region is a wooded steppe with peat bogs and mineral deposits. The Chuvash, who comprise about 70% of the population, are a Turkic-speaking people. Industries include engineering, oil and natural-gas refining, chemicals, and food processing, but the economy is predominantly agricultural, producing chiefly cereals and fodder crops; livestock is also important. Area: 7064 sq mi (18,300 sq km). Population (1991 est): 1,346,000.

Chu Xi (*or* Chu Hsi; 1130–1200) Chinese philosopher, born in Fujian province, the son of a government official. He was a precocious student and entered the government service, holding various important public posts for most of his life. His major work consists of four commentaries known as the *Ssu shu* or *Four Books*. These contain the formulation of *Confucianism that was adopted as the official philosophy of China until the communist revolution in the 20th century.

Chu Yuan (c. 343–c. 289 BC) Chinese poet, the earliest known by name. A nobleman of the state of Ch'u, he was banished to the S after court intrigues and drowned himself in the Mi-lo River. His contribution to the anthology *Ch'u tz'u* greatly influenced the development of early Chinese poetry.

CIA. *See* Central Intelligence Agency.

Ciano, Galeazzo (1903–44) Italian fascist leader. *Mussolini's son-in-law, Ciano was foreign minister from 1936 to 1943 and helped to form the military pact with Germany. In 1943 he voted against Mussolini in the Fascist Supreme Council and was shot by Mussolini's supporters in N Italy.

Ciardi, John (1916–86) US poet and editor. Poetry editor of *Saturday Review*, he wrote in contemporary poetic language for both adults and children. His works include *I Met a Man* (1961), *The Man Who Sang the Sillies* (1961), and *The Wish-Tree* (1964) for children; *Other Skies* (1947), *From Time to Time* (1951), *I Marry You* (1958), *39 Poems* (1959), *You Know Who* (1964), and *Lives of X* (1971), all poetry collections. He also translated Dante's *Divine Comedy* (*Inferno*, 1954; *Purgatorio*, 1961; *Paradiso*, 1970).

Cibber, Colley (1671–1757) British actor, dramatist, and theater manager. Son of a Danish sculptor, he wrote the sentimental comedy *Love's Last Shift* (1696) to supplement his earnings as an actor. His adaptation of Shakespeare's *Richard III* was the preferred acting version until the 19th century. His appointment as poet laureate in 1730 made him the target for satirical attacks by *Pope.

cicada An insect belonging to the mainly tropical family *Cicadidae* (over 2000 species). Cicadas are 0.8–2.0 in (20–50 mm) long and have large membranous wings. Males produce a variety of loud noises by vibrating two membranes at the base of the abdomen (this is called stridulation). Cicadas usually inhabit trees and the females lay eggs in the wood. The *nymphs (immature cicadas) drop to the ground and burrow underground to feed on plant juices from roots. After 1–17 years they emerge as adults. Order: *Hemiptera.*

cicely A perennial herbaceous plant, *Myrrhis odorata,* also called sweet cicely. 24–40 in (60–100 cm) high, it has umbrella-like clusters of white flowers and a strong aromatic smell. Cicely is native to Europe and also occurs in Chile (where it was probably introduced). Formerly widely used as a vegetable, it is still used for seasoning. Family: *Umbelliferae.*

Cicero, Marcus Tullius (106–43 BC) Roman orator and statesman. Established as a prominent lawyer by 70 BC, he was elected consul in 63 BC. His execution of the Catiline conspirators without trial lost him support and he was exiled in 58 BC for 18 months. During the civil war he supported Pompey against Caesar and lived privately in Rome during the latter's dictatorship. After the assassination of Caesar in 44 BC he made a series of attacks on Antony, the *Philippics,* for which he was later arrested and killed. The greatest of Roman orators, he also wrote treatises on rhetoric and philosophical works influenced by Greek political theory.

cichlid A freshwater fish of the family *Cichlidae* (over 6000 species), found in tropical regions, especially Africa. Cichlids have a brightly colored deep body, up to 12 in (30 cm) long, and a single long dorsal fin; they feed on plants or animals. Most build nests for their eggs and guard the young but some species carry the eggs in their mouths (*see* mouthbrooder). Many are popular aquarium fish. Order: *Perciformes.*

cider An alcoholic drink made from fermented apple juice. In England cider is made from apples grown specifically for cider making. They are crushed to press out the juice, which ferments spontaneously. Fermentation lasts weeks or months, varying according to the apples used. Cider is also made in France, especially in Normandy and Brittany, Spain, and the US, where cider denotes unfermented apple juice and hard cider denotes the English type of cider.

Cienfuegos 22 10N 80 27W A port in S Cuba, on the Caribbean Sea. A picturesque city with many fine buildings, it trades in tobacco, cattle products, and molasses and is the site of a naval base. Population (1989 est): 119,000.

cigar A cylindrical roll of tobacco leaf, smoked originally by the Indians of the Americas and copied by sailors from Portugal and Spain; by the 19th century they became common in N Europe. The most expensive cigars are still made by hand in Cuba and Jamaica, machine-made cigars being made extensively in the US, Europe, and the Far East. The cigar was replaced to some extent by the cigarette from the end of the 19th century, but small cigars have enjoyed some popularity in recent years.

cigarette A cylindrical roll of fine-cut tobacco, rolled in thin paper. Cigarettes became popular in the late 19th century and is now the form in which most tobacco is smoked. The tobacco most commonly used for cigarettes is Virginia-cut, a type that originated in the US, successfully grown in other countries. Since the 1960s there has been widespread concern over the effects that smoking has on health; it is associated with lung *cancer, lung disease, and *heart disease.

Ciliata A class of microscopic single-celled animals (*see* Protozoa) having two nuclei and tracts of hairlike cilia over the cell surface, used for feeding and swimming. Most are free-swimming (*see* Paramecium) but some are attached to the substrate by a stalk (*see* Stentor; Vorticella). Most ciliates feed on organic detritus, other protozoans, etc., but some are parasitic, especially on fish and other aquatic animals.

Cilicia The SE coastal region of Asia Minor. It was subject consecutively to the Hittites, the Assyrians, the Achemenians, the Macedonians, and the Seleucids. From the 2nd century BC pirates based on Cilicia seriously threatened Mediterranean trade until suppressed by Pompey in 67, after which the region was incorporated into a series of Roman provinces.

Cilician Gates (Turkish name: Külek Boğazi) 37 17N 34 46E A mountain pass in central S Turkey, in the Taurus Mountains. It lies on the route from Ankara to Adana and has been used for centuries.

Cimabue, Giovanni (Cenni de Peppi; c. 1240–c. 1302) Florentine painter, who introduced a degree of naturalism into the stylized *Byzantine art of his period. His only certain work is a mosaic of St John (Duomo, Pisa) but the fresco cycle in the upper Church of St Francis, Assisi, and the *Santa Trinità Madonna* (Uffizi) are attributed to him. *Giotto was probably is pupil.

Cimarosa, Domenico (1749–1801) Italian composer. He became court musician in St Petersburg and Vienna and was famous for his many operas. His best-known work is the *opera buffa *The Secret Marriage* (1792), which shows his flair for vocal ensemble writing and fine comic talent. He also wrote church music and chamber music.

cimbalom The traditional musical instrument of Hungary; a type of dulcimer. The cimbalom has ten pairs of wire strings stretched over a shallow three-sided soundbox. The strings are struck with a small hammer. The Hungarian composer Kodály used it in the suite *Háry János* (1927).

Cimbri A Germanic tribe from N Jutland. At the end of the 2nd century BC the Cimbri migrated southward, defeating Roman armies in 113 BC (Noricum), 110 BC (Rhône valley), and 105 BC (Arausio, now Orange, France). In 101 BC Marius destroyed them; a remnant survived in Jutland.

Cimon (died c. 450 BC) Athenian general and politician. The son of *Miltiades, Cimon opposed *Themistocles' policy of enmity toward the Spartans, believing Persia was the common Greek enemy, and in about 466 he scored a great victory against the Persians. His opponents, including *Pericles, caused him to be ostracized (461) but after his return to Athens, Cimon negotiated a truce with Sparta (c. 450) and died fighting the Persians in Cyprus.

Cinchona A genus of trees (40 species) of the South American Andes, now cultivated elsewhere in the tropics, especially India. One of the most important species is calisaya (*C. calisaya*). The bark yields powerful medicinal drugs, including cinchonidine and *quinine, used in the treatment and prevention of malaria, and cinchona, useful for coughs and sore throats. Cultivation, which is generally by coppicing, has lost importance since the development of similar synthetic drugs lacking side-effects. Family: *Rubiaceae*.

Cincinnati 39 10N 84 30W A city in SW Ohio, on the Ohio River. Founded in 1788, it developed as a meat-packing center in the 19th century. Today it is an important inland port and major manufacturing center best known as a producer of machine tools. The University of Cincinnati was established here in 1819. Population (1990): 364,040.

Cincinnatus, Lucius Quinctius (5th century BC) Roman statesman. He was made dictator to rescue a Roman legion that was besieged by an Italian tribe. After his victory he returned to his farm, despite pleas that he remain dictator. His rejection of autocratic rule made him a symbol of traditional Roman values.

Cinderella The heroine of a folktale, of which the first recorded version dates from 9th-century China. The story is of a girl treated cruelly by her stepfamily who receives help from a supernatural agent, in most versions an animal or her dead mother, and finally marries a prince.

cinema. *See* motion pictures.

cinematography The recording of moving pictures. Essentially a motion film records a rapid sequence of still pictures (each slightly different from the previous one) fast enough to appear continuous to the human eye. The film moves through the camera in a series of jumps. There are usually 18 pictures (frames) per second in silent film and 24 per second in sound film. The sequence of transparencies produced by developing the film is passed through a *projector in the same way. Sound can be carried as a magnetic or optical signal on a narrow strip at the side of the film, to synchronize with the picture. Various widths of film are used: 8 mm for educational and laboratory applications; 16 mm with portable equipment for amateur filming and many other uses; 35 mm for the professional cinema.

cineraria A herbaceous perennial pot plant developed from *Senecio cruentus* of the Canary Islands. There are numerous horticultural varieties, noted for their handsome, sometimes brilliantly colored, daisy-like flowers. Useful for spring and winter flowering, they require a cool moist draft- and frost-free atmosphere. Family: *Compositae.*

Cinna, Lucius Cornelius (d. 84 BC) Roman politician. Expelled from Rome by his opponent Sulla (87), Cinna with *Marius returned and captured Rome. He tried to restrain Marius's brutal revenge on their opponents and as consul (86–84) restored order. He was killed in a mutiny shortly before Sulla's return to Italy.

cinnabar (moth) A moth, *Callimorpha jacobaeae,* of Europe and Asia. Both the adults—scarlet and black—and the caterpillars—striped black and yellow—taste bad: their warning coloration discourages predators. The caterpillars feed on ragwort and have been used to control this weed. Superfamily: *Caradrinoidea* (noctuids, tiger moths, etc.)

cinnabar (ore) A mineral consisting of mercury sulfide, the chief ore of mercury. It is bright red and occurs in veins and impregnations associated with volcanic rocks. Spain, Italy, and Mexico are among the main producers.

cinnamon An evergreen tree, *Cinnamomum zeylanicum,* 23–35 ft (7–10 m) high, native to Sri Lanka and cultivated widely in the tropics. Before 1776 only wild plants were used, owing to the belief that cultivation would destroy its flavor. It is coppiced, the bark of the twigs being peeled off and rolled up to form the spice. Family: *Lauraceae.*

cinquefoil A shrub or herbaceous plant of the genus *Potentilla,* having leaves with five divisions each. Creeping cinquefoil (*P. reptans*) has been used medicinally, and shrubby cinquefoil (*P. fruticosa*) is often grown in gardens. Family: *Rosaceae.*

Cinque Ports An association of five English ports (Sandwich, Dover, Hythe, New Romney, Hastings) in Kent and Sussex formed during the 11th century to defend the Channel coast. After the Norman conquest they were granted considerable privileges in return for providing the nucleus of the navy. Winchelsea and Rye were added to their number and many other towns in the southeast became associate members. In the later Middle Ages their power declined both because of competition from other ports and the silting-up of their harbors. The Lord Warden of the Cinque Ports survives as an honorary office.

Ciompi, Revolt of the (1378) A rising of the poorer wage-earners of Florence against the oligarchic rule of the major guilds. The Ciompi (wool workers) seized power together with the minor guilds, but a split in this alliance allowed the major guilds to destroy the revolt and to abolish the Ciompi's newly formed guild.

Circassia An area in Russia, NW of the Great Caucasus. It is inhabited by the Circassian (*or* Cherkess) people, who, although Christian since the 6th century, adopted Islam under the influence of the Ottoman Empire in the 17th century and subsequently strongly resisted Russian rule until the Ottoman Turks ceded Circassia to Russia in 1829.

Circe Legendary Greek sorceress, who had the power to transform men into beasts. Odysseus, who visited her island of Aeaea on his voyage from Troy, was protected by the herb moly, and forced her to restore his men to human form.

circle A curve defined as the locus of all the points lying in a plane at a certain distance, called the radius, from a fixed point, called the center. Its diameter is any straight line joining two points on the circle and passing through the center. The ratio of the distance around any circle (the circumference) to its diameter is equal to the number π (*see* pi). The area of a circle, radius r, is πr^2.

circuit breaker A mechanism for breaking an electrical power circuit under load. Similar in function to a fuse, it has the advantage of being able to be reset immediately. It is used extensively in power stations and high-voltage distribution lines and now often replaces fuses in low-voltage circuits.

circulation of the blood The passage of blood through the □heart and the network of arteries and veins associated with it. By supplying the tissues with blood, the circulatory system effects the transport of oxygen, nutrients, etc., and the removal of waste products. Oxygen-rich blood is pumped out of the *heart into the aorta and then, via the arteries, to all the tissues of the body. Here oxygen is removed, and deoxygenated blood returns, through the veins, to the heart. This blood is then pumped to the lungs, where it is reoxygenated, and returned to the heart to repeat the circuit. The circulation of the blood was first discovered by William *Harvey in 1628.

circumcision The removal of all or part of the foreskin of the penis. In many primitive societies circumcision usually forms part of a ceremony initiating young men into adulthood. Among some Islamic peoples it is performed just before marriage; Jewish babies are circumcised in a religious ceremony when they are eight days old. Its origin is unknown but it has hygienic advantages, especially in hot climates, and cancer of the penis occurs infrequently among circumcised men. It is also carried out for medical reasons in certain circumstances. Female circumcision (the removal of the clitoris) is also practiced among some primitive peoples.

cire perdue (French: lost wax) A technique of metal casting used for small detailed castings, particularly statuary. A wax original model is encased in a mold. When molten metal is poured into the mold the wax melts and is replaced by metal. The process was already known in *Ur (c. 3000 BC) and was perfected in China about 500 BC.

cirque (*or* corrie) A rounded rock basin with steep sides, often containing a lake or cirque glacier. Common in glaciated mountain ranges, cirques form through freeze-thaw action on the headwall and basin floor together with abrasion by slipping ice and debris.

cirrhosis Destruction of the cells of the liver followed by their replacement with fibrous tissue, which eventually produces symptoms of liver failure (e.g.

jaundice, swelling of the legs and abdomen, and vomiting of blood). Cirrhosis may be caused by *alcoholism, *hepatitis, obstruction of the bile duct, and heart failure, but in many cases the cause is not known. The treatment of cirrhosis is determined by the underlying condition.

Cirripedia. *See* barnacle.

cirrocumulus cloud (Cc) A high *cloud with a mottled appearance composed of ice crystals; it is sometimes known as "mackerel sky."

cirrostratus cloud (Cs) A high thin veil of *cloud composed of ice crystals, visible as a halo around the sun or moon.

cirrus cloud (Ci) A high detached *cloud occurring in the troposphere above 20,000 ft (6000 m), composed of ice crystals and appearing wispy and fibrous. It is usually associated with fair weather.

Ciskei. *See* Bantu Homelands.

Cisneros, Henry (1947–) US political leader, secretary of housing and urban development (1993–). The first Hispanic-American to serve as mayor of San Antonio, Tex. (1981–89), he achieved a national reputation as an innovative social reformer while maintaining a pro-business stance.

Cistercians An order of Roman Catholic monks founded by St Robert of Molesme (c. 1027–1111) as a stricter offshoot of the *Benedictine order. The mother house at Cîteaux, France, from whence the order took its name, was founded in 1098. St *Bernard of Clairvaux contributed considerably to the order's prestige, and communities were established throughout W Europe in the 12th century. In the 17th century the order underwent a reform resulting in two groups: the monks of the Strict Observance, as opposed to the Common Observance, are known as *Trappists.

Citlaltépetl (Spanish name: Volcan Citlaltépetl) 19 00N 97 18W A dormant volcano in S central Mexico, the highest point in the country. Height: 18,697 ft (5699 m).

citric acid An organic compound that occurs in plant and animal tissues and is involved in the series of metabolic reactions called the *Krebs cycle. A commercial preparation of citric acid is used as a flavoring agent in foods.

citron A *citrus tree, *Citrus medica,* 7–10 ft (2–3 m) high. Originally from the Far East, it was introduced into the Mediterranean region in about 300 BC; this remains the main center of commercial cultivation. The rough yellowish sour fruits are used to make candied peel, produced by soaking in brine and preserving in sugar.

citronella A *grass, *Cymbopogon nardus,* cultivated in tropical regions of Africa and Asia and introduced into tropical America. It forms dense tufts and contains geraniol or citronella oil, which is used in cosmetics and insect repellents.

Citrus The largest and most important genus of tropical and subtropical fruits (10 species), originating in SE Asia. All the species are small evergreen trees or shrubs with simple glossy leaves and five-petaled, usually white, flowers. The juicy fruits are rich in vitamin C, citric acid, and pectin (used in jam making). The most important are the *orange, *lemon, *lime, *grapefruit, *citron, and *tangerine, of which commercial varieties as well as various hybrids have been developed. All contain essential oils used in perfumery and soap making (the *bergamot is grown especially for this). Family: *Rutaceae.*

city states Independent municipalities, each comprising a town and its surrounding countryside, characteristic of ancient Greece. There were several hundreds of city states, of which Athens was the largest. Each enjoyed autonomy, its own laws and constitution (democratic, as at Athens, or oligarchic, as at Sparta), and its own presiding deity. The geography of Greece encouraged life in small communities and the Greeks were so proud of their allegiance to the city state that Greek unity was somewhat precarious.

Ciudad Bolívar 8 06N 63 36W A port in E Venezuela, on the Orinoco River. Accessible to oceangoing vessels, its chief exports include gold, diamonds, and chicle. Population (1990 est): 226,000.

Ciudad Guayana (former name: Santo Tomé de Guayana) 8 22N 62 37W An industrial complex in E Venezuela, on the Orinoco River. Founded in 1961, it amalgamated several existing industrial centers into one; industries include iron and steel processing and gold mining. Population (1990 est): 537,000.

Ciudad Juárez 31 42N 106 29W A city in N Mexico, on the Rio Grande. Its importance is due to its location on the US border and as a marketing center for cotton. Its university was founded in 1973. Population (1980): 544,496.

Ciudad Real 38 59N 3 55W A city in S central Spain, in New Castile. It has a 13th-century gothic cathedral. An agricultural center, it produces flour and brandy. Population: 41,708.

civet A solitary nocturnal mammal belonging to the family *Viverridae*. The African civet (*Viverra civetta*) is cat-like, about 50 in (1.2 m) long with coarse grayish spotted fur. Mainly carnivorous, civets also eat some fruit and roots. The secretion of their anal glands is used in the manufacture of perfumes as a fixative, making other scents last longer. *See also* palm civet.

CIVET *A 2-month-old African civet cub.*

Civil Aeronautics Board (CAB) A federal agency that promoted, developed, and regulated commercial air transportation to, from, and within the US. Established in 1940, as an outgrowth of the Civil Aeronautics Authority (1938), it consisted of five members appointed by the president. The agency was abolished at the end of 1984.

civil engineering The branch of *engineering that deals with the design and construction of buildings and public structures, such as roads, railroads, dams, canals, etc. The term was first used in 1750 by John Smeaton (1724–92) to distinguish himself from military engineers, although the practice of civil engineering went back to ancient times. It has diversified into numerous branches calling on specialized mathematical and scientific knowledge and developing such new materials as prestressed concrete.

Civilian Conservation Corps (CCC) (1933–42) US federal work camp program, part of the New Deal, that gave conservation work to unmarried unemployed men. Established during the *Depression, projects included tree planting, dam building, and forest maintenance.

civil law The body of law governing the rights of private individuals and their relationships with each other rather than with the state. It is also called private law, as distinguished from public law and *criminal law. The term is especially used of the European legal systems derived from *Roman law, which are different from *common law in important respects. For example, in civil law court decisions have no legal force in the decision of similar cases. Roman law was revived in Europe from the 11th and 12th centuries and formed the basis of the *Code Napoléon* (1804), on which other European, Latin American, and some Asian states modeled their legal systems. English-speaking countries generally use common law, although the law of Scotland is more closely related to civil law.

civil rights The individual's rights to liberty, equality of treatment, education, etc., afforded to him under law and safeguarded by the state. In the US, the basic rights of all citizens are specifically protected by the first ten amendments to the Constitution, known as the *Bill of Rights. These include freedom of speech and religion, the right to bear arms, protection against unreasonable search and seizure by law enforcement authorities, the right to a jury trial, protection against self-incrimination, and protection against cruel and unusual punishment. These rights were developed from the English legal tradition of the *Magna Carta (1215) and of the English Bill of Rights (1689). In the US, the abolition of slavery in 1865 and the *Reconstruction programs after the end of the Civil War initiated a long struggle to ensure the civil rights of African Americans. In the 1950s and 1960s several important US Supreme Court decisions and the growth of the American *civil rights movement were instrumental in the establishment of legal protection for minority rights. On the international level, the United Nations proclaimed a Universal Declaration of Human Rights in 1948.

Civil Rights Acts (1957, 1960, 1964, 1968) US laws that guaranteed equal rights to African Americans. The 1957 law established the Civil Rights Commission, while the law of 1960 assured protection of voting rights for African Americans. The most important law, the Civil Rights Act of 1964, proscribed discrimination in public places and segregation in the schools and was followed in 1968 by a law that guaranteed fair and nondiscriminatory housing and real estate practices.

Civil Rights Cases (1883) A series of Supreme Court rulings that racial discrimination in private enterprise did not violate the 13th and 14th amendments. The decision voided the Civil Rights Act of 1875, which had outlawed discrimination in public places, and were not overturned until 1964 when the court ruled racial discrimination in the private sector unlawful in *Heart of Atlanta Motel* v. *US*.

civil rights movement In the US, the political and legal campaign for racial equality. Although the rights of African Americans were guaranteed by the 13th, 14th, and 15th Amendments to the US *Constitution, racial segregation in the public schools remained in effect in the South until the ruling of the US

Supreme Court in the case of *Brown* v. *Board of Education* (1954). Soon after that decision, Dr. Martin Luther *King, Jr, assumed the leadership of a movement to defend the rights of African Americans in every important aspect of public life. The first success of the civil rights movement came in Montgomery, Alabama, in the campaign to desegregate the city's buses (1955–56). During the following decade, the movement gained widespread public support, and its efforts led to the passage of wide-ranging federal laws against racial discrimination. One of the most important of these was the Civil Rights Act of 1964, which prohibited discrimination in housing, transportation, voting rights, and employment. Since that time, many federal programs have been established to provide funds to promote equal opportunity in education and business.

civil service The bureaucracy that implements government policy and provides governmental services. In the US, the civil service comprises government employees on the municipal, county, state, and federal levels who carry out the work of the various departments and agencies. During the 19th century, federal civil servants were customarily recruited by political patronage, but the establishment of the Civil Service Commission in 1883 introduced competitive examinations and a merit system as a means of hiring qualified candidates. In Great Britain, a Civil Service Commission was established in 1855 and was placed under the supervision of a special Civil Service Department in 1968. The secretariats of the various agencies of the UN are regarded as forming an international civil service.

Civil Service Commission (1883) US federal agency that regulates federal employment. Created to administer a merit system form of government employment, it is responsible for giving competitive exams, classifying jobs, and setting salaries, tenure, and benefits.

Civil War, English (1642–51) The war between Charles I and Parliament, which led to the execution of the king (1649) and the establishment of Oliver Cromwell's *Protectorate (1653). The Civil War was the outcome of a conflict between the king and Parliament that had steadily worsened during the reigns of James I (1603–25) and Charles. The struggle for power culminated in the events of the *Long Parliament (summoned in 1640). War was precipitated by Charles's rejection of Parliament's Nineteen Propositions in June 1642. The first battle, at Edgehill, ended indecisively but during 1643 the royalists (*or* *Cavaliers) gained ground. The parliamentarian alliance (*see* Roundheads) with the Scots led to a victory at *Marston Moor (1644). The formation of the *New Model Army brought about the decisive defeat of Charles at *Naseby (1645). In 1646 Charles surrendered to the Scots at Newark and the first Civil War was brought to an end. He was handed over to Parliament in January 1647, but escaped to the Isle of Wight. The second Civil War ensued (1648), with royalist uprisings in Wales and Kent, ending with Cromwell's defeat of the Scots at Preston. In the following year, Charles was tried and executed and the *Commonwealth was established by the Rump Parliament. The Civil War was concluded by Cromwell's subjection of Ireland (1649–50), his defeat of Charles's heir (later Charles II) at Dunbar (1650), and his victory against the Scots at Worcester in 1651. In 1653 he dismissed the Rump and established the *Protectorate, which governed England until preparations for the *Restoration of the monarchy were initiated in 1659.

Civil War, US (1861–65) The conflict between the US federal government and the 11 southern states that formed the *Confederate States of America. The war arose from an economic and political conflict of interest between the predominately agricultural slave-owning South and the industrialized North. The 1860 election of Pres. Abraham *Lincoln, who was opposed to slavery, precipitated the secession of the southern states in the following year. In February 1861, the Confederate States of America was established, its new constitution was adopted, and Jefferson *Davis was elected its president. War broke out in April when the Confederates opened fire on Fort Sumter, S.C., which the federal government had refused to evacuate. The opening skirmishes of the war took place in Virginia and culminated in the unexpected Confederate victory at the first battle of *Bull Run in July. Early in 1862 the Confederate general Thomas "Stonewall" *Jackson conducted a brilliant campaign in Virginia's Shenandoah Valley, but in April, Union general Ulysses S. Grant won an important victory at the Battle of *Shiloh in Tennessee and in May the federal Army of the Potomac under George B. *McClellan captured Yorktown, Va., and defeated Robert E. *Lee's force in the Seven Days' Battles near Richmond in July. The Confederates counterattacked in August, pushing northward into Maryland. Although Lee's forces were defeated at *Antietam in September, he gained an important victory at *Fredericksburg at the end of the year. In 1863, following his victory at *Chancellorsville, Va., Lee began his second invasion of the North, only to be defeated at *Gettysburg in July. In the West, Grant's forces captured Vicksburg, Miss., after a long siege and despite defeat at *Chickamauga, won the battle of Chattanooga in November. In 1864, Grant was appointed commander-in-chief of Union forces and he advanced against Lee in the *Wilderness Campaign and began the siege of Petersburg, Va. Gen. William *Sherman, who had succeeded Grant in command of Union forces in the West, captured Atlanta in September before making his historic March to the Sea. After taking Savannah in December, Sherman moved north through the Carolinas. In April 1865, he won a decisive victory at Five Forks, Va., the last major battle of the war. Lee surrendered to Grant at Appomattox Court House on Apr 9. By June, the federal victory was complete and the task of *Reconstruction lay ahead.

civitas Citizenship in ancient Rome acquired either by birth or by grant from the people or emperor. It was a much coveted privilege, entailing voting rights and facilitating an administrative or military career. As Rome expanded *civitas* was gradually extended to its Italian allies (89 BC) and to subjects of some Roman provinces (from 43 BC). In 212 AD all free inhabitants of the Empire were made citizens. An autonomous provincial city was also known as a *civitas*.

Civitavecchia 42 05N 11 47E A seaport in central Italy, in Lazio. It has Etruscan and Roman remains and a citadel designed by Michelangelo. There is a fishing industry. Population (1971): 48,460.

Clair, René (R. Chomette; 1898–1981) French film director. Both his early silent comedies and his pioneering sound films, such as *Sous les toits de Paris* (1930), were distinguished by his gifts for humor and fantasy. During World War II he worked in Hollywood, and his later films included *Les Belles de nuit* (1952).

Clairvaux (Latin: *clara vallis,* beautiful valley) The *Cistercian monastery founded (1115) by St *Bernard of Clairvaux in the Aube Valley (NE France), which remained the most influential Cistercian house until its suppression (1790) during the French Revolution.

clairvoyance. *See* extrasensory perception.

clam A *bivalve mollusk with two equal shells and a muscular burrowing foot. Burrowing clams live buried in sand and mud, mainly in shallow coastal waters; they feed by taking in water through a tube (siphon) extended into the water. The largest burrowing clam is the geoduck (*Panopea generosa*), weighing up to 11 lb (5 kg), while the giant clam (*Tridacna gigas*) can exceed 550 lb (250 kg).

clan A group tracing actual or putative descent in either the male or female line from a common ancestor. Clans are frequently important divisions in primitive societies, as in the pre-18th century Scottish Highlands. They are often exogamous (prohibiting marriage between members). Many have a totemic emblem taking the form of an animal or plant, from which members are believed to descend, and perform collective ceremonies.

The Scottish clans, until their suppression following the *Jacobite rebellions of 1715 and 1745, controlled distinctive territories and were frequently rivals. The members of a clan wore characteristic clothing (*see* Highland dress) and often bore the name of its founder preceded by Mac (son of), e.g. MacDonald. The clan chiefs are still officially recognized, both in Scotland and Ireland.

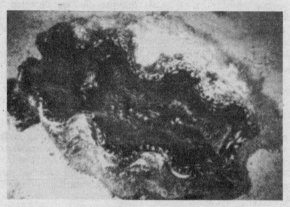

CLAM *The largest of the bivalve mollusks, the giant clam reaches 4 ft (1.2 m) across. This specimen is from the Great Barrier Reef.*

Clancy, Tom (Thomas L. Clancy; 1947–   ) US author noted for his high-tech thrillers. His first novel *The Hunt for Red October* (1984), an unexpected best seller, concerned a Soviet submarine commander who defects to the United States with his boat and officers. It subsequently became a successful film. Clancy's mastery of the technological apparatus of modern military forces virtually created a new genre of American popular fiction and inspired numerous other authors. Clancy followed this first success with the best sellers *Red Storm Rising* (1986); *Patriot Games* (1987), which concerned terrorism and was released as a film in 1992; *The Sum of All Fears* (1991); and *Without Remorse* (1993).

Clare (Irish name: Chláir) A county in the W Republic of Ireland, in Munster situated between Galway Bay and the Shannon estuary. It consists of a low-lying central plain rising E to mountains and W to the limestone area of the Burren. Agriculture is the chief occupation with cattle rearing and dairy farming. The salmon fisheries are important. Area: 1231 sq mi (3188 sq km). County town: Ennis.

Clarendon, Constitutions of (1164) Regulations concerning the relations between church and state issued by Henry II of England. They aimed to limit the power of the church, especially of the ecclesiastical courts, and to bring the church more firmly under royal authority. Thomas *Becket, Archbishop of Canterbury, repudiated his allegiance to the Constitutions, which action eventually led to his murder.

Clarendon, Edward Hyde, 1st Earl of (1609–74) English statesman and historian. In the events that led up to the English *Civil War he tried to influence Charles I toward moderation. He went into exile in 1646, settling eventually with the future Charles II in France. At the Restoration (1660) he became Lord Chancellor. His daughter Anne married the future James II. He was criticized for the sale of Dunkirk to France (1662) and for his handling of the second *Dutch War (1664–67). Forced again into exile, he completed his monumental *History of the Rebellion and Civil Wars in England* (1702–04).

Clarendon Code (1661–65) A series of Acts, passed by Charles II's government, that were directed against *Nonconformists (*or* Dissenters). They included the Corporation Act (1661), which excluded Nonconformists from municipal office, and the Act of Uniformity (1662), which enforced the use of the Church of England's Book of Common Prayer. The Code is named for the king's first minister, the Earl of *Clarendon.

Clare of Assisi, St (1194–1253) Italian nun, founder of the "Poor Clares." Influenced by the teaching of St *Francis of Assisi, she gave up all her possessions and followed him. St Francis established a community of women with Clare as abbess in 1215. They lived in absolute poverty without even communal property. She was canonized in 1255. Feast day: Aug 12.

clarinet A woodwind instrument with a single reed and a cylindrical bore. It is a transposing instrument existing in several sizes and generally has a fundamental of A- or B-flat; it has a range of three and a half octaves. The clarinet did not become a regular member of the orchestra until the late 18th century. Mozart popularized it, using it in several symphonies and writing a concerto and quintet for the instrument. The **bass clarinet** is pitched an octave lower than the B-flat clarinet. □musical instruments.

Clark, Champ (James Beauchamp C.; 1850–1921) US lawyer, politician, speaker of the House (1911–19). After attending schools in his native Kentucky and setting up a law practice in Missouri, he served in the US Congress (1893–95; 1897–1921). Democratic minority leader in 1907, he was elected speaker in 1911 after the Democrats became the majority. He ran unsuccessfully for the Democratic presidential nomination in 1912.

Clark, George Rogers (1752–1818) US pioneer, soldier, and surveyor. After doing survey work in the Ohio Valley, he served in the Virginia militia during the Revolutionary War and, participating in the Northwest Campaign, led successful attacks on key British-held posts in the Illinois country (now Illinois and Indiana).

Clark, Jim (James C.; 1937–68) British automobile race driver, who won a total of 25 Grand Prix races between 1959 and 1968, when he was killed in a crash. He was world champion in 1963 and 1965.

Clark, Joe (Charles Joseph C.; 1939–   ) Canadian politician; prime minister (1979–80). President of the Progressive Conservative Party Student Federation (1962–65), he served his party in the House of Commons (1972–76) and as leader of the Progressive Conservative Party. Elected prime minister in 1979 to succeed Pierre Trudeau, he held the position for nine months before his government fell to the Liberals.

Clark, Kenneth B(ancroft) (1914–   ) US psychologist, educator, and reformer; born in the Panama Canal Zone. After completing his education at Howard and Columbia universities, he taught psychology at City College of New York from 1942. His report on racial discrimination in the schools (1950) was used in the 1954 Supreme Court ruling on the unconstitutionality of public school segregation. His works include *Prejudice and Your Child* (1955), *Dark Ghetto* (1965), and *The Pathos of Power* (1974).

Clark, Kenneth (Mackenzie), Baron (1903–83) British art historian. As a young man, Clark worked with *Berenson in Florence. He was director of the National Gallery (1934–45), professor of fine art at Oxford (1946–50, 1961–62), and professor of art history at the Royal Academy, and the author of many works on individual artists and aspects of art. His television series *Civilization* greatly stimulated public appreciation of art.

Clark, Mark Wayne (1896–1984) US Army general. A West Point graduate (1917), he saw action in France during World War I and commanded US ground forces in Europe during World War II. He served under Gen. Dwight D. *Eisenhower and led invasions of North Africa (1942) and Italy (1943). He commanded US troops in Austria (1945–47) and UN troops in Korea (1952–53). After retiring from the Army (1953), he became president of the Citadel (1954–66).

Clark, Ramsey (1927–) US lawyer and public official; son of Tom C. *Clark. During his term as US attorney general (1967–69) he supported civil rights and opposed capital punishment, police violence, wiretapping, and the Vietnam War. He ran unsuccessfully for the Senate (1974) as a Democrat from New York and, defying a travel ban, headed a delegation to Iran (1980) to argue for the release of the American hostages held there. He wrote *Search and Destroy* (1972).

Clark, Tom C(ampbell) (1899–1977) US lawyer, associate justice of the Supreme Court (1949–67). After practicing law in his native Dallas, Tex., he worked in the US Department of Justice (1937–45) until he was appointed US attorney general (1945–49) by President Truman. Appointed by Truman to the Supreme Court in 1949, he is most noted for his opinion that upheld desegregation of public facilities as stated in the Civil Rights Act of 1964. He retired from the court in 1967 when his son, Ramsey *Clark, was appointed US attorney general.

Clark, William (1770–1838) US explorer and politician; younger brother of George Rogers *Clark. He traveled and explored the Northwest Territory with Meriweather *Lewis in 1804–06. He and Lewis left St Louis, crossed the Rocky Mountains, traveled to the mouth of the Columbia River at the Pacific Ocean, and returned to St Louis, mapping and chronicling the entire journey. He served as head of Indian affairs for the Louisiana Territory (1807–13; 1821–38) and as governor of Missouri Territory (1813–21).

Clarkia A genus of herbaceous plants (36 species) found naturally in semiarid environments in California and Chile. Horticultural varieties are grown as summer annuals. About 12 in (30 cm) tall, they are slender, showy, and mostly pink-flowered. Family: *Onagraceae* (willowherb family).

classical art and architecture. *See* Greek art and architecture; Roman art and architecture.

classical literature. *See* Greek literature; Latin literature.

classicism The aesthetic qualities that were embodied in the visual arts and literature of ancient Greece and Rome and served as ideals for various later European and American artistic movements. Qualities associated with this concept include harmony and balance of form, clarity of expression, and emotional restraint.

The Italian *Renaissance of the 15th and 16th centuries was the first and most general attempt to revive these qualities in the arts. Major productions of this period included the sculpture of *Michelangelo, the paintings of *Raphael and

*Titian, and the architecture of *Palladio. These achievements provided the artistic standards that other European artists attempted to emulate for the next two centuries. The art of the French 17th century painters *Poussin and *Claude Lorraine was greatly influenced by their study of Renaissance and classical models. Examples of the various neoclassical movements in the 18th century include the paintings of *David and *Ingres in France and the sculpture of *Canova in Italy, while in England the lectures of Sir Joshua *Reynolds at the Royal Academy were based on classical and Renaissance doctrines.

In literature, Renaissance interpretations of Aristotle's *Poetics* influenced writers throughout Europe in the 17th and 18th centuries, notably in the reigns of Louis XIV (1642–1715) in France and Anne (1702–14) in England. The tragic dramas of *Racine and *Corneille represent classicism in literature at its height.

Toward the end of the 18th century there was a general reaction against the rigid neoclassicist doctrines, but in England and the US, the popularity of the Greek Revival school of architecture continued the classical ideal in its use of columns, entablatures, and friezes.

clathrate A compound formed by the physical trapping of the molecules of one substance in the crystal lattice of another. No chemical bonds are formed between the host compound and the trapped molecule. Zeolites form clathrates with many simple compounds by virtue of their cagelike crystal structure. Ice can also form clathrate compounds with some of the *noble gases.

Claude Lorraine (Claude Gellée; 1600–82) French landscape painter. He was born in Lorraine but settled permanently in Rome (1626), where he had earlier received his training. His idealized paintings of the Roman countryside sometimes include small biblical or classical figures and his seascapes and harbor scenes are remarkable for their glowing sunlight. Both were highly esteemed by such patrons as Pope Urban VIII. His *Liber veritatis* (British Museum), dating from 1635, documents his career through drawings and notes and was intended to prevent later forgeries.

Claudian (c. 370–404 AD) Roman poet. Born in Alexandria, he went to Rome in 395. His praise for Stilicho, elected consul in 400, gained him high civil status. His works include panegyrics, satires, epigrams, and the epic poem *The Rape of Proserpine*.

Claudius I (10 BC–54 AD) Roman emperor (41–54). Claudius owed his accession to the chaos that followed the murder of his nephew Emperor *Caligula. His rule was generally efficient; he extended the Empire, taking part in the invasion of Britain (43), but his susceptibility to the influence of freed men and of his third wife Valeria *Messalina alienated the Senate. *Agrippina the Younger, his niece and fourth wife, was suspected of his murder. Claudius had been taught by Livy and he himself wrote histories.

Clausewitz, Karl von (1780–1831) Prussian general and military theorist. In 1812 Clausewitz negotiated the Treaty of Tauroggen, which set in motion the joint Prussian, Russian, and British war effort against Napoleon. In 1818 Clausewitz became director of the German War Academy. Of his many military works the posthumously published *Vom Kriege* is the most famous. Rejecting old ideas of strategy and systems of war in favor of total warfare backed by the will of the people, *Vom Kriege* became a military classic and had a profound influence up to World War I.

Clausius, Rudolf Julius Emanuel (1822–88) German physicist, who in 1854 formulated the concept of *entropy and used it in a statement of the second law of thermodynamics. He also contributed to the development of the *kinetic theory of gases and suggested that electrolysis involved the dissociation of molecules into charged particles.

clavichord A keyboard instrument, popular from the 15th to the 18th centuries and revived in the mid-20th century. Its delicate tone is produced by small brass plates (called tangents) fixed to the end of each key, which strike the strings. Its body consists of a rectangular wooden box, usually without legs, which is portable and able to be placed on a table. It is strung lengthways and has a range of about four octaves. It is said to have been J. S. Bach's favorite instrument.

clavicle The collar bone. There are two clavicles, each running from the upper end of the breastbone to form a joint with the shoulder blade. They brace the shoulders and help to support the arms. Fractures of the clavicle are fairly common, caused by any fall involving the upper arm.

clawed frog A South African aquatic frog, *Xenopus laevis,* also called platanna. Up to 5 in (12 cm) long, with a flattened head and body, it has three short black claws on its hind feet, probably used for stirring up mud to confuse enemies. It is well known as the frog originally used in pregnancy tests.

clay A sedimentary deposit that has plastic properties when wet and hardens and cracks when dry. It consists of fine rock particles (less than 0.0002 in [0.004 mm] in diameter), formed from the decomposition of other rocks. The principal minerals present in clays (the clay minerals) are hydrous silicates, mainly of aluminum and magnesium, which occur as crystals with a layered structure, capable of absorbing and losing water. The main groups of clay minerals are kaolinite, montmorillonite-smectite, illite, and vermiculite.

Clay, Cassius. *See* Ali, Muhammad.

Clay, Henry (1777–1852) US politician; secretary of state (1825–29). A lawyer, he served in the US Senate (1806–07, 1810–11) before moving to the House (1811), where he was elected Speaker (1811–20, 1823–25). In the House he was a leader of the War Hawks, who advocated the expansionist *War of 1812 with Britain. In the election of 1821 he supported John Quincy Adams and then became his secretary of state. Later he returned to the Senate (1831–42; 1849–52). Called "The Great Compromiser," he is best known for his various efforts (e.g. the Missouri Compromise of 1820 and the Great Compromise of 1850) to hold the Union together on the issue of slavery.

clay-pigeon shooting. *See* shooting.

Clayton Anti-Trust Act (1914) US law that strengthened anti-trust regulations and increased the power of unions. Passed to strengthen the *Sherman Antitrust Act (1890), it specifically prohibited such practices as price fixing, stock and directorate interlocking, and competitive contract exclusion. It increased the powers of the unions in regard to picketing, striking, and restricting court injunctions in labor disputes.

Clayton-Bulwer Treaty (1850) A US-British treaty regarding a shipping canal between North and South America. It stated that if either country built a canal in the isthmus separating the two continents certain rules must be observed: the canal would be jointly owned and controlled; Central America would not be colonized or fortified further; the canal would be considered neutral. Forged by Britain's Sir Henry Bulwer and John Middleton Clayton, US secretary of state, the compromise was quite controversial and unpopular.

Cleanthes (c. 310–230 BC) Greek philosopher and follower of *Zeno of Citium. Cleanthes taught that reason is inherent in the nature of living things and virtue is voluntary assent to natural reason. *See also* Stoicism.

Clear and Present Danger A doctrine, indicated in the US Supreme Court case *Schenck* v. *United States* (1919) that stated that freedom of speech could be restricted to preserve national security.

clearing house Any institution that settles debts between members. For example, banks establish clearing houses to exchange, usually each business day, checks drawn against each other. This procedure reduces the payments made to, or received from, other banks to a single payment rather than one for each check processed. Commodity markets often use a clearing house to avoid passing checks between strings of brokers, dealers, etc., all debts being settled by difference accounts through the clearing house on an appointed account day.

Clearwater 27 58N 82 48W A city in W central Florida, N of St Petersburg, on Clearwater Bay. Clearwater Beach Island separates Clearwater Bay from the Gulf of Mexico and is connected to Clearwater by a causeway. Although its main industry is tourism, the processing of citrus fruits and the canning of fish are important activities. Population (1990): 98,784.

clearwing moth A moth of the widely distributed family *Sesiidae* (about 700 species), also called wasp moth. Many have clear wings and dark slender bodies with red or yellow markings, resembling bees and wasps. The larvae bore into roots and stems and are often serious pests.

cleavage The repeated division of a fertilized egg cell (zygote) to produce a ball of cells that forms the *blastula. In egg cells with little yolk, such as those of frogs and mammals, the entire cell divides: this is termed holoblastic cleavage. Meroblastic cleavage occurs in yolky egg cells, such as those of birds, when only the yolk-free region divides.

Cleaver, (Leroy) Eldridge (1935–   ) US African-American activist and author. A convert to the Black Muslim religion, he served time in prison (1954–66) for various crimes; *Soul on Ice* (1968) is about his experiences. He was active in the Black Panther Party. In 1968, to avoid jailing for parole violation, he fled to Algeria and, subsequently, France and Cuba, and did not return to the US until 1975.

cleavers An annual herb, *Galium aparine,* also called goosegrass, native to Eurasia and widely introduced elsewhere; 6–48 in (15–120 cm) high, this pernicious weed is named because of its habit of clinging by means of tiny hooks on its stems and leaves. Its hooked fruits enable efficient seed dispersal via humans and animals. Family: *Rubiaceae* (madder family).

clef (French: key) The symbol placed at the beginning of a musical stave to indicate the pitch of the notes. The treble clef, a decorative G, indicates that the second line up of the stave is the G above middle C; the bass clef, an archaic F, indicates that the fourth line up is the F below middle C. The C clef can be set on any of the lines of the stave to establish it as middle C; the alto clef (used for viola music) has the C on the middle line; the tenor clef (used for cello music) has the C on the fourth line up.

cleft palate An abnormality caused by failure of the left and right halves of the palate to fuse during embryonic development. It leaves the nasal and oral cavities in continuity and it may be associated with a *harelip. The cleft can be repaired surgically at 16 to 18 months of age.

Cleisthenes (d. 508 BC) Athenian politician, regarded as the architect of Athenian democracy. Cleisthenes, a member of the *Alcmeonid family, achieved political power by appealing to the people for support and his democratic reforms (508) broadened the basis of political power in Athens. He is reputed to have introduced *ostracism.

Cleland, John (1709–89) English novelist. He served as consul in Turkey and as an agent for the East India Company, but was later several times imprisoned for debt. His best-known book is the pornographic novel *Fanny Hill* (1748–49).

Clematis A genus of herbaceous or woody plants (about 250 species), mainly climbing perennials, widely distributed in temperate regions. The fruits are often covered with persistent silky hairs, conspicuous and attractive in winter, as in traveler's joy, or old man's beard (*C. vitalba*) of Europe. There are many horticultural varieties, grown for their showy flowers, usually purple, pink, or white. Some species from which popular garden varieties have been developed are *C. alpina, C. montana,* and *C. patens.* Family: **Ranunculaceae.*

Clemenceau, Georges (1841–1929) French statesman; prime minister (1906–09, 1917–20). A member of the chamber of deputies from 1876 to 1893, when he became known as the Tiger for his attacks on other politicians, he subsequently devoted much of his energies to polemical journalism. During his first premiership he strengthened ties with Britain and broke irrevocably with the socialists at home. During the prewar years he urged military preparation against Germany and then attacked the World War I government for defeatism until again becoming prime minister, when he led France to victory. He condemned the failure of the Treaty of Versailles to provide for French security.

Clement I, St (late 1st century AD) The fourth bishop of Rome. He was the supposed author of several patristic texts, including a letter to the church of Corinth and the *Apostolic Constitutions,* which suggest that he was highly esteemed by the Church as a mediator and legislator. He probably suffered martyrdom. Feast day: Nov 23.

Clement V (Bertrand de Got; 1264–1314) Pope (1305–14), first of the Avignon popes (*see* Avignon papacy). Clement was appointed by the influence of *Philip IV of France. Although he was a patron of learning, his pontificate was marked by venality, nepotism, and high taxation.

Clement VII (Giulio de' Medici; 1478–1534) Pope (1523–34). A cousin of *Leo X, as pope he attempted to follow a middle course between the conflicting policies of Emperor *Charles V and *Francis I of France. This affected his ability to deal effectively with *Henry VIII's divorce from Catherine of Aragon and explains his failure to curb Protestantism. Like other early Renaissance popes, he was a patron of the arts and learning.

Clement IX (Giulio Rospigliosi; 1600–69) Pope (1667–69). His pontificate was marked by disputes with Louis XIV concerning control of the French Church and Louis's harsh policy toward the Jansenists, whose persecution was stopped by the Peace of Clement IX (1669). Clement wrote both sacred and comic opera libretti besides sacred poetry and drama.

Clement XI (Giovanni Albani; 1649–1721) Pope (1700–21). Although austere and pious, he largely failed in the exercise of papal diplomacy, especially in the War of the *Spanish Succession, in the latter stages of which he reluctantly supported the Habsburg candidate. He also met with little success in attempts to defeat *Jansenism.

Clementi, Muzio (1752–1832) Italian pianist and composer. After settling in England in 1766, he became famous as a virtuoso, a composer of piano music, a teacher, a music publisher, and a piano manufacturer.

clementine A small *citrus tree bearing edible fruits, regarded by some as a hybrid between the tangerine and sweet orange; by others as a variety of tangerine. It is grown mainly in N Africa.

Clement of Alexandria (c. 150–c. 215 AD) Greek Christian theologian. He was probably born in Athens and is known to have studied Christianity at the school at Alexandria, of which he became head in 190. He was succeeded by his pupil *Origen after he had been forced to flee from Alexandria in 202 because of persecutions. Clement's writings are much influenced by *Gnosticism and his importance lies in bringing Greek philosophical ideas in to supplement Christian belief.

Cleon (c. 422 BC) Athenian politician and demagogue. An artisan by birth, Cleon opposed the moderate imperialism of the aristocrats in the Peloponnesian War. He persuaded the Athenians to execute the rebellious citizens of Mytilene (427) but the decision was eventually reversed. Cleon opposed peace with Sparta (425) and was killed fighting at Amphipolis.

Cleopatra VII (69–30 BC) Queen of Egypt (51–48, 47–30), famous as the mistress of Julius Caesar and then of Mark Antony. Cleopatra was coruler with her brother Ptolemy XIII (61–48), who ousted her in 48. Restored by Caesar, she accompanied him to Rome and gave birth to (allegedly) his son Caesarion. After Caesar's murder, Cleopatra returned to Egypt and in 41 she met Antony. In 37 he abandoned his wife Octavia and lived with Cleopatra, who bore him three sons. In 31 Antony's brother-in-law Octavian defeated Antony and Cleopatra at *Actium and in 30 they both committed suicide. Shakespeare's reconstruction of their story follows Plutarch's romantic account.

CLEOPATRA *A relief at the temple of Horus at Edfu shows Cleopatra (second from the right) as the goddess of love.*

Cleopatra's Needles A pair of ancient Egyptian *obelisks carved in the reign of Thutmose III (c. 1475 BC) at Heliopolis. They were moved by *Augustus Caesar to Alexandria in 12 BC. They were moved again in 1878, one being set up on the Victoria Embankment, London, the other in Central Park, New York City.

Clermont-Ferrand 45 47N 3 05E A city in central France, the capital of the Puy-de-Dôme department. Founded by the Romans, it was the ancient capital of Auvergne in the 16th century. It has a fine gothic cathedral and its university was established in 1810. Clermont-Ferrand has France's largest rubber industry and manufactures textiles, chemicals, food products, and metal goods. Population (1982): 152,000.

Cleveland 41 30N 81 41W A city in the US, in Ohio on Lake Erie. It is a major Great Lakes port and the largest city in Ohio. One of the country's leading iron and steel centers, its other industries include oil refining, food processing, and the manufacture of motor vehicles. Population (1990): 505,616.

Cleveland, (Stephen) Grover (1837–1908) US statesman; 22nd and 24th President of the United States (1885–89, 1893–97). Trained as a lawyer, Cleveland served as mayor of Buffalo, N.Y. (1881–82) and as governor (1882–84) before receiving the Democratic nomination for president in 1884. After defeating Republican James G. *Blaine in the general election, Cleveland embarked on an ambitious program of civil service reform and tariff reduction. These policies provoked considerable opposition, and he was defeated for re-election in 1888 by the Republican candidate Benjamin *Harrison. Nominated again by the Democratic Party in 1892, Cleveland returned to office and supported the repeal of the Sherman Silver Purchase Act, which had permitted the free coinage of silver and which was believed to be largely responsible for the economic crisis of 1893. In 1894 he authorized the use of federal troops to put an end to the *Pullman Strike. In foreign affairs, Cleveland was opposed to US intervention abroad and opposed the annexation of Hawaii. He also helped to mediate the boundary dispute between Great Britain and Venezuela in 1895. Although he hoped to run for re-election in 1896, Cleveland lost the Democratic nomination to William Jennings *Bryan.

Cleveland Bay A breed of horse developed in the Cleveland region of N Yorkshire, England, and always reddish brown (bay) with black mane, tail, and legs. It has a deep muscular body with relatively short legs and was used as a pack and coach horse. Today Clevelands are used mainly for crossing with Thoroughbreds to produce showjumpers. Height: $15\frac{1}{2}$–$16\frac{1}{2}$ hands (1.57–1.68 m).

Clianthus A genus of shrubs (4 species) found in Australia, New Zealand, Indochina, and the Philippines. Several are cultivated for their attractive flowers. The glory pea (*C. formosis*) is an evergreen semiprocumbent shrub, 40 in (100 cm) high, with red and purple flowers. Family: *Leguminosae*.

Cliburn, Van (Harvey Lavan C., Jr.; 1934–   ) US pianist. He won the National Music Festival Award (1948) and from 1951 studied in New York City. In 1958 he became the first American to win the International Tchaikovsky Piano Competition in Moscow. He subsequently toured widely and made numerous recordings.

click beetle A long narrow flat beetle, also called skipjack beetle, belonging to a large and worldwide family (*Elateridae*; 8000 species). If upturned it is able to right itself by springing into the air, making a clicking sound in the process. The larvae, known as wireworms, are serious pests of root crops. Species of the genus *Pyrophorus* are luminous, resembling *firefly beetles.

cliffbrake A *fern of the genus *Pellaea* (about 80 species), found worldwide on rocks, mainly limestone. It has small elongated blue-green branched fronds, which overlap at the leaf margins to protect the spore capsules. Family: *Sinopteridaceae*.

climate The long-term weather conditions prevalent in an area. Climate is determined by three main factors. The first is latitude and the tilt of the earth's axis, which determines the amount of solar radiation received by an area. Second, the distribution of land and sea will affect climate as the land heats and cools far more rapidly than the sea. Ocean currents will also modify a region's climate. The third factor is the altitude and topography of an area; temperature will fall with increased altitude and hills and mountain barriers force clouds to rise and produce rainfall. Over long periods major changes in climate may occur, as in the *Ice Age. The study of the climate is called **climatology**.

climax In ecology, the final stage in the process of ecological *succession, in which a stable community of plants and animals becomes established. A typical climax community would be a deciduous woodland.

climbing perch A *labyrinth fish, *Anabas testudineus,* also called climbing or walking fish, that occurs in ponds and ditches of Asia. Its brownish-gray or greenish-gray body is about 10 in (25 cm) long. It can travel overland for short periods using its tail, pectoral fins, and gill covers and during the dry season it lies dormant in mud.

clingfish A *bony fish, also called sucker, belonging to the family *Gobiesocidae* (about 100 species), found mainly in salt water. Clingfish have an elongated scaleless body, up to 3 in (7.5 cm) long, a wide flattened head, and a suction disc formed from the pelvic fins with which it attaches itself to the bottom. Order: *Gobiesociformes.*

Clinton, De Witt (1769–1828) US statesman; governor of New York (1817–21, 1825–28). He became famous for his scheme to build the Erie Canal, "Clinton's Ditch," which was finished in 1825. It opened up the West by linking the Hudson River with the Great Lakes and made New York City the most important US port.

Clinton, George (1739–1812) US politician, soldier, governor of New York (1777–95; 1800–04) and US vice president (1805–12). He served in the French and Indian War, then studied law in his native New York, and eventually went to the Second Continental Congress. As governor of New York, he opposed ratification of the US Constitution, fearing a loss of states' rights. He served as vice president under Thomas *Jefferson and James *Madison.

Clinton, Hillary Rodham (1947–   ), US lawyer and wife of Pres. Bill Clinton, who was noted for her advocacy of national health-care reform. She graduated from Yale Law School, where she met her husband, and went into private law practice in Little Rock, Arkansas, where she became a leading attorney. Her strongly stated positions and active campaign involvement made her a target of Bill Clinton's political opponents. After his inauguration, she was named to head a commission to draft a national health-care plan, which was received with controversy.

Clinton, William Jefferson ("Bill") (Born William Jefferson Blythe 4th, (1946–   ) US statesman; 42nd President of the US (1993–   ). A Democrat, he ran with Albert Gore as his vice-presidential candidate and defeated Pres. George Bush in the 1992 election. He adopted his stepfather's name when he was 15. A Rhodes scholar and Yale Law School graduate, Clinton returned to his native Arkansas and was elected governor (1978–81; 1982–92). Emerging as a power in national Democratic politics, Clinton made a nominating speech for presidential candidate Michael Dukakis at the 1988 Democratic convention.

After announcing his presidential candidacy in 1991, Clinton campaigned extensively, overcoming a public perception that he was evasive about personal issues. The 1992 campaign against President Bush was complicated by the independent candidacy of H. Ross Perot. Clinton's emphasis on domestic issues, particularly the sagging economy, played a key part in his victory. Early in his term he faced problems in the Somalia relief effort, in reducing budget deficits, and in reforming national health care, while successfully pushing for approval of *NAFTA.

Clive of Plassey, Robert, Baron (1725–74) British soldier and colonial administrator. He joined the East India Company in 1743 and went to Madras, India. In 1757 he recaptured Calcutta from the Nawab of Bengal, whom he then defeated at *Plassey. This victory assured the East India Company control of Bengal, of which Clive was virtual ruler until 1760. He was appointed governor and commander in chief of Bengal (1764–67).

cloaca The posterior chamber of the body in all vertebrate animals except the placental mammals, into which the digestive, urinary, and genital tracts open. Feces, urine, and eggs or sperm are discharged through its vent.

clock A mechanical device for measuring the passage of time. Clockwork has two essential components: an energy store (a raised weight or a coiled spring) and an escapement that regulates the release of energy from the store. The earliest recorded escapement was in a giant Chinese astronomical clock (c. 1090 AD). Early European clocks were crude ironwork with verge escapements driven by falling weights and recording time by striking on the hour, but the 14th-century Italian family of Dondi introduced dials on their sophisticated astronomical mechanisms. The innovation of mainsprings about 1500 enabled portable clocks (*see also* watch) to be made. Refinements in the 17th century were the anchor escapement (1671) and the application of pendulums to clockwork (*see* Huygens). Both resulted in greatly increased accuracy and during the next 150 years clocks successfully challenged *sundials as the principal domestic timekeepers. Long-case (grandfather) and bracket clocks assumed their modern forms. Carriage clocks were introduced in 1810 by the French firm of Breguet. An important advance in the 18th century was the development of an accurate marine chronometer, used by navigators to determine position. Scientific advances in the 20th century have led to the development of clocks powered by the natural vibrations of atoms (*see* atomic clocks). The *cesium clock, first made in 1955, is so accurate that one specific line in the spectrum of cesium is now the standard by which time is defined (*see* second), replacing the period of the earth's rotation.

Clodion (Claude Michel; 1738–1814) French *rococo sculptor. Working in Rome (1762–71) and Paris, he enjoyed a wide reputation until the French Revolution, when the rococo style was superseded by *neoclassicism. Although he specialized in small terracotta sculptures of nymphs, satyrs, etc., he also produced more sober works, notably the lifesize marble sculpture of Montesquieu (1783; Versailles).

cloisonné (French: partitioned) A technique of decorating metal surfaces with polychrome *enamelwork. Thin metal strips are soldered edgewise to the surface following the outlines of the design and the resulting compartments filled with colored enamels. The work is then fired, fusion of the colors being prevented by the strips, and the surface ground smooth and polished. Beautiful cloisonné vases, brooches, etc., were produced in medieval Europe, while China and Japan perfected the technique in the 17th, 18th, and 19th centuries.

clone A population of organisms produced from a single parent cell by asexual division—for example by vegetative reproduction in plants or parthenogenesis in animals. The individuals of a clone are genetically identical. Thus cloning, if it could be achieved in humans, would provide the means of producing a whole generation of identical siblings—a concept that still remains in the realms of science fiction. However, some lower animals have been successfully cloned by inserting the nucleus of a somatic (body) cell of the animal to be cloned into an egg cell from which its own nucleus has been removed.

closed-end investment company A company that buys and sells *securities in order to make profits to distribute to its shareholders. The company has a fixed capital and its shares are bought and sold on the *stock exchange. In-

vestors (shareholders) have the advantage of being part owners of a profession-
ally managed portfolio of securities.

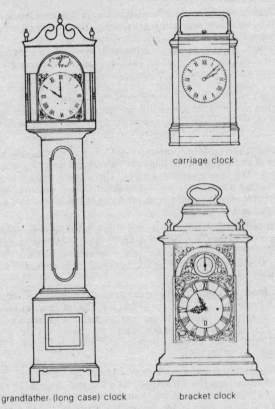

carriage clock

grandfather (long case) clock   bracket clock

CLOCK *Three traditional forms of domestic clock.*

closed shop A place of work in which all employees are required to be members of one or more specified labor unions. Closed shops are usually sanctioned
by the employer, whose *collective bargaining position may be made simpler if
the union (or unions) can speak for the whole workforce. The disadvantage of
closed shops is that they exclude from employment those who object to belonging to a labor union.

Clostridium A genus of rod-shaped spore-forming bacteria that occur widely
in soil and the gastrointestinal tract of animals and man. Some produce powerful
toxins (poisons), particularly *C. tetani*, which causes *tetanus, and *C. botu-
linum*, which causes *botulism.

clothes moth A small *tineid moth whose larvae feed on clothes, carpets,
blankets, etc. There are a number of species of widespread distribution. Adults
generally have a wingspan of 0.5–1.0 in (12–25 mm) and are pale gray-brown in
color. They prefer dark places. Pesticides, dry cleaning, and man-made fibers
have reduced their damaging effects.

Clotho. *See* Fates.

Clotilda. *See* Clovis.

cloud A mass of minute water droplets or ice crystals, or a combination of both, produced by the condensation of water vapor in the atmosphere. When conditions are favorable the droplets grow and precipitation may occur. Various classifications of clouds exist but the one internationally agreed upon and most extensively used by meteorologists is based on cloud appearance and height and comprises 10 principal forms. The high clouds, normally above 16,000 ft (5000 m) are *cirrus (Ci), *cirrostratus (Cs), and *cirrocumulus (Cc). The medium clouds at 6500–16,000 ft (2000–5000 m) comprise *altocumulus (Ac) and *altostratus (As). Below this level the low clouds are *stratus (St), *stratocumulus (Sc), and *nimbostratus (Ns). Some clouds grow vertically and cannot be classified solely by height; these are chiefly *cumulus (Cu) and cumulonimbus.

cloud chamber A device, invented by C. T. R. *Wilson, that makes visible the tracks of ionizing particles; it is used for studying their properties. It contains a chamber filled with a saturated vapor. The vapor is expanded adiabatically (usually using a piston) to cool it and so make it supersaturated. When an ionizing particle passes through the chamber drops of liquid condense along its trail, thus making the trail visible.

clouded leopard A large nocturnal forest *cat, *Neofelis nebulosa,* of SE Asia, Borneo, Sumatra, and Java. It is 48–75 in (120–190 cm) long including its tail 24–35 in (60–90 cm) and has a grayish or yellowish coat with black markings. It is an expert climber, using its heavy tail for balance, and feeds on birds and small mammals. □mammal.

Clouet, Jean (c. 1485–1540) Portrait painter, probably of Flemish origin. He worked in France as court painter to Francis I. The influence of Italian *Renaissance portraiture was stronger in the court portraits of his son **François Clouet** (c. 1515–72), who succeeded to his father's post in about 1540. François introduced informal poses, as in his portrait of *Diane de Poitiers (Washington), which shows her in her bath.

clove An evergreen Indonesian tree, *Eugenia caryophyllata,* growing to a height of 40 ft (12 m). The dried flower buds are used as spice. The whole tree is aromatic, clove oil being distilled from the buds, stalks, and leaves for use in medicine and as artificial vanilla. Clove production was once a Dutch Indonesian monopoly but the trees are now grown in many regions, including Madagascar, Brazil, and Tanzania. Family: *Myrtaceae.*

clover An annual or perennial plant of the genus *Trifolium* (about 290 species), which also includes the *trefoils. Clovers, which occur mainly in N temperate regions, have leaves divided into three leaflets and dense heads of flowers. Extensively cultivated as fodder plants, they are also valuable for their nitrogen-fixing ability. *Alsike, red clover (*T. pratense*), and crimson clover (*T. incarnatum*) are three widely grown and naturalized species. Family: *Leguminosae.*

Clovis (c. 466–511) King of the Salian *Franks (481–511), of the Merovingian dynasty, who conquered N Gaul (494), founding a kingdom that dominated western Europe. He married (c. 493) Clotilda, (c. 475–c. 545), a fervent Christian, whose efforts to convert him succeeded after an important victory over the Alamanni (496), when he was baptized with some 3000 warriors. He was regarded as defender of the faith against *Arianism. After defeating the Visigoths near Poitiers (507), he established his capital at Paris. Clovis sponsored the promulgation of the *Salic Law.

Clovis point A fluted stone weapon point found in sites in many parts of North America after about 10,000 BC. They vary in length from 1 in (2.5 cm) to 7½ in (19 cm). *Compare* Folsom point.

clubfoot A deformity in which the foot is abnormally twisted at the ankle joint, so that the sole cannot rest flat on the ground when the person is standing. Its medical name is talipes. When the defect is present at birth it can often be corrected by strapping the foot in the correct position. Surgical correction may be necessary for severe deformities.

clubmoss A perennial mosslike plant, also called ground pine, belonging to a genus (*Lycopodium*; about 200 species) of *pteridophytes, found mainly in tropical and subtropical forests and mountainous regions. It has a creeping stem with wiry branches, densely covered with green, yellowish, or grayish needle-like leaves. The spore capsules occur at the base of special leaves (sporophylls), which are often arranged in conelike clusters (strobili). Family: *Lycopodiaceae*; class: *Lycopsida. See also* Selaginella.

clubroot A disease, caused by the fungus *Plasmodiophora brassicae,* that affects the roots of plants of the family *Cruciferae,* especially brassicas (cabbages, etc.). The infected cells become greatly enlarged, resulting in the deformed nodular roots characteristic of the disease. Control measures include liming, growing in clean soil, and using appropriate fungicides.

Cluj (German name: Klausenburg, Hungarian name: Koloszvár) 46 47N 23 37E A city in NW Romania, on the Someşul River. A former capital of Transylvania, it possesses several educational institutions, including a university (1872). A major industrial center, its manufactures include metal products, chemicals, and textiles. Population (1992 est): 328,000.

Cluny 46 25N 4 39E A village in E France, in the Saône-et-Loire department. Its famous Benedictine abbey (founded 910 AD) became the center of the Cluniac order, a reformed Benedictine order that was widely influential in Europe (c. 950–c. 1130).

clutch A device enabling two rotating shafts to be coupled and uncoupled. Positive clutches have square or spiral jaws to transmit torque without slipping. They can be used where slow speeds and light loads are involved, but normally both shafts have to be at rest for engagement. Friction clutches provide a period of slipping while the shafts are being engaged, and they do not have to be stopped for engagement. The torque is transmitted by friction between attachments to each shaft: in a plate clutch the attachments are flat disks, which press against each other; in a hydraulic clutch they are radial vanes immersed in a fluid. In a motor vehicle a clutch is used between the engine and the gearbox, usually a plate clutch for manual gearboxes and a hydraulic clutch for automatic transmissions.

Clutha River A river in New Zealand, the longest river in South Island. It flows generally S from Lake Wanaka, in the Southern Alps, to enter the Pacific Ocean near Kaitangata. Length: 210 mi (340 km).

Clyde, River A river in W Scotland. Rising in SE Strathclyde Region, it flows NW through Glasgow and the Clydebank to enter the Atlantic Ocean at the Firth of Clyde. It is important for its large shipbuilding industries. Length: 106 mi (170 km).

Clydebank 55 54N 4 24W A city in W central Scotland, in Strathclyde Region on the River Clyde. Ship building and the manufacture of sewing machines are the main industries. Population (1981): 51,656.

Clydesdale A breed of horse developed in the Clydesdale region of Scotland in the 18th century. Used for draft purposes, it has a deep compact body with strong legs and feet and may be bay, brown, black, or chestnut. Height: about 17 hands (1.75 m).

Clytemnestra In Greek legend, the daughter of Tyndareus, King of Sparta, and Leda, and wife of *Agamemnon. She and her lover Aegisthus killed Agamemnon on his return from the Trojan War and she herself was killed by her son *Orestes.

Cnidos An ancient Greek city at the SW extremity of Asia Minor. Never politically important, Cnidos was known for its wine, *Praxiteles' statue of Aphrodite, and its medical school. The rebuilt city's rectangular street plan (c. 350 BC) is an outstanding example of Greek town planning.

coal A carbonaceous mineral deposit used as a fuel and raw material for the plastics and chemical industries. Coal results from the compaction and heating of partially decomposed fossil vegetable matter. During the coalification process the plant remains are changed progressively from a peatlike material into lignite (brown coal), sub-bituminous and bituminous coal, semianthracite, and anthracite. During this process the percentage of carbon present increases and the moisture and volatile content decreases; anthracite is about 90% carbon. These coals are known as the humic coals. The sapropelic coals (cannel coal and bog-head coal) are derived from finely divided vegetable matter (algae, spores, and fungal material). Most coal was formed in the Carboniferous period, although some of the younger coals, for example lignite, date from Mesozoic and Tertiary times.

Coal has been mined since Roman times but on a small scale until the industrial revolution. In about 1800 coal was being carbonized on a commercial scale for the first time, the resulting *coal gas being used for gas lighting and the coke for smelting iron ore. By the middle of the 19th century, interest in the by-products (coal tar, ammonia, and pitch) was awakening. The chemistry of the constituents of coal tar developed into the study of organic chemistry, and the use of aromatic compounds from coal tar led to the development of the dyestuffs and explosives industries. In the 20th century these products also became the foundation of the plastics industry. During the 1920s and 1930s processes were also developed (mainly in Germany) for converting coal into oil—providing Germany with valuable quantities of oil during World War II. Subsequently, *natural gas has largely replaced coal gas and petrochemicals (see oil) have to a considerable extent replaced coal tar as sources of organic raw materials. However, the rising price of oil products in the 1970s, reflecting their diminishing reserves, has reawakened a worldwide interest in coal. Recent world consumption is slightly in excess of 3000 million tons per annum and known reserves are capable of supplying this quantity for several centuries.

coal gas A gas consisting mainly of hydrogen (50%) and methane (30%), with some carbon monoxide (8%) and other gases. It is made by destructive distillation of coal, a process that involves heating it to 587°F (1000°C). Coal gas was formerly supplied to homes for heating and cooking, but it has now been largely replaced, in the UK, by *natural gas from the North Sea.

Coal Measures. See Carboniferous period.

coal tit A Eurasian *tit, *Parus ater.* It is about 4 in (11 cm) long with a gray back, buff underparts, a black crown and bib, and distinctive white cheeks and nape. It occurs in coniferous woodland, using its slender bill to extract insects from cones and beneath bark.

Coast and Geodetic Survey US agency of the Department of the Interior that measures the land and the earth's curvature and shape. It also conducts coastal area studies.

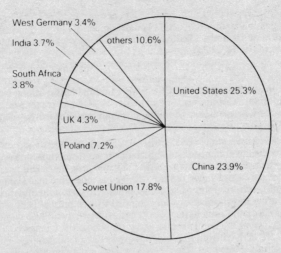

COAL *World production.*

Coast Guard A naval force established by many nations to prevent maritime evasion of customs duties and to ensure the safety of navigation. The US Coast Guard was established in 1790 as a division of the Department of the Treasury. Originally called the Revenue Cutter Service, it received its current name in 1915. The Coast Guard now provides meteorological information to mariners, maintains navigational aids and lighthouses, and is responsible for customs, immigration, pollution control, and the enforcement of maritime law. In 1967 the Coast Guard was placed under the supervision of the Department of Transportation. In wartime or at the request of the president, however, it functions as a branch of the US Navy.

Coast Mountains A mountain range of W Canada, extending from the US border 1000 mi (1600 km) N into Alaska. Very rugged, it rises steeply from the Pacific coast. It includes Canada's largest mountain mass and a long glacier belt. Mount Waddington at 13,260 ft (3978 m) is the highest point.

Coatbridge 55 52N 4 01W A city in central Scotland, in Strathclyde Region. It has important metallurgical industries. Population (1981): 50,866.

Coates, Joseph Gordon (1878–1943) New Zealand statesman; Reform Party prime minister (1925–28). He is best known for his stringent policies while minister of finance (1931–35), when he devalued the New Zealand pound, lowered interest rates, and encouraged trade within the British Commonwealth.

coati A carnivorous mammal, belonging to the genus *Nasua* (3 species), related to the *raccoons and occurring in Central and South American forests. About 39 in (1 m) long including a 19.7 in (50 cm) tapering tail, coatis have long snouts and grayish, reddish, or brown fur; they are good climbers, foraging in groups, in trees, or on the forest floor for seeds, eggs, and small mammals.

cobalt (Co) A transition metal similar to iron and noted for its deep-blue color when reacted in ceramics. It was discovered by G. Brandt (1694–1768) in 1735 and occurs naturally as cobaltite (CoAsS) and in copper, nickel, iron, silver, and lead ores. Cobalt is mined chiefly in Zaïre and Canada. It is used as an alloy in the manufacture of cutting steels and magnets. The chloride ($CoCl_2$) and oxides

(CoO and Co_3O_4) are used in the glass and ceramics industry. The isotope ^{60}Co is a strong gamma-emitter produced in nuclear reactors and used in radiotherapy (the **cobalt bomb**) and in industry. At no 27; at wt 58.9332; mp 2725°F (1495°C); bp 5203°F (2870°C)

Cobb, Ty (Tyrus Raymond C.; 1886–1961) US baseball player. Nicknamed the "Georgia Peach," he played the outfield for the Detroit Tigers (1905–26) and the Philadelphia Athletics (1927–28). With a lifetime hitting average of .367, a career total of 892 stolen bases, and a record 4191 hits, he set 90 records before retirement. He was a member of the first group elected to the Baseball Hall of Fame (1936).

Cobden, Richard (1804–65) British politician and economist, who was a leading advocate of free trade. A Manchester manufacturer, with John *Bright he formed the *Anti-Corn Law League (1839), which successfully fought for the repeal of the *Corn Laws (1846). A member of Parliament from 1843, he opposed Palmerston's "glory and gunpowder" foreign policy, negotiated an Anglo-French commercial treaty for the reduction of tariffs (1860), and campaigned for the 1867 Reform Act.

Coblenz. *See* Koblenz.

cob nut. *See* hazel.

COBOL (*c*ommon *b*usiness *o*riented *l*anguage) An international computer-programming language, developed in the US and used to express problems in commerce. A high-level language, it can describe business procedures in the form of readable English statements that are sufficiently standardized for presentation to a computer. *See also* program.

cobra A highly venomous snake occurring in warm regions of Africa and Asia and able to expand its neck ribs to form a hood. The king cobra (*Ophiophagus hannah*) of S Asia is over 12 ft (3.6 m) long, making it the largest venomous snake; it preys chiefly on other snakes. The common Indian cobra (*Naja naja*), used by snake charmers, is 6 ft (1.7 m) long and frequently enters houses at night in search of rats. The spitting cobra, or ringhals (*Hemachatus hemachatus*) and the black-necked cobra (*Naja nigricollis*), spit their venom into the eyes of attackers, causing blindness. Family: *Elapidae* (cobras, mambas, coral snakes). □reptile.

coca A Peruvian tree, *Erythroxylon coca,* cultivated in Java, South America, and Sri Lanka for its leaves, which—when dried—yield cocaine. Coca leaves have been chewed for centuries in South America for their effect in relieving fatigue and hunger; prolonged use can cause addiction and serious mental and physical deterioration. Family: *Erythroxylaceae.*

cocaine An alkaloid ($C_{17}H_{21}O_4N$) powder or solution derived from *coca leaves and also made synthetically. Cocaine was the first drug to be used for local anesthesia, but it has now largely been replaced for clinical use by safer, non-addictive drugs such as novocaine. Because cocaine is habit-forming and often causes dangerous side-effects, its non-medical use is strictly prohibited by law in most countries. *See* anesthesia; drug dependence.

coccus Any spherical bacterium. Cocci may occur singly, in clusters, or in chains. Examples are *Neisseria gonorrheae* (the gonococcus, which causes gonorrhea), *Staphylococcus,* and *Streptococcus.*

coccyx. *See* spine.

Cochabamba 17 26S 66 10W A city in Bolivia, situated in the E Andes. It is an important agricultural trading center (especially for grain). Industries include oil refining and it is the site of a university (1832). Population (1989 est): 404,000.

Cochin 9 56N 76 15E A major port in India, in Kerala on the Malabar Coast. Founded by the Portuguese in the 16th century, it achieved its greatest prosperity under Dutch rule (1663–1795). It is the Indian Navy's major training center. Population (1991): 564,038.

Cochin China A region in S Vietnam, long ruled from Saigon (now Ho Chi Minh City). It was divided for centuries before being annexed by *Annam in the 18th century. Following the dissolution of the Vietnamese empire it was a French colony (1867–1945) and then an overseas territory before becoming part of independent Vietnam (1949).

cochineal A natural red dye obtained from the dried bodies of certain female scale insects, especially *Dactylopius coccus* of Mexico. It has now been largely replaced by aniline dyes, but continues to be used for coloring foodstuffs and cosmetics.

Cochise (d. 1874) Apache Indian chief, who terrorized the SW US during the 1860s trying to prevent white settlement on his homeland. His band surrendered in 1871. His people were given a reservation on their own land. After his death there, his people were ordered to a more distant area.

cochlea. *See* ear.

Cockaigne An imaginary land of wealth and luxury, celebrated in medieval folklore. There are houses of barley sugar, roast pigs running in the streets with knives and forks in their backs, and a mountain of cheese. It features in some of the fairytales of the brothers Grimm.

cockatiel A small Australian *cockatoo, *Nymphicus hollandicus,* of interior grasslands. It is 13 in (32 cm) long and has a gray plumage with white wing patches, a yellow head and crest, and reddish ear patches.

cockatoo A *parrot belonging to a genus (*Cacatua*; 17 species) ranging throughout Australia, Malaysia, and the Philippines. Cockatoos are usually white, often with a pink or yellow blush, although some species are black; all have a long erectile crest and a large hooked bill used to crack open nuts and extract grubs from wood.

cockchafer A European beetle, *Melolontha melolontha,* also called maybug, that is very destructive to plants (*see* chafer). Up to 1.4 in (35 mm) long, it is black with reddish-brown legs and wing cases and has a loud buzzing flight. The larvae—which cause the most damage, particularly to cereals and grasses—are also called white grubs or rookworms.

Cockcroft, Sir John Douglas (1897–1967) British physicist, who shared the 1951 Nobel Prize with Ernest *Walton for their development of the first particle *accelerator. Their machine, built in 1932, was used for accelerating protons to split an atomic nucleus (of lithium) for the first time. In World War II he worked on the development of the atom bomb.

cocker spaniel A breed of gundog, thought to be of Spanish origin. It is compact with short legs, a short tail, and a square muzzle. The long flat silky coat is usually black, red, or cream, either plain or in mottled combinations. Height: 15–16 in (39–41 cm) (dogs); 15 in (38 cm) (bitches). □dog.

cockfighting A blood sport in which two or more gamecocks fight against each other, often to the death. Although illegal in some countries, it is still widespread in certain parts of the world. The cocks are carefully bred and trained, equipped with steel or bone spurs on their legs and set against each other in a cockpit. Being naturally fearless and very aggressive the cocks peck and gouge each other with intense fury. Heavy betting is a feature of the sport.

cockle A *bivalve mollusk of the widely distributed family *Cardiidae* (about 250 species). The ribbed shell valves, 0.4–9.2 in (1–23 cm) in diameter, are rounded, producing a relatively globular bivalve. Cockles burrow in sand or mud, straining food particles from water drawn in through their protruding siphons. The European cockle (*Cardium* [or *Cerastoderma*] *edule*) is edible.

cocklebur An annual plant, *Xanthium strumarium*, 8–30 in (20–75 cm) high, the fruiting heads of which are densely covered with hooked spines, which catch onto fur and clothing. It has been so widely and unintentionally dispersed by man and animals in warm and temperate regions that its place of origin is uncertain. Family: *Compositae*.

cockroach A nocturnal □insect belonging to the mainly tropical family *Blattidae* (3500 species). It has a black or brown flat body, 0.5–2.0 in (12–50 mm) long, with long antenne and leathery forewings. Cockroaches seldom fly; they feed on plant and animal materials and are household pests in dirty places. A widely distributed species is the common cockroach, or black beetle (*Blatta orientalis*). Order: *Dictyoptera*.

cocksfoot A perennial *grass, *Dactylis glomerata*, also known as orchard grass, cultivated throughout North America, Eurasia, and Africa as a pasture grass. It grows in dense tussocks, up to 40 in (1 m) tall.

cocoa and chocolate Foods derived from the seeds of the cacao □tree (*Theobroma cacao*), native to tropical South America and cultivated mainly in West Africa. The tree is pruned to a height of 16–20 ft (5–6 m) and woody pods, 10–12 in (23–30 cm) long, grow directly from its trunk. The pods contain 25–50 seeds (cocoa, or cacao, beans) embedded in a whitish pulp, which are scraped out, fermented, and dried before export. Manufacturing is carried out mainly in the importing countries, where the beans are shelled, roasted, and ground. From them cocoa powder and chocolate are made. Cocoa butter, a fat retained in chocolate but removed from cocoa powder, is a rich source of food energy. Molded chocolate is run into molds, which sometimes contain dried fruit, nuts, etc., to make blocks and bars of chocolate. Couverture (or confectionery) chocolate is used for covering cookies, dried fruit, or fruit fillings, etc. Family: *Sterculiaceae*.

cocodemer A *palm tree, *Lodoicea maldivica*, also known as double coconut, native to the Seychelles Islands. It grows 98 ft (30 m) tall and bears fleshy male and female flower spikes on separate plants. The female flowers produce the largest known fruit, up to 20 lb (9 kg) in weight, which takes 10 years to ripen. It consists of a fleshy fibrous envelope surrounding a hard two-lobed nut-like portion, containing edible flesh.

coconut The fruit of the coconut *palm, *Cocos nucifera*; one of the most important tropical crops. The tree has a slender trunk, up to 80 ft (25 m) high, which bears a crown of giant feather-like leaves. The coconuts, 12–18 in (30–45 cm) long and 6–8 in (15–20 cm) in diameter, take a year to ripen and have a thick fibrous husk surrounding a single-seeded nut. The hollow core contains coconut milk; the white kernel is eaten raw or dried to yield copra, from which coconut oil is extracted for use in soaps, synthetic rubbers, and edible oils. The residual coconut cake is used as a livestock feed and the coarse husk fiber (coir) is used for matting, etc.

coconut crab. *See* robber crab.

Cocos Islands (*or* Keeling Islands) Two Australian coral atolls in the E Indian Ocean. They were visited by Charles Darwin (1836). First settled in 1826, they were controlled by the family of a Scottish settler, John Clunies-Ross, from 1827 to 1972, although under Australian administration after 1955. Copra is produced and there is an important meteorological station. Area: 5 sq mi (13 sq km).

Cocteau, Jean (1889–1963) Immensely versatile French poet and artist. He made his name with the novel *Les Enfants terribles* (1929) and sketches written for *Diaghilev's ballet company, such as *Parade* (1917). In World War I he served as an ambulance driver and became acquainted with *Picasso, *Modigliani, *Apollinaire, and other leading painters and writers. In 1923 he was treated for opium addiction. His creative work includes poetry (*L'Ange Heurtebise*, 1925), plays (*Orphée*, 1926), novels, films (*Le Sang d'un poète*, 1929, and his own *Les Enfants terribles*, 1950), and graphic work in various media.

cod A carnivorous fish, *Gadus morhua*, that lives near the bottom in temperate N Atlantic waters and is commercially fished for food and liver oil. Its elongated body, up to 6 ft (1.8 m) long, is generally dark gray with spots and has three dorsal fins, two anal fins, and a whisker-like barbel on its lower jaw. *G. macrocephalus* is a similar N Pacific species. Family: *Gadidae* (haddock, ling, pollack, whiting, etc.); order: *Gadiformes*.

codeine An *analgesic drug used to relieve mild pain. It is a derivative of morphine but less toxic and less likely to become addictive. The combination of aspirin and codeine is a stronger pain killer than either of the two drugs used separately. Codeine combined with a chalky substance, such as kaolin, is an effective treatment for diarrhea. It depresses the cough center of the brain and is therefore often added to cough mixtures.

Code Napoléon The systematic collection of the *civil law of France. Drafted by a commission set up by *Napoleon I when he was first consul, the code—properly called the *Code Civil*—was brought into force in 1804. Representing the progressive legal thought of the time, it set out to be as clear and easily accessible as possible. It and the other codes subsequently produced under Napoleon's administration served as a model for civil law codes throughout Europe and the rest of the world and remain the basis of present French law.

codling moth A small European moth, *Cydia pomonella* (wingspan about 0.71 in [18 mm]), whose caterpillars eat apples and similar fruit. A serious economic pest, it has spread worldwide wherever apples are cultivated.

cod-liver oil A pale yellow fatty oil obtained from the liver of the cod. It is a rich source of vitamins A and D and is used in medicine to correct the effects of such diseases as rickets.

Cody, William F(rederick) (1846–1917) US showman, known as Buffalo Bill. An army scout and pony express rider, he gained his nickname from his success in supplying the men working on the Union (later Kansas) Pacific Railroad with buffalo—killing 4280 in 1867–68. In 1883 he began touring the US and Europe with his Wild West Show.

Coe, Sebastian (1956–) British middle-distance runner. He was a world record holder in the 800 m, the 1500 m, and the mile.

coeducation The education of both sexes together. Although support for the idea dates back to Plato, it has only recently been practiced to any extent. Coeducation could be found in some US elementary schools in the 17th century but it did not become widespread at all levels until the 20th century. Coeducation is also the norm in Scandinavia and in communist countries, and following World War II all Japanese schools became in principle coeducational. National attitudes still vary enormously, however, and many Muslim and Roman Catholic countries still favor the separate education of the sexes, especially during adolescence.

JEAN COCTEAU *With Sergei Diaghilev (right), about 1924. Cocteau's memoirs are one of the best sources of information on Diaghilev's circle and the Ballets Russes.*

coelacanth A *bony fish of the suborder *Coelacanthini.* Once thought to have been extinct for 60 million years, several living representatives have been found since the discovery, in 1938, of *Latimeria chalumne* off the coast of SE Africa. It has a heavy body, up to 5 ft (1.5 m) long, with a short head and limblike fins, and crawls on the bottom, feeding on other fish. Order: *Crossopterygii.*

coelenterate An aquatic invertebrate animal belonging to the phylum *Coelenterata* (or *Cnidaria*; about 9000 species), including *Hydra, *jellyfish, *sea anemones, *corals, etc. There are two different generations of the life cycle (*see* polyp; medusa) and either or both may occur. Coelenterates have a body cavity with a single opening (mouth) and stinging cells (nematocysts) used for defense or catching prey.

coelom The body cavity of many animals. In mammals (including man) the embryonic coelom is divided into three cavities, which become occupied by the lung, heart, and intestines. In the fully developed mammal the coelom is reduced to the virtually nonexistent spaces between the membranes lining the heart (the pericardium), the lungs (the pleura), and the intestines (the peritoneum).

Coen, Pieterszoon (1587–1629) Dutch colonial administrator; governor general of the Dutch East Indies (1618–23, 1627–29). He first visited the East

Indies in 1607, in the employ of the Dutch East India Company, which in 1614 appointed him to direct the Company's commerce in Asia. He was responsible for the conquest of the Banda Islands and for the first Dutch settlement in Formosa (now Taiwan).

coenzyme A nonprotein substance that forms a complex with certain enzymes and is essential for the proper functioning of these enzymes. Coenzymes include nucleotide derivatives, such as *ATP and NAD, coenzyme A (important in the *Krebs cycle), and *vitamins of the B complex.

Coeur, Jacques (c. 1395–1456) French merchant, who became *argentier* (court banker) to Charles VII of France around 1440. He helped to finance Charles's recapture of Normandy from the English (1450) but, disliked and envied for his wealth and power, he was arrested (1451) on a false charge. He escaped from prison and fled to Rome.

coffee The seeds (called beans) of certain tropical evergreen trees of the genus *Coffea*, which—when roasted, ground, and brewed in hot water—yield a stimulating drink. *C. arabica* is the most widely grown coffee tree, producing the best quality beans. It is pruned to a height of 10–16 ft (3–5 m) for easy harvesting. *C. canephora* is more disease resistant, longer living, and can be grown at lower altitudes. *C. liberica,* of still lower quality, is grown in Malaysia and Guyana. The coffee beans are usually fermented, then sun dried before export. The main coffee-producing areas are South and Central America, Jamaica, East Africa, and Mysore in India. Family: *Rubiaceae.*

cofferdam A temporary walled structure to hold back water or earth while excavation or construction work is carried out. Thus they may be used to protect workers during the construction of a permanent *dam or *bridge piers across a river. They are made by driving sheets of sectional steel vertically into the ground and bolting or welding the sheets together. Occasionally concrete is used.

Cognac 45 42N 0 19W A town in W France, in the Charente department. Under French law, the name Cognac may only be applied to brandy produced in a certain area around Cognac. Associated manufactures include bottles, corks, and barrels.

Cohan, George M(ichael) (1878–1942) US dramatist, songwriter, and entertainer. A native of Rhode Island, he was part of his family's vaudeville act as a child. He wrote the musicals *The Governor's Son* (1901), *Little Johnny Jones* (1904), *Forty Five Minutes from Broadway* (1905), *George Washington, Jr.* (1906), and *The Song and Dance Man* (1923). Popular songs written by him include "Give My Regards to Broadway," "I'm a Yankee Doodle Dandy," "Over There" (for which he received a congressional medal in 1940), "You're a Grand Old Flag," and "Mary's a Grand Old Name." He wrote nonmusical plays, such as *Broadway Jones* (1913) and *The Tavern* (1920) and acted in *The Phantom President* (1932) and *Ah, Wilderness!* (1933).

coherent radiation Electromagnetic radiation in which different waves have a constant *phase difference. Light from most sources is not coherent because it is emitted in random bursts. However, light from a *laser is coherent.

Cohn, Ferdinand Julius (1839–1884) German botanist, considered to be one of the founders of modern bacteriology. Following his early studies of algae and fungi, Cohn became interested in the identification of bacteria and established the basic elements of modern classifications. He also encouraged *Koch to publish his findings on anthrax.

Coimbatore 11 00N 76 57E A city in India, in Tamil Nadu. It is an agricultural processing center for hides, cotton, and oilseeds and has an expanding manufacturing sector. Population (1991): 853,402.

Coimbra 40 12N 8 25W A city in central Portugal. It was formerly the capital of Portgual (1139–1260). It has two cathedrals and Portugal's oldest university, founded in Lisbon (1290) and transferred in 1537. Industries include the production of beer, wine, and pottery. Population (1981 est): 72,000.

coke A fuel consisting mainly of carbon. It is made by heating coal in the absence of air and is produced as a by-product of *coal gas. Coke is used in *blast furnaces and other industrial processes as well as for domestic heating.

Coke, Sir Edward (1552–1634) English lawyer and politician. Initially a staunch supporter of the crown, Coke became speaker of the House of Commons in 1593 and attorney general in 1594. Under James I he was appointed chief justice (1613) but was dismissed in 1616 because of his defense of the common law against the royal prerogative. Reviving his political career in 1620, he became a leading spokesman for the protection of Parliament's liberties and was largely responsible for the Petition of Right.

cola. See kola.

Cola A dynasty that ruled S India from the 10th to the 14th centuries. The empire of the Cola kings centered on Kanci and Tanjore and was marked by cultural and artistic distinction and social stability. In the early 11th century Cola power spread to Ceylon and Indonesia.

Colbert, Claudette (Lily Claudette Chauchoin; 1905–) US film actress, born in France. She is best known for her performances in Hollywood light comedies during the 1930s and 1940s. These include *Three-Cornered Moon* (1933), *It Happened One Night* (1934), and *Midnight* (1939).

Colbert, Jean-Baptiste (1619–83) French statesman; an outstanding financial reformer. Rising to power through the influence of Cardinal Mazarin, Colbert became comptroller general of finance in 1665 and strove to make France under *Louis XIV the dominant power in Europe. An advocate of *mercantilism, he reformed taxation, tariffs, and financial administration, built roads and canals, and largely created a French navy. He was a lavish patron of the arts and sciences but his cold personality won him the nickname *le Nord* ("the North").

Colchester 51 54N 0 54E A market city in SE England, in Essex on the Colne River. Founded by Cymbeline (Cunobelinus) in about 10 AD, Colchester was an important Roman town (Camulodunum); the Roman walls remain in part and there is a Norman castle. Essex University (1961) is nearby. Colchester's industries include engineering and printing. Population (1981 est): 81,945.

colchicine. See autumn crocus.

cold (*or* common cold) A mild but widespread viral disease affecting the mucous membranes of the nose and throat. Symptoms include a sore throat, running nose, sneezing, headache, a slight fever, and general aches and pains. The disease, which is transmitted by coughing and sneezing, usually lasts about a week; rest and mild *analgesics such as aspirin provide the only treatment required.

cold-bloodedness. See poikilothermy.

Colden, Cadwallader (1688–1776) US scientist, writer, and politician; born in Scotland. He studied medicine there before coming to America in 1710. He wrote *History of the Five Indian Nations of Canada* (1727) and classified American plants according to the Linnaean System. The plant genus *Coldenia* is named for him. He served as lieutenant-governor of New York from 1761 until the Declaration of Independence in 1776 and was unpopular among the colonists for his support of the British-imposed Stamp Act of 1765.

Cold Harbor, Battles of Two battles in the *Civil War fought near Richmond, Va., the Confederate capital. In the first (June 27, 1862) the Confederate general, Robert E. *Lee, defeated the Federal forces under George B. *McClellan, both sides suffering heavy losses. In the second (June 3–12, 1864), the Federal advance on Richmond under Ulysses S. *Grant was temporarily halted when he encountered Lee's entrenched forces. Despite his losses (7000 of his 100,000 men), Grant resumed his advance.

Colditz 51 08N 12 49E A town in Germany, on the Mulde River near Leipzig. It is famous for its castle, built by *Augustus II on a cliff above the town, which was used as a top-security prisoner-of-war camp during World War II. Many escapes were attempted, some of which were successful.

cold storage A method of storing food or other perishables, such as photographic film, at a low temperature to prevent deterioration. *Refrigeration is used on a domestic scale in *freezing and also on an industrial scale in refrigerated warehouses, trucks, railroad wagons, and ships' holds.

Cold War The hostility between the US and the Soviet Union, and their respective allies, following World War II. The term was first used in 1947 by the US politician Bernard *Baruch. Fear of nuclear war prevented a military confrontation, and the Cold War was fought on economic, political, and ideological fronts. At its most virulent in the 1950s, it had given way by the 1970s to the movement toward detente.

Cole, Thomas (1801–48) US landscape artist, founder of the *Hudson River School of painting; born in England. He emigrated to the US in 1818. He frequently traveled the Hudson River Valley, sketching the landscape that he later incorporated in oil paintings. He traveled to Europe twice (1829–32; 1841–42), staying mainly in Italy; after the first trip he painted *The Course of Empire* (1836) and *The Voyage of Life* (1839–40). In his paintings he showed the overwhelming force of nature in intimate detail.

Coleoptera. *See* beetle.

Coleridge, Samuel Taylor (1772–1834) British poet and critic. In 1795 he met William *Wordsworth and their joint publication of *Lyrical Ballads* (first edition 1798) marked a decisive break with 18th-century poetry. His finest poems, such as *Kubla Khan* (1797) and *The Rime of the Ancient Mariner* (1797–98), were written at this time, but his personal life was troubled by his unhappy marriage, his poverty, and his increasing opium addiction. His subsequent creative energies were committed to journalism, lectures, and the writing of the critical and metaphysical *Biographia Literaria* (1817).

Colette (Sidonie-Gabrielle C.; 1873–1954) French novelist. After her divorce from her first husband, who had published her early novels (the *Claudine* series) under his own name, she became a music-hall performer in Paris. With *Chéri* (1920) and *La Fin de Chéri* (1926) she became an established writer, celebrated especially for her treatments of childhood and of the natural world, especially animals. Her long writing career was crowned with many official honors and awards.

Coleus A genus of herbaceous or shrubby plants (150 species) originating in the Old World tropics. Many cultivated varieties of the species *C. blumei* are grown for their variegated leaves of a diversity of colors, including red, purple, yellow, and green. They can easily be grown from cuttings at almost any time of year if kept at a temperature of 41°F (16°C). Family: *Labiatae*.

Colfax, Schuyler (1823–85) US politician; vice president (1869–73). He served in the US House of Representatives as a Republican from Indiana from 1855 until 1869, six of those years (1863–69) as speaker of the House. During his term as Grant's vice president, he was implicated in the Crédit Mobilier of America scandal (1872) in which several Congressmen had taken bribes.

colic A severe fluctuating abdominal pain, usually due to contraction of the wall of the intestines and caused by such conditions as constipation or obstruction. Colic in babies is quite common and usually due to air in the intestines.

Coligny, Gaspard II de, Seigneur de Châtillon (1519–72) French *Huguenot leader. He became an admiral of France in 1552 and was converted to Protestantism seven years later. He was chief commander of the Huguenots during the second and third *Wars of Religion but Catherine de' Medici, the mother of Charles IX, determined to end his influence over her son, arranged Coligny's murder in the *Saint Bartholomew's Day Massacre.

colitis Inflammation of the large intestine (the colon), causing abdominal pain and diarrhea (sometimes with the passage of blood). Colitis can be caused by bacterial infection (e.g. dysentery) or by *Crohn's disease. In ulcerative colitis the colon becomes ulcerated. The latter condition, which fluctuates in severity, is treated with corticosteroids or sulfasalazine (a sulfonamide drug). Surgery may be required for severe cases.

collage A picture composed of a variety of glued-on scraps of materials, such as newspaper, wallpaper, cloth, string, wood veneer, etc. The first collage was made by *Picasso in 1912 with a piece of oilcloth. It was later followed by the collages of the *dada painters *Arp, *Ernst, and *Schwitters.

collagen A structural protein that is the main component of the white fibers of connective tissue. Inelastic but with great tensile strength, it is found in tendons and ligaments and also in skin, bone, and cartilage.

collar bone. *See* clavicle.

collards. *See* kale.

collateral security Property (e.g. shares of stock, real estate, insurance policies, jewelry) pledged by a borrower, in addition to his promise to repay, as a safeguard for the repayment of a loan. On default the lender sells the collateral, deducts his debt and costs from the proceeds, and pays any balance to the borrower.

collective bargaining Bargaining between labor unions and employers on all matters relating to conditions of employment, rates of pay, etc. If agreement cannot be reached by bargaining, the dispute may be referred to *arbitration, or either side may take action against the other (*see* strikes;lockouts).

collective farms Agricultural cooperatives found especially in communist countries. Collectivization was instituted in the Soviet Union, with considerable ruthlessness, by Stalin in the late 1920s; widespread resistance necessitated some modifications in the mid-1930s. The farms and farm equpment belong to the state, which decides what is to be grown and in what quantities, but farmworkers, who live in surrounding villages, pay rent for their homes and are permitted to have their own garden plots and livestock; profits are shared in collective farms while in state farms workers receive wages. Collectivization was introduced into China in 1955. There, communes correspond to the Soviet collective farms, which are also found in Israel (*see* kibbutz).

collective unconscious In Jungian psychology, a body of images and ideas that are inherited and shared by all humans, rather than acquired by the individual. These ideas are called archetypes and *Jung believed them to be detected in the myths, dreams, and mental disturbances of mankind.

collie A breed of □dog originating in Scotland and widely used as a sheepdog. It has a streamlined body and a pointed muzzle. The rough-coated collie has a long dense coat and bushy tail; the smooth-coated variety has a shorter smooth coat and the bearded collie has a long coat with a shaggy beard. Collies are gray, fawn, or sandy, with or without white markings. Height: 22–24 in (56–61 cm) (dogs); 20–22 in (51–56 cm) (bitches).

collimator 1. A device used in conjunction with certain optical instruments for producing a beam of parallel light. A simple collimator consists of a slit placed at the focal point of a convex lens. **2.** A device used to produce a beam of radiation of the required dimensions in *radiotherapy.

Collingwood, Robin George (1889–1943) British philosopher, archeologist, and historian, who taught philosophy at Oxford. His *New Leviathan* (1946) defends free institutions. *Essay on Philosophical Method* (1933), *Idea of Nature* (1945), and *Idea of History* (1946) present his own *idealism in relation to that of *Plato, *Hegel, and *Croce.

Collins, Michael (1890–1922) Irish nationalist; leading member of Sinn Féin. He was imprisoned for his part in the *Easter Rising (1916) and subsequently became finance minister in the republican government (1919). He played a major part in the negotiations that led to the establishment of the Irish Free State (1921) but was shot by republicans who opposed the Anglo-Irish treaty.

Collins, (William) Wilkie (1824–89) British novelist. He worked in commerce and practiced law before publishing *Memoirs* (1848) of his father, a landscape painter. During the 1850s he enjoyed a mutually beneficial association with Dickens and in 1860 published his pioneering mystery novel, *The Woman in White*. His other novels include *No Name* (1862) and *The Moonstone* (1868).

colloid A solution in which the solute (*or* disperse phase) is present in the solvent (dispersion medium) in the form of particles 10^{-9}–10^{-6} m in length, rather than as single molecules or ions. If the disperse phase is solid and the dispersion medium is liquid the colloid is known as a **sol** (examples include milk, glue, and some drug preparations). If both are liquid the colloid is known as an **emulsion** (e.g. mayonnaise and most ointments). A colloidal suspension in which the particles of the disperse phase link together, with the dispersion medium circulating through the meshwork, is called a **gel** (e.g. a photographic emulsion). *See also* aerosols.

Colloids consist of charged particles. In lyophilic (solvent-loving) colloids, stability is achieved by attraction between the particles and the molecules of the dispersion medium. Lyophilic colloids are reversible in the sense that when the particles are removed from the solution, they will reform a solution by simply mixing with the dispersion medium. Lyophobic (solvent-hating) colloids usually consist of large inorganic particles (e.g. clays, metals, etc.). They maintain stability by repulsion between similarly charged aggregates. They often precipitate on the addition of a salt and are irreversible.

Colman, Ronald (1891–1958) British actor. He went to the US in 1920 after military service during World War I and played leading romantic roles in such films as *Lost Horizon* (1937) and *Random Harvest* (1943).

Colmar 48 05N 7 21E A city in E France, the capital of the Haut-Rhin department. It was held by Germany from 1871 to 1919, and from 1940 until 1945. It has many notable buildings, including a Dominican monastery (13th–14th centuries). A trading center for Alsatian wines, Colmar has an important cotton industry. Population (1983): 82,500.

colobus A leaf-eating *Old World monkey belonging to the genus *Colobus* (3 species), of African forests, also called guereza; 20–28 in (50–70 cm) long, colobus monkeys have long hands with small thumbs and their long silky fur is brightly marked. They have been widely hunted for their skins. □mammal.

colocynth The dried fruit of *Citrullus colocynthus*, a prostrate herbaceous perennial found in N Africa, the Middle East, and India and cultivated in Spain and Cyprus. It is a powerful laxative, used medicinally in very small amounts. It can cause poisoning. Family: *Cucurbitaceae*.

Cologne (German name: Köln) 50 56N 06 57E A city in western Germany on the Rhine River, the largest in North Rhine-Westphalia. A port and major commercial center, it is famed for its toilet water. Other industries include textiles, iron and steel, chemicals, and motor manufacture. It is the site of a university (1388) and the largest gothic cathedral in N Europe (founded 1248). The cathedral and the old gothic town hall were among the buildings reconstructed after World War II during which most of the city center was destroyed. *History*: founded by the Romans, it became the capital of the northern empire in 258 AD and later the seat of Frankish kings. During the Middle Ages its archbishops were powerful princes and it flourished as a mercantile and cultural center, where Albertus Magnus, Thomas Aquinas, and John Duns Scotus taught. In 1798 it was annexed by France, passing to Prussia in 1815. Population (1991 est): 954,000.

Colombia, Republic of A country in NW South America, on the Pacific Ocean and the Caribbean Sea. It consists chiefly of a hot swampy coastal plain, separated by ranges of the Andes from the pampas and the equatorial forests of the upper Amazon basin. The majority of the population is of mixed Spanish and Indian descent. *Economy*: mainly agricultural, the chief product is coffee, which accounts for over half the total exports. Although industry is largely undeveloped, the manufacturing section has expanded rapidly in recent decades and the export of such products as textiles and chemicals has risen sharply. The country is rich in mineral resources; gold production is the highest in South America and silver, copper, lead, and mercury are also mined. Colombia is one of the world's richest sources of platinum, as well as being the world's largest producer of emeralds. The most valuable natural resource, however, is oil. There are also large reserves of coal and natural gas. *History*: inhabited by Chibchas and other Indians before the Spanish colonization of the 16th century. In 1819 Simón Bolívar, after a 9-year war, secured the independence of Greater Colombia, which included what are now Panama, Venezuela, and Ecuador as well as present-day Colombia. This lasted until 1830 when Venezuela and Ecuador broke away; Panama became independent in 1903. Strife had plagued the country from the 19th century into the 20th, with a civil war of extreme violence erupting in 1899. Political parties, aligned along opposing conservative and liberal lines, had struggled for years with the conservatives emerging victorious after the war in 1902. In 1948 after more than 40 years of political peace, violent war once again tore the country and hundreds of thousands were killed. Gen. Gustavo Rojas Pinilla emerged as dictator. He was overthrown in a military coup in 1957 and a more democratic government was re-established the following year. Since 1975 there has been considerable unrest, including strikes, student rioting, and guerrilla activity. In 1980 the left-wing guerrilla organization M-19 took a number of hostages prisoner in the Dominican Republic's embassy in Bogotá, gradually releasing them in the next two months. In the 1982 presidential elections Belisario Betancur was elected to succeed Dr. Julio Cesar Tur-

bay Ayala, who had been in office from 1978. By the mid 1980s the once powerful M-19 had been isolated militarily and their leader killed in a plane crash.
Colombia distanced itself further and further from the US in response to US involvement in Central America. Liberal Party leader, Virgilio Barco Vargas, was
elected to the presidency in 1986. His administration was plagued by cocaine
cartels, violence, and assassinations. Under Cesar Gaviria Trujillo, elected in
1989, drug trafficking was somewhat curbed, and a new constitution was drafted
in 1991. The death of Colombia's most powerful drug lord in a 1993 raid increased hopes that the government could control trafficking. Official language:
Spanish. Official religion: Roman Catholic. Official currency: Colombian peso
of 100 centavos. Area: 456,535 sq mi (1,138,914 sq km). Population (1990 est):
32,598,800. Capital: Bogotá. Main port: Barranquilla.

Colombo 6 55N 79 52E The capital and main port of Sri Lanka, on the W
coast at the mouth of the Kelani River. Founded by the Arabs in the 8th century
AD, it was later developed by the Portuguese, the Dutch, and the British.
Colombo has one of the largest artificial harbors in the world, from which tea,
spices, and rubber are exported. The University of Sri Lanka was established
here in 1972. Population (1990 est): 615,000.

Colombo, Matteo Realdo (?1516–59) Italian physician, who first described
the circulation of blood between the heart and lungs. From his dissections of
human cadavers he also described the membrane surrounding the lungs (pleura)
and the membrane enclosing the abdominal organs (peritoneum).

Colombo Plan An agreement, signed in Colombo (Ceylon) in 1951, designed
to foster economic development in the countries of S and SE Asia. It now has 27
members—21 countries within the region and Australia, Canada, Japan, New
Zealand, the UK, and the US. There is an annual meeting of the Consultative
Committee, and financial arrangements are made between individual governments rather than from a central fund.

colon. *See* intestine.

Colón (former name: Aspinwall) 9 21N 79 54W A port in central Panama, at
the Caribbean end of the Panama Canal. It is a major commercial center; industries include oil refining. Population (1990 est): 54,500.

colophony. *See* rosin.

color The sensation produced when light of different wavelengths falls on the
human eye. Although it is actually continuous, the visible spectrum is usually
split into seven major colors: red, orange, yellow, green, blue, indigo, and violet,
in order of decreasing wavelength (from about 6.5×10^{-7} m for red light to
4.2×10^{-7} m for violet). A mixture of all these colors in equal proportions gives
white light; other colors are produced by varying the proportions or omitting
components. Colored pigments, dyes, and filters selectively absorb certain
wavelengths, transmitting or reflecting the rest. Thus a red book illuminated by
white light absorbs all the components of white light except red, which is reflected. This is a subtractive process, since the final color is that remaining after
absorption of the others. Combining colored lights, on the other hand, is an ad-
ditive process. A mixture of the whole spectrum gives white light, as will a mixture of lights of three *primary colors.

Colorado One of the Mountain States in the W central US. Wyoming lies to
the N, Nebraska to the N and E, Kansas to the E, Oklahoma and New Mexico to
the S, and Utah to the W. The flat, grass-covered Great Plains of the E are cut by
the South Platte and Arkansas rivers flowing eastward from the Rocky Mountains, which run N–S through the center of the state. Colorado's mean elevation
is the highest in the US and the majority of the Rockies loftiest peaks are located

within the state. The Rockies contain the valley of the Colorado River, and the Continental Divide forms the mountains' crest. The Colorado Plateau in the SE, an area of flat, semiarid land surfaces with stunted, sparse vegetation is cut by numerous majestic canyons. Much of the plateau region constitutes Indian reservations. Most of the population lives and works in a transition zone, the Colorado Piedmont, which divides the eastern and western regions. Manufacturing is the most important sector of Colorado's economy, especially the production of machinery, chemicals, military equipment, and food products. Mining is declining, although Colorado produces molybdenum, coal, oil, and sand and gravel. Tourism, especially winter sports, is of growing importance. The state's farmers are major cattle, pig, and lamb producers. As well as cultural and educational institutions the state has three important observatories. *History*: explored by the Spanish, part of Colorado was acquired by the US in the Louisiana Purchase (1803) and part from Mexico in 1848. Following the discovery of gold (1859), it became a territory in 1861 and a state in 1876. Colorado's cities grew rapidly during and after World War II and the energy crisis of the 1970s brought expansion of its coal and petroleum industries. The state's great natural beauty and outdoor lifestyle attracted many who sought escape from the cities. Colorado fared better than most states during the recession of 1980–82, although federal cutbacks caused a decline in its fuel-producing industries. Area: 104,247 sq mi (269,998 sq km). Population (1990): 3,294,394.

Colorado potato beetle A brown and yellow striped *leaf beetle, *Leptinotarsa decemlineata,* about 0.4 in (10 mm) long. Both the adults and larvae eat potato leaves: the larvae also attack the tubers. It is native to W North America but has spread eastward, throughout Europe, to become a serious pest of potato crops everywhere.

Colorado River A river rising in the Rocky Mountains and flowing SW through Colorado, Utah, and Arizona (where it passes through the *Grand Canyon) to the Gulf of California in Mexico. Its extensive use for irrigation and as a source of power (the many canyons providing ideal sites for dams, of which the Hoover Dam is one) is seen by conservationists as a serious threat to the natural landscape. Length: 1440 mi (2320 km).

Colorado Springs 38 50N 104 50W A health resort in Colorado situated at the foot of the Rocky Mountains. It is the site of the US Air Force Academy and the US Air Defense Command. Population (1990): 281,140.

coloratura (Italian: coloring) A style of vocal music characterized by elaborate and florid decorative passages. A **coloratura soprano** is a soprano whose voice is suited to such music. Donizetti and Verdi made effective use of the coloratura style in many of their operas; the Russian composer Reinhold Glière (1876–1956) wrote a concerto for wordless coloratura soprano voice and orchestra.

color blindness The inability to distinguish certain colors. There are various forms of color blindness, the most common of which is red-green color blindness (the inability to distinguish red and green). Color blindness is an inherited condition: because it is a recessive trait carried on the X chromosome it is far more common in men than women (about 8% of males of Caucasian origin are color blind). Very occasionally color blindness may be due to disease of the retina (the light-sensitive layer of the eye). Diagnosis depends on the use of charts in which symbols made of color dots are buried in a background of other dots. Inherited color blindness cannot be cured, and sufferers must avoid activities in which the distinction of color may be of importance.

color photography The recording of *color images on photographic *film that has three layers of light-sensitive emulsion, one for each of three *primary colors. Most color film uses a subtractive reversal process. Colored light entering the camera first falls on an emulsion sensitive only to blue light. On development of this layer, a black image is formed by deposition of silver where blue light has fallen. The unblackened areas are dyed yellow, the complementary color of blue, and the silver deposit is removed. Since silver halide emulsions cannot be made insensitive to blue light, there is a yellow filter (to remove blue light) between the blue emulsion and the next layer, which is green-sensitive. This is developed to form a magenta image of the parts where no green light has fallen. The bottom layer is red-sensitive and gives a cyan (blue-green) negative image. When white light shines through the three superimposed images, the cyan dye substracts red where it does not occur in the picture; the magenta subtracts green; and the yellow subtracts blue. The light emerging therefore reconstructs the original picture on a screen, in the case of a transparency, or onto printing paper.

COLORADO POTATO BEETLE *A specimen on potato leaves. A heavy infestation of this pest can completely strip a plant of its leaves, so that the tubers do not develop.*

color television. *See* television.

color vision The ability of the human eye (and that of some other animals) to detect differences in the wavelength of light. The ability is due to the presence in the retina of the eye of cells known as cones (*see* retina), of which three types are believed to exist; one type being sensitive to red light, one to blue, and one to green. Light stimulates one or more of these types of cones in varying amounts depending on its color. *See also* color blindness.

Colosseum An *amphitheater in Rome. Now one of the most impressive of all Roman remains, the Colosseum was begun (c. 70 AD) by the emperor *Vespasian. It is an elliptical building, four stories high, 617 ft (188 m) long, and 512 ft (156 m) wide. It could seat 47,000 people and was used mainly for gladiatorial and wild-beast fights, but could be flooded for mock naval battles.

Colossians, Epistle of Paul to the A New Testament book written by the Apostle Paul about 60 AD to the church in Colossae in W Asia Minor. Its theme is that the Christian faith is sufficient and that speculative philosophy, specifically ideas that appear to be derived from *Gnosticism, diverts attention from this truth.

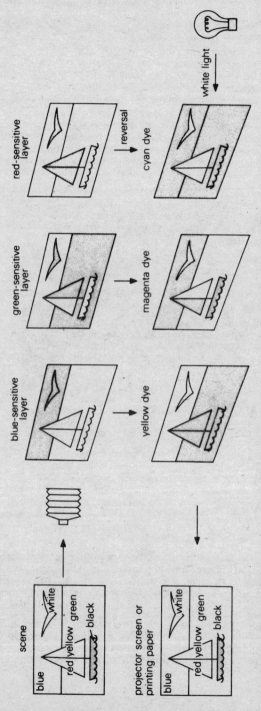

COLOR PHOTOGRAPHY *In color reproduction with subtractive reversal film, light from the different colored areas of the scene forms negatives for each primary color. These are dyed to form filters that subtract colors from white light to reconstruct the original picture.*

Colossus of Rhodes A gigantic statue of the sun god *Helios by the harbor of Rhodes. Cast in bronze by Chares of Lindos about 280 BC and standing about 100 ft (31 m) tall, it was counted among the *Seven Wonders of the World. An earthquake destroyed it 50 years after its completion.

Colt, Samuel (1814–62) US inventor. A native of Connecticut, his most famous invention was the Colt revolver, a gun with a revolving cylinder that would shoot six times before reloading. The gun became popular during the *Mexican War.

Colt revolver A *revolver with a multi-shot cylinder rotated and locked in line with the single barrel by cocking the weapon. Invented by the US engineer Samuel Colt (1814–62) in 1835, it became the .45 caliber Frontier Peacemaker (1873) and the standard .45 US army and navy revolver, remaining in service until 1945.

coltsfoot A perennial early-flowering herb, *Tussilago farfara,* 2–6 in (5–15 cm) high, bearing yellow single flower heads on scaly stems before the leaves appear. Found in Eurasia, N Africa, and North America (introduced), it can be a persistent weed. The dried leaves were previously smoked to cure coughs and asthma. Family: *Compositae.*

colugo An arboreal mammal belonging to the genus *Cyanocephalus* and order *Dermoptera* (2 species), also called flying lemur, found in Asia, Borneo, and the Philippines. About 24 in (60 cm) long, colugos have a membrane of skin, extending from the chin via the fore and hind limbs to the tail, with which they can glide up to 230 ft (70 m). Colugos feed on leaves and fruit.

Colum, Padraic (Patrick Colm; 1881–1972) Irish poet and folklorist. Associated with *Yeats, *Synge, and other members of the Celtic literary revival, he founded *The Irish Review* in 1911. From 1914 he lived in the US. His works include several volumes of lyrical poetry, plays, folklore anthologies, and a reminiscence of James *Joyce.

Columba, St (c. 521–597 AD) Irish missionary and abbot. Ordained in 551, he founded churches and monasteries in Ireland before setting up a monastery on Iona. From here, Scotland was evangelized. Feast day: June 9.

Columban, St (*or* St Columbanus; c. 543–615 AD) Irish missionary and abbot. Establishing himself with 12 companions in Gaul in 590, he founded monasteries in the Vosges. Because of a conflict with the king, his monks went first to Switzerland and then to Italy in 612, where they founded a monastery at Bobbio in N Italy, which became an important center of learning. Feast day: Nov 23. Emblem: a bear.

Columbia 38 57N 92 20W A city in central Missouri. The University of Missouri has been here since 1839 and is the chief industry of the city. Other higher education institutions include Stephens College (1833). Population (1990): 69,101.

Columbia 34 00N 81 00W The capital city of South Carolina. An important commercial center, its industries include textiles, plastics, and machinery. Fort Jackson (a major Army post) is adjacent to the city. The University of Carolina was established here in 1801. Population (1990): 98,052.

Columbia River A river in North America, flowing SW from British Columbia, through Washington State, to the Pacific Ocean at Oregon. It is an important source of hydroelectric power and forms the only deepwater harbor N of San Francisco. Length: 1200 mi (1930 km).

columbine. *See* Aquilegia.

columbium. *See* niobium.

Columbus 39 59N 83 03W The capital of Ohio, on the Scioto River. A major industrial and commercial center of a rich agricultural area, its manufactures include aircraft, machinery, and footwear. It is the site of the Ohio State University (1872). Population (1990): 632,910.

Columbus 32 28N 84 59W A city in W Georgia, on the Chattahoochee River. The state's second largest city, its industries include textiles, food processing, and chemicals. Population (1990): 178,681.

Columbus, Christopher (1451–1506) Italian navigator, who discovered America. He was born in Genoa, became a pirate, and in 1476 was shipwrecked off the coast of Portugal, where he settled. He conceived the idea of reaching the East by sailing westward but his plan was rejected by the Portuguese king (John the Perfect) and Columbus approached (1486) the Spanish monarchs Ferdinand and Isabella. He eventually won their patronage and on August 3, 1492, set sail in the *Santa Maria,* accompanied by the *Pinta* and the *Niña.* On October 12 he landed on Watling Island (now San Salvador Island, in the Bahamas) and in November visited Hispaniola. On his return to Spain he was greatly honored: Ferdinand and Isabella stood to receive him at court and offered him a seat. On his second voyage (1493–96) he discovered Guadeloupe, Puerto Rico, and Jamaica and founded the first town in the New World—named Isabella, after his patroness, it is now a ruin in the Dominican Republic. His third voyage (1498–1500) achieved the discovery of Trinidad and the mainland of South America but ended in disaster: in 1499, following a revolt against his command, a Spanish governor was dispatched to relieve Columbus, who was sent back in chains to Spain. On his arrival, however, he was released and compensated and shortly afterward set off on his last voyage (1502–04). From this he returned ill and disheartened, dying not long afterward in Valladolid. In 1542 his remains were taken to Hispaniola.

column. *See* orders of architecture.

coly A small gray or brown bird belonging to a family (*Coliidae*; 6 species) of Central and South Africa, also called mousebird because it creeps mouselike along branches. Colies are 12–14 in (30–35 cm) long, including the long stiff tail feathers, and have a short crest, a short curved bill, and red legs with long claws. Order: *Coliiformes.*

coma In medicine, a state of deep unconsciousness in which the subject is unrousable and does not respond to pain. Coma can be caused by a *stroke, drug overdosage, meningitis, or head injuries. Treatment is that of the underlying condition, with the maintenance of respiration.

Comanche A North American Indian people formerly inhabiting the southern Plains. Their language, a branch of the Uto-Aztecan liguistic family, is closely related to *Shoshone. During the 18th century, the Comanches migrated from the area of Wyoming, eventually spreading as far south as Texas and Mexico, where they gained a reputation as daring horsemen and raiders. In 1867, after a period of conflict with the US Army, the Comanches agreed to be resettled on reservations in Oklahoma, where the present Comanche population of approximately 3500 still resides.

Comaneci, Nadia (1961–) Romanian gymnast, who in the 1976 Olympic Games won gold medals on the beam, the asymmetrical bars, and also in the individual all-round competition for women.

Combination Acts (1799, 1800) The British laws that made illegal any association (combination) of working men for the purpose of improving their working conditions. They were unsuccessful in preventing the formation of labor unions and were repealed in 1824. An outbreak of strikes followed the repeal and another Act was passed (1825) allowing labor unions to exist but limiting their right to strike.

combine harvester A machine for harvesting grain crops that combines the operations of cutting the crop (reaping) and separating the grain (threshing) from the rest of the plant. Horse-drawn models originated in the US in the 1830s; in the 1940s, the predecessors of the modern self-propelled machines were introduced, replacing the earlier labor-intensive methods.

COMBINE HARVESTER

comb jelly. *See* ctenophere.

combustion A chemical reaction in which a substance combines with oxygen, producing heat and light. For a liquid or a solid to burn, the temperature must initially be high enough to release flammable vapor. To maintain combustion, the heat evolved must maintain this temperature to provide a constant supply of vapor. The oxidation reactions in combustion are generally chain reactions involving free radicals, the principal overall reactions being the oxidation of carbon to carbon dioxide and the oxidation of hydrogen to water ($C + 2H_2 + 2O_2 \geq CO_2 + 2H_2O$).

COMECON. *See* Council for Mutual Economic Assistance.

Comédie-Française The French national theater, founded in 1680 and reconstituted in 1803 by Napoleon. It is organized as a cooperative society, owned by its members. Probationary members are called *pensionnaires* and full members *sociétaires*; a pension is awarded on retirement after 20 years of service. Despite its strong emphasis on tradition, it has produced many of France's most original actors.

comedy A type of dramatic presentation that evokes amusement and laughter. Traditionally, it deals with ordinary characters in everyday situations and ends happily, usually with a marriage or unexpected good fortune. In the comedies of *Shakespeare these elements blend with a more romantic narrative vein.

The earliest surviving comedies are those of the Greek dramatist *Aristophanes and the Romans *Plautus and *Terence (*see* Old Comedy; Middle Comedy;

New Comedy; Roman Comedy). During the early 17th century the English dramatist Ben *Jonson pioneered the "comedy of humours" with characters who are gross caricatures of ruling passions. Examples of the satirical comedy of manners, in which more emphasis is placed on sophisticated witty dialogue, are the plays of *Congreve and *Wycherley in the late 17th century. The plays of Oscar *Wilde and Noel *Coward continued the tradition of the comedy of manners in the late 19th and early 20th century.

The development of motion pictures gave rise to a new medium for comedy. Among the most famous of the early silent film comedians were Charlie *Chaplin and Buster *Keaton. In the 1930s, the *Marx Brothers and W. C. *Fields became famous for their satirical, often iconoclastic form of humor. Among the most well-known modern American film comedians are Bob *Hope, Jerry Lewis, and Woody *Allen.

Comenius, John Amos (1592–1671) Czech theologian and educationalist. Comenius wrote widely on education, advocating a broad curriculum incorporating science, handicrafts, economics, and languages. He was commissioned by *Oxenstierna to reform Swedish schools (1641–48). A virulent opponent of the papacy, he was drawn to the mysticism of Jacob *Böhme.

comet A small body that moves, usually in a very elongated orbit, around the sun. A typical comet consists of a small nucleus of ice and dust surrounded by an immense tenuous luminous cloud of gas and dust, the coma. Tails of gas and of dust only appear when a comet is near the sun; they point away from the sun and may be millions of kilometers long. **Short-period comets** (such as *Halley's comet) have orbital periods of less than 150 years. The remainder have much longer periods, some exceeding 10,000 years, and move in approximately parabolic orbits. A comet eventually decays to produce a stream of meteoroids around its orbit. *See also* Oort cloud.

comfrey A perennial herbaceous plant, *Symphytum officinale,* also called boneset. Up to 40 in (100 cm) high, it has drooping creamy or purplish flowers. Native to Europe and temperate Asia and formerly used medicinally, it is now grown as a garden flower, as are the related plants *S. grandiflorum* (yellow flowers) and *S. peregrinum* (blue and pink flowers). Family: *Boraginaceae.*

comic opera An opera with a humorous or farcical plot. It is characterized by spoken dialogue and a comic or satirical libretto. Among the most famous comic operas are the Savoy Operas of *Gilbert and *Sullivan. *Compare* opéra comique; opera buffa.

Cominform (Communist Information Bureau) An international communist organization. Founded in 1947, it united the Communist Parties of the Soviet Union, Bulgaria, Czechoslovakia, Hungary, Poland, Romania, Yugoslavia, France, and Italy. In 1948 Yugoslavia was expelled because of its refusal to follow the Soviet line. In 1956, partly in order to improve relations with Yugoslavia, the Soviet Union dissolved the Cominform. *See also* International.

Comintern. *See* International.

comitia Assemblies of the Roman people summoned by magistrates and held at an official meeting place (*comitium*) on an appointed day (*comitialis*). The three *comitia* corresponded to the three divisions of the people into curiae (*see* curia), *centuries, and tribes. The Comitia Curiata was the earliest assembly but its legislative functions became largely formal. The Comitia Cenuriata elected the chief magistrates and had some judicial powers. The Comitia Tributa was the assembly of the *plebeians; its enactments had authority after 287 BC.

COMET *Comet Morehouse, discovered in 1908. (The short diagonal lines are the images left by stars in the background, as the telescope and camera were moved to follow the comet.)*

commedia dell'arte An Italian form of popular theater that flourished throughout Europe from the 16th to the 18th centuries. It was performed by professional actors whose comic and often vulgar improvisations were based on a set of stock situations, usually concerning romantic intrigues and stereotyped characters. These included the clown *Harlequin, the cuckold Pantaloon, and the lover Inamorato. Its influence can be seen in the works of such contemporary dramatists as Molière and in the dramatic forms of *pantomime and *farce. Its characters were popular subjects for 18th-century porcelain figures. *See also* Punch and Judy.

commensalism A relationship between two individuals of different species in which one (the commensal) lives in, on, or with the other (the host), from which it derives food, shelter, support, or transport. The association neither harms nor benefits the host. An example is provided by certain barnacles, which live attached to whales. *See also* symbiosis.

Commerce, Department of US government cabinet-level department that promotes international trade, economic growth, and technological advancement through programs that help increase exports, prevent unfair foreign trade competition, and provide statistics, analysis, and research. Headed by the secretary of commerce, it includes the National Bureau of Standards, Patent and Trademark Office, Bureau of the Census, and the US Travel and Tourism, International Trade, and National Oceanic and Atmospheric administrations. Created as the Department of Commerce and Labor (1903), it became the Department of Commerce in 1913.

commercial banks Institutions that accept demand deposits (checking accounts) and lend money to companies and private individuals. In addition to making loans, these banks offer trust departments, credit cards, safe deposit boxes, and many other services. The commercial banks make a profit by lending at a higher rate of interest than their borrowing rate. Commercial banks are chartered by both the federal and individual state governments.

commesso (*or* Florentine mosaic) A method of making mosaic pictures of flowers, landscapes, religious scenes, etc., with polished semiprecious hard stones, such as lapis lazuli, agate, and jasper. Commesso pictures, which were used chiefly as tabletops and small wall panels, have been made since 1588 at a special Florentine workshop, which is now state supported.

Committees of Correspondence Liaison committees originally appointed by the American colonies for communication with England. As the American Revolution neared, the committees encouraged colonial cooperation against the crown and provided leadership for the coming struggle. These intercolonial committees, first formed in Virginia, organized the first *Continental Congress (1774).

commode A low-level decorative chest of drawers or cupboard. As invented by André-Charles Boulle (1642–1732), the commode was an architectural piece of furniture, sarcophagus-shaped with heavy feet and fitted with drawers. It developed during the 18th century to become an elegantly curved chest of drawers. with *marquetry and *ormolu decoration. *Chippendale made important English examples.

commodity trading The buying and selling of products, such as metals, coffee, rubber, grains, sugar, and cocoa, conducted in commodity exchanges or markets by brokers on behalf of clients, who consist of producers, users, and speculators. The majority of dealings are in "futures" (goods for delivery at a stipulated date in the future) although "spots" (goods for immediate delivery) are also traded. Trading in futures rarely involves the exchange of goods, most transactions being closed out by equal sales or purchases on the same market. Commodity exchanges enable producers and users to hedge their transactions in goods and help to stabilize prices by regulating supply and demand.

Commodus, Lucius Aelius Aurelius (161–93 AD) Roman emperor (180–92). The son of Marcus Aurelius, Commodus showed increasing signs of mental imbalance, believing he was the incarnation of the demigod Hercules. He became increasingly unpopular and was finally assassinated.

common law The part of the law that was originally unwritten and based on the common customs of a country. US common law is largely descended from English common law, which developed with the rise of centralized government in England from the 10th to the 13th centuries.

Common Market. *See* European Economic Community.

commons Unenclosed land for the common use of the inhabitants of a particular district. Originally, in every manor there was a tract of uncultivated land over which the inhabitants had **rights of common**, such as the rights to pasture animals, to fish, and to cut wood.

Commons, House of. *See* Parliament.

common sense, philosophy of A philosophical movement particularly associated with certain Scottish followers of Thomas *Reid and promoted in the 20th century by G. E. *Moore. It rejected the traditional philosophical *skepticism that had raised doubts about such questions as to whether material objects exist unperceived or whether other people exist. Common-sense philosophers base their case on the universal nonphilosophical consent on such subjects; while particular beliefs may be mistaken, there is none the less a broad base of common-sense views that must be certain.

Commonwealth (1649–53) The period in English history between the execution of Charles I and the establishment of the *Protectorate; the term is sometimes used synonymously with Interregnum to refer to the entire period between the execution of Charles I and the *Restoration in 1660 of his son Charles II.

Commonwealth (British) A loose association of independent nations once subject to the imperial government of the UK (*see* Empire, British). The Commonwealth of Nations was established by the Statute of Westminster (1931), which was based on the principles, enunciated at the 1926 *Imperial Conference, of member states' autonomy, equality, and common allegiance to the English crown; its name was modified to the Commonwealth after World War II. Its member states, the populations of which comprise nearly a quarter of the world's population, are Antigua and Barbuda, Australia, the Bahamas, Bangladesh, Barbados, Belize, Botswana, Brunei, Canada, Cyprus, Dominica, The Gambia, Ghana, Grenada, Guyana, India, Jamaica, Kenya, Kiribati, Lesotho, Malawi, Malaysia, Maldives, Malta, Mauritius, Namibia, New Zealand, Nigeria, Pakistan, Papua New Guinea, St Kitts-Nevis, St Lucia, St Vincent, Seychelles, Sierra Leone, Singapore, Solomon Islands, Sri Lanka, Swaziland, Tanzania, Tonga, Trinidad and Tobago, Uganda, the UK, Vanuatu, Western Samoa, Zambia, and Zimbabwe; Nauru and Tuvalu are special members and are not represented at the meetings of Commonwealth heads of government. Commonwealth heads of government meet every two years but finance ministers meet annually. The Commonwealth Secretariat headquarters are in London.

Commonwealth of Independent States (CIS) Umbrella organization that sought to replace some of the functions of the Soviet Union. Founded in December 1991, its membership included 11 of the USSR's 15 republics: Azerbaijan, Armenia, Belarus (Byelorussia), Kazakhstan, Kyrgyzia, Moldova (Moldavia), Russia, Tajiskistan, Turkmenia, Uzbekistan, and Ukraine. Georgia did not initially adhere to the group, but agreed to join late in 1993, while the Baltic republics of Estonia, Latvia, and Lithuania had declared their independence in 1991 before the USSR dissolved. CIS members Russia (taking the Soviet seat), Belarus, and Ukraine were already members of the UN, and the others were admitted in 1992. Coordinated economic and foreign policies were the immediate CIS goals, but these were threatened by ethnic struggles in several republics and by economic problems.

commune An experimental community based on religious, social, political, or technological ideas, based on the abolition of private property and the sharing of community wealth and resources. In the 19th century, communes based on the philosophies of such men as Robert *Owen, Charles *Fourier, and William *Morris were established in the US, Europe, and South America. The members of these communities sought new physical environments, egalitarian principles of social organization, and a harmonious integration of family, work, and learning.

In the US, New Harmony and Brook Farm, of which Nathaniel *Hawthorne was a member, were founded on those principles but survived only a few years.

In the 20th century, there was a revival of interest in experimental communities in various parts of the world. In Israel, the *kibbutz became a successful form of agricultural settlement. In the US, during the 1960s and 1970s, many communes were established by groups dissatisfied with the way of life of modern technological society that turned, at least temporarily, to a way of life based on collective organization.

Commune of Paris (1871) A revolt in Paris against the conservative provisional government established at Versailles following French defeat in the Franco-Prussian War and the collapse of the Second Empire. Fearing a restoration of the monarchy, republican Parisians formed a revolutionary government in March that was reminiscent of the French Revolutionary Commune (1793). Defeated by government troops in May, the Communards lost some 20,000 supporters, 38,000 were arrested, and 7000 deported.

Communications Act (1934) US legislation that set up the Federal Communications Commission (FCC). The act regulated telephone, telegraph, radio, and, later, television transmissions.

communications satellite An unmanned artificial satellite by which long-distance live television broadcasting and telephone communications are achieved. Radio signals, suitably modulated (*see* modulation), are sent from one transmitting station to the satellite, where they are amplified and retransmitted (at a different frequency) to one or more receiving stations. The orbits of communications satellites lie above the earth's atmosphere so that high-frequency radio waves (microwaves), which can penetrate the *ionosphere, must be used. The electronic equipment on board is powered primarily by solar cells (*see* solar power).

The first active satellite was the US Telstar 1, launched in 1962. Telstar and other early satellites were in relatively low elliptical orbits and were only visible for a short portion of their orbit. A communications satellite is now usually placed in a geostationary orbit. This is a circular orbit lying about 22,370 mi (36,000 km) above the earth's equator. The satellite completes such an orbit in the same time (24 hours) as the earth rotates on its axis and thus to a ground-based radio station appears to remain nearly stationary in the sky. Three or more satellites, suitably placed around the equatorial orbit, can provide worldwide communications links.

Communications Satellite Corporation (COMSAT) US international satellite communications system, privately owned but controlled by the US government. Established in 1962, COMSAT, with the cooperation of 13 other countries, launched the Intelsat I (Early Bird) satellite in 1965. Other satellites followed.

communism A movement based on the principle of communal ownership of all property. More specifically, it is associated with *The Communist Manifesto* (1847) of Karl *Marx and Friedrich *Engels according to which the capitalist profit-based system of private ownership is replaced by a communist society in which the means of production are communally owned. This process, initiated by the revolutionary overthrow of the bourgeoisie (*see* Marxism), passes through a transitional period marked by the dictatorship of the proletariat (*see* Leninism) and the preparatory stage of *socialism.

In the late 19th century, Marxist theories motivated several social democratic parties in Europe, although their policies later developed along the lines of reforming *capitalism rather than overthrowing it. The exception was the Russian Social Democratic Workers' Party. One branch of this party, commonly known as the *Bolsheviks and headed by Vladimir *Lenin, succeeded in overthrowing the Czar's regime in the Revolution of November 1917. In 1918 this party changed its name to the Communist Party of the Soviet Union, thus establishing the modern distinction between communism and socialism.

After the success of the Russian Revolution, many socialist parties in other countries became communist parties, owing allegiance of varying degrees to the Soviet Communist Party (*see* International). In 1944–46 communist regimes were set up with the aid of the Soviet army in Poland, East Germany, Czechoslovakia, Hungary, Romania, Yugoslavia, Albania, and Bulgaria. In 1949 the communists in China, led by *Mao Tse-tung, came to power and established the People's Republic of China. Among the other countries in the *Third World that adopted a communist form of government at some point were Cuba, North Korea, Vietnam, Cambodia, Angola, Ethiopia, South Yemen, and Nicaragua.

Communism never became a popular philosophy in the US, either before or after the establishment of the Communist Party of America in 1919. Federal legislation such as the Smith Act (1940) and the Communist Control Act (1954) greatly restricted the party's activities and controversial hearings conducted by Senator Joseph *McCarthy further reduced its influence.

From the early 1970s until the 1990s, the term **Eurocommunism** was used to refer to the policies of communist parties in Western Europe, which sought to break with the tradition of uncritical and unconditional support of the Soviet Union. Such parties were politically active and electorally significant in France and Italy.

With the collapse of communist governments in Eastern Europe from the late 1980s and the breakup of the Soviet Union, communism's influence decreased.

Communism Peak (Russian name: Pik Kommunizma) 38 59N 72 01E The highest mountain in the Pamir range in Tajikistan, near the Afghan and Chinese borders. Height: 24,589 ft (7495 m).

community In ecology, an interdependent group of living organisms that occupies a particular habitat. The plants and animals of a community are closely associated with each other in various ecological relationships: for example, they depend on one another for food (*see* food chain). The size and composition of the community depend on the nature of the habitat and its climate; it may show seasonal changes. During ecological *succession, the structure of a community constantly changes until the stable climax community is established. *See also* ecology; ecosystem.

community service A form of sentence that requires an offender to work for a prescribed number of hours on behalf of the community instead of being imprisoned.

commutative law The mathematical rule, obeyed by addition and multiplication but not division, that the result of an operation combining two quantities is independent of the order in which they are taken: for addition, $a + b = b + a$, and for multiplication, $ab = ba$.

Commynes, Philippe de (c. 1445–1511) French statesman and chronicler. He served Charles the Bold, Duke of Burgundy, from 1464 and Louis XI from 1472. On the accession of Charles VIII in 1483 he was imprisoned but later returned to favor. His *Mémoires* (1524) are important historical records of the reign of Louis XI and the Italian expedition of Charles VIII, and embody his advanced political theories.

Como 45 48N 09 05E A city and resort in N Italy, in Lombardy on Lake Como. Known as Comum in Roman times, it is the birthplace of the elder and younger Pliny. It fell to the Visconti in 1335 and in 1859 was liberated from Austrian occupation by Garibaldi. It has a 15th-century marble cathedral and a gothic town hall. Como is an important tourist center and has several industries, including the famous silk factories. Population (1990 est): 90,000.

Como, Lake A lake in central N Italy, lying in a narrow forked valley at the S foot of the Alps. It is about 31 mi (50 km) long, dividing into two arms about halfway along, with a maximum depth of 1345 ft (410 m). There are many fashionable resorts on its shore such as Bellagio, Como, and Lecco. Area: 55 sq mi (145 sq km).

Comoros, Federal and Islamic Republic of the A country consisting of a group of islands in the Indian Ocean, between the NW coast of Madagascar and the African mainland. The main islands are Grand Comoro, Anjouan, and Mohéli and exclude the island of Mayotte, which has remained French. The population is of mixed African and Arab descent. *Economy*: almost entirely agricultural. The soils are fertile but the relatively undeveloped farming has suffered since French aid was withdrawn in 1975. Sugar cane was formerly the main crop but others, such as vanilla and perfume plants, are now increasing in importance. Exports include vanilla, sisal, and essential oils such as ylang-ylang. *History*: there were successive African, Malay, Malagasy, Arab, and other immigrations to the islands before they became a French colony in the 19th century. At first joined to Madagascar, the Comoros became a separate French overseas territory in 1947. Moves toward independence in the early 1970s culminated in a referendum in 1974 in which the majority voted in favor of independence, except for the island of Mayotte, which voted to remain French. Mayotte has since been made an overseas department of France. Ahmed Abdallah became the first president in 1975 but later that year he was overthrown in a military coup led by Ali Soilih. The government was taken over by a National Revolutionary Council. In 1976 the independence of the three islands was recognized by France and Soilih was elected president. He was overthrown (and later killed) in a military coup in 1978 and a Political-Military Directorate took over. The exiled Ahmed Abdallah and Mohammed Ahmed were invited to return and appointed copresidents. In October, Ahmed Abdallah was elected as the first president of the Federal Islamic Comoro Republic for a six-year term, following the approval of a new federal style constitution, with provision for the inclusion of Mayotte. Under Abdallah's leadership, Comoros was a one-party republic. Abdallah was reelected in 1984, but was killed during a coup attempt in 1989. In 1991, an attempt to unseat Pres. Said Mohammed Djohar was unsuccessful. A new constitution was approved in 1992. Official languages: French and Arabic; Swahili is also used commercially. Official currency: CFA franc of 100 centimes. Area: 719 sq mi (1862 sq km). Population (1990 est): 459,000. Capital and main port: Moroni.

compass A device for determining the direction of magnetic north. The magnetic compass, which has been in use as an aid to navigation probably since the 2nd century BC, consists of a magnetic needle balanced on a point, allowing it to pivot freely. The S end of the magnet indicates magnetic N, as shown on a card (called a compass card) marked with the points of the compass and fixed below it. In some magnetic compasses, the entire card pivots, indicating direction against a mark on the fixed housing. Such compasses are often filled with a fluid (usually alcohol) for damping. A more sophisticated kind of compass, used on larger vessels and in aircraft, is the **gyrocompass**, which employes the effect of the earth's rotation on the orientation of a spinning object's axis of rotation. Magnetic compasses are subject to interference from nearby ferrous metal objects and fittings, and compasses must be adjusted to compensate for distortion. Compensation must also be made, in the reading of a compass, for magnetic N not being in the same direction as geographic N in most longitudes. Up-to-date navigation charts mark on a compass rose the annual correction for position that must be allowed in various longitudes.

compass plant A perennial herbaceous plant, *Silphium laciniatum,* of the North American prairie. Its oval leaves are orientated N–S to avoid the intense midday radiation. 40 in–7 ft (1–2 m) high, it is sometimes cultivated and is also known as turpentine plant, from the substances that ooze from the stem. Family: *Compositae.*

Compiègne 49 25N 2 50E A city and resort in N France, in the Oise department on the Oise River. Joan of Arc was captured here by the English in 1430. A railroad coach in the forest of Compiègne was the scene of the signing of the Armistice (1918) ending World War I and of the agreement made between the Pétain government and Hitler in 1940. Industries include machinery, printing, and rubber. Population (1975): 40,720.

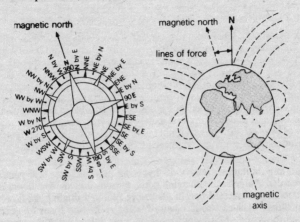

magnetic compass

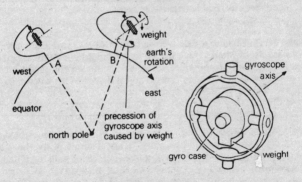

gyro compass

COMPASS *In the magnetic compass, the magnetized needle lines up with the earth's magnetic field. In the gyrocompass a spinning gyroscope is suspended on three mutually perpendicular frames. The axis of spin of a free gyroscope shifts around as the earth rotates: as the axis of the gyrocompass moves from the horizontal at position A to position B, a weight pulls it downward. As a result of the gyroscopic effect, the axis shifts around at right angles to the gravitational force (precesses) and describes a circle around the N–S direction. When the precession is damped, the gyroscope axis settles down pointing N.*

complementarity principle The principle, proposed by Niels *Bohr, that an elementary particle may be regarded as either corpuscular or wavelike. Thus an experiment designed to detect a corpuscular property cannot, at the same time, detect a wave property, and vice versa. *See also* de Broglie wave.

complex In psychoanalysis, a group of associated ideas that are unacceptable to the conscious mind and have therefore been repressed into the *unconscious. Although the individual is no longer aware of these ideas they continue to influence his (or her) behavior. *See* inferiority complex; Oedipus complex.

complex numbers Quantities that consist of a real number and an imaginary number. They may be written in the form $a + ib$, where a and b are real numbers and $i = \sqrt{-1}$. Two complex numbers can be added and subtracted: for example $(a + ib) + (c + id) = (a + c) + i(b + d)$. They may also be multiplied and divided into each other. A complex number $a + ib$ may be thought of as a pair of ordered numbers (a,b) similar to a pair of *Cartesian coordinates (x,y). Then (a,b) can be regarded as a point on a plane called the complex plane or Argand diagram in which the real axis is taken as horizontal and the imaginary axis as vertical. Complex numbers are widely used in the physical sciences, particularly in electrical engineering in calculations concerning alternating current.

Compositae The largest family of flowering plants (about 900 genera and 14,000 species). They vary from small herbs to trees and are found worldwide. The tiny flowers are grouped into heads that resemble a single large flower. The individual florets may be similar, as in thistles, or of two types (disk and ray flowers), as in daisies. Many composites are cultivated as ornamentals (e.g. chrysanthemums and dahlias); others are agricultural weeds (daisies, dandelions, etc.) and some are edible (such as lettuce).

Composite order. *See* orders of architecture.

compressor A machine for delivering high-pressure gas. They have a wide variety of uses, from small garage machines for inflating tires to large industrial machines for supplying compressed-air lines. The piston compressor resembles an internal-combustion engine in reverse and is driven by an electric motor or a diesel engine. The centrifugal compressor uses radial vanes to increase the momentum of the gas; they are extensively used in *gas driven by the turbine shaft (turbines) to supply pressurized air to the combustion chambers.

Compromise of 1850 US legislation passed to settle disputes between pro and antislavery forces. Drafted by Henry *Clay, a series of five laws evolved that admitted California to the Union as a free (nonslave) state; admitted the territories of New Mexico and Utah with no mention of slavery; established stricter regulations regarding fugitive slaves; and banned the slave trade in Washington, D.C. The issues that had split the political parties were solved, although only temporarily.

Compromise of 1877 US agreement that ended the Reconstruction period. It stated that Federal troops in the South would be withdrawn if southern Congressmen would give their support to Republican presidential candidate Rutherford B. *Hayes.

Compton, Arthur Holly (1892–1962) US physicist, who discovered the *Compton effect (1923) while analyzing the scattering of X-rays by matter. He could only explain the effect by assuming that the X-rays consisted of photons, then still a novel idea. He shared the 1927 Nobel Prize with C. T. R. *Wilson.

Compton-Burnett, Dame Ivy (1892–1969) British novelist. *Pastors and Masters* (1925) was the first of a series of 17 novels set in a stylized Victorian-Edwardian upper-class world. The series includes *Brothers and Sisters* (1929), *Manservant and Maidservant* (1947), and *Mother and Son* (1955).

Compton effect The increase in the wavelength of electromagnetic radiation when it is scattered by free electrons. The effect can only be explained by regarding the radiation as consisting of particles called photons. Part of the photon's energy is transferred to the electron, the velocity of which is thereby increased. Named for Arthur *Compton.

computer A device for performing calculations at high speed, usually by electronic methods. The principles behind the modern computer were conceived by Charles *Babbage in the 19th century. The first practical machines were built in the US and Britain during World War II. During the immediate postwar years, the developments in *information theory and the invention of the *transistor set the scene for the computer revolution of the next 20 years.

There are two main types of computer: digital and analog. Of these the **digital computer** is the more widely used. It processes information in the form of groups of the binary numbers 1 and 0, which represent the on and off positions of electronic switches. A digital computer requires programming, or *software, to convert the information fed into it into binary form (*see* bit). Computer languages, such as *COBOL, *FORTRAN, and *ALGOL, have been developed to transcribe the *programs from English and mathematical symbols into a notation that a machine can read. The physical equipment, or hardware, of a digital computer system generally has three main components: the central processing unit (CPU), the memory, and the peripheral devices that enable information to be fed into the machine and to be displayed by it after processing. Input is generally by magnetic tape, punched paper tape, or cards. Output is by printout, cathode-ray-tube (CRT) displays, or magnetic tape.

Analog computers deal with continuously varying physical quantities, such as current or voltage. They are used mainly for simulating or monitoring and controlling continuous processes in industry or scientific research.

Hybrid computers use both digital and analog elements. Frequently, an analog input is converted into numbers (the digital form) for processing as digital computation is considerably faster and more efficient.

Advances in solid-state electronics have continually extended the application of computer techniques. Large computers were made possible when vacuum tubes were replaced by solid-state *transistors. Integrated circuits using silicon chips of decreasing size and increasing complexity led to the introduction of *microcomputers, minicomputers, and portable laptop and notebook computers.

Comte, Auguste (1798–1857) French philosopher. Often said to be the founder of sociology, he coined and defined the term, although work of a sociological nature had been done long before his time. He is best remembered for his positivism (the view that society could be studied scientifically by natural-science methods and was subject to general laws); his Law of the Three Stages of intellectual development (theological, metaphysical, and positive); and his view that the theoretical sciences formed a hierarchy, with sociology at the peak providing a basis for social planning and reorganization. His principal work is *Cours de philosophie positive* (6 vols, 1830–42).

Conakry (*or* Konakry) 9 25N 13 56W The capital of Guinea, a port in the SW on Tombo Island, which is linked to the mainland by a causeway. It was founded by the French in 1884 and became capital of French Guinea in 1893. Population (1983): 705,280.

Conant, James Bryant (1893–1978) US educator and statesman. After serving in the US Army (1917–18) during World War I, he taught at Harvard University (1919–33) before becoming its president (1933–53). He was high commissioner to Germany (1953–55) and then ambassador to West Germany

(1956–57). After that, funded by Carnegie Corporation, he conducted studies of the US public school system and advised the Ford Foundation on education (1963–65). His many reports on education include *The American High School Today* (1959), *Slums and Suburbs* (1961), and *The Education of American Teachers* (1963).

concentration camps Prisons in which people are held without trial, usually on account of their politics or race. From 1900 to 1902, during the second *Boer War, the British detained civilian Afrikaners in concentration camps, with the loss of some 20,000 lives.

In Germany, camps were first established by the Nazis in 1933 to detain communists and Social Democrats; they were later used to imprison minority groups, such as Gypsies, homosexuals, and, above all, Jews. In 1940 the Nazis established extermination centers, the most notorious being Auschwitz and Treblinka in Poland and Belsen and Buchenwald in Germany. An estimated 20 million people were gassed or died of disease or starvation in Nazi camps, of which some 6 million were Jews—two-thirds of European Jewry. Notorious for their torture, medical experiments on living people, and the cruelty of their jailers, the Nazi camps and the *holocaust that took place within them have raised serious doubts as to the moral validity of western civilization.

In the Soviet Union forced labor camps were first established in 1917 and expanded greatly during Stalin's purges in the 1930s. Although many camps were closed following his death in 1953, they continue to be used for the detention of political dissidents.

Concepción 36 50S 73 03W A city in S Chile, on the Bío-Bío River. It suffered damage (1939 and 1960) from earthquakes. It is an important industrial center situated near Chile's chief coalfield; industries include steel processing and oil refining. Its university was founded in 1919. Population (1992 est): 312,000.

concertina A hexagonal musical instrument of the reed-organ family, invented in 1829 by Sir Charles Wheatstone. Similar to the *accordion in construction, the concertina is hand held and notes are produced by pressing buttons on panels at either end of the bellows.

concerto A musical composition for one or more solo instruments and orchestra, usually in three movements (a *sonata form movement, a slow movement, and a rondo finale). In the late 18th century Mozart perfected the form in his piano concertos; 19th-century composers treated it more freely and in the 20th century concertos have been written in a number of different styles and forms. In the baroque period and in the 20th century the word concerto has been applied to a variety of other compositions.

concerto grosso. *See* Corelli, Arcangelo.

conch A heavy-shelled marine *snail of the family *Strombidae* (about 80 species). Conch ☐shells have a roughly triangular outer whorl with a broad lip and can be 0.8–14 in (2–35 cm) long. Indo-Pacific spider conchs (genus *Lambis*) have long horns around the aperture of their shell.

conciliarism The view of those Roman Catholics who regarded a general council of the Church as a superior authority to the pope. First proposed in the early 13th century, the theory gained support especially in the 15th century. Pius II refuted the doctrine in his bull *Execrabilis* (1460).

Concord 43 13N 71 34W The capital city of New Hampshire. Founded in 1725, it was the home of Mary Baker Eddy (the founder of Christian Science). Industries include printing and publishing. Population (1990): 36,006.

Concord 42 28N 71 17W A city in Massachusetts, on the Concord River. The first battle of the American Revolution occurred here on April 19, 1775. Ralph Emerson, Nathaniel Hawthorne, Louisa May Alcott, and Henry Thoreau all lived in Concord. Population (1990): 17,076.

concordance An index of words used in a single book or all the works of an author, with accompanying citations. Originally used for study of the Bible, concordances are now used as a method of textual analysis of major literary authors.

concrete A building material that was used by the Romans but in its modern form came into use after the invention of Portland *cement in 1824. Concrete consists of a mixture of a cement, usually Portland cement, and an aggregate of sand, gravel, and broken stones. The strength of the concrete depends on the proportion of cement to the quantity and type of aggregate. Water is added to this mixture and complex hydration reactions cause the cement to dry out and harden around the aggregate. The material can be reinforced with steel bars (usually up to 2 in [50 mm] in diameter) to increase its tensile strength. **Reinforced concrete** was invented in France in about 1850. In **prestressed concrete** the concrete is maintained in a state of compression by stretching the steel reinforcing wires (usually 0.24 in [6 mm] in diameter) and keeping them in a state of tension after the concrete has set around them. Prestressed concrete is now widely used as a structural material as it has a reduced tendency to bend under load. Concrete parts may be precast in a factory or poured wet on site to harden, usually inside wooden shuttering, into any desired shape.

concussion The sudden and temporary loss of consciousness that may follow a head injury. On recovering consciousness the patient may be disorientated and confused, possibly with some loss of memory. Headache and blurred vision are other possible consequences.

Condé A French princely family, a branch of the *Bourbon royal house. Its first prince **Louis I** (1530–60) was a Huguenot leader during the French *Wars of Religion and was shot after being taken prisoner in battle. He was succeeded as Huguenot leader by his son **Henri I** (1552–88), who fled to Germany following the *St Bartholomew's Day Massacre of Huguenots (1572). Henri's grandson was the general **Condé the Great** (Louis II; 1621–86). During the Thirty Years' War he won victories against Spain at Rocroi (1643) and Lens (1648), subsequently being recalled to suppress the first *Fronde (civil war). In the second Fronde he joined the rebels and fled to Spain. After being defeated by *Turenne at the battle of the Dunes Condé was pardoned and became one of Louis XIV's outstanding generals.

condensation 1. A change of physical state from a gas or vapor to a liquid. Thus as a gas is cooled below a certain temperature it may (depending on the pressure) condense to the liquid. Condensation occurs in buildings when warm moist air comes in contact with cold surfaces, such as windows and uninsulated walls. **2.** A type of organic chemical reaction in which two molecules combine to form a larger molecule with elimination of a smaller molecule, such as water or methanol. Condensation reactions are the basis of a type of *polymerization process.

Condillac, Étienne Bonnot de (1715–80) French philosopher and psychologist. His ideas in *L'origine des connaissances humaines* (1746), *Traité des systèmes* (1749), and *Traité des animaux* (1755) resemble *Locke's; all knowledge springs from the senses and association of ideas. After 1800 his high reputation waned, but modern psychology largely vindicates his work.

condition A statement in logic that determines the truth of another statement. A **sufficient condition** always ensures the truth of the second statement. A **necessary condition** must be true if the second statement is true.

conditioned reflex A *reflex response that is evoked by a stimulus other than that which normally produces it. A classic example is provided by *Pavlov's experiments with dogs. The normal stimulus causing salivation (i.e. food) was paired with a different stimulus (a ringing bell) so often that eventually the bell by itself caused the dogs to salivate. A conditioned reflex gradually disappears if the stimulus is presented repeatedly; this process is called extinction. *See also* conditioning.

conditioning The process of modifying behavior by changing the stimuli (and therefore responses) associated with it. Classical conditioning occurs when a response is associated with a stimulus by pairing the stimulus with an event that causes the response by reflex (*see* conditioned reflex). Operant conditioning is brought about by either rewarding or punishing an action by the subject, which thus either encourages or discourages the behavior (*see also* aversion therapy). *Behaviorism uses both forms of conditioning to explain how people learn.

condominium 1. The joint exercise of sovereignty over a territory by two or more sovereign states, usually brought about by treaty to resolve a territorial dispute. The New Hebrides (now the Vanuatu Republic) was the subject of a condominium created by Britain and France in 1906. **2.** The multiple ownership of a building by the residents. Condominiums have become increasingly popular as residences as single family homes have become more expensive.

condor A huge South American *vulture, *Vultur gryphus,* found high in the Andes. It is black with a white ruff, bare pink head and neck, and has a wingspan of 10 ft (3 m). It feeds chiefly on carrion but also takes lambs and young deer. The very rare Californian condor (*Gymnogyps californianus*) is smaller with a bare yellow head and red neck.

Condorcet, Marie Jean Antoine de Caritat, Marquis de (1743–94) French philosopher and politican. Distinguished as a mathematician and progressive man of letters in the 1770s and 1780s, after the outbreak of the French Revolution he was elected to the Legislative Assembly (1791). As a moderate *Girondin he was arrested when the *Jacobins became dominant in 1793 and died, perhaps by his own hand, in prison. His most famous work, *Esquisse d'un tableau historique des progrès de l'esprit humain,* was published posthumously (1795).

condottiere A leader of a mercenary army employed by an Italian city or lord between the 14th and 16th centuries. The earliest condottieri (from Italian *condotta,* contract) were foreign, one of the most famous being Sir John Hawkwood (d. 1394), the English adventurer, but by the end of the 14th century the Italians began to raise their own mercenary armies. Condottieri, among them Francesco *Sforza of Milan and Cesare *Borgia, began to conquer territories for themselves. The system disappeared with the foreign invasions and new methods of warfare in the late 15th century.

conductance. *See* resistance.

conduction 1. (thermal) The transfer of heat from a region of high temperature to one of lower temperature, without the transfer of matter. It occurs as a result of the transfer of kinetic *energy by collisions between atoms and molecules in gases, liquids, and nonmetallic solids. In metals, which are the best thermal and electrical conductors, the energy is transferred by collisions between the free electrons that move through the crystal lattice and the ions of the lattice. **2.** (electrical) The passage of an electric current through a substance. In metals, the best conductors, it results from the passage of free electrons moving in one direction under the influence of an electric field. In a liquid conductor it is due to the passage of positive ions in one direction and negative ions in the other. In gases it is due to positive ions flowing in one direction and electrons in the other. In *semiconductors it results from the passage of electrons in one direction and positive holes in the other.

cone (botany) The structure, also called a strobilus, that bears the reproductive organs (sporophylls) in some pteridophytes (club mosses, horsetails, etc.) and the gymnosperms (conifers and related plants). In conifers both male and female cones are produced: the familiar woody cones of pines, larches, etc., are female strobili, made up of overlapping woody structures called bract scales, which bear the sporophylls in their axils.

coneflower. *See* black-eyed Susan.

cone shell A carnivorous marine *gastropod mollusk of the family *Conidae* (about 400 species), occurring in warm seas; 0.4–12 in (1–30 cm) long and cone-shaped, the highly colored and patterned shells are prized by collectors. The mollusks have a venomous sting and some can be dangerous to man.

Coney Island 40 35N 73 59W A resort in New York City on the S shore of Long Island. With its amusement parks, fine beach, and the New York Aquarium it attracts many tourists.

Confederate States of America (CSA) The 11 southern states of the US that seceded from the Union (1860–61), precipitating the *Civil War. The government of the Confederate States of America was established in February 1861 by South Carolina, Mississippi, Florida, Alabama, Georgia, and Louisiana. Jefferson *Davis of Mississippi was elected president and Alexander *Stephens of Georgia, vice president. The states of Texas, Virginia, Arkansas, North Carolina, and Tennessee joined the Confederacy soon afterward, and Confederate governments were temporarily established in Missouri and Kentucky. The capital of the CSA was originally Montgomery, Alabama, but it was later moved to Richmond, Virginia. The Confederate constitution protected the institution of *slavery and the principle of *states' rights. Its loose organization, however, made efficient conduct of the war with the US difficult. Unable to levy taxes, the government issued unbacked paper currency and caused massive inflation. No foreign government ever recognized the sovereignty of the CSA, and the Confederate government was dissolved soon after the surrender of Gen. Robert E. *Lee in April 1865.

Confederation of the Rhine (1806–13) The union of the German states (except Austria and Prussia) under *Napoleon I. It facilitated the subsequent movement for German unification, which was achieved in 1871.

Conference on Environment and Development, United Nations. *See* Earth Summit.

Confessing Church A movement among German Evangelicals opposed to the rise of Nazism in the 1930s and to the pro-Nazi German Christian Church. Led by Martin *Niemöller, it was openly active until the start of World War II, but lost influence as it was forced underground by the Nazis during the war. It continued as a movement within the Evangelical Church after 1945.

confession The admission of sins made by a penitent seeking forgiveness of them. As a religious practice it originated in Judaism and was taken over by the early Christian Church, in which public confession was customary. The fourth *Lateran Council (1215) made auricular confession (private confession to a priest, who is empowered to grant absolution) incumbent on all Christians once a year. In the Roman Catholic and Orthodox Churches auricular confession is part of the *sacrament of penance. Many Protestant Churches use a form of general confession, made by the whole congregation in public worship, although auricular confession is also practiced in some Anglican and Lutheran Churches.

confirmation A Christian rite generally held to complete the initiation of a member into the Church. Originally associated with *baptism, it became separated with the spread of infant baptism and in the Middle Ages came to be regarded as one of the seven *sacraments. In the Eastern Orthodox Church, it is administered by a priest immediately after baptism and followed by Holy Communion; in the West, it is conferred by a bishop—in the Roman Catholic Church not before the seventh birthday and customarily at the age of 11 or 12.

Confucianism The traditional philosophy and, until recently, the state religion of China. It was founded in the 5th century BC by *Confucius, whose teaching is contained in five classical works or canonical books (not all of which were actually written by Confucius). While retaining the idea of a divine will (*ming*), Confuciansim emphasizes the moral duty of man to his fellows. Man is born good; the superior man follows his true nature and develops sincerity, fearlessness, compassion, and wisdom. Precise rules of conduct are recorded, regulating social intercourse and establishing the forms of ritual sacrifice to one's ancestors. The canonical books also include works on divination, poetry, and history. Although not sanctioned in China since the Cultural Revolution of 1966–68, Confucianism is still practiced by expatriate Chinese and, as a fundamental ethical attitude, continues to influence Chinese culture.

Confucius (Kong Zi *or* K'ung-fu-tzu; c. 551–479 BC) Chinese philosopher, the founder of *Confucianism. As a minor official in his native Lu, a small state situated in modern Shandong province, he gathered numerous disciples, mainly young gentlemen who wished to enter government service. Promoted to ministerial rank, he became famous for his just and effective policies, but on the ruler's refusing to heed his advice, he left Lu (c. 496) and spent many years wandering from court to court, seeking a prince receptive to his ideas. Most of the works attributed to him are later compilations but the *Analects (Lun Yu)* is probably an authentic collection of his sayings and conversations.

conga A modern Cuban dance in march time in which the second beat in alternating measures is accompanied by a sixteenth note. Originally a parade dance performed by a line of people, it was popularized by bandleader Xavier Cugat.

conger eel A voracious *eel belonging to a family (*Congridae*; about 100 species) found in all oceans; 40 in–10 ft (1–3 m) long, conger eels have a grayish or blackish body with a paler belly, a large head, and a wide mouth with strong teeth.

conglomerates Sedimentary rocks consisting of rounded fragments of former rocks cemented together, usually in sand. These fragments are over 0.08 in (2 mm) in diameter and generally consist of hard material, such as quartzite or granite. Some conglomerates are used for crushed stone for road making and other purposes.

Congo, Republic of (name until 1960: Middle Congo) A country in W central Africa, bordering on the Zaïre River. The narrow coastal plain rises to hills inland and lower valleys in the E provide fertile grasslands. The uplands give way to plains in the NE. The population is composed chiefly of Bantu tribes. *Economy*: largely agricultural, the main cash crops being sugar cane, palm oil, cocoa, and tobacco. Minerals include lead, zinc, and gold, and oil was discovered in 1969. Forests cover about half the country and timber is one of the main exports; others include sugar. The discovery of oil brightened the country's eco-

Congress of Industrial Organizations

nomic outlook considerably, encouraging foreign investment. In the 1980s efforts to decentralize the economy and lessen dependence on oil were aided by loans from the World Bank and other European and African lending agencies. *History*: in the 15th century the Portuguese established trading relations with the Congo kingdom. In the 19th century the exploration of the Frenchman de *Brazza led to the establishment of the colony of Middle Congo, which in 1910 became one of the four territories of French Equatorial Africa. In 1958 it attained internal self-government as a member of the French Community and in 1960 became independent as the Republic of Congo. In 1968 Maj. Marien Ngouabi came to power in a military coup. Ngouabi was assassinated in 1977 and the government was taken over by a military committee under Col. Joachim Yhombi-Opango until his resignation in 1979. A one-party marxist state from 1970, the Congo lessened its dependence on the USSR during the 1980s. In 1992 a new constitution was adopted, and multi-party elections were held. Official language: French. Official currency: CFA (Communauté financière africaine) franc of 100 centimes. Area: 132,018 sq mi (342,000 sq km). Population (1992 est): 2,695,000. Capital: Brazzaville. Main port: Pointe-Noire.

Congo River. *See* Zaïre River.

Congregationalism In Christianity, a form of church government that opposes centralized authority and in which each congregation is democratically autonomous. Congregationalist groups first became active at the time of the *Reformation in the 16th century and played an important role in the opposition to King Charles I in England in the 17th century. They were active supporters of Oliver *Cromwell and became one of the most important forces in the early settlement of New England. Congregationalists founded the Plymouth Colony in 1620 and were the dominant political force in the Massachusetts Bay Colony. Now officially called the United Church of Christ, American Congregationalists now number more than 2,000,000. In Great Britain, the unification of the Congregationalists and the Presbyterians in 1972 led to the establishment of the United Reformed Church.

Congress The legislative branch of the US government established by the US *Constitution (1789) and comprising the Senate and the House of Representatives. According to Article I of the Constitution, all legislation must be passed by both the House and the Senate and be signed by the president before being enacted into law. The House of Representatives has the exclusive power to initiate proposals for new taxes, while the Senate has the sole authority to confirm presidential appointments and ratify treaties. There are 435 members of the House of Representatives, allocated among the states according to population. Members must be at least 25 years of age and serve for terms of two years. The House of Representatives is headed by the Speaker of the House and the chairmen of various committees, who are elected by the members of the majority party. The Senate comprises 100 senators, two from each state regardless of population. All senators must be at least 30 years of age and serve for terms of six years. The vice president presides over the Senate and casts the deciding vote in the case of a tie, but a president pro tempore and the Senate committee chairmen are elected by the majority party. In addition to their legislative duties, the two houses of Congress are empowered to remove federal officials from office through the process of impeachment. This proceeding, used only when an official is accused of serious crimes or misconduct, begins with the presentation of formal charges and a vote by the House of Representatives and is decided by a trial in the Senate.

Congress of Industrial Organizations (CIO) A US labor organization. Originally established in 1835 as a part of the *American Federation of Labor to coordinate mass production worker industries, it became a separate organization by 1938. Its first president, John L. *Lewis (1935–40), was successful in unionizing the automobile, steel, textile, rubber, electric, and mining industries. In 1955 it merged with the American Federation of Labor.

Congress Kingdom of Poland (1815–32) A Polish state, formed at the Congress of *Vienna, having administrative autonomy under the Russian crown. Polish nationalists twice attempted to overthrow Russian dominance but were unsuccessful: after the November Insurrection (1830), Congress Poland lost its autonomy and following the January Insurrection (1863–64), it became a Russian province.

Congreve, William (1670–1729) British dramatist. Educated in Ireland, he returned to England in 1688 to study law but under the patronage of *Dryden entered the literary world instead. The comedies *Love for Love* (1695) and *The Way of the World* (1700) are his best-known plays, although his contemporaries most admired his tragedy *The Mourning Bride* (1697). He wrote little after 1700.

conic section Geometrical figures produced by the intersection of a plane and a cone. If the plane cuts the cone at right angles to its axis the figure is a *circle. If the plane is tilted slightly an *ellipse is formed. If the plane is tilted further, until it lies parallel to the side of the cone, the figure is a *parabola. Tilted more, the figure becomes a *hyperbola. In the case of a hyperbola, the plane also intersects another cone the vertex of which touches the vertex of the first cone, the axes of the two cones being parallel. In this case two conic sections are produced. Therefore a hyperbola has two branches.

conifer A *gymnosperm tree of the widely distributed order *Coniferales* (400–500 species), most abundant in the colder temperate zones, especially in the north; elsewhere they are usually found at high altitudes. Conifers are typically pyramidal in form, with a straight continuously growing stem that can reach great heights (*see* Sequoia). Nearly all conifers are *evergreen (larches are exceptions), with simple needle-like or scalelike leaves. The reproductive organs are typically borne in separate male and female *cones, usually on the same tree, and produce winged seeds that are dispersed by wind (the yew and juniper are exceptions). The wood of conifers—called softwood—is economically important, being used for construction and as a source of paper pulp, etc. (*see* timber).

The principal families are the *Pinaceae* (pines, cedars, spruces, firs, larches, hemlocks, etc.); *Cupressaceae* (cypresses, junipers, arbor vitae, etc.); *Taxodiaceae* (sequoias, swamp cypress, etc.); *Taxaceae* (yews); and *Araucariaceae* (monkey puzzle, etc.)

conjugation The process by which exchange of genetic material occurs in certain lower organisms by means of a connection between the cytoplasm of the two "mating" individuals. In ciliate protozoa and certain algae it is a type of sexual reproduction, the gametes (or gametic nuclei) passing through a cytoplasmic bridge (protozoa) or a conjugation tube (algae). In bacteria the connection between "male" and "female" cells is by means of special hairs (pili) or cell-to-cell bridges.

conjunction An alignment of two celestial bodies in the solar system, usually the sun and a planet, that occurs when the angular distance between them as seen from earth (i.e. the angle planet-earth-sun) becomes zero.

conjunctivitis Inflammation of the conjunctiva—the membrane that covers the surface of the eye and lines the eyelids. Popularly known as pinkeye, it is marked by itching, redness, and watering of the eye. It may be caused by allergy to drugs or pollen; bacterial infection (in which case it usually spreads to the other eye); or mechanical irritation.

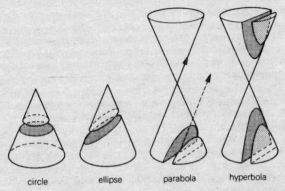

circle   ellipse   parabola   hyperbola

CONIC SECTION *The circle, ellipse, parabola, and hyperbola are produced by slicing through the cone as shown.*

Conkling, Roscoe (1829–88) US politician, lawyer, and orator. A lawyer in New York and a leader in the state Republican Party, he served in the US House of Representatives (1859–63; 1865–67) and the Senate (1867–81). He was a strong advocate of *Reconstruction and worked for the passage of the 14th Amendment. He resigned from the Senate when his leadership of the Republican Party was threatened by federal civil service reform.

Conn (2nd century AD) King of Leinster and High King of Ireland. A tireless warrior, known as Conn of the hundred battles, he gained control over the northern half of Ireland and then, shortly before his death, the whole island.

Connacht (*or* Connaught) A province and ancient kingdom of the NW Republic of Ireland. It consists of the counties of Galway, Leitrim, Mayo, Roscommon, and Sligo. Area: 6611 sq mi (17,122 sq km). Population (1991): 422,909.

Connaught. *See* Connacht.

Connecticut A state in the NE US, in New England. It is bordered by Massachusetts on the N, Rhode Island on the E, Long Island Sound on the S, and New York State on the W. Uplands in the E and W are separated by the central lowlands, forming the fertile Connecticut River valley. It is one of the most densely populated states in the US with a fairly even demographic distribution; 90% of the inhabitants living in cities. The populous SE forms part of the New York City metropolitan area. Connecticut is highly industrial and manufacturing is an important source of revenue. Traditionally produced goods include clocks, silverware, and brass products, as well as military equipment. Hartford, the capital, is one of the principal US insurance centers. Farming is only a minor activity, producing dairy products, eggs, poultry, and vegetables for local markets with some tobacco for export. The state has a rich tradition and culture dating back to colonial times. Yale University at New Haven is the most famous of its large number of universities and colleges. *History*: one of the original 13 colonies, it was first explored by the Dutch in the early 17th century. The first settlement was by English colonists from the Massachusetts Bay Colony (1633–35). Connecticut joined the other colonies in the American Revolution and was one of the first states to ratify the Constitution. It abolished slavery in 1848. In 1974

Connecticut elected Ella Grasso as governor, the first woman to be elected a governor in her own right. Area: 5009 sq mi (12,973 sq km). Population (1990): 3,287,116. Capital: Hartford.

Connecticut Compromise (1787) A proposal set forth at the US Constitutional Convention by Connecticut delegates that solved the problem of equal representation of states in the federal government. Each state would have representation in the House of Representatives proportionate to its population, while the Senate would have an equal number of representatives from each state.

Connecticut River 41 17M 72 21W A river that rises in the Connecticut Lakes in N New Hampshire and flows S to Long Island Sound at Old Saybrook, Conn. It forms the entire New Hampshire-Vermont border and passes by Springfield, Mass., and Hartford, Conn. Length: 407 mi (656 km).

Connecticut Wits A group of US writers in Hartford, Conn., in the late 1700s and early 1800s. Federalists in favor of strong central government, they grouped together to write satirical verse, such as *The Anarchiad* (1786–87) and *The Political Greenhouse* (1799). *The Echo* (1791–1805) was a series. Members included Theodore Dwight, Joel Barlow, John Trumbull, David Humphreys, and Richard Alsop.

connective tissue The tissue that supports, binds, or separates the specialized tissues and organs of the body. Connective tissue consists of a semifluid ground substance of polysaccharide and protein in which are embedded white collagen fibers, yellow elastic fibers, and various cells (including fibroblasts, which produce the ground substance and the fibers). The amount of collagen determines the toughness of the tissue. Specialized connective tissue includes fatty tissue, blood, bone, and cartilage.

Connelly, Marc (Marcus Cook C.; 1890–1980) US dramatist. He began writing plays with George S. *Kaufman in the 1920s, while he was a newspaper theater reporter in New York City. In 1930 he wrote *The Green Pastures* for which he received a Pulitzer Prize. Other works include *The Wisdom Tooth* (1926) and, in collaboration with Frank B. Elser, *The Farmer Takes a Wife* (1934).

Connemara An area in the W Republic of Ireland, in Co Galway bordering on the Atlantic Ocean. It contains many lakes, peat bogs, and the Twelve Bens, a group of quartzite mountains.

Connery, (Thomas) Sean (1930–) British film actor, who first achieved fame as the sophisticated spy James Bond in a series of movies that included *Dr. No* (1962), *From Russia with Love* (1963), and *Goldfinger* (1964). Subsequently, he established a reputation as a versatile actor in such films as *The Name of the Rose* (1986), *The Untouchables* (1987; Academy Award, best supporting actor), *The Hunt for Red October* (1990), and *The Russia House* (1990).

Connors, Jimmy (1952–) US tennis player, who won the US singles title in 1974, 1976, 1978, and 1982 and the doubles title in 1975. He also was a Wimbledon singles champion in 1974 and 1982 and doubles champion in 1973.

conquistador (Spanish: conqueror) One of the men who conquered the Indians of Central and South America for Spain in the first half of the 16th century. Few in number, the conquistadores were driven by a fanatical desire to find fame and gold and to serve the Roman Catholic Church. The most famous were Hernán *Cortés and Francisco *Pizarro.

Conrad II (c. 990–1039) German king (1024–39), who founded the Salian dynasty (1024–1125), and Holy Roman Emperor (1027–39). He conquered part of Poland (1028) and Burgundy (1033–34). While attempting to suppress a rebellion in N Italy (1036–38), he lost most of his army in an epidemic.

Conrad III (1093–1152) The first Hohenstaufen German king (1138–52). He was proclaimed antiking (1127) in opposition to Lothair, after whose death (1137) he became king. His election was opposed by the Welf family and although peace was made in 1142 the conflict between the two families was renewed, giving rise to the *Guelf and Ghibelline struggle. In 1147 Conrad joined the second Crusade.

Conrad, Joseph (Teodor Josef Konrad Wątęcz Korzeniowski; 1857–1924) Polish-born British novelist, who knew no English before he was 20. Orphaned at the age of 11, he went to Marseilles in 1874, where he became a sailor, serving for 16 years in the British Merchant Navy. He became a naturalized British subject in 1886, and published his first novel, *Almayer's Folly,* in 1895. His seagoing experiences influenced both the themes of his fiction and his own moral outlook. His major novels include *Lord Jim* (1900), *Heart of Darkness* (1902), *Nostromo* (1904), *The Secret Agent* (1907), and *Under Western Eyes* (1911).

consanguinity Relationship by blood, either real or putative. However, many societies do not consider everyone to whom they are genetically related to be blood kin. For example, some societies do not consider a father to be genetically related to his children and therefore they are not his consanguines. Consanguinity affects laws regarding property inheritance and prohibits marriage between close blood relatives.

Conscience, Hendrik (1812–83) Flemish novelist. The author of over a hundred novels, he began writing sketches in Flemish in the late 1830s, and his historical romance *The Lion of Flanders* (1838) was the first major Flemish novel.

conscientious objection. *See* pacifism.

conscription The compulsory enlistment of citizens for military service. Conscription was used in the ancient world and during the Middle Ages, when short-term *militia service was enforced for local defense. Universal male conscription was introduced in 1793 in Revolutionary France and was adopted by Prussia in the early 19th century. During the *Civil War, both the Union and the Confederacy used conscription as a means of gaining recruits. There was considerable opposition to this practice, however, especially in the North, where *Draft Riots broke out in 1863. With the entry of the US into World War I in 1917, Congress enacted the first of the *Selective Service Acts, which required the registration of all men between the ages of 18 and 45 for possible military service. Conscription was also used by the US for its participation in *World War II, the *Korean War, and the *Vietnam War. It was officially abolished in 1973, although young men are still required to register with the Selective Service upon reaching the age of 18.

Consejo Real (Spanish: Royal Council) The central organ of government in Spain, created in 1386 in *Castille by Juan I. It was dominated by the clergy and nobility until the reforms of Isabella I in 1480 replaced them with lawyers loyal to the crown. It survived, with diminishing power, until the 19th century.

Consentes Dii The 12 major Roman and Etruscan gods, six male and six female. They are Jupiter and Juno, Neptune and Minerva, Mars and Venus, Apollo and Diana, Vulcan and Vesta, Mercury and Ceres. They were first collectively mentioned in 217 BC.

conservation The rational use of the earth's resources so that life can be sustained indefinitely. Pressure on both mineral and natural resources, resulting from increased agricultural and industrial activity, has required urgent examination of the consequent effects on the world ecosystem. The prudent use of fossil fuels and minerals and the search for alternatives are becoming both political and economic necessities. The destruction of many natural habitats has led to the creation of nature reserves and national parks where wildlife can be protected. Such areas are also often of aesthetic value and serve as recreational areas for urban populations. Legislation can protect some rare species of animals and plants from extinction but international cooperation is needed to protect economically important species (including whales), to conserve fish stocks, and to prevent pollution of the atmosphere and the oceans. In most cases the technological means to solve these problems are available but their high costs, or conflict with sectional interests, prevent their implementation.

conservation of energy supplies The more efficient use of increasingly scarce fuel supplies. In the 1970s several governments began to encourage home-insulation improvements and research into new sources of energy, as well as ways to reduce waste from industrial processes. Similar interest developed in *alternative energy sources. Thus, most new buildings are now designed to minimize heat losses. In electricity-generating stations the warm water produced from condensed steam may be used for local domestic heating in combined heat and power (co-generation) projects. More efficient burners and boilers have been developed for coal-fired power stations. The introduction of transport systems that are less wasteful than the private gasoline-driven car is also likely to become a necessity. *See also* solar power; wave power; wind power.

conservation of mass and energy The principle that, in any closed system, the total of the mass and energy remains constant. It replaced the older laws in which mass and energy were held to be separately conserved, since the special theory of *relativity demonstrates that mass and energy may, in certain circumstances, be interconvertible. The energy (E) equivalent to a mass (m) is given by Einstein's equation: $E = mc^2$, where c is the speed of light in a vacuum.

Conservative Party A UK political party that grew out of the *Tory Party in the 1830s under the leadership of Sir Robert *Peel. Under the leadership of *Disraeli the Conservatives acquired a distinct philosophy that combined identification with the monarchy, the British Empire, and the Church of England with social reform. The party was almost continuously in power from 1886 to 1905 and again from 1922 to 1945. It was again in office in 1951–1964, 1970–74, and from 1979 under *Thatcher and John *Major. The party is now firmly committed to the furtherance of private enterprise and individualism rather than *nationalization.

consols. *See* gilt-edged securities.

Constable, John (1776–1837) British landscape painter, he trained in London at the Royal Academy schools. He painted the Suffolk countryside, Hampstead Heath, and Salisbury Cathedral with a particular concern for changing weather conditions, exemplified in *The Leaping Horse* and *Dedham Vale*. Although he exhibited regularly at the Royal Academy, he was only elected a member in 1829. He achieved greater recognition in France, where his *Haywain* won a gold medal and influenced *Delacroix.

Constance (German name: Konstanz) 47 40N 9 10E A city in SW Germany, in Baden-Württemberg on Lake Constance. Its 11th-century church was formerly a cathedral. Manufactures include textiles, computers, and chemicals. Population (1983): 69,100.

Constance, Council of (1414–18) The 16th ecumenical council of the Roman Catholic Church, which ended the *Great Schism by electing Pope *Martin V (1417). It decreed that the authority of a general council was superior to that of the pope. The heretics *Wycliffe and *Hus were condemned, and Hus was burned at the stake.

CONSTABLE *Self-portrait in pencil and watercolor.*

Constance, Lake (German name: Bodensee) A lake on the Rhine River in Germany, Switzerland, and Austria. Area: 205 sq mi (531 sq km).

Constant, Benjamin (1767–1830) French novelist, born in Switzerland and educated in Germany and Britain. He supported the French Revolution but opposed Napoleon and went into exile. After the restoration of the monarchy he returned to France in 1818 as a leading liberal politician and journalist. His novel *Adolphe* (1816) was based on his passionate affair with Mme de *Staël. Several volumes of his private journals have also been published.

Constanţa 44 10N 28 40E The chief seaport of Romania, situated on the Black Sea. Founded by the Greeks in the 7th century BC, it was rebuilt by Constantine the Great in the 4th century AD. Oil is pumped here from the Ploieşti fields to be refined and exported. Population (1992): 350,000.

constantan An alloy of 55% copper and 45% nickel. It is used in electrical equipment, such as resistors and *thermocouples, because it has a high electrical resistance that does not change with temperature.

Constantine (ancient name: Cirta) 36 23N 6 29E A city in N Algeria. It was destroyed in 311 AD but rebuilt by Constantine the Great in 313 and renamed for him. The old town is popular with tourists and noted for its handicrafts. Population (1987): 440,842.

Constantine I (1868–1923) King of Greece (1913–17, 1920–22). Constantine led Greece to victory in the *Balkan War (1912–13) but unpopularly maintained neutrality in World War I and was forced to abdicate (1917). Recalled in 1920, he again abdicated following a military revolt against his war with Turkey.

Constantine II (1940–   ) King of Greece (1964–67). In 1967, following a military coup, Constantine went into exile, eventually moving to Britain. In 1973 he was officially deposed and Greece became a republic. He married (1964) Princess Anne-Marie of Denmark (1946–   ).

Constantine VII Porphyrogenitus (905–59 AD) Byzantine emperor (913–59). Constantine reigned (919–45) with his father-in-law and coemperor, Romanus I Lecapenus (d. 948), and while Romanus ruled Constantine devoted himself to studying and writing. His works *On Imperial Administration* and *Ceremonies of the Byzantine Court* are invaluable sources for Byzantine social and economic history.

Constantine the Great (?285–337 AD) Roman emperor in the West (312–24) and sole emperor (324–37). The son of Constantius (c. 250–306), Roman emperor in the West (305–06), Constantine was acclaimed as his father's successor by his troops at York but did not secure his position until he had defeated his rival Maxentius (d. 312). He became sole emperor after defeating the Eastern emperor Licinius (c. 270–325; reigned 311–24). Constantine was the first Roman emperor to adopt Christianity. During his campaign against Maxentius he was reputed to have had a vision of the Christian cross with the words "In this sign, conquer." In 313 Constantine issued the Edict of Milan, which established toleration of Christians, and in 325 summoned the Council of *Nicaea, the first general council of the Church. He was baptized on his deathbed. Constantine introduced administrative and military reforms and founded Constantinople (*see* Istanbul).

Constantinople. *See* Istanbul.

Constantinople, Councils of Three general councils of the Christian Church. **1.** (391) The council that was summoned to end the Arian dispute (*see* Arianism) and assert the doctrine of the Council of *Nicaea. **2.** (553) The council that attempted to resolve the conflict between the *Nestorians and *Monophysites. **3.** (680) The council that condemned the *Monothelite heresy and asserted the doctrines of the Council of *Chalcedon concerning the dual nature of Christ's will.

constellations The 88 areas into which the N and S hemispheres of the sky are now divided, using established boundaries. Each star, galaxy, or other celestial body lies within, or sometimes overlaps, the boundaries of one of the constellations and is often named in terms of this constellation. The constellations all have Latin names. They originally had no fixed limits but were groups of stars forming a distinctive pattern outlining a mythological hero, animal, etc. The constellations that can be observed at night depend on the latitude of the observer and change with the time of night and the time of year.

constipation The conditon in which emptying of the bowels occurs infrequently: feces are often hard and dry and there may be pain in passing them. Constipation is often associated with advancing age and a diet deficient in vegetable fiber (probably the most common cause in the Western world). It is also caused by some drugs (e.g. codeine) and by obstruction of the bowel. Longstanding constipation not due to disease of the bowel is treated by increasing the amount of vegetable fiber (e.g. bran) in the diet. *Laxatives may also be used.

constitution The principles according to which a country is governed. Constitutions may comprise the sum of a country's laws and its customs of government, as in the UK, where government is by the monarch in *Parliament, or be contained in a single document, as in the US.

Constitution, US (1787) The document that embodies the fundamental laws of the US. It was drawn up in 1787, ratified in 1788, and came into effect in 1789. Framed by James *Madison, it contains seven articles, which define separation of powers, a system of checks and balances between the legislature (*see* Congress), the executive (*see* president), and the judiciary (*see* Supreme Court). There are 26 amendments, the first 10 of which constitute the *Bill of Rights. Subsequent amendments dealt with prohibiting a citizen of one state from suing another state government (11, 1795), revision of methods for electing the president and vice president (12, 1804), abolition of slavery and full citizenship and voting rights (13,1861; 14, 1868; 15, 1870), income tax (16, 1913), popular election of senators (17, 1913), prohibition of alcohol (18, 1919), woman suffrage (19, 1920), convening of Congress to eliminate "lame duck" situation (20, 1933), repeal of amendment 18 (21, 1933), number of presidential terms (22, 1951), District of Columbia residents' right to vote for president (23, 1961), prohibition of poll tax (24, 1964), presidential succession (25, 1967), and lowering the voting age to 18 (26, 1971). *See* Connecticut Compromise; New Jersey Plan; Virginia plan.

Constitutional Act of 1791 British act that divided Canada into Upper (English-speaking) and Lower (French-speaking) Canada. It was drawn up by Prime Minister William Pitt the Younger (*see* Pitt the Elder, William, 1st Earl of Chatham) in an effort to keep the colonists under British rule. Under the act the colonists had an elective assembly that worked with a legislative council appointed by the crown.

Constitutional Convention (1787) An assembly of delegates from 12 of the original states (Rhode Island choosing not to participate) that met in Philadelphia to draft a new constitution for the US. Since the original form of federal government for the US, set down in the *Articles of Confederation, had proved to be too weak to permit an effective central authority or a unified foreign policy, an effort was made to create a strong federal government while preserving the rights of the individual states. During the debates at the Constitutional Convention, which lasted from May to September, James *Madison played an instrumental role in shaping the new US *Constitution. The cornerstone of the new system of government was a division of federal power among three separate branches: the executive, the legislative, and the judicial. In order that there be some balance between the influence of the larger states and the smaller states, the legislative branch was to consist of a bicameral *Congress with both proportional and equal representation. After debates in state constitutional ratification conventions, the US Constitution was adopted in 1788.

constrictor A snake belonging to the family *Boidae* (70 species) occurring chiefly in tropical regions. Constrictors are nonvenomous and kill their prey by coiling their thick muscular body around it and squeezing until it suffocates. They often have claws, which are vestigial limbs. The family comprises two subfamilies, *Boine* (*see* boa) and *Pythonine* (*see* python).

constructivism A movement in abstract sculpture, architecture, and design, which was launched in Russia by the *Realist Manifesto* (1920) of the brothers Naum *Gabo and Antoine *Pevsner with the aim of freeing contemporary art from political and social overtones. The chief principles of constructivism were functionalism, the articulation of space, and the use of modern materials, such as plastic and steel. Many Russian constructivists left their country for Germany or France in 1922 because of state opposition to the movement. The architect, painter, and designer El *Lissitzky was influential at the *Bauhaus school in Germany, while Gabo spread the style to the UK and the US.

consubstantiation In Christian theology, a doctrine concerning the presence of Christ in the *Eucharist, especially associated with the teaching of Martin *Luther. Traditionally, the consecrated bread and wine were held to become, substantially, the body and blood of Christ (*see* transubstantiation). According to the doctrine of consubstantiation, the substances of the body and blood of Christ and of the bread and wine were held to coexist together in the consecrated Host.

consuls The two magistrates who held supreme civil and military authority under the *Roman Republic. They were elected annually by the Comitia Centuriata (*see* comitia) and presided over the Senate. Under the Empire they were nominated by the emperor and held office for only two to four months, the posts becoming honorary.

Consumer Affairs, The Office of US agency within the Department of Commerce that works with the business community on behalf of consumers and assists consumers with marketplace problems. It develops cooperative projects with companies, trade and professional associations, consumer organizations, and federal, state, and local agencies to help businesses improve their relations with consumers.

consumerism The idea that consumers should influence the design, quality, service, and prices of goods and services provided by commercial enterprises. Movements based on this idea have developed in the US (*see* Nader, Ralph) and in Europe as a response to the concentration of economic power in modern corporations and to the increased technical complexity of many contemporary consumer goods.

consumption (economics) Expenditure on goods and services, excluding expenditure on capital goods (*see* investment). A country's national income is spent either on consumption or on investment. Public consumption consists of government spending on services, such as education, health, defense, etc. Private consumption is money spent by individuals on nondurables, such as food and drink, durables, such as cars and washing machines, and services, such as entertainment. There is some controversy as to whether private consumption is determined by an individual's lifetime prospects or his current income. This controversy has important consequences in economic planning: for example, whether or not tax cuts would reduce unemployment by increasing consumption.

contact lenses A removable form of lens worn directly against the eye to replace spectacles for long or short sight or to protect the eye in some disorders of the outer transparent layer (cornea). Originally made of glass, modern contact lenses are made of plastic and become molded to the shape of the individual's eye. At first the lenses may irritate the eyes, but most people can adapt to them with time.

containerization The use of large cuboid containers built to internationally accepted dimensions (usually $8 \times 8 \times 20$, 30, or 40 ft [$2.4 \times 2.4 \times 6.1$, 9.1 or 12.2 m]) for the transport of goods. These containers are transported from the producing factory to the user, distributor, or export dock without being unpacked: thus they cut down on the cost and time involved in handling and reduce the chances of loss through pilferage or damage. Containerization has revolutionized international shipping, as specialized ships are needed to transport the containers efficiently; this has led to the decline of the many docks that are only equipped to handle conventionally packed goods.

conté crayon A stick of soft crayon, named for its inventor, the French scientist Nicholas Jacques Conté (1755–1805). Unlike pastel, its color is durable and nonsmudging, while its size makes it suitable both for line drawing and shading large areas.

contempt of court An act or omission that is designed to obstruct a court in its administration of justice or which is designed to lessen its authority or its dignity. There are two types of contempt: direct and constructive. Direct contempts are committed in court (such as insulting language or acts of violence). Constructive (or indirect) contempts arise from matters occurring out of court, but which tend to obstruct the administration of justice (such as failure or refusal to obey a lawful order, injunction, or decree). Contempt is punishable by fine or imprisonment.

continent One of the major land masses of the earth. The following are usually given as distinct continents: Asia, Africa, North America, South America, Europe, Australia, and Antarctica. (These divisions do not correspond to the rigid plates into which the whole of the earth's crust is divided.) The continents occupy about 30% of the earth's surface area. The crust of which they are formed (mainly granitic) is less dense than the oceanic crust (basaltic). The constituents of the continental crust are called sial and those of the oceanic crust, sima. The continents have not always occupied their present positions; the approximate "fit" of the coastlines of the present continents provided the first evidence for the theory of *continental drift.

Continental Congress (1774–89) The body of representatives of the American colonies, which met in Philadelphia. The first Continental Congress (1774–75) was convened as a response to the passage of the *Intolerable Acts and the *Quebec Act by the British parliament. The members of the First Continental Congress agreed to organize an economic boycott of Great Britain and to reconvene if further action proved to be necessary. Since the British government refused to offer any concessions to the colonists, the Second Continental Congress (1775–76) met to consider the question of American independence and the coordination of a plan for military defense. Its members named George Washington commander of the Continental Army and adopted the *Declaration of Independence on July 4, 1776. With this action, the Continental Congress became the provisional government of the US. It continued to meet yearly until 1789, when it was replaced by the US *Congress established by the Constitution.

continental divide A major *watershed separating the drainage basins of a continent. In North America a continental divide extends generally N–S along the Rocky Mountains dividing the rivers flowing E from those flowing W.

continental drift The theory, first set out in 1912 by Alfred *Wegener and now widely accepted by earth scientists, that the continents are not fixed in position but drift slowly over the earth's surface (*see also* plate tectonics). Wegener's work was based on similarities in rock types, geological structures, flora and fauna, and the coastal outlines of the continents; in recent years geophysical data, particularly from geomagnetic studies, have provided firmer evidence for continental drift. It is believed that about 200 million years ago a supercontinent (termed Pangaea), into which all the continents were joined, began to break up and the fragments drifted apart until the continents reached their present positions. It is probable that continents have been joining together and breaking up throughout the earth's history.

continental shelf The area of sea floor adjacent to the continents, dipping gently from the shoreline to a depth of about 650 ft (200 m). At this depth, the shelf edge, the continental slope begins, dipping more steeply to the ocean bottom. Shelves tend to be wider off low-lying regions than mountainous regions; the average width is about 42 mi (70 km).

Continental System The trade blockade of Britain introduced by Napoleon in 1806 to ruin Britain's commerce and thus force peace on his own terms. Napoleon used his control of the coast from the Baltic to the Adriatic to forbid French allies or neutrals to trade with Britian or its colonies. Britain subjected all countries in alliance with France to counterblockade. The Continental System ultimately failed because of the contraband trade and the new British markets in South America.

contraception The prevention of unwanted pregnancy, also known as birth control and family planning. Of the numerous methods available for preventing conception, the rhythm method and coitus interruptus are the most simple but least reliable. In the former sexual intercourse is avoided around the middle of the menstrual cycle, when ovulation is most likely to occur; in the latter the penis is withdrawn from the vagina before ejaculation. Both the condom (or sheath), which is worn over the penis, and the diaphragm, which is fitted over the cervix of the womb, are more effective since they prevent the sperm from entering the womb. A far more reliable contraceptive is the intrauterine device (IUD)—a loop or coil, often impregnated with copper, that is inserted by a doctor into the womb. Its method of action is not known. Some women, however, are unable to use an IUD as it causes unacceptable side effects (such as heavy menstrual bleeding or recurrent infection). The most efficient means of preventing pregnancy is by taking hormonal pills (*see* oral contraceptive), but this, too, may produce side effects and is unsuitable for some women. Another hormonal contraceptive method is the injection, at three-monthly intervals, of a synthetic hormone (progestogen). The selection of any contraceptive method depends on its suitability for the individual: there is no universally acceptable method. Permanent contraception is achieved by *sterilization, which includes vasectomy for men and cutting of the Fallopian tubes for women. A contraceptive pill to be taken by men and a morning-after pill for women are actively being sought.

Family planning has had a long history, with early methods ranging from infanticide and abortion to the use of such preventive devices as sheep's bladders as condoms. The need for it, however, was not formally discussed until the beginning of the 19th century, when the writings of *Malthus drew attention to the problems of overpopulation. Moral objections and the absence of an appropriate technology delayed the advent of the first family-planning clinics until 1916. They were pioneered in the US by Margaret Sanger (1883–1966). Until the 1960s and the appearance of the Pill, contraception was almost entirely dependent upon rubber devices (the condom and the diaphragm).

contract In law, an enforceable promise or bargain, usually written but sometimes verbal. A simple promise for which nothing is given in exchange is not a contract and is only enforceable at law as a *deed. Something of value, called "consideration," must be exchanged in return for the promise; the value must be real but need not be equivalent. If a house is sold for a pound of sugar, that sugar represents sufficient consideration. Breach of contract, meaning failure to fulfil its conditions, may result in the offender being sued for damages by the other party to the contract.

contralto The deepest female singing voice. Range: F below middle C to D an octave and a sixth above.

contrapposto A technique in sculpture for resting a figure's weight on one leg to tilt the body in a realistic pose. Practiced by *Polyclitus of Argos (5th century BC), it was revived during the Renaissance, notably in *Michelangelo's statue of David (Accademia, Florence).

Contreras, Battle of (Aug 19–20, 1847) A battle of the *Mexican War fought near Mexico City. US forces under Gen. Winfield *Scott (1786–1866) put the Mexican forces to flight and gained control of the road to the Mexican capital.

convection The transfer of heat within a fluid by means of motion of the fluid. Convection may be natural or forced. In natural convection, the fluid flows by virtue of the warmer part being less dense than the cooler part. Thus the warmer fluid rises and the colder fluid sinks under the influence of gravity. In forced convection, some external cause, such as a fan or impeller, drives colder fluid into a warmer one, or vice versa.

convergence (*or* convergent evolution) The development in unrelated animals of similarities resulting from adaption to the same way of life. Thus whales (mammals) and fish have evolved similar features independently, associated with their aquatic habitat.

conversos (Spanish: converts) The Spanish Jews who were forced to become Roman Catholics during the persecution of Jews in the late 14th and 15th centuries. The Spanish Inquisition was created to prevent the apostasy of *conversos* and the Muslim *Moriscos.

Convolvulus A widely distributed genus of annual or perennial twining plants (about 250 species). The flowers are funnel or bell-shaped and attractive. The Eurasian *bindweed (*C. arvensis*) is a noxious weed, now widely introduced, with deep persistent roots and rapidly growing stems. Some species, such as *C. altheoides,* are cultivated in gardens. Some have medicinal (purgative) properties. Family: *Convolvulaceae.*

cony. *See* hyrax; pika.

Cook, Captain James (1728–79) British navigator and cartographer. He joined the Royal Navy (1755) and served in the Seven Years' War (1756–63), during which he surveyed the St Lawrence River. His observations on the eclipse of the sun in 1766 were presented to the Royal Society, which gave him command of an expedition to Tahiti to observe the transit of the planet Venus across the sun and to discover Terra Australis, a presumed southern continent. The expedition set sail in the *Endeavour* in 1768 and, Venus observed, Cook went on to discover and chart New Zealand and the E coast of Australia, returning to England in 1771. The voyage was remarkable not least for the absence of scurvy among his crew—the result of a diet, devised by Cook, that was high in vitamin C. His second voyage (1772–75), in the *Resolution,* accompanied by the *Adventure,* achieved the circumnavigation of the Antarctic. He charted Easter Island and discovered New Caledonia, the South Sandwich Islands, and South Georgia Island. Cook's third voyage (1776–79) ended in tragedy; he was killed in a quarrel with Hawaiians.

Cook, Sir Joseph (1860–1947) Australian statesman, born in England; Liberal prime minister (1913–14) He was hampered by a majority of only one in the House of Representatives and a minority in the Senate.

Cook, Mount (Maori name: Aorangi) 43 37S 170 08E The highest mountain in New Zealand, in South Island in the Southern Alps. It is permanently snow capped and flanked by glaciers. Height: 12,349 ft (3764 m).

Cook, Thomas (1808–92) British travel agent, who introduced conducted excursions and founded the travel agents Thomas Cook and Son. He organized his first excursion in 1841, a railroad journey from Leicester to Lowborough for a temperance meeting.

Cooke, Jay (1821–1905) US financier. After working for a banking firm in Philadelphia, he formed his own banking company in 1861. He aided the US Treasury Department during the Civil War by selling war bonds and raising millions of dollars for the war effort. His firm was also instrumental in setting up the new national bank system under the National Bank Act of 1863. The company went bankrupt in 1873, due to railroad speculations, and Cooke turned to other ventures.

Cook Islands A group of scattered islands in the SE Pacific Ocean, a New Zealand dependency. The chief islands are Rarotonga, Atiu, and Aitutaki. Fruit, copra, and mother-of-pearl are exported. Area: 93 sq mi (241 sq km). Capital: Avarua.

coolabar A tree, *Eucalyptus microtheca,* growing to 80 ft (25 m), common inland in W Australia. The leaves are mainly persistent and the wood is gray near the outside, deep red within. Called locally by many names, including jinbul, moolar, blackbox, and dwarf box, it is used for building. Family: *Myrtaceae. See also* Eucalyptus.

Coolidge, John Calvin (1872–1933) US statesman; 30th President of the United States (1923–29). After beginning his political career as a Republican member of the Massachusetts legislature, Coolidge was elected governor in 1918 and gained national prominence for his uncompromising and efficient handling of the Boston police strike (1919). Chosen as the vice-presidential running mate of Warren G. *Harding in 1920, Coolidge succeeded to the presidency after Harding's death in 1923. While Harding's administration was marred by scandal and corruption, Coolidge acted decisively to restore the integrity of the federal government and was elected by a large majority to a full term in 1924. In accordance with the belief that "the business of America is business," the Coolidge administration promoted the interests of private industry and, for the most part, avoided active intervention in foreign affairs. While the country achieved unprecedented prosperity, dangerous stock market speculation created the conditions that later resulted in the 1929 financial crash. As a modest, self-effacing individual, popularly known as "Silent Cal," Coolidge chose not to run for reelection in 1928.

cool jazz (*or* progressive jazz) A style of US *jazz developed on the W coast in the early 1950s. Cool jazz was characterized by subtle rhythms as well as by instruments and harmonies borrowed from European classical music. Less frenetic than *bop, cool jazz was also quieter and more economical. Important cool-jazz musicians include Stan Getz, Miles Davis, and Dave Brubeck.

Cooper, Gary (Frank James C; 1901–61) US film actor. He is noted for his portrayals of tough but sensitive heroes in Hollywood westerns. His best known films include *The Virginian* (1929), *The Westerner* (1940), *Sergeant York* (1941), and *High Noon* (1952).

Cooper, James Fenimore (1789–1851) US novelist. Expelled from Yale, he served briefly in the navy before his marriage in 1811. Financial need prompted him to start writing, and in *The Pioneers* (1823), his third novel, he portrayed frontier life. Sequels included *The Last of the Mohicans* (1826) and *The Pathfinder* (1840). A parallel series of sea novels, a form that he pioneered, included *The Red Rover* (1827) and *The Sea Lions* (1849). His democratic sympathies were strengthened during his stay in Europe from 1826 to 1833 but his nonfiction writings met with little success.

cooperative societies Organizations set up to manufacture, grow, buy, or sell produce, either without profit or with profits distributed to all members or shareholders as dividends. The cooperative movement was inspired by the ideas of the British philanthropist Robert *Owen in the early 19th century. Owen believed that the pooling of funds and the sharing of expensive equipment by small farmers and tradesmen might eliminate the economic hardships that seemed to be caused by unrestricted competition. Cooperative societies in agriculture, in which heavy farm machinery is shared and produce is marketed jointly by the societies' members, have become common throughout the world. In the US, the *Granger Movement, established in the 1860s, provides the members of local societies, or "Granges," with such agricultural services as low-cost grain storage and cooperative meat packing plants. It also protects the economic interests of small farmers through lobbying activities in Congress. Retail cooperative societies have also been established for consumers in many American cities, providing members with food and other products at reduced prices by bulk purchasing and low merchandising costs.

Cooper Creek (*or* Barcoo River) An intermittent river in E central Australia, in the *Channel Country. Rising in central Queensland it flows generally SW into Lake Eyre. Actual water flow in its lower reaches is irregular, occurring only in times of flood. Length: 880 mi (1420 km).

Cooperstown 42 42N 74 56W A resort town in E central New York where the headwaters of the Susquehanna River flow from Lake Otsego. Here James Fenimore Cooper's *Leather-stocking Tales* took place and Abner Doubleday popularized the game of baseball (1839). It is the home of the National Baseball Museum and Hall of Fame. Population (1990): 2,180.

coordinate systems Geometrical systems that locate points in space by a set of numbers.

In **Cartesian coordinates**, devised by René *Descartes, a point is located by its distance from intersecting lines called axes. In a plane (two dimensions) there are two axes and in space (three dimensions) there are three. Usually the axes are at right angles to each other and are known as rectangular axes, but oblique axes are also used in exceptional circumstances.

Polar coordinates denote position by distance and direction. A fixed point, called the origin, and a fixed line, called the polar axis, are taken as the references. For any point, the polar coordinates are the length, r, of the radius of the circle centered at the origin and passing through the point, and the angle, θ, between this radius and the polar axis. In three dimensions, spherical polar coordinates are used. The radius of a sphere centered at the origin and the two angles it makes with the polar axis define the point.

coot An aquatic *rail of the genus *Fulica* (9 species). Coots have broadly lobed toes, diving deeply to feed on invertebrates and aquatic plants. The European coot (*F. atra*) occurs throughout the Old World and is 14 in (37 cm) long with black plumage and a white bill and frontal shield.

copal Any one of the many resins collected from living or fossilized tropical trees and used in the manufacture of varnishes and inks. Copals can vary from brownish-yellow to colorless.

Copán 14 52N 89 10W A town in Honduras. Extensive ruins with temples, pyramids, astronomical stelae, and a ceremonial stairway remain from its heyday as a *Mayan city (c. 300–900 AD).

Copenhagen (Danish name: København) 55 40N 12 35E The capital and chief port of Denmark, on the E coast of Sjælland. It is an industrial as well as a commercial and shipping center, with engineering, food processing, and brewing. Notable buildings include the 17th-century Charlottenborg Palace (now the Royal Academy of Arts) and Christiansborg Palace (now the parliamentary and government buildings). An important center of Scandinavian culture, Copenhagen possesses a university (1479) and several museums. *History*: already a human settlement in the year 900 AD, it became capital of Denmark in 1443. Over the centuries it has been involved in many wars; it was attacked by the Hanseatic League in the Middle Ages and by Sweden in the 17th century. In 1801 the Danish fleet was destroyed by Nelson at the battle of Copenhagen. In 1728, and again in 1795, it was badly destroyed by fire. Occupied by the Germans in World War II, it became the center of a strong resistance movement. Population (1990 est): 1,337,000.

Copepoda A subclass of *crustaceans (7500 species), mostly 0.02–0.08 in (0.5–2 mm) long, that have long antennae, a single median eye, and no carapace. There are 11 pairs of appendages on the head and thorax and forked tail filaments (furca). Copepods occur in abundance in fresh and salt water, forming a constituent of plankton. Most feed on microscopic plants or animals but some are parasitic on fish, other crustaceans, etc.

Copernicus, Nicolaus (1473–1543) Polish astronomer, formulator of the modern heliocentric theory of the solar system. After studying mathematics and music at Cracow and Bologna, Copernicus became interested in the problem of calculating planetary positions, since existing tables were out of date. He noticed that by using a system in which the earth revolved round the sun, instead of *Ptolemy's geocentric system, these calculations would be much easier to make. He then realized that such a system could actually describe the solar system, rather than providing a simple working model of it, since it explained the occasional backward motion of the planets. Copernicus, realizing that these ideas were at variance with the Church's view that the earth was at the center of the universe, only circulated them to a few friends. The full text of his book *De revolutionibus orbium coelestium* was not published until 1543: legend has it that Copernicus was presented with the first copy on his deathbed.

Copland, Aaron (1900–90) US composer, a pupil of Nadia Boulanger. He was active as a teacher, pianist, and champion of contemporary music. He is best known for his compositions in a popular style, such as the ballets *Billy the Kid* (1938), *Rodeo* (1942) and *Appalachian Spring* (1944) and the operas *The Second Hurricane* (1937) and *The Tender Lane* (1954). Many of his themes are based on American folklore. His other works employ a variety of styles and include *Piano Concerto* (1927) in a jazz idiom and *Piano Fantasy* (1957) using *serialism.

Copley, John Singleton (1738–1815) US portrait painter. Born in Boston, he worked as an artist from the age of 15 and by his late 20s had become well known for his realistic portraits in America and Europe. In 1774 he brought his family to England and began painting historical subjects. Among these massive works are *The Death of the Earl of Chatham, The Death of Major Peirson,* and *The Siege of Gibraltar.* He is best known, however, for his American portraits, such as *Paul Revere* and *John Hancock.*

copper (Cu) A reddish-brown metal, known from prehistoric times and named for the island of Cyprus, which was the principal source in Roman times. It occurs naturally as the native element, the sulfide chalcopyrite ($CuFeS_2$), the carbonate malachite ($Cu_2CO_3(OH)_2$), and other minerals. It is mined in Zambia, Zaïre, Chile, Australia, New Guinea, and elsewhere. Copper is extracted by smelting and electrolysis. It is malleable, ductile, and is important because of its good electrical (second only to silver) and thermal conductivity. Copper is widely used in the electrical industry and in the form of copper pipes in plumbing. It is contained in coins, and in the alloys *brass and *bronze. Common compounds are the oxides (Cu_2O, CuO) and copper sulfate ($CuSO_4$). At no 29; at wt 63.546; mp 633°F (1083°C); bp 1472°F (2595°C).

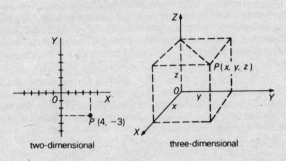

Cartesian coordinates

two-dimensional   three-dimensional

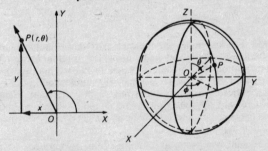

polar coordinates

two-dimensional   three-dimensional

COORDINATE SYSTEMS *In two-dimensional Cartesian coordinates, a point* P *is located by giving its x- and y-coordinates, in this case 4 and –3 (always given in this order, as shown). In three-dimensional Cartesian coordinates,* P *is located in terms of three axes. In polar coordinates,* P *is located by a radius* r *and an angle* θ. *In three dimensions a second angle,* φ, *is required. In the diagrams, Cartesian coordinates are superimposed on the polar coordinates.*

copperhead A North American *pit viper, *Agkistrodon contortrix,* occurring in swampy or wooded regions. Up to 40 in (1 m) long, it is reddish with a coppery head and brown bands on its back. The name is also given to a S Australian snake, *Denisonia superba,* which is about 5 ft (1.5 m) long and usually coppery-brown.

Copperhead A Northerner sympathetic to the South during the *Civil War, especially one who opposed Lincoln's military or civil policies. Mostly midwestern Democrats, the Copperheads were accused of disloyalty to the northern cause and the Democratic Party suffered by association with them. The name derives from a newspaper reference comparing antiwar Democrats to snakes.

Coppermine River A river in N Canada, in Mackenzie district. Rising in Lac de Gras, it flows NW past copper deposits into Coronation Gulf (an arm of the Arctic Ocean). Length: 525 mi (845 km).

copra. *See* coconut.

Coptic A *Hamito-Semitic language spoken in Egypt from the early Christian period until the 8th century AD. It was the last stage of ancient Egyptian and was written in Greek characters with seven additional *demotic letters. There were six dialects of which Sahidic became the standard form in Upper Egypt after the 5th century. Bohairic of Lower Egypt was used for religious purposes by the Coptic Christians and has a literature of scriptural translations from Greek and original writings that reflect Gnostic and Manichaean tendencies within early Christianity.

Coptic Church The largest Christian Church in Egypt. The Copts trace the history of their Church to St *Mark. As a result of its *Monophysite beliefs, which were condemned at the Council of Chalcedon (451), the Coptic Church became somewhat isolated from other Christian bodies. The Muslim conquest of Egypt in 642, together with language and cultural differences, widened the division. The Church suffered some persecution under Arab dominion. In 1741 a number of Copts entered the Roman Catholic communion, becoming the Uniat Coptic Church. Alexandria held an eminent position in the early Church and remains the seat of the Coptic patriarch, who presides over the Church with 12 diocesan bishops. The Copts are in communion with the Armenian and Syrian (Orthodox) Churches.

copyright law The law protecting the exclusive right of authors, composers, artists, publishers, and others who create or publish original literary, dramatic, and artistic works to reproduce them (in whole or in part) and to exploit them. Infringement of copyright is known as piracy. The protection lasts for a certain number of years after the death of the owner of the copyright. Many nations adopted the Universal Copyright Convention in 1952, whereby each signatory undertook to give the same protection to the authors of the other signatories as it gave its own authors.

coracle An ancient boat, usually round, made of wickerwork or laths over which a waterproofed animal skin has been stretched and fitted. Coracles were used in Ireland and in Wales and other parts of W Britain.

coral A sedentary marine animal belonging to a class (*Anthozoa*) of *coelenterates. Individual corals—*polyps—produce a protective skeleton that may be soft and jelly-like, horny, or stony. They usually occur in colonies and are found in all oceans, particularly warm shallow waters, feeding mainly on small animals. Reproduction can be asexual (by budding) or sexual, the eggs being fertilized in the water.

The stony (*or* true) corals (order *Madreporaria*; about 1000 species) secrete a rigid external skeleton made of almost pure calcium carbonate. **Coral reefs** (*see* reef) are produced by succeeding generations of stony corals, occurring in dense colonies. The principal reef building occurs at depths of less than 165 ft (50 m) and at temperatures above 68°F (20°C). Within this zone symbiotic algae (zooxanthellae) are present in coral tissues and stimulate the secretion of calcium carbonate, accelerating the growth of coral skeletons. The Great Barrier Reef off NE Australia is the best-known example.

Coralli, Jean (J. C. Peracini; 1779–1854) Italian ballet dancer and choreographer. He trained in Paris and was choreographer at the Paris Academy (1831–45). He choreographed many of the most celebrated Romantic ballets, including *Giselle* (1841) and *La Peri* (1843).

Coral Sea A section of the SW Pacific Ocean between NE Australia, New Guinea, and the New Hebrides. It contains many coral reefs, including the *Great Barrier Reef. During World War II it was the scene of a US victory over the Japanese (1942).

coral snake A New World burrowing venomous snake having a boldly patterned skin. They occur chiefly in the tropics and are generally secretive, preying on other snakes. The main genus, *Micrurus* (40 species), ranges from the S US to Argentina; most species are ringed with red, black, and yellow or white. Old World coral snakes are similar and found in SE Asia (genus *Calliophis*) and Africa (genus *Elaps*). Family: *Elapidae* (cobras, mambas, coral snakes).

The rear-fanged false coral snakes have similar patterning but belong to the family *Colubridae* (grass snakes, etc.)

coral tree A Brazilian tree, *Erythrina crista-galli,* 7–10 ft (2–3 m) high, with clusters of deep-scarlet flowers, for which it is often grown as an ornamental. Family: *Leguminosae.*

cor anglais A double-reeded musical instrument, the alto member of the oboe family. It is a transposing instrument, the notes sounding a fifth lower than written. It has a range of two and a half octaves from the E below middle C. Sibelius used its rich tone in the symphonic poem *The Swan of Tuonela.*

Corbusier, Le. *See* Le Corbusier.

Cordaitales An order of extinct *gymnosperm trees that—with *Calamites*—formed vast forests during the Carboniferous and Permian periods (370–240 million years ago); coal was formed from their fossilized remains. The trees probably grew up to 98 ft (30 m) high, with a tall columnar trunk and strap-shaped leaves, up to 40 in (1 m) long.

Corday, Charlotte (1768–93) French noblewoman, who assassinated Jean-Paul *Marat in his bath on July 13, 1793. She was guillotined on July 17. She sympathized with the Girondins, the revolutionary party that opposed the more radical Jacobins.

Cordeliers, Club of the A French Revolutionary club founded in Paris in 1790 to defend the rights of man. It was temporarily disbanded following a demonstration against Louis XVI in 1791. After it was restored, it became more radical and was finally disbanded in 1794 following an unsuccessful insurrection.

cordgrass. *See* Spartina.

Córdoba 31 25S 64 11W A city in central Argentina. Founded in 1573, it has many notable old buildings, including the cathedral (1758) and the university (1613). A commercial and industrial center, its manufactures include automobiles, tractors, and textiles. Population (1991): 1,179,067.

Córdoba 37 53N 4 46W A city in S Spain, in Andalusia on the Guadalquivir River. It became the capital of Moorish Spain in 756 AD and by the 10th century was Europe's largest city and a major cultural center. Its immense Moorish cathedral (8th–10th centuries) was originally a mosque. Industries include silverware and textiles. Population (1991): 300,229.

Cordon Bleu Originally, the blue ribbon of the knight's grand cross of the Order of the Holy Spirit, the first order of the Bourbon kings. The term is now used to describe food, or a chef, that achieves an (unspecified) degree of excellence.

Corelli, Arcangelo (1653–1713) Italian violinist and composer. He rationalized contemporary violin technique and wrote sonatas for the instrument. He also established the concerto grosso, in which a small group of soloists (typically two violins and cello) is contrasted with the full orchestra, a form much used by baroque composers. His most famous work is the *Christmas Concerto* for strings and continuo.

Coreopsis A genus of North American, tropical African, and Hawaiian plants (120 species) commonly known as tick-seeds (because of the shape of their seedlike fruits). Annual or perennial herbs, they are often grown in gardens for their daisy-like flowers, which are usually yellow with a darker center. Family: *Compositae*.

Corfu (Latin name: Coreyra; Modern Greek name: Kérkira *or* Kérkyra) A Greek island in the NE Ionian Sea, in the Ionian Islands. It has belonged to many powers, including Venice (1386–1797) and Britain (1815–64). The local produce includes olives, figs, and citrus fruit, and tourism is important. Area: 250 sq mi (641 sq km). Chief town: Corfu.

corgi One of two breeds of working □dog originating in SW Wales. Both are low-set: the Cardigan Welsh corgi has a long tail, rounded ears, and a shortish coat, which may be reddish brown, streaked brown, or black and tan; the Pembroke Welsh corgi has a short tail, pointed ears, and a finer coat of red, sable, fawn, or black and tan. Both breeds can have white markings. Height: 12 in (30 cm) (Cardigan); 10–12 in (25–30 cm) (Pembroke).

coriander An annual plant, *Coriander sativum*, 8–28 in (20–70 cm) high, with umbrella-like clusters of small pink or white flowers. Probably native to the Mediterranean, it is widespread in waste places and is also cultivated for its fruits, used in curries, alcoholic beverages, as a condiment, and medicinally for flatulence. Family: *Umbelliferae*.

Corineus A legendary Trojan hero after whom the region of Cornwall, England, is named. According to the medieval chronicler *Geoffrey of Monmouth he was a companion of Brutus, the grandson of Aeneas and legendary founder of Britain, and the killer of the giant Gogmagog (*See* Gog and Magog).

Corinth (Greek name: Kórinthos) 37 56N 22 55E A port in S Greece, in the Peloponnese on the Isthmus of Corinth. The modern port was founded in 1858 near the site of the ancient city; its trade includes wine. *History*: a settlement before 3000 BC, the ancient city of Corinth developed in commercial importance during the 8th century BC. It became the second largest and richest of the Greek city states after Athens, rivalry between the two culminating in the *Peloponnesian War. Corinth resisted Roman pressures but was destroyed by them in 146 BC, later to be revived as a Roman colony (44 BC). The city declined during the Middle Ages. Extensive excavations have taken place since 1896. Population: 20,733.

Corinth, League of (*or* Hellenic League) An alliance of Greek states formed in 338 BC at Corinth under the leadership of *Philip II of Macedon. The League was formed for a joint Greek and Macedonian campaign against Persia and contributed to the Asian campaign of *Alexander the Great, who succeeded Philip in 336. The League was disbanded after Alexander's death (323), being briefly revived in 303.

Corinthian order. *See* orders of architecture.

Corinthians, Epistles of Paul to the Two New Testament books written by the apostle Paul to the Christian Church at Corinth in about 57 AD. In the first he deals with problems that had arisen in the Church and answers questions on a number of practical and doctrinal issues, for example marriage and celibacy, the resurrection of the dead, and the Eucharist. In the second he explains the nature of his own apostolic ministry and defends himself against his opponents at Corinth.

Coriolanus, Gnaeus Marcius Roman general, who defeated the Volsci and captured the town of Corioli. Exiled in 491 BC for his contempt for the common people during a famine, he led the Volsci against Rome but was dissuaded from sacking the city by his wife Virgilia and mother Volumnia. The story is the subject of Shakespeare's *Coriolanus* (1607).

Coriolis force A *force required to account for the motion of a body as seen by an observer in a rotating frame of reference. It is often referred to as a fictitious force as it disappears on changing to a nonrotating frame. For example, a shell shot from a gun at the center of a rotating table appears to an outside observer to travel in a straight line. To an observer on the table it appears to have a curved path. The Coriolis force is required to account for this apparent tangential acceleration. The Coriolis force is responsible for the formation and direction of rotation of anticyclones and whirlpools. Named for the French physicist Gaspard de Coriolis (1792–1843).

cork Tissue that forms the outer layer of *bark in woody plants. Cork provides extra insulation and physical protection to the internal cells of the plant. The cork oak (*Quercus suber*), an evergreen oak tree of S Europe and N Africa, is cultivated in Portugal and SW Spain as the source of commercial cork. The cork is stripped from the tree every 8–10 years and is used for shock absorbers, bungs, fishing floats, floor and wall coverings, shoe soles, etc.

Cork (Irish name: Corcaigh) The largest county in the Republic of Ireland, in Munster bordering on the Atlantic Ocean. Mountains in the W extend eastward intersected by valleys, notably that of the Blackwater River. Its many coastal inlets include Bantry Bay and Cork Harbour. Fishing is important; Ballycotton is noted for its game fishing. Agriculture is varied with dairy and arable farming. Its many castles include Blarney Castle, famous for the Blarney Stone. Area: 2880 sq mi (7459 sq km). Population (1991): 409,814. County town: Cork.

Cork (Irish name: Corcaigh) 51 54N 8 28W The second largest city in the Republic of Ireland and county town of Co Cork, on Cork Harbour. The settlement grew up around a monastery (founded in about the 6th century AD) and it has remained important as a center of learning with the presence of University College (founded 1845), part of the National University of Ireland. It has many notable buildings, especially its cathedrals and St Ann's Shaldon Church, famous for its bells. It is an important industrial and trading center with a fine harbor. Exports include bacon, dairy produce, and livestock and it has bacon-curing, car assembly, and brewing and distilling industries. Population (1991): 127,024.

corkwood: *See* balsa.

corm A fleshy underground stem base of certain perennial herbaceous plants, such as the crocus and gladiolus, that acts as an overwintering structure. Growth the following season occurs by one or more buds: if two or more plants are produced the corm is acting as an organ of vegetative reproduction.

cormorant A slender long-necked waterbird belonging to a family (*Phalacrocoracidae*; 30 species) and found on most coasts and some inland waters 20–40 in (50–100 cm) in length, cormorants are typically glossy black with white throat markings and have short legs, webbed feet, a long stiff tail, and a long slender hook-tipped bill; they feed mainly on fish caught underwater. Order: *Pelecaniformes* (gannets, pelicans, etc.).

corn An annual *cereal grass, *Zea mays*, also called Indian corn, sweet corn, or maize, native to the New World and widely cultivated in tropical and subtropical regions, 3–13 ft (1–4.5 m) high, it bears a tassel of male flowers at the top of the stem and spikes of female flowers in the leaf axils; these develop into cobs, each comprising long parallel rows of grains. Corn is used as a vegetable, in breakfast cereals, flour, and livestock feed and for the extraction of corn oil. Cultivated as a grain crop in Central America since at least 2000 BC, corn is a staple food in Latin America and many other countries throughout the world. In terms of world production, it is the third most important cereal crop (after wheat and rice), the US being the chief producing country.

CORMORANT *The common cormorant* (Phalacrocorax carbo) *breeds in colonies, usually on cliffs. The eggs are incubated for a month by both parents.*

Corn Belt An area in the central US, S and W of the Great Lakes, extending mainly through Indiana, Illinois, Iowa, and Nebraska. It possesses a distinctive agriculture with intensive corn and soybean production used in the raising of fat cattle and pigs.

corn borer A small European *pyralid moth, *Pyrausta nubilalis,* accidentally introduced to North America. It is a serious economic pest, attacking over 200 plant species, including beans, celery, corn, and potatoes. The larvae burrow into plant stems near ground level, sometimes causing them to break off.

corncockle An annual purple-flowered weed of arable land in most temperate regions, *Agrostemma githago,* growing to a height of 40 in (100 cm). Once abundant, it is now rare due to efficient seed clearing. Family: *Caryophyllaceae.*

corncrake A migratory bird, *Crex crex,* also called landrail, that breeds in Eurasian grasslands, wintering in S Africa and Asia. It is 10 in (26 cm) long with a streaked brown plumage and chestnut wing patches and is easily identified by its harsh rasping call. Family: *Rallidae* (rails).

cornea The transparent outer layer at the front of the eyeball, through which light enters the □eye. Corneal grafts have been used successfully to replace diseased areas of cornea; since the cornea has no blood supply the graft cannot be rejected by blood-borne antibodies.

Corneille, Pierre (1606–84) French dramatist. After a Jesuit education he worked in government service in his home town of Rouen from 1628 to 1650. His early comedies, beginning with *Mélite* (1629), were much admired by Cardinal Richelieu. *Le Cid* (1636), the seminal play of French classical tragedy, excited much controversy. Here and in *Horace* (1640), *Cinna* (1641), and

Polyeucte (1643) he pioneered a dramatic genre the main emphasis of which was on moral conflicts expressed in majestic formal verse, a genre later perfected by his younger contemporary *Racine. In 1647 he moved to Paris and continued to write prolifically until his last play, *Suréna*, in 1674.

Cornelius, Peter von (1783–1867) German painter, born in Düsseldorf. In Rome (1811–19) he was associated with a group of German artists, the Nazarenes, in the revival of fresco painting. He worked subsequently in Munich on frescoes for the museum of classical sculpture and in Berlin.

cornet A valved brass instrument, with cup-shaped mouthpiece and conical bore. Pitched in B-flat, it is similar to the trumpet but less brilliant. It has a range of two and a half octaves from the E below middle C and plays an important role in the brass band.

cornetfish A tropical marine *bony fish, also called flutemouth, belonging to a family (*Fistulariidae*; about 4 species) related to *pipefish and *seahorses. It has a slender body, up to 6 ft (1.8 m) long, a long threadlike filament extending from the tail fin, and a long siphon-like snout. Order: *Gasterosteiformes*.

cornett A woodwind instrument with a cup-shaped mouthpiece and finger holes. The brilliant tone of the treble cornett was much favored by composers of the 16th and 17th centuries, such as Giovanni Gabrieli.

cornflower An annual, sometimes overwintering, herbaceous plant, *Centaurea cyanus*, growing to about 30 in (75 cm) high. Flower heads are bright blue with a purplish center. Probably native in most of Europe and the Near East, it is widely introduced as a cereal crop weed but is now becoming rare due to improved seed clearing. Horticultural garden varieties are popular. Family: *Compositae*.

Cornforth, Sir John Warcup (1917–) Australian chemist, who shared the 1975 Nobel Prize with Vladimir Prelog (1906–) for their work on stereochemistry. Cornforth showed the importance of stereoisomers in biological systems, using *radioactive tracers to follow the course of their reactions.

Cornish A *Celtic language of the Brythonic group, formerly spoken in Cornwall and Devon, that became extinct in about 1800. It was closely related to Breton, which was introduced to Brittany from this area. A number of miracle and morality plays dating from the 15th century were written in Cornish.

Corn Laws The British laws that regulated (1360–1846) the import and export of wheat and other cereals to guarantee farmers' incomes. These laws were bitterly resented by the working classes, because they kept the price of bread high, and the manufacturers, who argued that little money was left for the purchase of manufactured goods. Opposition to the Corn Laws was led by the *Anti-Corn Law League and in 1846 Sir Robert *Peel's government repealed them. A nominal duty continued to be levied until 1869.

Cornplanter (c. 1746–1836) US Seneca Indian chief. Born of a Dutch or English father and a Seneca mother, he led his people against the white settlers, but gradually sought more peaceful means of resisting the takeover of Indian lands. He signed treaties with the US and tried to prevent other tribes from warring against the Americans. By 1791 he was replaced as chief of the Senecas and was granted land and an annuity by the US government.

corn poppy An annual, or sometimes biennial, poppy, *Papaver rheas,* with scarlet (occasionally pinkish) flowers. Also called field poppy, it grows to a height of 20 in (50 cm). It is a weed of arable and waste places, occurring throughout much of Eurasia and N Africa and introduced to North America, New Zealand, and Australia.

corn salad A slender branching annual plant, *Valerianella locusta,* also called lamb's lettuce; 3–16 in (7–40 cm) high, with small pale-lilac flowers, it grows in dryish places and is sometimes cultivated for salads. It is native to Europe, N Africa, and W Asia and introduced to North America. Family: *Valerianaceae.*

cornucopia A decorative motif from Greek antiquity denoting abundance and wealth. It consists of a goat's horn filled with fruit and flowers and was reputedly presented to the nymph Amalthaea by Zeus or vice versa.

Cornwall (Celtic name: Kernow) The most southwesterly county of England, bordering on the Atlantic Ocean and the English Channel and including the Isles of *Scilly. It consists mainly of rugged hills rising to Bodmin Moor in the E. Dairy farming and market gardening are the main agricultural activities, the equable climate encouraging the growth of early fruit and vegetables. Tourism is a chief source of income and the county is popular for second homes and retirement. Tin mining, important since early times, was revitalized in the 1960s. In 1974 the Cornish nationalist movement led to the revival of the Stannary or Tinners' Parliament and also to attempts to resurrect the Cornish language. Area: 1369 sq mi (3546 sq km). Population (1991): 469,300. Administrative center: Truro.

Cornwallis, Charles, 1st Marquess (1738–1805) British general in the *American Revolution. Although he opposed the taxation of the American colonies, he took a command when the revolution broke out and was at first successful, defeating Gates at *Camden (1780). In 1781, however, he was disastrously defeated at Yorktown. He served twice as governor general of India (1786–93, 1805).

Coromandel Coast The SE coast of India between the Krishna Delta and Point Calimere.

Coromandel screens Large 17th-century Chinese screens named for the Coromandel Coast of India, from which they were shipped to Europe. They have up to 12 panels with brown or red lacquer grounds and incised polychromatic decoration.

corona The outer layer of the sun's atmosphere. The **inner corona** lies above the *chromosphere and consists of rapidly moving electrons. Its temperature reaches about 1,110,000°F (2,000,000°C) some 46,500 mi (75,000 km) above the solar surface. The **outer corona** extends for millions of miles and consists of comparatively slow-moving dust particles. The corona cannot be seen without special equipment, except at a total solar *eclipse. It then appears as a pearly usually unsymmetrical halo around the darkened solar disk, the shape depending on the time of the *sunspot cycle. *See also* solar wind.

coronary heart disease The most common form of *heart disease in the western world. It is caused by *atherosclerosis of the coronary arteries, which reduces the blood flow to the heart. This may precipitate the formation of a blood clot in these arteries—**coronary thrombosis.** The patient experiences sudden pain in the chest (*see* angina pectoris) and the result may be a heart attack, when the blood flow to the heart is suddenly stopped (*see* myocardial infarction). Coronary heart disease is associated with smoking, lack of exercise, high-fat diets, hypertension, and middle age; it is commoner in men.

Corot, Jean Baptiste Camille (1796–1875) French landscape painter. After training under two minor landscapists (1822–25), he visited Italy (1825–28), the subject of many of his landscapes. Although he exhibited at the Paris Salon from 1827, he did not achieve critical acclaim until the 1850s, with his poetical misty landscapes populated by nymphs. More popular today are his open-air sketches, small landscapes, and figure studies. He was friendly with the *Barbizon school of painters and influenced the impressionists.

corporate state (*or* corporative state) A society in which the individual is represented in government by the economic group (corporation) to which he belongs rather than according to his geographical location. The ideas were adopted as a system of government by fascist dictators, such as Mussolini, Franco, and Salazar, and the term now has pejorative implications.

Corpus Christi 27 47N 97 26W A city in Texas on Corpus Christi Bay. A popular resort, its port exports cotton, petroleum, and sulfur. Industries include cement and chemicals as well as fishing. Population (1990): 257,453.

Corpus Christi, Feast of (Latin: body of Christ) A Christian feast honoring the institution of the Eucharist, observed in the West on the second Thursday after *Whit Sunday. Originally a local festival in Liège, it was extended to the whole Church by Pope Urgan IV in 1264. The chief rite of the feast is the procession of the Blessed Sacrament. It is not generally observed by Protestant Churches.

Corpus Juris Canonici A collection of papal and conciliar decrees comprising the main body of the canon law of the Western Church. It is composed of six collections compiled between the 12th and 15th centuries. Pope Gregory XIII revised it in 1582. It was superseded in 1917 by the Codex Juris Canonici, a revision of the whole of canon law.

Correggio (Antonio Allegri; c. 1494–1534) Italian Renaissance painter, born at Correggio, near Modena. Initially influenced by *Mantegna, he later studied *Leonardo and *Michelangelo. He worked chiefly in Parma, where he decorated the Camera di San Paolo, the domed vaulting of San Giovanni Evangelista, and the cathedral with frescoes that anticipate the *baroque. Using strong contrasts between light and shade, he painted religious subjects, e.g. *Adoration of the Shepherds* or *Night* (Dresden), and sensuous nudes, e.g. *Jupiter and Io* (Kunsthistorisches Museum, Vienna), which later influenced *rococo painters.

Corregidor An island in the N Philippines, in the mouth of Manila Bay. Strategically important, it has been fortified since Spanish times. During World War II US troops on it held Manila harbor against the Japanese for five months although bombed continuously.

Correns, Carl Erich (1864–1933) German botanist and geneticist, whose work on breeding garden peas confirmed the principles of heredity first established by *Mendel. In 1900, simultaneously with *de Vries, he rediscovered Mendel's original paper, which had been ignored since 1865.

Corrientes 27 30S 58 48W A port in NE Argentina, on the Río Paraná. It is an important export center for agricultural products, including cotton, rice, and tobacco. It has a university (1957). Population (1991): 267,742.

corrosion. *See* rust.

Corsica (French name: Corse) An island in the Mediterranean Sea, separated from Sardinia by the Strait of Bonifacio. Together with 43 islets it comprises a region of France. It is mountainous with a rugged coastline and much of the island is covered with *maquis*, a dense thorny scrub type of vegetation. Agriculture is relatively undeveloped, producing citrus fruits, olives, vegetables, and tobacco; sheep and goats are extensively reared and tourism is a major source of income. *History*: under Genoese control from the 14th century, it was sold to France in 1768. During World War II it came under Italian occupation but was liberated by the French in 1943, weakening the German position in Italy. Area: 22,364 sq mi (8722 sq km). Capital: Ajaccio.

Cortes The Spanish Parliament, which first met in the kingdom of Léon in 1188. This was the first time that representatives of the townsmen attended the king's court together with the clergy and nobility. The regional Cortes lost their influence during the 16th century. The first national Cortes met in 1810.

Cortés, Hernán (1485–1547) Spanish conquistador. In Hispaniola and Cuba from 1504, he led a small expedition to Mexico in 1519 and reached Tenochtitlán, the capital of the Aztec Empire. In Cortés's absence, dealing with an attack from a Spanish force from Cuba, the Aztecs launched an attack on Tenochtitlán, forcing the Spaniards' retreat—the *noche triste* (night of sorrows). Cortés eventually rebuilt his forces and destroyed Tenochtitlán (1521) and the Aztec Empire, founding New Spain. After an expedition to Honduras (1524–26) Cortés returned to Spain (1528) but renewed his Pacific explorations in the 1530s. He died in poverty in Spain.

cortex The outer tissues of an animal or plant organ. In plants the cortex is situated between the *epidermis and vascular (conducting) tissues of stems and roots. Its cell walls may contain corky and woody materials or silica, providing strength, and also stored food, usually starch. Other substances that may be present include resins, latex, tannins, and essential oils. In animals the outer tissue of the *adrenal gland, the cerebrum, and the *kidney is called the cortex.

corticosteroids Steroid hormones secreted by the cortex of the adrenal glands (the term also includes synthetic drugs with similar properties). There are two main groups. The glucocorticoids (e.g. cortisone, prednisolone, and dexamethasone) affect carbohydrate metabolism. As anti-inflammatory drugs, they are used to treat allergic conditions (e.g. asthma), inflammatory disorders (e.g. ulcerative colitis and rheumatoid arthritis), and autoimmune diseases. They are also used to treat some cancers. The mineralocorticoids (e.g. aldosterone, fludrocortisone) control the balance of salt and water in the body.

Cortona 43 17N 11 59E A town in Italy, in Tuscany. It is famous for its Etruscan and Roman remains and has a cathedral dating from the 15th century. Population: 21,830.

corundum A mineral consisting mainly of aluminim oxide, the accessory minerals giving rise to a variety of colors. Sapphire is a blue variety containing iron and titanium; ruby contains chromium. It occurs in silica-poor igneous rocks, in metamorphosed shales, and in some metamorphosed limestone veins. The nongem varieties are used as abrasives (corundum is the second hardest mineral to diamond).

corvette A small highly maneuverable lightly armed warship displacing approximately 1600 tons and carrying a complement of a hundred officers and men. They were used mainly for antisubmarine escort duty during World War II. In the days of sail, the corvette, smaller than a *frigate, was a sloop rigged as a ship.

Corvo, Baron. *See* Rolfe, Frederick William.

Corybant One of the Corybantes, the eunuch priests or attendants of the goddess *Cybele, whose worship was accompanied by wild dancing and orgies. They castrated themselves in imitation of the self-mutilation of Cybele's lover, the fertility god Attis.

Corydalis A genus of mainly N temperate herbs (320 species), mostly perennials with underground tubers. The flowers, usually yellow, grow in clusters and resemble those of peas. Garden varieties, 6–24 in (15–60 cm) high, prefer shady cool positions. Family: *Fumariaceae*.

Cos (Modern Green name: Kos) A Greek island in the SE Aegean Sea, in the Dodecanese. It was a member of the Delian League and the home of the Greek physician Hippocrates. It produces chiefly fruit but also silk and tobacco. Cos lettuce originally came from here. Area: 109 sq mi (282 sq km).

Cosby, Bill (William Henry Cosby, Jr.; 1937–) US entertainer and author. His primary success was on television, where he was the star of "I Spy" (1965–68), variety shows (1969–73), and the immensely popular "The Cosby Show" (1984–92), in which he played a middle-class doctor with several children. Cosby also starred in movies, including *Ghost Dad* (1990); produced the "Fat Albert" animated cartoon shows for television; made numerous television commercials; and wrote several books of reminiscences, including *Love and Marriage* (1989).

Cosgrave, William Thomas (1880–1965) Irish statesman. A member of *Sinn Féin, he took part in the *Easter Rising (1916) and was elected to the first Irish Assembly (1918). He was first president of the Irish Free State (1922–32) and then led the *Fine Gael opposition until 1944. His son **Liam Cosgrave** (1920–) became leader of Fine Gael in 1965 and was prime minister from 1973 until 1977.

Cosmas and Damian, SS (early 4th century AD) Christian martyrs. Nothing certain is known of their lives, but according to tradition they were twin brothers who practiced as physicians in Asia Minor, refused to accept payment from their patients, and were martyred under Diocletian. They are patron saints of physicians. Feast day: Sept 27 or Oct 27.

cosmetics Beauty aids and preparations intended to improve the appearance of face, hair, or nails or the texture of the skin. Historically, among the most common cosmetics have been kohl, for shading around the eyes, and henna, for dyeing hair, fingertips, and toes; their use dates back at least to ancient Egypt. Rouge and face powders were used by the ancient Greeks and Romans. Although periodically cosmetics have met with public disapproval, as in Puritan and Victorian times, during the 20th century the manufacture of cosmetics has become an important industry, catering increasingly to men as well as women.

Although modern western cosmetics no longer contain such dangerous ingredients as the lead compounds found in ancient Greek face powders, some ingredients can nevertheless irritate sensitive skins. Many modern cosmetics, such as eyebrow pencils, are wax-based; lipsticks also contain nondrying oils. Petroleum jelly, liquid paraffin, and coloring are also widely used. Creams and lotions are emulsions of wax or oil in water, which evaporates on application; the oily film left prevents the skin from drying out. Face powder consists principally of zinc oxide, precipitated chalk, talc, and zinc stearate. Nail polish consists of a nitrocellulose base, a plasticizer, and a modifying resin, all in a volatile solvent. Astringent lotions (including aftershave), which close the openings of the hair follicles, are based on alcohol solutions; antiperspirants are usually based on an aluminum salt, which prevents sweat from leaving the sweat ducts.

cosmic rays A continuous stream of very high-energy particles that bombard the earth from space. The primary radiation consists of *protons and light nuclei with smaller numbers of neutral particles, such as *photons and *neutrinos. These particles collide with atomic nuclei in the earth's atmosphere producing large numbers of elementary particles, known as secondary radiation. One primary particle may produce a large number of secondary particles on colliding with a nucleus. This effect is called a shower. Some cosmic rays are believed to originate from the sun, others from outside the solar system.

cosmogony The study of the origin and evolution of the universe and the astronomical objects it contains, or a theory concerning the origin and development of a particular system, especially the solar system.

cosmology The study of the origin, evolution, and structure of the universe. A great variety of cosmological models have been put forward through the ages, based on the observations of astronomers. Ranging from the flat earth draped by a canopy of stars and the earth-centered (geocentric) universe (*see* Ptolemaic system), these models have changed and evolved as more powerful instruments have been developed to study the heavens (*see* astronomy). The current model of the universe has emerged from the observation of the *redshift, the advent of *radio astronomy, as well as the discovery of *quasars (1964), the microwave background (1965), and *pulsars (1967). Its origin is seen as a superdense agglomeration of matter that exploded (*see* big-bang theory), flinging fragments far and wide into space. These fragments passed through various stages to form *stars and galaxies, which are still flying apart from each other like fragments from a bomb (*see* expanding universe; Hubble constant; steady-state theory).

Cossacks A people of S and SW Russia descended from independent Tatar groups and escaped serfs from Poland, Lithuania, and Muscovy. They established a number of independent self-governing communities, which were given special privileges by Russian or Polish rulers in return for military service. Known for their horsemanship, each Cossack community provided a separate army. The Cossacks slowly lost their autonomy as Russia expanded in the 17th and 18th centuries and there were occasional rebellions. Many fled Russia after the Revolution (1918–21) and collectivization subsumed remaining Cossack communities.

Costa Brava A coastal region in NE Spain, bordering on the Mediterranean Sea. It extends from Barcelona to the French border and is a popular tourist area with many resorts.

cost accounting. *See* accountancy.

Costa Rica, Republic of A country in the Central American isthmus between Nicaragua and Panama. It includes the island of Cocos, 186 mi (300 km) to the SW. The Caribbean lowlands rise to a central plateau area, with volcanic peaks reaching 12,529 ft (3819 m). The inhabitants are mainly of Spanish and mixed descent, with a dwindling Indian population. *Economy*: chiefly agricultural, the main crops being coffee, bananas, and sugar (the principal export). Livestock is important and crops, such as cocoa, are being introduced as part of a plan to diversify the economy. Almost 75% of the land is forested with valuable woods, such as mahogany, rosewood, and cedar. Mineral resources include gold, hematite ore, and sulfur; many small industries are being encouraged. *History*: discovered by Columbus in 1502, it became a Spanish colony in the 15th century and the native Indian population was practically wiped out. It was part of the captaincy general of Guatemala until gaining independence in 1821. From 1824 until 1838 it formed part of the Central American Federation. In 1948 José Figueres Ferrer, leader of the socialist National Liberation Party, came to power at the head of a junta. A new constitution brought more democratic rule—the army was abolished and banks nationalized. Since then government has been more stable than in most Latin American countries, each election being won by the party in opposition at the time. Costa Rica endeavored to maintain its neutrality in the face of the growing turmoil in Latin America, at the same time seeking to establish closer ties with the US. In 1983 relations with neighboring Nicaragua deteriorated as that country accused Costa Rica of support of anti-Sandinista guerrillas. Oscar Arias Sanchez, president from 1986 to 1990, was awarded the 1987 Nobel Peace prize for his efforts to bring together Central

American countries to work for peace. President: Rafael Calderon. Official language: Spanish. Official religion: Roman Catholic. Official currency: colon of 100 centimos. Area: 19,653 sq mi (50,900 sq km). Population (1990 est): 3,032,000. Capital: San José. Main ports: Limón (on the Caribbean) and Puntarenas (on the Pacific).

cost-benefit analysis An investigation to determine whether a certain investment project is of net benefit to the community or to decide between competing projects. This type of analysis is useful because a purely commercial assessment does not always take account of all the costs and benefits involved; for example, it would not show the benefit of reduced road congestion that might be entailed in building an underground railroad. The weakness of cost-benefit analysis is that it is not always possible to quantify all the consequences, such as the destruction of the breeding grounds of a rare bird.

Costner, Kevin (1955–) US actor and director, who received an Academy Award in 1991 as best director for *Dances with Wolves*. From the mid-1980s he built an outstanding reputation as a film actor with such movies as *Silverado* (1985), *The Untouchables* (1987), *Bull Durham* (1988), and *Field of Dreams* (1989). After *Dances with Wolves* (1990), his roles continued to demonstrate his versatility, ranging from *Robin Hood: Prince of Thieves* (1991), *JFK* (1991), in which he played attorney Jim Garrison; and *The Bodyguard* (1992) to *A Perfect World* (1993), in which he portrayed a murderer.

cost of living A measure of the income required to purchase essential goods. Usually the Consumer Price Index based on a standard "basket" of goods, is used as a guide to the cost of living. The cost of living can vary geographically (e.g. depending on whether heating oil is essential) and with time (e.g. as a result of price inflation or revised definitions of what is essential).

Cotoneaster A genus of shrubs and small trees (about 50 species) of N temperate regions of the Old World. Some species are evergreen. Many are grown in gardens for their attractive foliage and red or black berries. *C. horizontalis* is a popular ground and wall cover; *C. hybrida pendula* is a weeping standard. Family: *Rosaceae*.

Cotonou 6 24N 2 31E The chief city in Benin, on the Gulf of Guinea. A deepwater port, it is the nation's main commercial and financial center and industries include textiles and brewing. Its university was founded in 1970. Population (1982): 487,000.

Cotopaxi 0 40S 78 28W The world's highest active volcano, in N central Ecuador, in the Andes. It is noted for the beauty of its symmetrical snow-capped cone. Height: 19,457 ft (5896 m).

Cotswold Hills A range of limestone hills in SW central England, mainly in Gloucestershire. It is noted for its picturesque towns and villages, such as Stow-on-the-Wold, built in the local limestone.

Cottbus (*or* Kottbus) 51 45N 14 24E A city in eastern Germany, on the Spree River in the state of Brandenburg. Cottbus has several medieval churches and is a railroad junction and industrial center. Population (1990): 128,000.

cotton A herbaceous plant of the genus *Gossypium* (20 or 67 species, according to the classification system), native to tropical and subtropical regions. Several species are cultivated for the whitish outer fibers of their seeds. Usually 40 in–7 ft (1–2 m) high, cotton plants bear whitish flowers and produce seed pods (bolls), which burst when filled with the soft masses of fibers. The bolls are harvested mechanically and the fibers separated from the seeds (ginning) and cleaned and aligned (carding), ready for spinning into yarn. The longest and most lustrous fibers are obtained from varieties of Sea Island or Egyptian cotton (*G. bardadense*). Cotton forms a light durable cloth used in a wide range of garments, furnishings, and other products. The seeds are crushed to yield cottonseed oil, used in margarines, cooking oils, soaps, etc., and the residual meal is used as a livestock feed. Family: *Malvaceae.*

cottonmouth. *See* water moccasin.

cotton stainer A black and red *plant bug belonging to the genus *Dysdercus,* widely distributed in warm regions. They are serious pests of cotton plants in North America and India, staining the bolls with excrement and rendering them useless. Family: *Pyrrhocoridae.*

cottonwood A North American poplar the seeds of which resemble cotton seeds, especially *Populus deltoides,* which grows in rich woods and river bottoms and reaches a height of 100 ft (30 m). Its lightweight wood is used commercially.

cotyledon The seed leaf of seed-bearing plants (gymnosperms and angiosperms): a food store within seeds providing the embryo plant with sufficient energy to germinate. In some plants the cotyledons become the first leaves of the seedling and are often different in form from subsequent leaves. Flowering plants with one cotyledon are classified as *monocotyledons; those with two as *dicotyledons. *See* germination.

couch grass A *grass, *Agropyron repens,* also known as quack grass or twitch, native to Europe and naturalized in other N temperate regions; 12–48 in (30–120 cm) high, it spreads by underground rhizomes and is a serious weed of arable crops, being difficult to eradicate.

cougar A red-brown *cat, *Felis concolor,* of North and South America, also called puma, mountain lion, and catamount. It is a slender muscular animal, 5–10 ft (1.5–3 m) long including its tail (20–30 in [50–80 cm]), with long hind legs enabling a powerful leap. It prefers deer, but feeds on a variety of animals.

Coughlin, Charles Edward (1891–1979) US churchman; born in Canada. He became a Roman Catholic priest in 1916 and came to the US (1926) where, by the 1930s, he was known as the "radio priest" because of his broadcasts expressing his political views. By 1936 he had formed the Union Party to oppose Franklin D. *Roosevelt and by the early 1940s was expressing pro-Nazi and anti-Semitic views. His magazine *Social Justice* and his radio broadcasts were silenced by his superiors in 1942.

coulomb (C) The *SI unit of electric charge equal to the quantity of electricity transferred by a current of one ampere in one second. Named for Charles de *Coulomb.

Coulomb, Charles Augustin de (1736–1806) French physicist, who invented the torsion balance and used it to show that the force between charged particles is proportional to the product of their charges and inversely proportional to the square of the distance between them (*see* Coulomb's law). He developed a similar law for magnetic poles. The unit of charge (*see* coulomb) is named for him.

Coulomb's law The force between two electrically charged bodies is proportional to the product of their charges (q_1 and q_2) and inversely proportional to the square of the distance (d) between them. In free space the law is $F = q_1 q_2 / 4\pi \in_0 d^2$, where $\in_0$ is the *electric constant. The law is named for its discoverer Charles de *Coulomb. The force is known as the **Coulomb** (or electrostatic) **force. Coulomb scattering** is the scattering of a charged particle by a nucleus due to the Coulomb force between them.

Council for Mutual Economic Assistance (COMECON) An economic association of communist countries founded in 1949 and dissolved in 1991, in the aftermath of the breakup of the Soviet Union. Its members included the Soviet Union, Bulgaria, Czechoslovakia, East Germany, Hungary, Mongolia, Poland, Romania, Cuba, and Vietnam; Albania ceased to participate in 1961.

Council of Europe An association of European states, founded in 1949, that is pledged to uphold the principles of parliamentary democracy and to promote the economic and social progress of its members (Austria, Belgium, Cyprus, Denmark, Finland, France, Greece, Iceland, the Republic of Ireland, Italy, Liechtenstein, Luxembourg, Malta, the Netherlands, Norway, Portugal, San Marino, Spain, Sweden, Switzerland, Turkey, the UK, and Germany). Eastern European countries joined after the collapse of communist regimes from 1989, including the Czech Republic, Hungary, Poland, and Slovakia. Its seat is in Strasbourg.

counterfeiting The illegal production of false money for gain. Counterfeiting is a form of forgery, distinguished because of the unique position of *money as a general medium of exchange. Most banknotes are produced with exceptionally fine printing on watermarked paper, often with a strip of metal inserted, in an effort to make them difficult to counterfeit. Many countries are signatories to an agreement of 1929 that allows extradition of counterfeiters.

counterpoint The art of combining two or more melodic lines simultaneously in music. The word derives from the Latin *punctus contra punctum,* point against point (i.e. note against note). The use of counterpoint continued beyond the end of the polyphonic period (*see* polyphony). Composers continue to make use of it today; contrapuntal techniques have been used by Stravinsky, Hindemith, Tippett, and others.

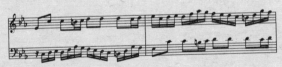

COUNTERPOINT *An example of counterpoint from J. S. Bach's* Fantasia in C Minor.

Counter-Reformation A movement within the *Roman Catholic Church dedicated to combating the effects of the Protestant *Reformation by reforming abuses within the Church and eradicating heresy by conversion, etc. Extending from the mid-16th to about the mid-17th century, it witnessed the emergence of the *Jesuits as a leading missionary body throughout the world, the reforms instituted by the Council of *Trent, the extension of the *Inquisition from Spain to other countries, and in general a revival of Catholic spirituality. Although most of N Europe remained Protestant, Poland and S Germany were stabilized as Catholic during this period.

countertenor A natural high male singing voice, higher than tenor, common in England in the 17th and 18th centuries. It is distinguished from the male *alto voice, which is produced by falsetto, but has the same range. The art of countertenor singing has been revived in the 20th century by Alfred Deller (1917–79) and James Bowman (1941–   ).

country and western A type of US popular music that evolved from the hillbilly ballads of the Appalachian Mountains and the cowboy songs of the West. Country and western is predominantly vocal music, relating the everyday experiences of the common man in sentimental texts. The singer is accompanied by the guitar and other stringed instruments. Influenced by other styles of popular music, country and western has its own offshoots, such as bluegrass. Famous country hits include "Your Cheatin' Heart" and "Mule Skinner Blues."

country house In England, a large house on a country estate. The great country houses were mainly built between the reigns of Elizabeth I and Victoria; before about 1550 feudal conditions caused the aristocracy to live in *castles or fortified *manor houses and after 1860 political reform and industrialization shifted the major landowners' power base and attention to the towns. Country houses displayed their owners' wealth and status, enabling them to entertain their political allies in impressive style. Some country houses exhibit the architectural opulence of small palaces (e.g. *Castle Howard and *Chatsworth), contain notable art collections, and are set in magnificent grounds (see Blenheim Palace).

Country Party. See National Country Party.

Count's War (1533–36) The last war of succession in Denmark, constituting a revolt led by Count Christopher of Oldenberg (c. 1504–66) against Christian, heir to the throne. Oldenberg finally surrendered Copenhagen in July 1536, after which Christian became king as *Christian III.

county A geographical unit of local government. The US does not have a comprehensive county system and the powers of counties differ widely between states. In Britain counties are long established: the name was applied by the Normans to the Anglo-Saxon *shire. England is divided into 45 counties, Wales into eight, and Scotland into nine regions and three island areas. Northern Ireland has six counties.

Couperin, François (1668–1733) French composer, called le Grand, the most famous member of a family that produced five generations of musicians. He was organist to Louis XIV and at St Gervais and is best known for his harpsichord music, a series of ordres consisting of pieces in dance forms with descriptive titles. He also wrote organ music, church music, and a book on the art of playing the harpsichord.

Courbet, Gustave (1819–77) French painter, born in Ornans. Self-taught, through copying paintings in the Louvre, he became leader of the school of realism. He painted portraits, including one of his friend Baudelaire, nudes, seascapes, hunting scenes, and everyday life, e.g. Burial at Ornans (Louvre) and Bonjour Monsieur Courbet (Montpellier). Reacting against academic criticism of his work, in 1855 he organized his first private exhibition. A political radical, he was imprisoned for his participation in the Commune of Paris (1871) and in 1873 he fled to Switzerland, where he died.

Courrèges, André (1923–) French fashion designer, who opened a fashion house in Paris in 1961 after training with *Balenciaga. In 1964 he presented his "space-age" collection, which included close-fitting silver trousers, worn with short-sleeved jackets and calf-length boots. He helped to promote the unisex fashion.

courser A brownish bird belonging to the subfamily Cursoriine, having long legs and a pointed curved bill and occurring in arid regions of Africa, India, and Australia. The cream-colored courser (Cursorius cursor) of Africa is 10 in (25 cm) long with white underparts and eye stripes and feeds chiefly on insects and lizards. Family: Glareolidae (pratincoles and coursers).

Court, Margaret (born Smith; 1942–) Australian tennis player, the first Australian to win the women's singles at Wimbledon (1963). Wimbledon champion again in 1965 and 1970, she was US singles champion five times, French champion five times, and Australian champion a record 11 times, winning 90 titles in all.

Courtauld Institute of Art An art gallery and college for the study of art history in Portman Square, London. It was originally the home of the manufacturer and art collector Samuel Courtauld (1876–1947), who donated the building and his collection of impressionist paintings to London University.

court cupboard A set of three open shelves supported by corner columns and frequently having a recessed cupboard between the top two. Popular throughout N Europe during the 16th century for displaying plates, they were usually made of oak.

courtly love Essentially a literary convention describing passionate love, arising in 12th-century Provence in the poems of the *troubadors. (The term itself was coined in the 19th century.) It is not certain to what extent courtly love actually existed as a social phenomenon in feudal courts. In the literary convention both lover and beloved are of aristocratic rank. The lover is abjectly devoted as a vassal to his chosen lady, whose virtues are idealized with quasi-religious fervor and who remains unobtainable because she is married to someone else. The lover is bound by rules of gallantry and *chivalry and is ennobled by his attachment to the beloved. On the other hand, his love-sickness may be devastating and he can only be cured if his lady takes pity on him, that is, consents to an adulterous affair. Although the lover's virtue is supposed to be exalted by his love, he suffers enormously from fear of exposure, from the capricious behavior of his lady, etc. The convention, which owes much to the influence of *Ovid, spread from Provence to Italy, influencing the *dolce stil nuovo; to N France, where it formed an important theme in the romances of *Chrétien de Troyes and in the 13th-century *Roman de la Rose*; to Germany in the work of the *Minnesingers; and to England, where it was treated in detail by Chaucer, especially in *Troilus and Criseyde*. It continued as an important element in the Elizabethan sonnet through the influence of *Petrarch.

court-martial Legislative criminal courts established in the armed forces. Their jurisdiction is entirely penal and disciplinary. They may be convened by the president, secretaries of military departments and by senior commanders to try and punish offenses committed by members of the armed forces. Appeals are made to the Court of Military Appeals.

Court Packing Bill (1937) A proposal to add six justices to the US Supreme Court. Initiated by Pres. Franklin D. *Roosevelt in an attempt to create a court more sympathetic to his New Deal reforms, the bill was rejected by Congress.

Courtrai (Flemish name: Kortrijk) 50 50N 3 17E A city in Belgium, on the Lys River. It was the site of the battle of the Spurs (1297), in which the French army was defeated by the burghers of Bruges and Ghent. It is an important textile center. Population (1981 est): 76,072.

courts of law Any duly constituted tribunal responsible for administering the law of the state or nation.

court tennis A racket-and-ball indoor court game that originated in France in the 12th–13th centuries as *jeu de paume*. It was originally played with the bare hand; the strung racket was developed c. 1500, when the game became highly popular in France. Many other handball and racket-and-ball court games developed from it. Its world championships are the oldest of any sport, dating back to about 1750, although it is now very much a minority sport. The stone or concrete floor area is approximately 96×32 ft (29×10 m). The cloth ball is hit over a central net, as in *tennis and *badminton, but it also bounces off the side walls, as in *squash rackets and *fives.

Cousin, Victor (1792–1867) French philosopher. He enjoyed a brilliant career, despite anti-establishment sympathies, and was a superb lecturer and prolific writer. As a minister under *Thiers (1840) he reformed French education. His talents were eclectic rather than analytic and his only truly original work is *Du vrai, du beau, et du bien* (1854).

Cousin the Elder, Jean (1490–1560) French artist and craftsman, who designed tapestries and stained-glass windows. The nude study *Eva Prima Pandora* (Louvre) is attributed to him. His son **Jean Cousin the Younger** (c. 1522–c. 1594) was also a painter, engraver, and stained-glass designer, known particulary for *The Last Judgment* (Louvre).

Cousteau, Jacques Yves (1910–) French naval officer and underwater explorer. He shared in the invention of the aqualung (1943) and invented a way of using television under water. In 1945 he founded the Undersea Research Group of the French navy at Marseilles and in 1950 became commander of the oceanographic research vessel *Calypso*. He became director of the Oceanographic Museum and Institute in Monaco, 1957. He is famous for such films as *The Silent World* (1953), *The Living Sea* (1963), and for popular television series.

couvade A custom, common in many parts of the world among primitive peoples, in which the father retires to bed during his wife's confinement and simulates the pain of childbirth. Its intention is presumably to establish a role for the father and, by magical association, to lessen the pain of the mother. In the 20th century it has been reported among Basques and in Brazil.

covenant A binding agreement between two parties whereby each promises to do something for the other (*see also* deed). In the Old Testament, the covenant between God and Israel forms the basis of the Jewish religion. In return for obedience to the Law (the *Ten Commandments) as delivered to Moses, the Israelites were promised a privileged relationship with God as the chosen people. The symbol of this agreement was the *Ark of the Covenant containing the tablets of the Law. In the New Testament, this belief is interpreted in Christian terms as including all men, who are regarded as having been redeemed by Christ.

Covenanters Scottish Presbyterians who in the 16th and 17th centuries bonded together (or covenanted) to defend their church. The National Covenant of 1638 was signed by thousands of Scottish Presbyterians after Charles I's attempt to introduce the English Prayer Book. In the English *Civil War the Covenanters joined the parliamentarians in 1643 in return for the promise of church reform. After the Restoration (1660) they were persecuted and suppressed until 1688.

Coventry 52 25N 1 30W A city in central England. Heavily bombed during World War II, the city center was almost entirely rebuilt. Its famous cathedral, designed by Sir Basil Spence, was opened in 1962 and retains the ruins of the old cathedral, which was bombed in 1940. Formerly a weaving town, Coventry is now an important center for the automobile industry and also produces motorcycles, machinery, electrical equipment, and synthetic fabrics. Population (1986 est): 337,000.

Coverdale, Miles (1488–1568) English Protestant reformer. While an Augustinian friar at Cambridge, he was converted to Protestantism. In exile he published an English translation of the Bible (1535) and was largely responsible for the revisions resulting in the Great Bible of 1539. He was Bishop of Exeter from

1551 until exiled again under Queen Mary. After returning in 1559 he became a Puritan leader.

Covilhã, Pêro da (c. 1460–c. 1526) Portuguese explorer sent by John II to find *Prester John and explore Africa and the East, he left Portugal in 1487 and traveled via Aden to India, visiting Cannanore, Calicut, and Goa. He returned to Ormuz in the Persian Gulf and from Cairo set off for Ethiopia. There he ended his days, honored but forcibly detained.

Coward, Sir Noël (1899–1973) British dramatist, composer, and actor. He first established his reputation with *The Vortex* (1924), an intense domestic drama, but his best-known plays are witty and elegant comedies of manners, such as *Hay Fever* (1925) and *Blithe Spirit* (1941). He also contributed as writer, director, composer, and performer to revues, musicals, and films, notably *In Which We Serve* (1942) and *Brief Encounter* (1946). His best-known songs include "Mad Dogs and Englishmen" and "Mad about the Boy."

cowboys Mounted cattle herders and folk heroes of the American West, who from about 1820 worked in the open grassland W of the Mississippi River, from Canada to Mexico. Cowboys used horse, spur, rope, and branding iron to "round up" the herds and drive them to market. The legendary cowboy of Western films, drinking and fighting in a saloon, derives from his twice-yearly spree after the round-ups. Rail transport and barbed wire fences rendered the cowboy's jobs of herding and range riding obsolete. *Compare* gaucho.

SIR NOËL COWARD *At Montreux, Switzerland (1967).*

Cowley, Malcolm (1898–1989) US literary critic, editor, and author. He was an editor on the *New Republic* (1929–44) and edited collections of writers, such as William *Faulkner, F. Scott *Fitzgerald, and Ernest *Hemingway, and greatly advanced the career of John *Cheever. His works include *Exile's Return* (1934) about his years with the "lost generation" of American writers in Paris in the 1920s, *Dry Season* (1941), *And I Worked at the Writer's Trade* (1978), and *The Dream of the Golden Mountains* (1980).

cow parsley A biennial herb, *Anthriscus sylvestris,* up to 40 in (100 cm) high, with conspicuous umbrella-like clusters of white or pinkish flowers. It is found in hedgerows, wood edges, and waste places throughout much of Eurasia and N Africa and has been introduced to North America. Family: *Umbelliferae.*

cowpea An annual African plant, *Vigna unguiculata,* widely grown in tropical areas and the S US. Having a high protein content, cowpeas are an important food crop, especially in Africa. There are two forms: a short erect one grown in Africa and America, whose seeds are used dried, and a tall climbing one grown in SE Asia, whose long pods are eaten when young. Family: *Leguminosae.*

Cowpens, Battle of (Jan 17, 1781) A battle in the American Revolution in which the Americans defeated the British. Led by Gen. Daniel Morgan (1736–1802), the Americans inflicted a surprise defeat on the British force, slowing down *Cornwallis's invasion of North Carolina.

Cowper, William (1731–1800) British poet. With John Newton, he published *Olney Hymns* in 1779. "John Gilpin's Ride" (1783), a comic ballad, and "The Task" (1785) a long discursive poem on rural themes, were both very successful. He was mentally unstable throughout his life. After the death in 1796 of Mary Unwin, a widow with whom he had lived for many years, he expressed his despair in "The Castaway."

cowpox A contagious viral disease of cattle that can be contracted by man. Resembling a mild form of smallpox, it appears as blisters on the teats and udder. Animals should be isolated and recovery is usually complete. Edward *Jenner used fluid from cowpox blisters to produce the first effective smallpox vaccine.

cowrie A *gastropod mollusk of the family *Cypraeidae* (about 160 species), mostly found in warm seas; 0.4–6 in (1–15 cm) long, cowries have glossy □shells with inrolled lips that are covered by the mantle, which is withdrawn inside the shell when the animal is disturbed. Cowries feed at night on small animals. The shell of the tropical money cowrie (*Cypraea moneta*), about 1.2 in (3 cm) long, is used as a form of currency in Africa and India.

cowslip A perennial spring-flowering Eurasian herb, *Primula veris,* growing to a height of 8 in (20 cm). It has a rosette of crinkled leaves and hanging clusters of bright-yellow five-petaled flowers. It is found from lowland meadows to alpine pastures. Family: *Primulaceae* (primrose family).

Coxey's Army (1894) US unemployed workers, led by Jacob S. Coxey (1854–1951), marched on Washington, D.C., to protest against unemployment and to urge the passing of laws to create more jobs and to circulate more paper money. Also known as the Commonwealth of Christ, the group disbanded when Coxey was arrested and accused of treason.

coyote A wild *dog, *Canis latrans,* of Central and North American grassland, also called prairie wolf. Coyotes are about 48 in (120 cm) long, including the bushy tail (12 in [30 cm]), and have yellowish fur. They hunt alone or in packs and take food ranging from insects to small deer.

coypu A South American aquatic *rodent, *Myocaster coypus.* About 24 in (60 cm) long (excluding a long hairless tail), it has thick brown fur and webbed hind feet. The underfur of the belly is known as nutria, and coypus are farmed for fur. In Britain escaped coypus are becoming a pest, especially in East Anglia, eating vegetation and undermining river banks by burrowing. Family: *Capromyidae.*

Cozzens, James Gould (1903–78) US novelist. He was born in Chicago and grew up in New York. *Confusion* (1924) was published while he was in his second year at Harvard University. By 1949 he had won the Pulitzer Prize for *Guard of Honor* (1948). His works include *S. S. San Pedro* (1931), *The Last Adam* (1933), *The Castaway* (1934), *Men and Brethren* (1936), *The Just and the Unjust* (1942), *By Love Possessed* (1957), and *Morning, Noon and Night* (1968).

crab A *crustacean belonging to the tribes *Brachyura* (true crabs; about 4500 species) or *Anomura* (about 1300 species, including the *hermit crab). True crabs have a wide flat body covered by a hard carapace, with the small abdomen tucked underneath. There is a large pair of pincers and four pairs of legs used for walking (typically in a sideways scuttle) or swimming. They are carnivores or scavengers and most species are marine (the *land crab is an exception). The European species *Cancer pagurus* is edible. Order: *Decapoda.*

crab apple A □tree, *Malus sylvestris,* 7–33 ft (2–10 m) high: one of the species from which cultivated *apples have been developed. It has pinkish-white five-petaled flowers that bloom in spring and small sour greenish fruits, used to make jelly. A native of Europe and Asia, it is sometimes grown as an ornamental. Family: *Rosaceae.*

Crabbe, George (1754–1832) British poet. His native Suffolk was the scene of many of his poems. *The Village* (1783) was a brutally realistic portrayal of rural life, in stark contrast to conventional idealized treatments. This theme he took up again in the verse tales of *The Borough* (1810), source of *Britten's opera *Peter Grimes,* and *Tales of the Hall* (1819).

crabeater seal A common Antarctic seal, *Lobodon carcinophagus,* that feeds entirely on krill. About 8.2 ft (2.5 m) long, crabeater seals are dark in winter and almost white in summer; they are slender and can travel fast over ice. □oceans.

Crab nebula A turbulent expanding mass of gas, lying about 6000 light years distant in the constellation Taurus. It is the remnant of a *supernova that was observed in 1054. It emits radiation from all spectral regions and is an especially strong source of radio waves and X-rays. Within the nebula, and supplying energy to it, lies the **Crab pulsar.** This optical pulsar was produced by the supernova and has the fastest period (0.033 seconds) of all known pulsars.

Cracow. *See* Kraków.

Craig, Edward Henry Gordon. *See* Terry, Ellen.

Craiova 44 18N 23 47E A city in S Romania, on the Jiu River. Industries include heavy engineering and food manufacture. Its university was established in 1966. Population (1992 est): 303,500.

crake A small shy bird belonging to the *rail family. Crakes have a short conical bill and are commonly found in marshes and swamps. The Eurasian spotted crake (*Porzana porzana*) is 9 in (23 cm) long and has a streaked olive back, a lightly spotted breast, buff underparts, and a red ring at the base of the bill.

Cram, Ralph Adams (1863–1942) US architect, writer, and reformer. An advocate of a return to the Gothic style in architecture, he designed buildings at Princeton University, the US Military Academy at West Point, Rice University, and other schools. With his partner F. W. Ferguson he redesigned in Gothic style New York City's St John the Divine cathedral. As a reformer he advocated social customs from medieval times. He wrote *The Gothic Quest* (1907), *The Min-*

istry of Art (1914), *The Nemesis of Mediocrity* (1918), and *The End of Democracy* (1937).

cramp Painful spasmodic contraction of a muscle. Cramp is often caused by overexercise, often of the legs (in swimmers) or hands (writers' cramp). It may also be due to salt deficiency or poor circulation.

Cranach the Elder, Lucas (Lucas Müller; 1472–1553) German artist, born in Kronach (Bavaria). He studied painting under his father before moving to Wittenberg in 1505 to become court painter to Frederick the Wise, Elector of Saxony, and later to his two successors. Because of his portraits of Reformation leaders including his friend Luther, he is sometimes called the Reformation painter. He is also noted for his stylized but sensuous nudes, e.g. *Adam and Eve* (Courtauld Institute, London).

cranberry A low evergreen shrub of the genus *Vaccinium,* bearing red edible berries and growing in acidic boggy areas. *V. oxycoccus* occurs in Europe, N Asia, and North America. *V. macrocarpon* of North America has larger fruits (about 0.6 in [1.5 cm] across). The fruits of both are made into cranberry sauce, eaten with turkey and venison. Family: *Ericaceae* (heath family).

crane (bird) A large long-legged bird belonging to a family (*Gruidae*; 14 species) occurring in Old World regions and North America. Standing up to 56 in (140 cm) tall with a wingspan of over 80 in (200 cm), cranes vary from gray to white with black wingtips; some species are crested. They have heavy bills, feeding in marshes and plains on grain, shoots, and small animals, and are strong fliers; northern species are migratory. Order: *Gruiformes* (rails, etc.) *See also* demoiselle; whooping crane.

crane (machinery) A machine for raising, lowering, or moving heavy objects. It is used in construction work, loading cargoes onto ships, etc. There are many types but most have an engine to wind cables supported by an inclined or horizontal jib or boom, which either has a pulley system at one end or, in the case of a traveling crane, a pulley system that can move along the whole length of the jib. In a gantry crane the jib is fixed on supports at both ends, which themselves travel along rails. Cranes are often mounted on trucks or locomotives.

Crane, Hart (1899–1932) US poet. After an unhappy childhood in Ohio, he settled in New York in 1923 and began writing poems expressive of the personal conflicts caused by his homosexuality and alcoholism. He published *White Buildings* in 1926. *The Bridge* (1930), an epic poem in 15 parts, unites myth, history, and dream in a celebration of contemporary America. He went to Mexico to write another epic and drowned himself on the return voyage.

Crane, Stephen (1871–1900) US novelist. His early work as a journalist in New York provided him with first-hand knowledge of the poverty and destitution portrayed in his novel *Maggie: A Girl of the Streets* (1893). He is best known for the Civil War novel *The Red Badge of Courage* (1895) and his short stories, especially "The Open Boat." He worked as a war correspondent in Cuba and Greece, lived in England, and died in Germany of tuberculosis.

cranefly A harmless fly, also called daddy longlegs, belonging to the family *Tipulidae*. Craneflies are 0.24–3 in (6–75 mm) long with long delicate legs and wings. They are found near water or vegetation and are attracted to light. The larvae generally occur in water or rotting vegetation. However some—the leatherjackets—live in the soil and are plant pests, feeding on the roots of cereals and grasses. □insect.

cranesbill A herbaceous plant of the genus *Geranium* (about 400 species), widely distributed, especially in temperate regions, and usually having pink or purple flowers. They take their name from the long slender beaklike carpels. The meadow cranesbill (*G. pratense*), a perennial up to 24 in (60 cm) high, has violet-blue flowers, 0.6–0.7 in (15–18 mm) long, and is widespread throughout Eurasia and North America. Family: *Geraniaceae.*

Cranmer, Thomas (1489–1556) Anglican reformer and martyr. He was consecrated Archbishop of Canterbury in 1532. He is especially remembered for his contributions to the Prayer Books of 1549 and 1552. Under Queen Mary he was tried as a heretic and, after initially recanting, burned at the stake.

crannog An artificial island of stone, timber, and peat, constructed as sites for houses in Ireland from the early Neolithic to the medieval eras. A notable example is the Low Gara crannog.

craps A dice game used for gambling, especially in the US. It was developed in the 19th century by African-American workers from the more complex game of *hazard. Two dice are used. Each player attempts to throw a "natural," a 7 or 11, which wins. 2, 3, or 12 ("craps") are losing combinations. If he throws a 4, 5, 6, 8, 9, or 10 he continues to throw until he wins by throwing the same number again or loses by throwing a 7. Bets are made by the other players against the thrower, among themselves, or (in a casino) against the house.

Crassus, Marcus Licinius (c. 115–53 BC) Roman politician and ally of Caesar, nicknamed *Dives* (wealthy). Crassus suppressed Spartacus's revolt (71), although Pompey took the credit. Failing to manipulate political affairs on his own, Crassus joined Pompey and Caesar in the first Triumvirate (60). He was killed during an invasion of Parthia.

Crater Lake National Park 42 49N 122 08W A national park in SE Oregon, in the Cascade Mountains. Crater Lake, almost 2000 ft (610 m) deep, was formed in the crater of an extinct volcano and is one of the deepest lakes in North America. The lake is surrounded by lava rock cliffs, some as high as 2000 ft (610 m). Other features of the park, which was established in 1902, are Pumice Desert and the Pinnacles. Area: 250 sq mi (648 sq km).

Crawford, Joan (Lucille le Sueur; 1908–77) US film actress. She started her film career in musicals but became famous during the 1930s and 1940s for her dramatic portrayals of ambitious women in such films as *Grand Hotel* (1932), *The Women* (1939), *Mildred Pierce* (1945), *Humoresque* (1946), and *The Best of Everything* (1959).

Crawley 51 7N 0 12W A city in SE England, in West Sussex. Designated a new town in 1947, it has light engineering, electronics, plastics, and furniture industries. Population (1981): 72,756.

crayfish A freshwater *crustacean, also called crawfish and crawdad, belonging to the superfamily *Nephropidea*. It has a small lobster-like body, 1–3 in (25–75 mm) long, and occurs under rocks or debris or in burrows in mud banks during the day. At night it feeds on plant and animal material. Some species are edible. Order: *Decapoda.*

Crazy Horse (c. 1849–77) Leader of the Oglala Sioux, who organized active resistance to the US Army. After their defeat in the First Sioux War (1866–68), the Sioux agreed to be resettled in a permanent reservation in the Dakota Territory. However, the extension of the Northern Pacific Railroad and the arrival of gold miners in the Black Hills was seen by the Sioux as a violation of their treaty with the US government and the Second Sioux War ensued (1875–76). In this war, Crazy Horse joined forces with *Sitting Bull, leader of the Northern Sioux, and they defeated and massacred the troops of Gen. George *Custer at the Battle of Little Bighorn in 1876. Crazy Horse surrendered to the US Army in the following year, but he was killed while resisting imprisonment.

cream of tartar Potassium hydrogen tartrate that occurs in the later stages of the fermentation of grape juice as a deposit on the sides of the cask. After purification and crystallization it is used for culinary (*see* baking powder) and medical purposes.

Crécy, Battle of (August 26, 1346) The first land battle of the *Hundred Years' War, fought in N France, in which the English, led by *Edward III, defeated the French under *Philip VI. It was a triumph for the English longbowmen over heavily armored French knights; about 1500 French soldiers were killed. The victory enabled Edward to move N and beseige Calais.

credit and credit ratings The loan of money to an individual or company by a bank, credit-card organization, retailer, etc. Much consumer purchasing, especially of durables (*see* consumption), in industrial countries is on credit terms. The amount of credit that a person or company can command depends on his credit rating at the bank or on that given by an agency that specializes in listing the creditworthiness of companies. Credit ratings will depend on the applicants' known assets and liabilities, income (profitability for a company), and past record for trustworthiness. Influencing credit is a central part of a government's monetary policy.

credit card A card that enables the holder to obtain goods or services on credit. They are issued by retail stores, banks, and credit-card companies to approved clients. The bank or credit-card company settles the client's bills, invoicing him monthly and usually charging interest on any outstanding debts. The high rate of interest charged, the card-holders' subscriptions, and the fees paid by some organizations that accept cards provide the profit for the credit-card companies and banks.

Cree An Algonquian-speaking North American Indian people closely related to the *Ojibwa and formerly inhabiting large areas of central Canada. Supporting themselves by trapping and hunting in small wandering bands, the Cree nation gradually split into two groups, the Plains Cree and the Woodlands Cree. The Plains Cree migrated southward where they acquired horses and guns and adopted the buffalo-hunting culture of the Great Plains. The Woodlands Cree maintained their traditional way of life, and many became guides for British and French fur-trappers in their territory. The present Cree population, settled mostly in the Canadian province of Manitoba, is approximately 10,000.

Creed, Frederick (1871–1957) Canadian inventor, who moved to Scotland in 1897 and developed the Creed teleprinter (*see* Telex). The first such device was installed in 1912 and was soon in widespread use.

creeds In Christianity, formal summaries of the principal items of belief, often recited as part of the eucharistic service in many Churches. They originated as professions of faith said at baptism and were gradually formalized. The two most widely used are the Apostles' Creed (probably 3rd century AD) and the Nicene Creed, probably a revision by the Council of Constantinople (381) of the creed promulgated at the Council of *Nicaea (325) and accepted by both Western and Eastern churches. The Athanasian Creed, probably dating from the 5th century, is used in the Anglican catechism.

Creek A group of Muskogean-speaking North American Indian peoples, whose main sub-divisions are the Muskogee of Georgia and the Hitchiti of Alabama. Formerly inhabiting extensive territories throughout the SE, the Creek were advanced farmers and villagers who built towns in which rectangular houses were constructed around a central square that often contained a temple mound. Among their characteristic customs was the practice of elaborate body tattooing. In 1813–14 a confederacy of Creek towns began armed resistance to

the US Army and were defeated by the forces of Gen. Andrew *Jackson in a series of engagements known as the *Creek War. The Creek were later resettled in
Oklahoma. The present Creek population numbers approximately 15,000.

Creek War (1813–14) A war between US settlers and the Creek Indians.
Aided by the British and carrying Spanish weapons, the Creek Indians in Alabama, Georgia, and Florida attacked and massacred over 500 settlers at Ft
Mims, Ga. US troops under Gen. Andrew *Jackson defeated the Creeks at Tal-
lasahatchee, Talladega, and finally Horseshoe Bend, Ala. The Creeks ceded
parts of Alabama and Georgia to the US and ultimately were moved to reservations in Oklahoma.

cremation The disposal of the dead by burning. Practiced by many ancient
European peoples, cremation was forbidden by the Christian Church on account
of the doctrine of bodily resurrection of the dead. With 19th-century urban over-
crowding in the West, cremation was revived and the practice has grown rapidly.
The Roman Catholic Church formerly disapproved of cremation but it is now
accepted as it is among most Jews. In the East it has remained the most general
method of corpse disposal.

Cremona 45 08N 10 01E A city in N Italy, in Lombardy on the Po River. It
has a 12th-century cathedral and a 13th-century palace. From the 16th to the
18th centuries it was famous for the manufacture of violins, including those of
Stradivari. Population: 81,983.

creodont An extinct primitive carnivorous mammal of the early Tertiary period
(55–45 million years ago). They were mostly short-legged and slow-moving,
preying on herbivores.

creole 1. Originally a white person born in Spanish America during the colonial period (16th to 18th centuries). They suffered social and commercial disad-
vantages in comparison with the Spanish administrative class. 2. A person of
mixed blood living in the Caribbean area or in Latin America, extending to en-
compass a descendant of slaves in Surinam, a French-speaking descendant of
French or Spanish settlers in Louisiana, and various other groups. More loosely,
the term refers to people of Caribbean culture. 3. A patois based on French, English, or Dutch and spoken especially in the West Indies as a mother tongue
(*compare* pidgin English).

creosote A substance produced by distilling tar. The creosote used for preserving wood is obtained from *coal tar and is a brownish mixture of aromatic
hydrocarbons and *phenols. Creosote made from wood tar is a mixture of phenols and is used in pharmacy.

creosote bush A shrub of the genus *Larrea* (5 species), of arid and semiarid
areas of North and South America, where it is the dominant feature of the landscape. Up to 7 ft (2 m) high, these plants contain resinous phenolic substances
that deter grazing animals, although some insects are adapted to living and feeding on them. Family: *Zygophyllaceae*.

cresol ($CH_3C_6H_4OH$) A liquid *aromatic compound obtained from *coal tar. It
has three *isomers, a mixture of which is used as a disinfectant.

cress A plant of the mustard family (*Cruciferae*) the sharp-tasting leaves of
which are used in salads, especially garden cress, or peppergrass (*Lepidium
sativum*), believed to be native to W Asia but widely cultivated and naturalized
in Europe. The seedlings are eaten, often with those of white mustard (*Sinapis
alba*), with which it may be grown in containers. The European winter, or land,
cress (*Barbarea verna*) grows to a height of 40 in (100 cm). Its leaves can be
picked throughout the winter.

Cressent, Charles (1685–1768) French cabinetmaker. After working with *Boulle he became official cabinetmaker (1715) to the regent, the Duc d'Orléans, and also made furniture for foreign courts. The leading designer of the period, he made popular the use of colored-wood marquetry and *ormolu mountings.

crested tit A dull-brown and gray *tit, *Parus cristatus,* of European conifer-ous forests. It is about 4 in (11 cm) long and has a pointed black-and-white crest and black C-shaped marking bordering its face. It feeds on insects and seeds, often storing them for winter use.

Cretaceous period A geological period of the Mesozoic era, between about 135 and 65 million years ago, following the Jurassic and preceding the Tertiary (when the Cenozoic era began). It is divided into the Lower and Upper Creta-ceous. The period saw a widespread gradual marine transgression, the rocks of the Upper Cretaceous culminating in the thick chalk deposits of N Europe and the midwestern US. The dinosaurs and other giant reptiles, as well as the ammonites and many other invertebrates, became extinct at the end of the Cretaceous.

Crete (Modern Greek name: Kríti) The largest of the Greek islands, in the E Mediterranean Sea approximately 63 mi (100 km) SE of the mainland. It is gen-erally mountainous, rising over 7874 ft (2400 m). The economy is based primar-ily on agriculture producing olives, wines, and citrus fruits; the raising of sheep and goats is also important. There is a thriving tourist industry, based on Irák-lion. *History*: colonized probably in the 6th millennium BC from Asia Minor, Crete achieved extensive maritime power during the Middle Minoan period (c. 2000–c. 1700 BC), from which many artifacts, inscriptions, and buildings have been discovered (*see* Minoan civilization). The most notable are the palace at *Knossos and clay tablets bearing two different scripts known as *Linear A and *Linear B. Politically insignificant in the history of classical Greece, it fell to Rome (67 BC), Byzantium (395 AD), and the Muslims (826). In 1204 it was sold to the Venetians, who gave both the island and Iráklion the name Candia. It fell to Turkey in 1669 and was officially incorporated into Greece in 1913. Dur-ing World War II it was the scene (1941) of the first ever large-scale airborne in-vasion, in which the Germans took the island from British and Commonwealth troops, who had been evacuated here from the Greek mainland. Area: 3217 sq mi (8332 sq km). Population (1991): 536,980. Capital: Khaniá.

cretinism The condition resulting from a deficiency of thyroid hormone, which is present from birth. Affected children are mentally retarded dwarfs with coarse skin and facial features. Cretinism is treated with injections of thyroxine, which must be started early and continued throughout life. *See also* hypothyroidism.

Crèvecoeur, Michel-Guillaume-Jean de (*or* J. Hector St John; 1735–1813) French-American writer. After military service in Canada he stayed in America, where he served as French consul between 1784 and 1790. His *Letters from an American Farmer* (1782) and *Sketches of Eighteenth-Century America* (1925) are the thoughtful records of an early immigrant in the New World.

cribbage (*or* crib) A card game attributed to Sir John *Suckling. It is played by 2, 3, or 4 players with a standard pack of 52 cards. The rules vary in detail, but play basically consists of each player alternately playing a card until the total value of the cards played approaches 31. The last player able to play a card without exceeding 31 scores. Points are also scored for having certain combina-tions of cards in a hand or for playing during certain sequences of cards. The crib (consisting of cards discarded from each hand) scores for the dealer. The score is kept with small pegs on a cribbage board containing rows of holes.

Crick, Francis Harry Compton (1916–   ) British biophysicist, who (with James D. *Watson) proposed a model for the molecular structure of *DNA

(1953). Following this breakthrough, Crick continued to work on DNA, helping to determine the mechanism of protein synthesis. He shared a Nobel Prize (1962) with Watson and Maurice *Wilkins.

cricket (sport) An 11-a-side bat-and-ball team game, in which the object is to score the most runs. It originated in England among shepherds using their crooks as bats; its rules were laid down in 1744 and the game is played almost exclusively in the UK and its former empire. Presided over by two umpires, it is played on a large field; the pitch is a strip of grass 22 yd (20.12 m) long having at each end a wicket of three stumps surmounted by two bails. The ball is made of cork and twine, encased in leather. The members of one team take turns to bat in pairs, one defending each wicket; the batsmen's objective is to score runs by hitting the ball and exchanging ends before the ball is returned to the pitch. Each player bats until he is bowled, caught, stumped, run out, or judged lbw (leg before wicket). The members of the other team field, some taking turns to bowl the ball. After every over of six balls (eight in Australia) the bowler changes, the new bowler bowling from the other wicket. A match consists of one or two innings and may last for a few hours or up to six days, depending on the type of competition. International cricket, governed by the International Cricket Conference, is played mainly in Test matches between England, Australia, the West Indies, New Zealand, India, and Pakistan.

cricket (zoology) An insect, resembling a grasshopper but with longer antennae, belonging to one of several families of the order *Orthoptera*. The males stridulate (i.e. make a chirping noise) by rubbing the front wings together. True crickets (family *Gryllidae*; 2400 species) have black or brown flattened bodies, 0.12–2 in (3–50 mm) long, with long tail appendages (cerci) and short forewings (they do not fly). The females have long needle-like ovipositors for depositing eggs in soil or crevices. True crickets are omnivorous and live in burrows or among vegetation; some, for example the widely distributed house cricket (*Acheta domesticus*), frequent buildings. *See also* bush cricket; mole cricket.

Crimea (Russian name: Krym) A peninsula and autonomous region (*oblast*) in Ukraine, almost totally surrounded by the Black Sea and the Sea of Azov and connected to the mainland in the N by the Perekop Isthmus. It is mainly flat but rises to 5069 ft (1545 m) in the S. Iron ore is mined here and wheat, tobacco, and wine are produced. The chief towns are Feodosia, Kerch, Sevastopol, Yalta, Yevpatoria, and the capital of the *oblast*, Simferopol. *History*: colonized by Greeks in the 6th century BC, the Crimea was continually invaded by Goths, Huns, and others and in 1239 was made a khanate by Tatars of the *Golden Horde. This was overthrown by Turks in 1475, and the area was annexed by Russia in 1783. Many Tatars emigrated then, and the remainder were deported in 1945 for alleged collaboration with the German forces of occupation between 1941 and 1943. Area: about 10,423 sq mi (27,000 sq km). *See also* Crimean War.

Crimean War (1853–56) The war between Russia, on one side, and Britain, France, the Ottoman (Turkish) Empire, and (from 1855) Sardinia-Piedmont, on the other. Caused by Russia's expansionist ambitions in the Balkans, the war was precipitated by Russia's desire to establish a protectorate over Orthodox Christians in the Ottoman Empire. In July 1853, Russia occupied Moldavia and Walachia, in October, Turkey declared war, and in March 1854, following the destruction of a Turkish fleet at Sinope, Britain and France entered the war. The major battles of the year-long siege of Sevastopol, in the Crimea, were of *Balaclava and *Inkerman, and the Russians eventually evacuated the port in September 1855. Peace was formally concluded at Paris (1856). Over

250,000 men were lost by each side, many from disease in the appalling hospitals of the Crimea. The British Government dispatched Florence *Nightingale to inspect those at Scutari, where her work had a considerable effect in improving conditions.

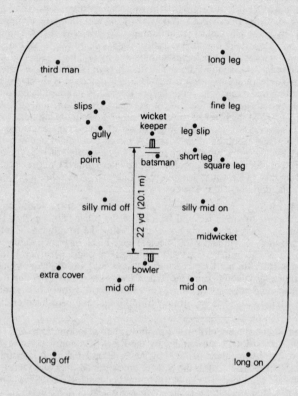

CRICKET *The pitch, as the field is called, showing the usual fielding positions (for a right-handed batsman).*

criminal law *See* penal law.

criminology The study of the cause, nature, and prevention of crime. Crime was generally equated with immorality until the 19th century, when the pioneer Italian criminologist Cesare *Lombroso suggested, in *L'uomo delinquente* (1876), that criminals are born and can be recognized by such physical attributes as a receding forehead. Although this view is no longer accepted, at various times evidence has been produced to suggest that such physiological abnormalities as an extra Y chromosome or an endocrine abnormality do predispose to criminality. Poverty, psychological stress, lack of parental affection in childhood, working mothers, and the decline of the extended family have all been suggested as additional or alternative predisposing factors, and some evidence has been produced to support each of them. But none of this evidence can explain why some people succumb to predisposing factors and become criminals while others, exposed to the same factors, do not.

Deep ethical problems are also involved. To what extent, for example, do predisposing factors affect culpability? To what extent should crime be regarded merely as a deviation from social norms? Should punishment fit the crime or the criminal and to what extent should it attempt to be therapeutic? Criminologists have, as yet, no satisfactory answers to most of these questions.

crinoid A marine invertebrate animal belonging to a class (*Crinoidea*; about 700 species) of *echinoderms, including the sea lilies and feather stars. It has a small cup-shaped body covered with calcareous plates and with five radiating pairs of feathery flexible arms surrounding the mouth at the top. Sea lilies, most of which are now extinct, are fixed to the sea bottom, coral reefs, etc., by a stalk. Feather stars, e.g. *Antedon,* are free-swimming and are usually found on rocky bottoms. Crinoids occur mainly in deep waters and feed on microscopic plankton and detritus caught by the arms and conveyed to the mouth. The larvae are sedentary. ☐fossil.

Cripps, Sir (Richard) Stafford (1889–1952) British Labour politician. Cripps became solicitor general in 1930, before entering Parliament in 1931. In 1939 he was expelled from the Labour Party for campaigning against Neville *Chamberlain's appeasement policy. He was ambassador to Moscow (1940–42), and chancellor of the exchequer (1947–50), when his austere economic policy set Britain on the road to recovery after World War II.

Cristofori, Bartolommeo (1655–1731) Italian harpsichord maker and inventor of the *piano. He constructed the escapement system in which the hammer falls away from the string immediately after striking it, leaving it free to vibrate. A damper stops the sound when the key is released.

critical mass The mass of fissile substance that is just capable of sustaining a *chain reaction within it. Below the critical mass, too many of the particles that might have induced a reaction escape and the chain reaction dies away.

critical-path analysis A planning method based on the use of a schematic representation of the network of activities and events involved in a project. Its aim is to aid coordination by identifying the optimum schedule. A critical path is a sequence of activities in which the key parameters, usually time and cost, cannot be increased without endangering the whole project. In large networks, which often need to be analyzed by computer, there may be more than one critical path. The method is commonly used in large construction projects.

critical state The state of a gas at its critical temperature, pressure, and volume. The critical temperature is the temperature above which a gas cannot be liquefied by increased pressure alone. The vapor pressure of the gas at this temperature is the critical pressure and its volume, the critical volume. In the critical state the density of the vapor is equal to the density of the liquid.

Crivelli, Carlo (c. 1430–95) Venetian painter, who settled in the Marches of Italy in the late 1460s. He is set apart from the Venetian school by his sharp linear style, influenced by *Mantegna, and the decorative detail that appears in such paintings as *The Annunciation* (National Gallery, London).

croaker. *See* drumfish.

Croatia (Serbo-Croat name: Hrvatska) A country in SE Europe, formerly a constituent republic of Yugoslavia, bordering on the Adriatic Sea. It is chiefly mountainous, descending to plains in the NE, where it is drained by the Drava River. It is primarily agricultural, producing cereals, potatoes, tobacco, fruit, and livestock. Industries, centered on the larger towns, include metallurgy and textile manufacture. *History*: settled by the Croats in the 7th century AD, the region was successively controlled by Hungary, Turkey, and Austria until the formation of the kingdom of the Serbs, Croats, and Slovenes (later Yugoslavia) in 1918. Following the occupation of Yugoslavia by the Axis Powers in World War II, Croatia was proclaimed an independent state (1941), ruled over by the fascist dictator Ante Pavelić (1889–1959). In 1945 Croatia once more became part of Yugoslavia as a people's republic. Croatia was recognized as an independent country in 1992. An ongoing civil war among the various ethnic factions continued, particularly involving the large Serbian population that was opposed to breaking away from Yugoslavia. Area: 22,050 sq mi (56,538 sq km). Population (1991): 4,784,265. Capital: Zagreb.

Croatian. *See* Serbo-Croat.

Croce, Benedetto (1866–1952) Italian philosopher. Orphaned at 17 by an earthquake, he attended Rome University, studying art, philosophy, and history. His system is expounded in the four-volume *Philosophy of Mind* (1900–10). The only reality is mental and this reality is divided into theoretical and practical. Theoretical reality comprises intuition (art and aesthetics) and conception (philosophy or history—essentially the same, both being accounts of reality). Practical reality comprises individual will (political and economic activity) and universal will (morality). His aesthetic ideas, aired in numerous other works, are the most influential.

Crockett, Davy (1786–1836) US frontiersman. He was a colonel in the Tennessee militia under Andrew Jackson, elected to the state legislature (1821–26), and Tennessee representative to Congress (1827–31, 1833–35). He cultivated the image of a rough frontiersman and became known for his skill as a scout and hunter. He fought for Texas in its struggle for independence from Mexico and was killed at the *Alamo.

crocodile A □reptile belonging to either of two genera, *Crocodylus* or *Osteolemus*, and distinguished from alligators and caymans by having a more pointed snout and fewer teeth, the fourth tooth of the lower jaw remaining visible when the mouth is closed. Crocodiles occur chiefly in tropical fresh waters although the estuarine crocodile (*C. porosus*), which reaches a length of 20 ft (6 m), occurs in coastal waters of SE Asia and Australia.

Crocodiles belong to the order *Crocodilia* (about 20 species), along with alligators and caymans. Crocodilians are amphibious mainly nocturnal carnivores living in tropical and subtropical swamps and rivers, where they prey chiefly on fish but also on water birds and land animals. They have long powerful jaws and a covering of thick protective bony plates; the ears and nostrils are placed high on the head and can be closed by valves when under water. The female builds a nest of mud or vegetation in which over a hundred shelled eggs may be laid. She guards the nest until the young, measuring 8–10 in (20–25 cm) in length, begin to hatch. Crocodilians may live for over a hundred years. Their skins are used to make leather goods and this has caused a decline in their numbers.

crocodile bird An African riverbank *courser, *Pluvianus aegyptius,* that feeds on parasites picked from crocodiles. It is 9 in (23 cm) long and is black with white markings on the throat and above the eyes.

Crocus A genus of low-growing plants (75 species), native to Mediterranean regions and widely planted in gardens. They grow from *corms to produce long thin leaves and six-lobed flowers in spring or autumn. Spring-flowering species include *C. vernus,* with white, blue, or purple flowers, and *C. aureus,* with deep-yellow flowers. *C. speciosus* is a purple autumn-flowering species. An Asian species (*C. sativus*) is the source of *saffron. Family: *Iridaceae. Compare* autumn crocus.

Croesus (died c. 546 BC) The last king of *Lydia (c. 560–c. 546 BC), famous for his wealth. He conquered the Greek cities on the coast of Asia Minor but was defeated by the Persian king *Cyrus (II) the Great in 546. According to legend, Croesus was saved by Apollo from execution by Cyrus, whose counsellor he then became.

crofting A system of subsistence farming that involves the cultivation of a small parcel of land together with access to common grazing land. Crofting was widely practiced in the Scottish Highlands until the introduction of sheep farming together with the eviction of many crofting families in the late 18th century.

Crohn's disease An inflammatory disorder that can affect any part of the intestinal tract, most usually the terminal part of the small intestine (ileum). Crohn's disease, named for the US physician B. B. Crohn (1884–1983), occurs most commonly between the ages of 20 and 40 years; symptoms commonly include abdominal pain and diarrhea. Its cause is not known but it may be a form of *autoimmunity. Patients are treated with drugs, such as prednisolone (a steroid) and sulfasalazine (a sulfonamide); some cases require surgical removal of the affected part of the intestine.

Cro-Magnon A prehistoric race of men believed to be ancestral to modern men. Skeletal remains were found (1868) at Cro-Magnon near Les Eyzies-de-Tayac in the Dordogne (SW France) and similar bones of tall broad-faced individuals have been found at other European sites. They first appeared in Europe about 35,000 years ago and were associated with *Aurignacian and subsequent cultures. They hunted reindeer, bison, and wild horse. They were often cave dwellers but seem also to have constructed huts. They produced the earliest known examples of cave art (*see* Lascaux). *See also* Homo.

cromlech (Welsh: bent stone) A former name for a megalithic table grave or *dolmen and other prehistoric stone monuments. *See also* megalith.

Crompton, Samuel (1753–1827) British inventor of the spinning mule (1779), so called because it was a cross between *Arkwright's water frame and *Hargreaves's spinning jenny. It was able to produce yarn of a higher quality and at a greater speed than had previously been possible. Unable to afford a patent, Crompton sold his idea for very little money but in 1812 he was awarded a parliamentary grant of £ 5,000.

Cromwell, Oliver (1599–1658) English soldier and statesman; Lord Protector of England (1653–58). Cromwell, a country gentleman, was a member of Parliament in the parliament of 1628–29. He emerged as a convinced Puritan and critic of Charles I in the *Long Parliament, summoned in 1640. After the outbreak of the *Civil War he raised a troop of cavalry, and fought at Edgehill (1642). As second in command he decisively defeated Charles at *Naseby (1645). Cromwell acted as mediator between the king, Parliament, and the army but his conciliatory attitude hardened after Charles's flight to the Isle of Wight; when the second Civil War ended in Charles's defeat (1648), Cromwell signed the king's death warrant. In the power struggle between Parliament and the army, he sided with the army and after the establishment of the Commonwealth turned to the final mopping-up campaigns of the Civil War. He ruthlessly subjected Ireland (1649–50) and, after defeating Charles's heir at Dunbar (1650), finally subdued the Scots at Worcester (1651). In 1653 he expelled the Rump of the Long Parliament and following the failure of the Barebones Parliament accepted the Instrument of Government, which established the *Protectorate. As Lord Protector, Cromwell established Puritanism but permitted religious toleration, allowing the Jews to return to England (1656). His foreign policy was dictated by religious and commercial considerations: he ended the first *Dutch

War, allied with France against Spain (gaining Dunkirk), and conquered Jamaica (1655). His relations with Parliament were strained. He failed to find a workable constitutional basis for his rule, refusing Parliament's offer of the crown in 1657. He was succeeded as Lord Protector by his son **Richard Cromwell** (1626–1712), who was forced by the army to abdicate in 1659 and lived in exile in France until 1680.

OLIVER CROMWELL *Dismissing the Rump of the Long Parliament (1653).*

Cromwell, Thomas, Earl of Essex (c. 1485–1540) English statesman, who drafted the legislation that made the English Church independent of Rome (*see* Reformation). He entered Wolsey's service in 1514, became a member of Parliament in 1529, and by 1532 was Henry VIII's chief adviser; he became chancellor of the exchequer in 1533. He gained Henry's divorce from Catherine of Aragon by a series of acts that made the king, rather than the pope, head of the English Church. Between 1536 and 1540 he organized the dissolution of the monasteries, after which his negotiation of Henry's disastrous marriage to the uncomely Anne of Cleves led to his execution for treason.

Cronin, A(rchibald) J(oseph) (1896–1981) British novelist. He practiced medicine until he published his successful first novel, *Hatter's Castle* (1931). His later novels include *The Citadel* (1937) and *The Judas Tree* (1961).

Cronje, Piet Arnoldus (c. 1840–1911) South African general in the *Boer Wars. He captured Potchefstroom (1881) and the raiders led by *Jameson (1896) and delayed (Magersfontein, 1899) the British advance to relieve Kimberley. He was captured at Paardeburg (1900).

Cronus A Greek deity, the youngest of the Titans. He ruled the universe after castrating his father Uranus. He swallowed all the children he fathered by his sister Rhea except Zeus, for whom a stone was substituted. Zeus was reared secretly in Crete and eventually overthrew Cronus.

Crook, George (1829–90) US general. After graduation from West Point, he served in the Northwest and then saw action as a Union officer in the Civil War from 1862, participating in the battles of Antietam, Chickamauga, Shenandoah, and Petersburg. He was then reassigned to the Western frontier where he successfully fought against Indian uprisings and was victorious against the Apaches and their leader, *Geronimo. He was made brigadier general in charge of the Department of the Platte in 1886 and major general in command of the Division of the Missouri in 1888.

Crookes, Sir William (1832–1919) British physicist, whose work on vacuums led him to investigate the newly discovered phenomenon of *cathode rays. Crookes showed that cathode rays consisted of charged particles rather than electromagnetic radiation, since they were deflected by a magnetic field. He invented the Crookes radiometer and Crookes glass, containing cerium, to protect the eyes of the industrial workers. He also discovered the element thalium.

crop rotation The growing on the same land of different crops in sequence. Crop rotation helps maintain soil fertility, prevents the build-up of crop pests, and enables cultivation of the soil to clear weeds. Nowadays, mechanized farming and the use of artificial fertilizers and pesticides have encouraged monocropping (the repeated growing of the same crop).

croquet A ball-and-mallet game that probably developed from *paille-maille*, a French game played certainly by the 13th century. Croquet was particularly popular in Britain and in the US in the mid- to late-19th century. It is played on a grass court or lawn, ideally 35 × 28 yd (32 × 25.6 m), with an arrangement of six hoops and one peg. Two to four players attempt to follow a prescribed course through the hoops, each using a distinctively colored ball, the winner being the first to hit the peg with his ball. If a player's ball hits (roquets) another ball, the player may croquet this ball by placing his own ball next to it and striking his own ball so that the opponent's ball is also moved; the object is to advance his own ball toward the peg and to drive his opponent's ball off course. After passing through a hoop or scoring a roquet a player has another turn.

Crosby, Bing (Harry Lillis C; 1904–77) US popular singer. He achieved worldwide fame during the 1930s and 1940s as a crooner and is associated with the best-selling recording of all time, Irving Berlin's *White Christmas* (1942). He starred in many films, including *Going My Way* (1944) for which he won an Academy Award, and the "Road" series with Bob *Hope, and also in his own radio and television shows. □Sinatra, Frank.

crossbill A finch of the genus *Loxia* (3 species), 6–7 in (14.5–17 cm) long, whose unique cross-tipped bill is specialized for extracting seeds from unopened cones. The common crossbill (*L. curvirostra*) of Eurasia and North America feeds on spruce seeds. The male is red and the female gray-green; both have dark-brown wings and tail. The parrot crossbill (*L. pytyopsittacus*) feeds exclusively on pine seeds, and the Eurasian two-barred crossbill (*L. leukoptera*) feeds on fir seeds.

crossbow A short bow mounted on a stock, used in Europe throughout the Middle Ages. Crossbows were composite, made of wood, horn, tendons, and by the early 15th century of steel (called an arbalest). They were drawn by hand, a belt hook, or a winch. The bolt or *quarrel* was short, iron-tipped, fletched with wood, leather, or brass, and capable of penetrating armor. Slower and less accurate than the *longbow, it could be fired from behind cover. It is now used for sport.

crosses Figures formed by a vertical line or bar intersected by a horizontal. As a symbol, the cross is found in the art of several ancient cultures. One of the earliest Egyptian hieroglyphs is the cruciform ankh (*crux ansata*), the symbol of life. The primary association of the cross is with Christianity, in which it represents the instrument used at Christ's *crucifixion. This had several forms, conventionally distinguished by their Latin names: a simple upright stake (*crux sim-*

plex); a stake with a transverse beam toward the top (*crux immissa*), which is known as the Latin cross and is the common form in the Western Church; a stake topped by a transverse beam (*crux commissa*), also known as the tau cross or cross of St Anthony; and an X-shaped structure (*crux decussata*), known as the cross of St Andrew. In European art, the crucifixion is usually depicted with a Latin cross, and the crucifixes (crosses with the image of the crucified Christ) used on altars, rood screens, etc., are given this form. The Greek cross or cross of St George has vertical and horizontal arms of equal length and is the traditional form in use in Orthodox Churches. The cross has influenced innumerable aspects of religious ritual, dress, and art, including the cruciform plan of churches and cathedrals. It is also one of the earliest of monumental designs (*see* Ruthwell Cross). As a charge in *heraldry, it is given various elaborated forms; a familiar example is the Maltese cross, the insignia of the *Hospitallers and, in Britain, of the St John Ambulance Association.

Crossopterygii An order of bony fish—the lobe-finned fishes—most of which are now extinct. Their fins were fleshy and contained elements of the internal skeleton, permitting movement both on land and in water. The suborder *Rhipidistia* were predatory freshwater fishes of the Devonian and Carboniferous periods (about 400–280 million years ago), some of which evolved into the amphibians. The suborder *Coelacanthini* contains *Latimeria,* the only surviving member of the order (*see* coelacanth). Subclass: *Sarcopterygii.*

ankh   Greek   Latin   tau

St Andrew's   Celtic   papal   Maltese

CROSSES *As a Christian symbol the cross was popularized by Constantine the Great and came into wide use in the 4th century.*

crossword puzzles A word puzzle with a series of clues, the answers to which are written into a diagram divided into squares, some of which are blacked out. (In most puzzles the pattern of the black squares has to be symmetrical.) The first modern crossword was devised by Arthur Wynne and published in the New York *World* in 1913. They became very popular in the US during the 1920s. They are now a feature of many newspapers, each one having its own style and idiosyncrasies. The more sophisticated puzzles have clues based on literary references, puns, and cryptic sentences as well as anagrams and synonyms.

Croton A genus of tropical trees and shrubs (750 species) many of which are of economic importance. *C. tiglium* of SE Asia produces croton oil, a powerful laxative now considered unsafe. The bark of *C. cascarilla* and *C. eluteria,* trees of the Bahamas, produces cascarilla, used in tonics. *C. laccifer* from India and Sri Lanka provides a lac used in varnishes. Several Brazilian species produce dragon's-blood resin. Family: *Euphorbiaceae* (spurge family).

The evergreen ornamental plants called crotons are members of the genus *Codiaeum,* grown as pot plants for their variegated foliage.

Crotone (ancient name: Croton) 39 05N 17 08E A city in S Italy, in Calabria on the Gulf of Taranto. It was founded in about 700 BC by the Achaeans. There are chemical and zinc industries. Population: 50,970.

crottle A large leafy *lichen belonging to the genus *Parmelia,* which is widely distributed from seashores to mountain tops and resembles crumpled leather. It has a black underside and sometimes reaches 35–48 in (90–120 cm) in diameter. It is used as a dye for fabrics.

croup An acute infection of the respiratory tract, usually caused by viruses, resulting in inflammation and obstruction of the larynx (voice box). Croup occurs most commonly in children under five years of age; symptoms include difficulty in breathing, which is harsh and noisy. Treatment consists of steam inhalations and sedatives; severe cases may require a tracheostomy—an operation in which a tube is inserted through a hole in the trachea (windpipe).

crow A large songbird of the widely distributed family *Corvidae* (102 species); 12–26 in (30–65 cm) long, crows typically have a black or brightly colored plumage and a stout bill. They take a variety of food, which often includes carrion, and have a distinctive harsh call. The typical crows are the *carrion, *hooded, and American crows but the family also includes the *rooks, *ravens, *choughs, *jays, and *jackdaws.

Crow A *Siouan-speaking North American Indian people formerly inhabiting the Yellowstone River region. Early in the 18th century, the Crow moved westward, where they adopted the culture of the Great Plains and became traders of guns, horses, and other commodities between the village Indians and the *Shoshoni. In addition to trade, the Crow supported themselves by buffalo hunting. Their religion emphasized a personal quest for a spirit guardian experienced through fasting and other ordeals. They were led by chiefs who had distinguished themselves by acts of personal bravery. The present Crow population, residing mainly in Montana, now numbers approximately 4500.

crowberry A dwarf procumbent shrub, *Empetrum nigrum,* of N temperate and arctic heathlands; 6–18 in (15–45 cm) high, it has oblong leaves, tiny pinkish flowers, and black edible berries. The name derives from the reputation of the fruit for attracting crows. Family: *Ericaceae* (heath family).

crowfoot A widely distributed herbaceous annual or perennial plant of the genus *Ranunculus,* which also contains the buttercups. They have deeply lobed leaves (hence the name) and white or yellow five-petaled flowers. Some species, such as the European water crowfoot (*R. aquatilis*), are aquatic. Family: *Ranunculaceae.*

crown colony A territory that is under the direct legislative control of the UK. Most crown colonies have now been granted independence: the most important one remaining is *Hong Kong; most of the others are small islands, chiefly in the Caribbean and the Pacific.

crown jewels Royal insignia and regalia and the personal jewelry inherited or acquired by a sovereign. They are now frequently museum pieces. The British Crown Jewels, among the most famous, are housed in the Tower of London. Those owned by the czars of Russia are in the Kremlin in Moscow. In Britain they are used for state occasons such as coronations.

crown of thorns 1. A Madagascan shrub, *Euphorbia splendens,* often cultivated for ornament. Up to 40 in (100 cm) high, it has spiny stems at the tips of which are a few leaves and clusters of small flowers, each surrounded by rounded scarlet bracts. *See* Euphorbia. **2.** A spiny vigorous shrub, *Zizyphus spina-christi,* forming thickets or growing singly as a tree. It is widespread in the Mediterranean region and is said to be the source of Christ's crown of thorns. Family: *Rhamnaceae* (buckthorn family).

crown-of-thorns starfish A reddish starfish, *Acanthaster planci,* that has a spiny body, up to 18 in (45 cm) across, with 12–19 arms. With the decimation of its chief predator—The Pacific triton (*Charonia tritonis*)—by shell collectors, it has spread throughout the South Pacific since the mid-20th century and now threatens destruction to the coral reefs and islands on which it feeds.

Cruciferae A family of plants (about 1900 species), mainly annual or perennial herbs, particularly abundant in N temperate regions. The flowers are four-petaled and cross-shaped. Many crucifers are of economic importance as food plants, cattle food, ornamentals, and weeds. Some, such as cabbage and other brassicas, have been grown since ancient times. In some European countries up to 30% of vegetable crop acreage is devoted to crucifers.

crucifixion A form of capital punishment carried out by nailing or binding a person to a *cross by the wrists and feet and leaving him to die from previously inflicted wounds or from exhaustion. It was commonly used in Carthage and adopted in the Roman Empire, where it was regarded as a scandalous form of death and so restricted to slaves and the worst criminals; it could not be inflicted on anyone holding Roman citizenship. Scourging customarily preceded crucifixion and the victim's legs were sometimes broken to hasten death. As a legal punishment it was abolished by the emperor Constantine. The crucifixion of Christ is reported in the four Gospels of the New Testament; the mockery, the crown of thorns, and the piercing of his side with a spear are not typical elements of this form of punishment. According to tradition, St Peter was also crucified, but head downward, and St Andrew was executed on the X-shaped cross that bears his name. In Christian legend, the cross on which Christ was crucified was discovered in 326 AD by St *Helena.

Cruikshank, George (1792–1872) British caricaturist, painter, and illustrator. He achieved early success with his satirical political cartoons. He illustrated such books as Dickens's *Oliver Twist* and Ainsworth's *Tower of London.* His etchings of *The Bottle* and painting of *The Worship of Bacchus* are moralizing sermons on alcoholism.

cruiser A fast heavily armed warship, smaller than a *battleship but larger than a *destroyer and designed for a larger cruising radius. Cruisers with increased firepower, nuclear power that extends their range almost without limit, and greater versatility are replacing the battleships in the world's major navies.

Crusades The military expeditions organized in western Christendom primarily to recover the Holy Places of Palestine from Muslim occupation. The first Crusade (1095–99) was launched under the aegis of the papacy. Jersusalem was captured and the Crusader states of the Kingdom of Jerusalem, the County of

Edessa, Antioch, and Tripoli were created. The fall (1144) of Edessa inspired the unsuccessful second Crusade (1147–48) and the capture of Jerusalem by *Saladin in 1187 led to the inconclusive third Crusade (1189–92), led by *Phillip II Augustus of France, Emperor *Frederick I Barbarossa, and *Richard (I) the Lionheart of England. The fourth Crusade (1202–04) was diverted from its initial objective, Egypt, and sacked Constantinople (1204). The four Crusades of the 13th century failed to recover lost ground and Acre, the last foothold of the West in Palestine, was lost in 1291. The Crusades failed in their stated objective, but Europe benefited greatly from the resultant growth of E–W trade and the introduction of eastern concepts into medieval culture. *See also* Children's Crusade.

crustacean An *arthropod of the class *Crustacea* (over 35,000 species), which includes the *barnacles, *woodlouse, *shrimps, *lobsters, *crabs, etc. The head bears two pairs of antennae and three pairs of jaws; the head and thorax together are usually covered by a chitinous carapace. There are numerous pairs of forked appendages, which are modified for different functions. Crustaceans are predominantly aquatic, breathing by means of gills. A few, such as the *fish louse, are parasitic on fish, whales, and other aquatic animals. During reproduction the male transfers sperm to the female, which often carries the fertilized eggs until they hatch. The larvae are mainly free-swimming and pass through several stages (*see* metamorphosis) to reach the adult form.

Crux (Latin: cross) A small conspicuous constellation, also called the Southern Cross, in the S sky, lying in the Milky Way. The four brightest stars form a cross, the longer arm of which points approximately toward the S celestial pole.

Cruz, Sor Juana Inéz de la (1651–95) Mexican poet. An infant prodigy, she lived at the Spanish viceroy's court before entering a convent in 1669. She died while nursing nuns during an epidemic. In addition to her metaphysical religious poems she wrote a defense of intellectual freedom and of women's rights to education.

cryogenics The production, effects, and uses of very low temperatures, usually meaning from −150°C down to *absolute zero. The most common method of producing cryogenic temperatures is to use *adiabatic processes. In adiabatic demagnetization, a magnetized paramagnetic substance is thermally isolated and demagnetized, thus cooling it. In adiabatic expansion, a thermally isolated gas is expanded. Cryogenic effects include changes in electrical properties, such as *superconductivity, and changes in mechanical properties, such as superfluidity (*see* superfluid). Cryogenics has been applied to new methods of food preservation, life-support systems in space, and the use of liquid propellants.

cryolite A rare mineral of composition Na_3AlF_6. It is colorless or white and occurs in pegmatite veins. It is only mined in significant quantities in Greenland, although it is known to occur elsewhere. It is used in aluminum refining. Synthetic cryolite is manufactured from hydrofluoric acid, sodium carbonate, and aluminum.

cryptogam Any plant that does not produce flowers or seeds but reproduces by means of spores. The nonvascular cryptogams include the mosses and liverworts (bryophytes), lichens, fungi, and algae; the vascular cryptogams are the ferns, horsetails, and related plants (pteridophytes) *Compare* phanerogam.

Cryptomeria. *See* Japanese cedar.

Cryptozoic time Geological time prior to the *Phanerozoic, i.e. the Precambrian, ending about 590 million years ago. It is the eon of "hidden life"; fossils are rare and obscure.

Crystal Palace A building designed by Joseph Paxton to house the *Great Exhibition of 1851. The Crystal Palace, which had an area of 772,289 sq ft (69,892 sq m), was built in Hyde Park, London, with the highly advanced use of prefabricated glass and iron. It was later dismantled and reassembled at Sydenham (a suburb of London) but burned down in 1936.

crystals Solids that have a regular geometrical shape because the constituent atoms, ions, or molecules are arranged in an ordered repeating pattern, known as a crystal lattice. Salt grains, for example, are cubic crystals of sodium chloride with sodium and chlorine ions alternating at the corners of a cubic lattice. There are seven crystal systems, into which all crystals are classified. Crystal structures are studied by a variety of techniques, including *X-ray diffraction and electron microscopy. Specialized mathematical notation and stereographic projections are used to describe lattice structure and symmetry. Many crystalline solids are polycrystalline, i.e. they consist of many small crystals. The physical properties of crystals have found many uses, ranging from *piezoelectric transducers to gemstones. **Crystallography** is concerned with the study of the structure and properties of crystals. Noncrystalline solids, such as glass, are said to be amorphous.

Csokonal Vitéz, Mihaly (1773–1805) Hungarian poet. His autobiographical play *Tempeföi* (1793) records the struggles and failures of his life as a poet. His work includes a cycle of love poems addressed to "Lilla," a volume of odes, and the highly popular comic epic *Dorottya* (1804).

ctenophore A marine invertebrate animal, also called comb jelly, sea gooseberry, and sea walnut, belonging to the phylum *Ctenophora* (about 80 species). Its transparent gelatinous body is usually rounded and bears eight rows of ciliated comblike plates, used for locomotion. Ctenophores are mainly free-swimming and often occur in swarms in coastal waters, feeding on other planktonic animals captured by long branched tentacles. Ctenophores were formerly classified as a subphylum of *coelenterates.

Ctesiphon The capital of *Parthian and *Sasanian kings near Baghdad (Iraq). Taken temporarily by the Roman emperors *Trajan (115 AD) and Carus (283), it fell to the Arabs in 637. The remains of the palace of Khosrow I (reigned 531–79) incorporate the largest known brickwork vault, spanning over 82 ft (25 m).

Cuba, Republic of A country in the Caribbean Sea, off the S coast of Florida. It consists of two main islands, Cuba (the largest in the Caribbean) and the Isla de Pinos, together with over 1500 small islands and keys. On the island of Cuba fertile plains rise to mountains in the center and SE and there are some lower hills in the NW. The population is mainly of European origin, with large African and mixed minorities. *Economy*: state controlled, it is primarily agricultural and very much dependent upon its sugar crop (its main source of export revenue); production levels have been generally low and attempts to increase efficiency include the part mechanization of the cane-cutting process. Tobacco (especially for cigars) is another important export crop and meat production is very important in the domestic economy. Fishing has expanded with government help and in 1977 fishing limits were extended to 200 mi (320 km). Important mineral resources include nickel (the second largest export). Largely dependent upon the former Soviet Union for its oil supplies, Cuba has undertaken a program of oil exploration. The fastest growing industries include metallurgy, construction, and textiles. The Cuban economy was heavily subsidized by the Soviet Union but despite this aid it had suffered serious economic declines by the end of 1983. A dramatic drop in the world price of sugar, debts to Western lenders, and high

689

CRYSTALS

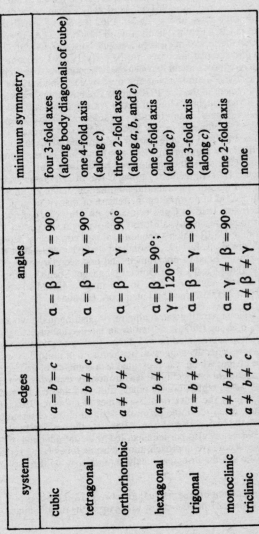

unit cell

system	edges	angles	minimum symmetry
cubic	$a = b = c$	$\alpha = \beta = \gamma = 90°$	four 3-fold axes (along body diagonals of cube)
tetragonal	$a = b \neq c$	$\alpha = \beta = \gamma = 90°$	one 4-fold axis (along c)
orthorhombic	$a \neq b \neq c$	$\alpha = \beta = \gamma = 90°$	three 2-fold axes (along a, b, and c)
hexagonal	$a = b \neq c$	$\alpha = \beta = 90°$; $\gamma = 120°$	one 6-fold axis (along c)
trigonal	$a = b \neq c$	$\alpha = \beta = \gamma = 90°$	one 3-fold axis (along c)
monoclinic	$a \neq b \neq c$	$\alpha = \gamma = 90°$, $\beta \neq 90°$	one 2-fold axis
triclinic	$a \neq b \neq c$	$\alpha \neq \beta \neq \gamma$	none

CRYSTALS *The classification of crystals.*

unemployment and inflation forced severe cutbacks and placed the country in a precarious economic position. *History*: discovered by Columbus in 1492, it was a Spanish colony (except in 1762–63, when it was occupied by the British) until 1898, when Spain was forced to withdraw following war with the US. After three years of US occupation Cuba became a republic (1901) but the US, which had invested heavily in the country's economy, continued to intervene in Cuba's internal affairs and to control its foreign policy until 1934. In 1940 *Batista became president, taking Cuba into World War II on the Allied side. His corrupt dictatorship was threatened by Fidel Castro's unsuccessful revolt of July 26, 1953, and in Castro's second attempt (1959) with the aid of Che Guevara, Batista was overthrown. Relations between Castro's socialist government and the US were increasingly strained and Cuba moved closer in international relations to the Soviet Union. In 1961 an invasion by Cuban exiles with US support was defeated at the *Bay of Pigs and in 1962 the Soviet installation of nuclear missile bases in Cuba resulted in a US naval blockade. The Cuban missile crisis aroused worldwide fear of nuclear catastrophe but was resolved when the Soviet Union agreed to remove the bases. In the early 1970s US economic sanctions were lifted and rapprochement between the two countries seemed more possible. In 1976 a socialist constitution was approved by a referendum. As a result of serious unemployment in the late 1970s many Cubans emigrated to countries in E Europe and some sought asylum in South America. In 1980 a flotilla of boats carried Cuban refugees, many of them regarded as "undesirables" by both the US and Cuban governments, to Key West in Florida. In the early 1980s relations between Cuba and the US were further jeopardized by Cuban involvement in Africa (particularly Angola and Ethiopia) and in Central America (mainly Nicaragua and Granada). Increasing drug traffic from Cuba to the US and air piracy worsened US sentiments regarding Cuba. In 1984 Jesse Jackson, a candidate for the Democratic presidential nomination, made an unofficial visit to Cuba and succeeded in negotiating the release of many Cuban political prisoners and Americans held in Cuba primarily on drug charges. Despite a 1989 Cuba-Soviet friendship treaty, all forms of Soviet aid stopped in 1991 with the dissolution of the USSR. Cuba's economy, almost completely dependent on Soviet aid, was shattered. In 1993, Cuba held its first secret-ballot election since Castro took power. Head of government and first secretary of the Cuban Communist Party: Fidel Castro Ruz. Official language: Spanish. Official currency: Cuban peso of 100 centavos. Areas 46,736 sq mi (148,124 sq km). Population (1990 est): 10,582,000. Capital and main port: Havana.

cubism A style of painting and sculpture, originating in the works of *Picasso and *Braque in about 1907. It started as an intellectual investigation of how a solid form can be represented in two dimensions without resorting to illusionism. Volume was generally suggested by the fusion of multiple viewpoints of an object in one image, which was presented as a complex of geometrical shapes. The subject matter of early cubism was invariably everyday objects of simple form, such as vases, tables, books, pipes, fruit, and musical instruments, many being suggested by the work of a forerunner of cubism, *Cézanne. Figures, which are rare, often resemble primitive sculpture, the observation of which helped Picasso to break with tradition. After 1911 the development of cubism, in which Juan *Gris now also participated, led to the introduction of *collage and also to a more decorative approach, monochrome tones being replaced by rich colors. Cubism was the principal catalystic influence on the evolution of *abstract art.

cubit An ancient unit of length equal to between 18–22 inches (46–56 cm); it is based on the distance from the elbow to the tip of the middle finger.

Cuchulain (*or* Cú Chulainn) A legendary Irish hero, resembling *Achilles in his strength and courageous exploits. He was the son of the god Lug (*see* Lugus) but was brought up by his mortal uncle, Conchobar, King of Ulster. Cuchulain is the central subject in a series of ancient Gaelic epics and romances known as the Ulster cycle.

cuckoo A bird belonging to a family (*Cuculidae*; 127 species) occurring worldwide and ranging from 6–28 in (16–70 cm) in length. The European cuckoo (*Cuculus canorus*), gray with distinctive white barring and a long tail, belongs to a subfamily of parasitic cuckoos (*Cuculine*; 47 species); these lay their eggs in the nests of other birds, which rear their young. Parasitic cuckoos' eggs resemble those of the host in order to deceive the host bird. On hatching, the young cuckoo removes the other nestlings from the nest, thus obtaining sufficient food from its adopted parents. Order: *Cuculiformes* (cuckoos and turacos).

cuckoo-shrike A gregarious arboreal songbird of the family *Campephagidae* (70 species), occurring in tropical regions of the Old World; 5–12 in (13–32 cm) long, they have a mainly gray plumage, long pointed wings, and a notched bill and feed on insects and fruit.

cucumber An annual vine, *Cucumis sativus,* probably originally from Asia but widely cultivated since ancient times. The long green juicy fruits, up to 24 in (60 cm) long, are eaten raw, cooked, or pickled (*see* gherkin). In northern regions both glasshouse and outdoor (ridge) varieties are grown. Indoor cucumbers produce fruit without fertilization; if pollinated, the fruits taste bitter. Family: *Cucurbitaceae* (gourd family).

cucumber tree A slender North American tree, *Magnolia acuminata,* 53–98 ft (16–30 m) high. Hardiest of all magnolias, it is found in moist rich woodlands, often on mountain slopes. It has tulip-shaped greenish-white flowers and cucumber-like fruit—greenish at first, ripening to dull crimson. The light yellow satiny textured wood is used for furniture, flooring, etc. Family: *Magnoliaceae*.

Cúcuta (*or* San José de Cúcuta) 7 55N 72 31W A city in N Colombia, on the Pan-American Highway. It is an important commercial center (especially for coffee). Its university was founded in 1962. Population (1985 est): 380,000.

Cudworth, Ralph (1617–88) English scholar, a leading member of the *Cambridge Platonists. His *True Intellectual System of the Universe* (1678) defends Christianity as the only genuine source of knowledge against the atheism and materialism of *Hobbes.

Cuernavaca 18 57N 99 15W A city and resort in S central Mexico. It is the site of Cortés's palace (now government offices), a Franciscan cathedral (1529), and a university (1939). Many writers, artists, and film stars have resided here. Its varied industries include flour milling, textiles, and sugar refining. Population (1986 est): 385,000.

cuisine minceur A recently developed style of gourmet cookery in which the traditional generous use of butter, cream, and other rich ingredients is minimized. Cuisine minceur was elaborated by the French chef Michel Guérard in the 1970s at his restaurant at Eugénie-les-Bains in SW France. This entirely new approach to elegant cooking recommends using fresh herbs, concentrated stocks, and puréed vegetables to give flavor and texture to sauces and casseroles.

Culbertson, Ely (1891–1955) US bridge authority, born in Romania. He influenced the development of contract bridge. Imprisoned in the Caucasus in his youth for anarchist activity, he emigrated after the Russian Revolution. His life after 1938 was devoted to campaigning for world peace. He founded the magazine *The Bridge World* (1929) and wrote many books on bridge, as well as an autobiography, *The Strange Lives of One Man* (1940).

Culiacán 24 50N 107 23W A city in W Mexico. It is the commercial center for an irrigated agricultural area. Population (1978 est): 302,229.

Cullen, Countee (1903–46) US poet and writer. He wrote about African-American society in the Harlem section of New York City and was a leading figure in the Harlem Renaissance. By his senior year at New York University he had published a poetry volume, *Color* (1925), and had won national poetry contests. His poetry is collected in *Copper Sun* (1927), *The Ballad of the Brown Girl* (1927), *The Black Christ* (1929), and *The Meda and Other Poems* (1935). He also wrote a novel, *One Way to Heaven* (1932).

Cullinan diamond An exceptional diamond weighing 3106 metric carats (c. 621 g) when found in the Premier Mine, South Africa, in 1905. It was cut into 9 major and 96 small stones.

Culloden Moor A moor in N Scotland, in the Highland Region near Inverness. In 1746 it was the scene of the last land battle to be fought in Britain, in which the Young Pretender, Charles Edward Stuart, was defeated by the Duke of Cumberland, thus ending the *Jacobite cause in Britain.

Culpeper's Rebellion (1677–79) An American colonial uprising, in which tobacco growers in North Carolina opposed British restrictions on their markets. John Culpeper seized the British deputy governor and governed capably himself until his voluntary surrender for trial in England, at which he was acquitted.

cultivator A farm implement used to till the soil, so destroying weeds and promoting crop growth. Horse-drawn models date from the 19th century but modern tractor-drawn machines consist of a steel frame with curved steel tines to penetrate and disrupt the soil.

Cultural Revolution, Great Proletarian (1966–68) A political rather than cultural movement launched in China by Mao Tse-tung in opposition to bureaucracy and to reinvigorate revolutionary attitudes. Many leading officials were dismissed, the formal educational system was abolished, and reforms to foster correct political views were introduced. Many universities were closed and young people, mobilized as *Red Guards, attacked Party officials and destroyed cultural objects.

culture In microbiology, a colony of microorganisms grown in a solid or liquid medium for experimental or diagnostic purposes. A widely used medium is agar gel (contained in petri dishes) supplemented with required nutrients, which is inoculated with microorganisms and incubated. Sterile conditions are essential to avoid contamination.

Cumae The first Greek colony in Italy. Founded near Naples about 750 BC by settlers from Chalcis, Cumae expanded rapidly, spreading Greek civilization in S Italy. It repulsed Etruscan influence but was subsequently subject to Rome (from c. 340 BC).

Cumaná 10 29N 64 12W A city in N Venezuela. Exports, through its port of Puerto Sucre on the Caribbean Sea, include sugar, cocoa, and tobacco. Its university was founded in 1958. Population (1990 est): 212,500.

Cumans A nomadic Turkish people, who dominated the W steppes for two centuries until they were driven into Hungary by the Mongol invasions (1237–39). They were absorbed into the Hungarian kingdom in which they had considerable influence.

Cumberland, Richard (1631–1718) English moral philosopher. One of the *Cambridge Platonists, he was renowned for scholarship and virtue. His *De legibus naturae disquisitio philosophica* (1672) opposed *Hobbes's egoism in its principle of universal benevolence and anticipated *utilitarianism.

Cumberland Gap National Historical Park 36 36N 83 40W A national park in the Cumberland Mountains that encompasses an area in SW Virginia, SE Kentucky, and NE Tennessee. A natural pass through the mountains, the Cumberland Gap was part of the 18th century Wilderness Trail, and later played a strategic role during the Civil War. The park includes a paved road through the gap and a tunnel beneath the mountains. Area: 20,177 acres (8166 hectares).

Cumberland River A river that flows from SE Kentucky in the Cumberland Mountains E and S to Nashville, Tenn., and then NW to the Ohio River in southwest Kentucky. Shipping is important along the river as are the Tennessee Valley Authority hydroelectric and flood control projects. Length: 687 mi (1106 m).

cumin An annual herb, *Cuminum cyminum,* up to 12 in (30 cm) high with umbrella-like clusters of small whitish flowers and oblong bristly fruits. Native to the Mediterranean, it has long been cultivated in Europe, India, and China for its fruits, which resemble caraway seeds but are more bitter and are used in curry powders, to flavor liqueurs, etc. Cumin was formerly used medicinally as a stimulant and liniment and in veterinary medicine. Family: *Umbelliferae.*

cummings, e(dward) e(stlin) (1894–1962) US poet. His highly experimental lyric verse is characterized by typographical innovations and eccentric punctuation, which he employed to reinforce the verbal element of his poetry. His works include *Tulips and Chimneys* (1923), *Eimi* (1933), *No Thanks* (1935), and *1 × 1* (1944). He also wrote an experimental novel, *The Enormous Room* (1922), a poetic drama, *Him* (1927), and a ballet, *Tom* (1935).

cumulus cloud (Cu) A low type of *cloud of convective origin having a heaped appearance and developing vertically from a flat base. Fair-weather cumulus clouds are shallow but others are deep and may develop into **cumulonimbus cloud**. This cloud is heavy and dense, extending vertically to about 20,000 ft (6000 m), and is associated with thunderstorms. Its upper part often spreads out to form an anvil shape.

Cunaxa, Battle of (401 BC) The battle fought between *Cyrus the Younger and his elder brother Arsaces, who had seized the Persian throne as *Artaxerxes II in 404 BC. Cyrus gathered an army of Greek mercenaries (including the historian, Xenophon) and met Artaxerxes at Cunaxa, 42 mi (70 km) N of Babylon. Cyrus was defeated by Artaxerxes' superior cavalry forces and died in the battle.

cuneiform The oldest *writing system of which records survive, used to represent a number of ancient Near Eastern languages. The name derives from the wedge-shaped marks (Latin *cuneus,* a wedge) made by the imprint of a stylus in soft clay. Originally pictographic, by the 3rd millennium BC cuneiform pictures had become stylized in the form of groups of wedge-shaped imprints, many representing the sounds of syllables. Once hardened the clay tablets were almost indestructible and many are extant today. Probably devised by the Sumerians not later than 3100 BC, cuneiform spread to other language groups in the area. By 100 BC, however, it had largely been superseded by the North Semitic script that was used to represent the increasingly dominant Aramaic language.

Cunningham, Merce (1919–) US dancer and choreographer. He joined the Martha Graham Company in 1945 and founded his own company in 1952. He has frequently collaborated with the composer John *Cage. His works, which include experimental abstract ballets, include *Suite for Five* (1956), *Antic*

Meet (1958), *Aeon* (1961), *Scramble* (1967), *Landrover* (1972), *Travelogue* (1977), and *Arcade* (1985).

pictographs		cuneiform		
c. 3500	c. 3000	c. 2800	c. 800	
				mountain
				fish
				barley grain

CUNEIFORM *The wedge-shaped strokes of cuneiform writing developed gradually from pictographs.*

Cunobelinus (*or* Cymbeline; died c. 42 AD) British ruler (c. 10–c. 42) of the Catuvellauni tribe. Their lands embraced much of SE England after they overcame the Trinovantes. He founded Colchester (c. 10).

cup fungus A fungus, belonging to the order *Pezizales,* that produces a cup- or saucer-shaped fruiting body. Cup fungi may or may not have a stalk and the spores are released from the upper surface of the cup. The distinctive scarlet elf cup (*Peziza coccinea*), found on dead branches, is a smooth-rimmed cup, 0.8–2.4 in (2–6 cm) in diameter, deep red inside and whitish gray or pink outside. Class: **Ascomycetes.*

Cupid The Roman god of love, identified with the Greek Eros, and lover of Psyche. He is usually portrayed as a winged boy shooting arrows of love.

cuprite A red to black mineral of composition Cu_2O, found where deposits of copper have been subject to weathering.

cupronickel A corrosion-resistant alloy of 75% copper and 25% nickel (by weight). It is often used in coins.

Curaçao A West Indian island, the largest in the Netherlands Antilles. Discovered in 1499, it was settled by the Spanish before being colonized by the Dutch in 1634. The refining of oil from Venezuela is of major importance; other industries include the production of Curaçao liqueur and calcium-phosphate mining. Area: 173 sq mi (444 sq km). Population (1992 est): 144,000. Chief town: Willemstad.

curare A resinous substance obtained from South American trees of the genera *Strychnos* and *Chondodendron,* used as an arrow poison by South American Indians. Curare blocks the action of **acetylcholine, which is released at the junctions of nerve endings and muscles and causes muscular contraction. Curare therefore causes a relaxed paralysis of muscle. Curare-like compounds (e.g. tubocurarine) are injected during general anesthesia to relax muscles and provide the surgeon with better access to the part of the body on which he is operating.

curassow A long-tailed tropical American gamebird belonging to the family *Cracidae.* Curassows have a long neck and long legs and may reach 40 in (100 cm) in length. The black males have a crest of curly feathers and a yellow bill ornament; females are smaller and brownish in color. They are mostly arboreal, feeding on buds, insects, and frogs. Chief genera: *Crax, Pauxi, Mitu*; order: *Galliformes* (pheasants, turkeys, etc.).

curia An ancient division of the Roman people. There were 30 *curiae,* each with a meeting place that was also known as a *curia.* The Senate house of Rome, attributed to Tullus Hostilius, was called the Curia Hostilia and its replacement, built by Julius Caesar, was known as the Curia Julia.

Curia, Roman. *See* Roman Curia.

Curia Regis The king's court of early medieval Europe. It fulfilled all the functions of royal government—administrative, legislative, and judicial—and from its specialist departments developed the public government offices, such as, in England, the Chancery and the Exchequer, as well as the courts of law and parliament.

curie (Ci) A unit of radioactivity equal to the amount of an isotope that decays at the rate of 3.7×10^{10} disintegrations per second. Named for Marie *Curie.

MARIE CURIE *The discoverer of radium working with her husband, Pierre, in their laboratory in 1903, the year they were awarded a Nobel Prize.*

Curie, Marie (1867–1934) Polish chemist, renowned for her research into *radioactivity. Born Marya Sklodowska, she emigrated to France in 1891, studied at the Sorbonne, and married (1895) **Pierre Curie** (1859–1906), a French physicist. Interested in *Becquerel's discovery of radioactivity, Marie Curie noticed in 1898 that one particular uranium ore emitted an anomalously large amount of radiation. Realizing that the radiation was caused by a new element, she and her husband spent four years isolating one gram of radium salt from eight tons of the ore. The Curies, together with Becquerel, were awarded the 1903 Nobel Prize for Physics and, for her discovery of radium and polonium, she won the 1911 Nobel Prize for Chemistry. Pierre Curie, before joining his wife's work, had discovered the *piezoelectric effect (1880) and shown that ferromagnetism reverts to paramagnetism (*see* magnetism) above a certain temperature, now known as the Curie point (1895). He was killed in a road accident; she died as a result of the radiation to which she had been exposed. Their daughter **Irène Joliot-Curie** (1896–1956) married the French physicist **Frédéric Joliot** (1900–59) in 1926. Working together in the same field as her parents, they were the first to produce radioactivity artificially. For this work they were awarded the Nobel Prize in chemistry (1935).

Curie's law The susceptibility of a paramagnetic substance is inversely proportional to its thermodynamic temperature. The **Curie point** (*or* Curie temperature) is the temperature above which a ferromagnetic substance becomes paramagnetic. Named for Pierre Curie.

Curitiba 25 24S 49 16W A city in SE Brazil, the capital of Paraná state. It has two cathedrals and is the site of the Federal University of Paraná (1894). Curitiba is a commercial and industrial center producing chiefly furniture, tobacco, and maté. Population (1980): 843,733.

curium (Cm) An artificial transuranic element discovered by Seaborg and others in 1944 and named for Marie and Pierre Curie. All 13 isotopes are radioactive and some intensely so; ^{242}Cm gives out about three watts of heat per gram. Curium is a silvery reactive metal. Its compounds include the oxides (CmO_2, Cm_2O_3) and halides (CmF_3, $CmCl_3$). At no 96; at wt 247; mp 2444 ± 104°F (1340 ± 40°C).

curlew A streaked brown or gray bird belonging to the genus *Numenius* (8 species). Curlews have a long neck and long curved bill. They breed in inland subarctic regions and migrate south in winter to marshes and mudflats, feeding on worms and crabs. The common Eurasian curlew (*N. arquata*) is almost 24 in (60 cm) long and ranges from Britain to central Asia. Family: *Scolopacidae* (snipe, sandpipers, etc.).

Curley, James Michael (1874–1958) US politician. A Democrat, he served in the US House of Representatives (1911–14) before becoming mayor of Boston in 1914. He served until 1918 and again from 1922–1926 and 1930–1934, at which time he was elected Massachusetts governor (1935–37). After that he again served in the House (1943–46) and as mayor of Boston (1946–50) for the fourth time. During this last term as mayor he was convicted of mail fraud and spent five months in jail.

curling A game played on ice with stones fitted with handles, played since at least the early 16th century and strongly associated with Scotland, but also played in the US and Canada. Two teams of four players take turns sliding two curling stones, each up to 39 yd (36 m), along the ice toward the "house," a series of concentric circles at the end of the rink. A team scores one point for each stone finishing nearer the center of the house than any of its opponents'. Teammates are allowed to sweep the ice ahead of a moving stone to remove impediments and influence its course.

currant 1. One of several species of shrubs belonging to the genus *Ribes*. Some are cultivated for their fruit, for example *blackcurrant and *redcurrant, and others, such as the *flowering currant, are grown as ornamentals. Family: *Grossulariaceae*. 2. The dried berry of a small seedless *grape, grown in the Mediterranean region and used in cooking.

currawong An Australasian songbird of the genus *Strepera* (6 species). About 20 in (50 cm) long, currawongs are usually black, sometimes with white markings, and have a long hook-tipped bill. They feed on insects, small mammals, and birds and frequently destroy fruit crops. Family: *Cracticidae* (Australian magpies).

currents Flows of water masses moving in a particular direction. The major ocean currents form part of the general circulatory system in the oceans and are permanent, although they may vary with the seasons. They result mainly from the action of the prevailing winds on the sea surface; an example is the North Atlantic Drift. Currents are also induced by the tides, by differences in water density (densities vary with temperature, salinity, and turbidity levels), and by rivers discharging into the sea.

curricle A light two-wheeled carriage usually drawn by two horses harnessed abreast to a pole. Curricles were favored in the 18th and 19th centuries as rapid and stylish conveyances, equivalents to modern sports cars.

Currier & Ives US lithographic company. Founded by Nathaniel Currier (1813–88) in 1834 and joined by James Merritt Ives (1824–95) in 1857, the company published prints of current events and of aspects of everyday American life. Today the lithographs stand as a documentation of life during the second half of the 19th century.

curry A spicy stew of meat, chicken, vegetables, etc., originating in the Indian subcontinent. Long slow cooking over a gentle heat allows the meat to become tender and the different ingredients to intermingle. The essence of curry is the balanced mixture of aromatics: spices (especially yellow turmeric but also cumin, coriander, cardamoms, and ginger), herbs, and seasonings (peppers, chilies, and salt; or sweet seasonings made from sugar or honey; and acid seasonings made from citrus fruit juices). Curries are usually eaten with rice and chutneys. In the West premixed curry powder is often used.

Curtin, John Joseph (1885–1945) Australian statesman; Labor prime minister (1941–45). He implemented many social-welfare policies and developed the military defenses of Australia, introducing wide-ranging conscription measures during World War II. He died in office.

Curtiss, Glenn (Hammond) (1878–1930) US aviator and aeronautical engineer. Curtiss made the first 1-mile flight in the US (1908) and designed and constructed the earliest US seaplanes. He manufactured aircraft for the Allies in World War I.

Curzon, George Nathaniel, 1st Marquess (1859–1925) British politician. As viceroy of India (1898–1905) he made administrative changes but resigned following disagreements with *Kitchener. In World War I he was a member of the War Cabinet (1916–19). As foreign secretary (1919–24) he established a short-lived British protectorate over Persia.

Curzon line A line between Poland and the Soviet Union, which they recognized as the border between them in 1945 after World War II. The boundary, named for Lord *Curzon, had initially been suggested during the Russo-Polish War (1919–20).

cuscus A cat-sized *marsupial mammal belonging to the genus *Phalanger,* found in forests of NE Australia, New Guinea, and nearby islands. Cuscuses have a prehensile tail and climb slowly around trees at night, eating mainly leaves and fruit but sometimes catching lizards or roosting birds. Family: *Phalangeridae* (*see* phalanger).

Cushing, Harvey Williams (1869–1939) US surgeon, noted for his contributions to brain surgery, particularly of the pituitary gland, and his classification of brain tumors. He was the first to describe the hormonal disorder known as *Cushing's disease.

Cushing's disease A disorder resulting from excess *corticosteroid hormones in the body, named for H. W. *Cushing. The symptoms include obesity, loss of minerals from the bones, and reddening of the face and neck; it may be associated with the symptoms of *diabetes mellitus and high blood pressure. It may be caused by a tumor of the pituitary gland or the adrenal gland or by prolonged therapy with high doses of corticosteroids: the treatment is determined by the cause.

Cushitic languages A subgroup of the *Hamito-Semitic languages. They are spoken in the Sudan, Somalia, Ethiopia, and Eritrea, and include Beja and *Somali. This group is the closest in sound to the common ancestor Proto-Hamito-Semitic.

custard apple A small tree of the genus *Annona* of the American tropics, so called because of the custard-like flavor of its fruits. The common custard apple (*A. reticulata*), 16–26 ft (5–8 m) high and widely grown in the West Indies, produces reddish many-seeded fruits, 3–5 in (8–12 cm) in diameter, with a sweetish pulp. *See also* soursop; sweetsop. Family: *Annonaceae*.

Custer, George Armstrong (1839–76) US cavalry general. A graduate of West Point, he had a distinguished Civil War record, becoming the Union's youngest brigadier general. After the war he became a lieutenant colonel in the Seventh Cavalry during the Western campaigns against the Indians. Sent to round up Sioux and Cheyenne forces under Sitting Bull in South Dakota's Black Hills in 1876, an erroneous reconnaissance report led him to divide his force. He and his force of about 260 were massacred by the main Indian strength at the *Little Bighorn (Custer's Last Stand).

customs and excise duties Indirect taxes (*see* taxation) applied to goods and services. Customs (*or* tariffs) are duties payable on import of foreign goods. They may be either specific duties assessed according to the weight or quantity, or ad valorem duties assessed according to the foreign or domestic price of the imported goods. They raise revenue and restrict imports. An excise tax is a duty chargeable on specific goods produced or consumed within a country, e.g. gasoline, liquor, and tobacco.

customs unions Associations of countries that agree to abolish customs duties and tariffs for each other's products and to institute *free trade between themselves. They usually also agree to common external tariffs for nonmembers. The *European Economic Community is an example of a customs union.

Cuthbert, St (c. 635–87 AD) Celtic churchman and missionary. As a monk and later a prior at Melrose, Ireland, he evangelized, earning a reputation as a miracle worker. With his abbot, St Eata, he moved to Lindisfarne, a coastal island, in 664 and became its bishop in 685. He died on the island of Farne, where he had earlier lived as a hermit. His body was reburied in Durham Cathedral in the 10th century. Feast day: Mar 20.

cutter 1. A sailing vessel, similar to a *sloop, but with the mast stepped about halfway between the bows and the stern. **2.** A fast armed powerboat used by the US Coast Guard for patrolling coastal waters in the enforcement of customs regulations, to rescue vessels in distress, etc.

cuttlefish A *cephalopod mollusk belonging to the family *Sepiidae* (about 100 species), of temperate coastal waters; 1–35 in (2.5–90 cm) long, the body is supported by an internal calcareous leaf-shaped shell—the cuttlebone—which gives buoyancy. When alarmed, the animal emits an inky fluid.

cutworm The larva of a *noctuid moth belonging to the widely distributed genus *Agrotis*. Cutworms destroy crops, such as cabbage, corn, and pasture grasses, by biting through the stems, often at ground level.

Cuvier, Georges, Baron (1769–1832) French zoologist and father of the sciences of comparative anatomy and paleontology. His studies at the Museum of Natural History in Paris showed him how the different parts of an animal skeleton were related to each other and to their functions. By extending this to fossils he was able to reconstruct entire skeletons from the incomplete ones in existence. His classification system, described in *Le Règne animal* (1817), grouped animals (including extinct fossil species) into four phyla. This was an advance on the system of Linneus although it was later superseded.

Cuyp, Aelbert Jacobsz (1620–91) Dutch landscape painter. He was born in Dordrecht, the son and pupil of **Jacob Gerritsz Cuyp** (1594–1651), a portrait and landscape painter. Aelbert's paintings of cattle, river scenes, etc., are distinguished by their glow of golden light, a fine example being *Herdsmen with Cows by a River* (National Gallery, London).

Cuzco 13 32S 71 57W A city in S Peru, in the Andes 11,207 ft (3416 m) above sea level. It was the capital of the Inca Empire prior to the Spanish conquest in 1533; Inca ruins include the Temple of the Sun. It is now a commercial center serving an agricultural region. It has a university (1962). Population (1990 est): 275,000.

cyanide process The extraction of gold from its ores by chemical treatment with potassium cyanide. The ore is crushed to a fine powder and mixed with a weak solution of cyanide in water. Once the gold is dissolved by the cyanide the resulting compound is precipitated from the solution and the metallic gold separated out by chemically displacing it from the compound with zinc.

cyanocobalamin. *See* vitamin B complex.

cyanogen (C_2N_2) A colorless highly poisonous flammable gas with a smell of bitter almonds. It can be prepared by heating mercury cyanide and has been used as a fumigant, war gas, and rocket fuel.

Cybele An Asiatic earth goddess identified by the Greeks with *Rhea. The center of her worship was Phrygia, whence her cult spread to Athens and later to Rome. She represented the powers of nature and was a protectress of wild animals. Her priests were eunuchs known as Corybantes.

cybernetics The study of communication and control between men, machines, and organizations. The name was derived from the Greek word meaning "steersman" by Norbert *Wiener, who was largely responsible for pioneering the subject. It is an aspect of *bionics, in which the human ability to adapt to changing circumstances and to make decisions is simulated in the design of computer-controlled systems. Ultimately, the application of cybernetics may extend the process of *automation to the point at which almost every operation in a factory is automatic, with very little human supervision.

Cybernetics has also been used as a link between the physical and life sciences, for instance in using *information theory to explain how messages are transmitted in nervous systems and in genetic processes.

cycad A *gymnosperm plant belonging to the order *Cycadales* (about 100 species), native to warm and tropical regions. They resemble small palms or tree ferns, having short stout stems with a crown of frondlike leaves. Reproductive organs are in the form of separate male and female cones borne on different trees, the female cones often being very large (up to 99 lb [45 kg]). The stems of some species yield a type of *sago.

Cyclades (Modern Greek name: Kikládhes) A group of some 220 Greek islands in the S Aegean Sea, including Andros, Delos, Íos, Míkonos, Melos, Náxos (the largest), Páros, and Syros. Total area: 995 sq mi (2578 sq km). Capital: Hermopolis (on Syros).

cyclamate A salt of cyclamic acid ($C_6H_{11}NHSO_3H$). Sodium and calcium cyclamates were formerly extensively used as artificial sweeteners in soft drinks and for diabetics, but their excessive consumption has been shown to have dangerous side effects and their use has been discontinued.

Cyclamen A genus of perennial plants (15 species) native from the European Mediterranean to Iran and widely cultivated as pot and garden plants. The pot varieties are grown from *C. persicum*. The garden cyclamens include attractive dwarf varieties, 2–3 in (5–8 cm) high. All cyclamens produce corms but most can be grown from seed. They have marbled heart-shaped leaves and drooping flowers with red, pink, or white reflexed petals. Family: *Primulaceae*.

cycloid The curve traced out by a point on the circumference of a circle as it rolls along a flat surface.

cyclone An area of relatively low atmospheric pressure with a series of closed isobars around its center. In the N hemisphere wind circulates in an anticlockwise direction around its center, in the S hemisphere it is clockwise. Except in the tropics, cyclones are now usually referred to as *depressions or lows. Tropical cyclones form over the tropical oceans and are accompanied by strong winds; they include *hurricanes and *typhoons.

Cyclops (Greek mythology) Storm gods who made thunderbolts for Zeus. Homer describes them in the *Odyssey* as one-eyed man-eating giants who lived on an island later identified as Sicily. *See also* Polyphemus.

Cyclops (zoology) A genus (44 species) of very small freshwater crustaceans of the subclass *Copepoda*, so named because of their single median eye. In Africa and Asia they transmit the parasitic Guinea worm larvae to man if accidentally swallowed.

cyclostome An eel-like jawless aquatic vertebrate of the class *Cyclostomata*, which includes the *lamprey and *hagfish. Cyclostomes have a long smooth cylindrical body with fins arranged not in pairs but singly (*compare* fish), a cartilaginous skeleton, and a sucking mouth with numerous horny teeth. They occur mainly in temperate fresh waters and salt waters and many are parasitic on fish. Subphylum: *Agnatha*.

cyclotherms Series of beds of sedimentary rocks deposited in a single cycle (in cyclic sedimentation) or repeated group (in rhythmic sedimentation). Carboniferous strata, particularly the Coal Measures, show such sequences, representing the changes in conditions from terrestrial to marine that repeatedly occurred in the period.

cyclotron A type of particle *accelerator in which charged particles are accelerated in an outward spiral path inside two hollow D-shaped conductors (called dees) placed back to back. A magnetic field at right angles to the plane of the dees causes the particles to move in a spiral and, at the same time, they are accelerated by an alternating electric field applied across the gap between the two dees. When the particles reach the edge of the device they are deflected onto the target. The maximum energy of the particles is about 25 MeV. *See also* synchrocyclotron.

Cygnus (Latin: swan) A large conspicuous constellation in the N sky, lying in the Milky Way. The brightest star, *Deneb, and four other bright stars form the **Northern Cross.** The constellation contains many interesting *variable stars, *binary stars, and dark and emission *nebulae—including the old supernova remnant, the **Cygnus Loop. Cygnus A** is an intense double radio source while **Cygnus X-1**, thought to be a *black hole, is one of several strong X-ray sources.

cymbals Circular metal percussion instruments of indefinite pitch. Orchestral cymbals are clashed together, struck with a drumstick, or suspended and rolled with felt-covered timpani sticks. **Choke cymbals** (*or* hi-hat) are a pair of cymbals on a stick, operated by a foot pedal; they are used in dance bands and pop groups. Small tuned cymbals are known as **ancient cymbals.** □musical instruments.

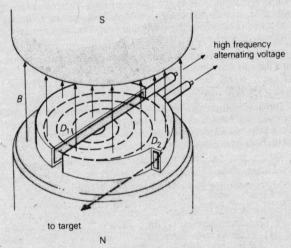

CYCLOTRON *The charged particles are accelerated in the two D-shaped conductors* (D_1 *and* D_2), *which are supported in the magnetic field B.*

Cymbeline. *See* Cunobelinus.

Cymbidium A genus of tropical and subtropical *orchids (40–70 species), native to Asia and Australia. Most species have pseudobulbs, straplike leathery leaves, and long-lasting sprays of 6–20 flowers on each flower stalk. Ornamental and very adaptable, cymbidiums are among the most popular orchids in cultivation today. They are popular as ornamentals.

Cynewulf (early 9th century AD) One of the earliest Anglo-Saxon religious poets (*compare* Caedmon). His work shows him to have been a native of Mercia or Northumbria and from a learned background. Four surviving religious poems, preserved in 10th-century manuscripts, carry his runic signature. They are *Elene, The Fates of the Apostles, The Ascension,* and *Juliana.* All are based on Latin sources and are distinguished by their clear narrative form. Many other Old English poems have been attributed to him.

Cynics The followers of the Greek moral philosopher *Diogenes of Sinope, who were active from the early 3rd century BC. They are notable less as a coherent school with systematic doctrines than as a succession of flamboyant individuals whose characteristic concern was to discount the pursuit of worldly wealth and success and to demonstrate that basic human needs can be very simply satisfied. They were outspoken critics of accepted social values and often lived notably unconventional lives. Positive freedom could be attained by self-realization, but often it was the negative destructive side of the Cynics' beliefs that was emphasized. Their distinction between natural and artificial values strongly influenced other ancient philosophies, such as *Epicureanism.

cypress A conifer of the genus *Cupressus* (true cypresses; 20 species), native to S Europe, E Asia, and North America and widely planted for ornament and timber. Cypresses have tiny scalelike leaves, which densely cover the branches and twigs, and rounded cones, 0.4–1.6 in (1–4 cm) in diameter, usually ripening from green to brown. The Italian or funeral cypress (*C. sempervirens*), of the Mediterranean region, is 80–145 ft (25–45 m) high. Cultivated forms, usually narrow and columnar, are planted in gardens and cemeteries. Its strong fragrant long-lasting wood is used for chests, furniture, etc. Family: *Cupressaceae*.

Similar and related trees of the genus *Chamaecyparis* (6 species), of North America and SE Asia, are known as false cypresses. The most important species is Lawson's cypress (*C. lawsoniana*), of W North America, where it grows to a height of 198 ft (60 m). There are many cultivated varieties, up to 125 ft (38 m) high, widely planted for shelter and ornament. *See also* swamp cypress.

Cypress pine A coniferous tree of the genus *Callitris* (about 16 species), native to Australia and New Caledonia. Their branches are densely covered with small scale leaves and the cones are small and globular. Several species yield a useful timber. Family: *Cupressaceae*.

Cyprian, St (c. 200–58 AD) African churchman; Bishop of Carthage (from c. 248) and Father of the Church, martyred under the Emperor Valerian. In his treatise, *De unitate ecclesiae,* he argues that the bishop's authority provides the basis for the Church's unity. Feast day: Sept 16.

Cyprus, Republic of (Greek name: Kypros; Turkish name: Kıbrıs) An island state in the E Mediterranean Sea, off the S coast of Turkey. A central plain, the Messaoria, rises to the Kyrenia Range in the N, and in the SW the Troödos Massif rises over 6000 ft (1800 m). Most of the population is Greek or Turkish, the former being in the majority. *Economy*: mainly agricultural. Mineral resources include iron pyrites, asbestos, chromite, and copper ores. Though mining is on the decline, other (mainly light) industries are being rapidly developed. Tourism is important, although, like the rest of the economy, it has been badly affected by the unrest of recent years. There is now an intensive development program in the Turkish sector, largely based on agriculture and especially citrus fruit for export, with the aim of creating a self-sufficient economy. Exports include wine, citrus fruits, potatoes, and metals. *History*: there was already a Greek colony on Cyprus almost 4000 years ago. It was conquered by Egypt in the 6th century BC and later formed part of the Persian, Macedonian, Roman, Byzantine, and Arab empires. In 1193 it became a Frankish kingdom and in 1489 a Venetian dependency. In 1571 it was conquered by the Turks and this occupation lasted until 1878 when it came under British administration. It became a crown colony in 1925. In the 1930s Greek Cypriots began advocating Enosis (Union with Greece), and in 1955 a Greek Cypriot organization (*see* EOKA), led by Archbishop *Makarios and General Grivas, began guerrilla warfare against the British. Cyprus became a republic in 1960 and a member of the Commonwealth in 1961. The UK, however, retained sovereignty over several military bases. There were fierce clashes between the Greek and Turkish communities in the 1960s and in 1964 a UN peacekeeping force was sent to the island. Greek and

Turkish talks in 1968 aimed unsuccessfully at better relations between the two sides. In 1971 General Grivas began a further terrorist campaign in favor of Enosis; he died in 1974. Following a Greek-supported military coup of the same year, in which Makarios was temporarily overthrown, Turkey invaded the island leading to its virtual partition. In 1975 the Turks set up their own government in the N as the Turkish Federated State of Cyprus, with Rauf Denktash as president. It has not, however, received international recognition. On the death of Makarios in 1977, Spyros Kyprianou was elected president. Cyprus remained divided, with the Turkish-occupied territory in the N constituting about 40% of the country. The rest of the island, occupied by Greek Cypriots, remained under the government of the Republic of Cyprus, internationally recognized as the official government. In 1984 Denktash, president of the Federated States, unilaterally declared the independence of Turkish Cyprus, plunging Cyprus into its worst political crisis since the Turkish invasion. Peace talks between Greek and Turkish factions continued into the 1990s. Official languages: Greek and Turkish; English is also widely spoken. Official currency: Cyprus pound of 1000 mils. Area: 3572 sq mi (9251 sq km). Population (1992 est): 755,000. Capital: Nicosia. Main port: Limassol.

Cyrano de Bergerac, Savinien (1619–55) French writer and dramatist. He became famous in his youth as a soldier and fighter of duels. He wrote a comedy, *Le Pédant joué* (1654), some tragedies on classical subjects, and two fantastic satirical romances describing visits to the moon and sun (published posthumously). He was noted for his comically long nose as well as his chivalrous nature; the conflict between his appearance and his noble character is captured in *Rostand's famous play, *Cyrano de Bergerac* (1897).

Cyrenaica A region of E Libya, bordering Egypt on the E, largely desert to the S and inhabited mainly by tribesmen of the Senussi, a puritanical Islamic sect. From early pre-Christian times Cyrenaica was colonized or conquered by Greeks, Egyptians, Romans, Vandals, Arabs, Turks, and Italians successively. The scene of many battles in World War II, it was occupied by the British from 1943 until united with Libya in 1951. It was a province of Libya until 1963.

Cyrenaics A school of Greek philosophers, founded about 400 BC by *Socrates' disciple, Aristippus of Cyrene. The Cyrenaics identified virtue with pleasure and, adopting the *Sophists' view that truth and morality are matters for individual judgment, held that the only purpose of life was immediate gratification of the senses. Among them, Anniceris stressed the pleasures of friendship and family affection, whereas Hegesias, believing that pure pleasure was unattainable, advocated rather the avoidance of pain. Their ethical doctrines foreshadowed those of *Epicureanism.

Cyrene The chief city of ancient Cyrenaica (now in Libya). Founded by colonists from Thera about 630 BC, Cyrene quickly became prosperous, basing its wealth on trade. Its monopoly in silphium, an important Greek medicinal spice, brought the Cyreneans fame as doctors. It fell under the control of the Ptolemies of Egypt in the 4th century BC and was bequeathed by Ptolemy Apion to Rome in 96 BC. Excavations of its extensive remains have provided valuable information about ancient art, architecture, and society.

Cyril, St (c. 827–69 AD) Greek missionary, traditionally the inventor of the *Cyrillic alphabet. With his brother **St Methodius** (c. 825–84) he was sent to Moravia to evangelize the Slavs by the Patriarch of Constantinople in 863. Although highly successful, the brothers initially incurred much hostility from the German rulers and ecclesiastics for their use of the vernacular in the liturgy. After Cyril's death, Methodius translated the Bible into Slavonic. Feast day: July 7.

Cyrillic alphabet The alphabet used for Russian, Belorussian, Ukrainian, Bulgarian, Serbian, and various other languages of the Soviet Union. It was developed from a Greek alphabet of the 9th century AD in the course of Christian missionary work and is traditionally attributed to the Greek brothers St *Cyril and St Methodius. It originally consisted of 43 letters, but modern versions have reduced this number to about 30.

Cyril of Alexandria, St (c. 375–444 AD) Christian theologian; Patriarch of Alexandria (from 412) and Doctor of the Church. He became a champion of Christian orthodoxy, expelled the Jews from Alexandria, and opposed Nestorius (*see* Nestorians) on the question of Christ's divinity, eventually succeeding in having him banished as a heretic. He produced numerous works, including biblical commentaries and refutations of paganism. Feast day: Feb 9.

Cyrus (II) the Great (d. 529 BC) King of Persia (559–529), who founded the Achemenian Empire. He staged a successful revolt against his overlord Astyages (reigned c. 584–c. 550), gaining control of the empire of the Medes (*see* Media). He then conquered Lydia, Ionia, and Babylonia (539), thereby gaining Syria and Palestine, and territories in Central Asia. He was noted for his humane and tolerant policies toward conquered peoples and permitted the Jews to return to Jerusalem in 537. He was killed fighting in Central Asia: his tomb at *Pasargadae is still to be seen.

Cyrus the Younger (d. 401 BC) The son of Darius II (reigned 423–404) of Persia. Appointed commander of Persian forces in Asia Minor in 407, he helped the Spartan admiral *Lysander defeat Athens in the *Peloponnesian War. When in 404 Cyrus's brother succeeded their father as *Artaxerxes II, Cyrus led a Greek mercenary army, which included the historian *Xenophon, against him. He died leading a cavalry charge at *Cunaxa.

cyst 1. A close fluid-filled sac within the body. Cysts may be caused by blockage of the duct of a gland (e.g. a sebaceous cyst in the skin), dilation of an existing body space (e.g. in the ovary), or by parasitic infection. Some cysts are present from birth. **2.** A structure formed during the life cycle of certain lower animals, such as parasitic protozoans and worms. The cysts usually protect the animals when they are most vulnerable.

cystic fibrosis A hereditary disease affecting the mucus-secreting and sweat glands. Symptoms, which appear in early childhood, are due to the production of thick mucus, which obstructs the pancreatic duct, intestinal glands, and bronchi. Patients suffer from malnutrition (because the production of digestive enzymes is blocked) and recurrent chest infections. The sweat contains large quantities of salt, which confirms the diagnosis. Treatment of cystic fibrosis, aimed at relieving its effects, includes antibiotics to combat infections, daily physiotherapy, a low-fat high-protein diet, and the administration of pancreatic enzymes.

cystitis Inflammation of the bladder, usually caused by a bacterial infection. Cystitis is most common in women: symptoms include frequent painful urination and occasionally blood in the urine. It is treated with antibiotics.

cytochromes A group of heme-containing pigments found in the mitochondria of plant and animal cells and involved in cell respiration. Cytochromes b, c_1, c, a, and a_3 form an electron transport chain that captures the energy (in the form of electrons) released by the *Krebs cycle and conserves it for use by the cell through the formation of *ATP molecules. The electrons are transferred ultimately to oxygen with the formation of water.

cytokinins A group of plant growth-stimulating compounds derived from purines. They act in conjunction with *auxins to promote cell division and retard senescence. Synthetic cytokinins, such as kinetin, are used commercially in the storage of vegetables.

cytology The study of the structure and function of cells. It began with the development of techniques for the sectioning, fixation, and selective staining of materials for study under the light microscope, which enabled the *nucleus and other organelles to be observed. This led to the identification of chromosomes within the nucleus and of their role in heredity. More recent developments have included the use of phase-contrast and electron microscopy, and the biochemistry and physiology of cells has been studied using such techniques as cell separation and analysis, autoradiography, and tissue culture. Cytology has an important function in medicine. The study of diseased cells can reveal the nature of a disease and how it may be controlled, and cytological tests provide the basis for diagnosis of many diseases, including cancer. *See also* biological sciences.

cytoplasm *See* cell (biology).

cytotoxic drugs Drugs used to kill cancer cells. These drugs, which include nitrogen mustard and vincristine, have led to major improvements in the treatment of some cancers (e.g. leukemia). They act by interfering with the multiplication of the malignant cells, but since they may also affect nonmalignant cells they often cause severe side effects, including damage to bone marrow.

Czech A West Slavonic language related to Slovak and Polish and spoken by nine million people in the Czech Republic. It is the official language of the republic and is written in the Latin alphabet in a standardized form based on the dialect of Prague. Its development as a literary language dates from the 15th and 16th centuries.

CZECHOSLOVAKIA *The Cathedral of St Vitus (left) and Hradcany Castle (center) in Prague. The statue in the foreground is of the Czech painter Josef Manes (1820–71).*

Czechoslovakia (Czech and Slovak Federal Republic) A landlocked country of 49,365 sq mi (127,855 sq km) in central Europe, divided in 1993 into the Czech Republic and Slovakia. It was mainly wooded and mountainous, the central lowlands surrounding the Morava River rising to the Bohemian plateau in the W and the Slovakian highlands in the E. The capital was Prague. The population was about two thirds Czech and almost a third Slovak, with small minorities of Hungarians, Germans, Poles, and others. *History*: Czechoslovakia was created, under the leadership of Tomáš *Masaryk and Edvard *Beneš, in 1918 following the collapse of the Austrian Empire. It comprised the former Austrian possessions of *Bohemia, *Moravia, part of *Silesia, and (from 1920) *Ruthenia. The new state encountered threats from the diverse national minorities that peopled it and was unable to withstand the expansionist ambitions of Hitler's Germany. In 1938, Hitler secured the *Munich Agreement to his annexation of the *Sudetenland and in 1939 took possession of the rest of Czechoslovakia. During World War II a provisional Czechoslovak government existed in London under Beneš's presidency. Following the war the Allies recognized its former territories, except for Ruthenia, which was ceded to the Soviet Union, and some three million Germans were expelled from Czechoslovakia. By 1948 the Communist Party was in power and Czechoslovakia was closely allied with the Soviet Union. In 1968 a liberalization program initiated by Dubček provoked a Soviet invasion and Dubček's overthrow. In 1977 Czech dissidents protested against the violation of human rights in Czechoslovakia in a manifesto entitled Charter 77. By 1989, political reform sweeping through Eastern European countries prompted the communist government to begin negotiations with opposition groups. A new government was formed and in late 1989 writer Vaclav Havel was chosen its leader. He was reelected in 1990. Issues facing Czechoslovakia in the early 1990s were a faltering economy and a growing movement for Slovakian independence. In mid-1992, the two regions agreed to separate, and Havel resigned as president. An interim government ran the country until Jan 1, 1993, when the Czech and Slovak republics became independent. *See also* Czech Republic, Slovakia.

Czech Republic Independent nation in central Europe, the western portion of the former country of Czechoslovakia, which dissolved on January 1, 1993. It consists of the historic regions of Bohemia, with mountains, plains, and plateaus, and Moravia, a more lowland area. The population is about 80% Czech and 13% Moravian, with other small minorities. The breakup of the Communist regime brought economic hardship with the movement toward a free-market economy, but the republic's balanced industrial and agricultural base kept unemployment low. Initially, the government concentrated on securing foreign investment and on reaching agreements with Slovakia on the disengagement of the two countries. President: Vaclav Havel. Premier: Vaclav Klaus. Currency: koruna. Area: 30,440 sq mi (78,840 sq km). Population (1992 est): 10,315,000. Capital: Prague. For history prior to 1993, *see* Czechoslovakia. *See also* Slovakia.

Czerny, Karl (1791–1857) Austrian pianist, composer, and teacher. A child prodigy, he had lessons with Beethoven and was influenced by Clementi and Hummel. He was a prolific composer but is best known for his piano studies. He was the teacher of Liszt.

Częstochowa 50 49N 19 07E A city in S Poland, on the Warta River. Formed from two separate communities in 1826, it has a monastery that was defended against the Swedes in the Thirty Years' War and to which Roman Catholics make pilgrimages. Its industries include iron and steel production. Population (1992 est): 258,000.

D

dab One of several *flatfish of the family *Pleuronectidae,* especially the genus *Limanda* found in N Atlantic and N Pacific waters. The European *L. limanda,* up to 12 in (30 cm) long, is light brown, sometimes with dark spots, and is an important food fish.

dabbling duck A *duck that feeds near the surface of water, rarely diving and frequently feeding on land. With relatively small feet and legs set well forward, dabbling ducks walk efficiently on land; they include the *mallard, *pintail, *shoveler, *teal, and *wigeon. Drakes are usually brightly colored and generally have a distinctive patch (speculum) on the wing. *Compare* diving duck.

dabchick A small *grebe, *Tachybaptus ruficollis,* common in quiet inland waters of Europe, S Asia, and Africa. It is 9 in (23 cm) long and has a dark-brown back, pale underparts, and a bright chestnut breast, neck, and cheeks. It feeds on small fish and aquatic invertebrates.

Dacca (Name from 1982: Dhaka) 23 42N 90 22E The capital of Bangladesh, situated in the SE of the country, on the Burhi Ganga River. It is a riverport and commercial and industrial center producing various textiles and jute. The university was founded in 1921. *History*: with a long history of human settlement, it became the capital of the Bengal province of the Mogul Empire in the 17th century. In the 18th century it came under British rule, and upon independence in 1947 was made capital of East Pakistan. Population (1991): 3,397,187.

dace A slender lively fish, also called dart or dare, belonging to the family *Cyprinidae,* which includes chub, roach, minnow, etc. The European dace (*Leuciscus leuciscus*) is up to 12 in (30 cm) long, silvery colored, and lives in fast-flowing streams and rivers, eating plant and animal material.

Dachau 48 15N 11 26E A town in Germany, in Bavaria. It was the site of a notorious Nazi *concentration camp (1933–45).

dachshund A breed of □dog originating in Germany, where they were developed to pursue badgers to earth. There are two size varieties—standard and miniature—and three coat types—long-haired, smooth-haired, and wire-haired. Dachshunds are usually brownish or black and tan. Height: 7–10 in (18–25 cm) (standard); miniatures are smaller, not exceeding 11 lb (5 kg) in weight.

dacoit An armed robber in a gang in India; the term is also applied to members of guerrilla groups in Burma.

dada A European art and literary movement, beginning in Zürich in 1916 and aimed at deflating the status of the art-object. Dada was originally the name of a Zürich literary periodical published by the poet Tristan Tzara (1896–1963) and *Arp. Since it had no coherent style, much of its ideology was more effectively transmitted in poetry periodicals, such as *L'Intransigeant* in France. Manufactured objects were favored both in graphic art and sculpture. Their violent effect is shown in the collages of Arp, *Ernst, and *Schwitters and the *ready-mades of *Duchamp, who exported dada to the US. For its most fanatical adherents dada was also a way of life, characterized by calculatedly absurd behavior. Although dada petered out in the early 1920s, *surrealism absorbed many of its characteristics.

daddy longlegs. *See* cranefly.

Daedalus A legendary Greek craftsman and sculptor, said to have built the labyrinth for King *Minos of Crete. Minos imprisoned him, but he created wings for himself and his son Icarus and flew away; Icarus was killed when the sun melted his wings, but Daedalus reached Sicily safely.

daffodil A perennial European plant, *Narcissus pseudonarcissus,* widely grown as a garden bulb. It has narrow leaves and yellow flowers, each with a trumpet-shaped central crown surrounded by six segments. The bulbs are poisonous and were once used in medicine as an emetic and cathartic. Family: *Amaryllidaceae.*

Dafydd ap Gwilym (c. 1320–c. 1380) Welsh poet. Born into an aristocratic family in S Wales, he traveled widely and was acquainted with the work of the continental troubadours. He was trained in the bardic tradition but introduced a personal humor and originality into the intricate and obscure conventional forms of his odes.

Dagestan Autonomous Republic Former Soviet administrative division, now in the Russian federation, on the Caspian Sea. The Caucasus Mountains lie in the S, and much of central and N Dagestan is also mountainous. Over 30 different nationalities inhabit the republic, many of whom are Muslim. Its mineral resources remain largely unexploited, although sizeable quantities of oil and natural gas have been extracted in coastal areas. There are large engineering, oil, chemical, and food industries and power stations are under construction. Agriculture is varied and crops include wheat and fruit—cattle breeding is also important. *History*: conquered by Arabs, Turks, Mongols, and Persians, Dagestan was annexed by Russia in 1813. It became an autonomous republic in 1921. In 1970, the area suffered a severe earthquake. Area: 19,416 sq mi (50,278 sq km). Population (1991 est): 1,854,000. Capital: Makhachkala.

Dagly, Gerhard (c. 1653–1714?) Belgian artist, a master in baroque lacquer work. At the courts of Electors Frederick William and Frederick III in Berlin (1687–1713) he became known for his cabinet cases, making *chinoiserie popular throughout Europe.

Daguerre, Louis-Jacques-Mandé (1789–1851) French inventor of the first practicable photographic process (the daguerreotype). Working initially with Joseph Niepce (1765–1833), who had produced the first permanent photographic image (the heliograph), Daguerre succeeded during the 1830s in producing a photograph by focusing light onto a copper plate that had been coated with a silver salt. Daguerreotypes were widely made in the mid-19th century.

Dahl, Roald (1916–90) British author, whose work is pervaded by an ironic and frequently very black humor. Of Norwegian parentage, he served in the RAF during World War II. He has published many collections of short stories, including *Kiss Kiss* (1959) and *Switch Bitch* (1974), and several popular children's books, including *Charlie and the Chocolate Factory* (1976) and *James and the Giant Peach* (1961).

Dahlia A genus of herbaceous perennial tropical American plants (12 species) up to 7 ft (2 m) high, originally cultivated as a food crop for their tubers but now grown mainly for ornament. The brightly colored flowers, 2–20 in (5–50 cm) across, may be single or double and are of two main types. The varieties known as flat heads and pompoms are derived from *D. pinnata*; cactus-type flowers with pointed petals are varieties of *D. juarezii*. Family: *Compositae.*

Dahomey. *See* Benin, People's Republic of.

Daigo II (1287–1339) Emperor of Japan (1318–39), who attempted to restore the power of the throne at the expense of the *shoguns (military overlords). Despite superficial success in 1333, Daigo's plans provoked fierce feudal resistance and led to prolonged civil war and his own exile.

Dáil Éireann The representative assembly of the Republic of Ireland. It is the more important house in the National Parliament, the other house being the Seanad Éireann (the Senate). There are 144 members elected by proportional representation, at least once every 5 years. The president (the nominal head of state) summons and dissolves the Dáil on the advice of the prime minister.

Daimler, Gottlieb (Wilhelm) (1834–1900) German inventor, who contributed to the development of the internal-combustion engine. Daimler started to build his own engines in 1883, which were soon sufficiently light and efficient to power machines; in 1890 he founded a company to manufacture *automobiles. ▢motorcycles.

daimyo The feudal lords who rose to control one or more provinces of Japan between the 14th and 16th centuries. Their constant warfare was ended by the triumph of *Tokugawa Ieyasu in 1600 but over 250 *daimyo* remained in charge of their own domains until 1871. They were then given pensions and titles and their lands were incorporated into prefectures by a modernizing government.

Dairen. *See* Lüda.

dairy farming The maintenance and management of cattle, goats, and sheep for *milk production. Man has used the milk of his animals as a food for thousands of years and the modern dairy cow is an efficient converter of grass into milk. Herds of 50–200 are milked by machine in milking parlors and the milk passes by pipeline under hygienic conditions to await collection in refrigerated bulk tanks.

Advances in breeding and management of dairy cows have resulted in current annual yields of about 1050 gallons (4000 liters) per cow. *See also* dairy products.

dairy products Foods and other products derived from the processing of milk. Separation of milk by centrifugation yields skimmed milk and cream. Churning the cream disrupts the fat globules, removes water, and produces butter, containing over 80% fat, and buttermilk. Cream is retailed in various stages of concentration, for example light cream and heavy cream; other less concentrated forms include evaporated milk (containing about 65% water) and condensed milk (about 26% water).

Yogurt (*or* yoghurt) is produced by inoculating whole milk with bacteria, principally of the genera *Streptococcus* and *Lactobacillus*. The acid they produce during incubation at about 56°F (43°C) for four to five hours coagulates the milk, to which sweetening and flavoring may be added. Whey is a by-product of *cheese manufacture and, as with skimmed milk, may be dried to a powder form for use in the food industry or fed to farm animals in the fresh liquid state. *See also* dairy farming; milk.

daisy A herbaceous plant of the genus *Bellis* (15 species), native to Eurasia, with flower heads consisting of small central yellow disk florets surrounded by white or purple petal-like ray florets. The entire head is surrounded by bracts (small leaflike structures). The flower heads are solitary, arising on long stalks from a basal rosette of simple leaves. Many species are garden ornamentals, some with double-flowered varieties. The common wild Eurasian daisy is *B. perennis*, a perennial up to 24 in (60 cm) high, common in grasslands and lawns. Family: *Compositae*.

Dakar 14 45N 17 08W The capital and main port of Senegal, on Cape Verde peninsula. It was the capital of French West Africa (1904–59). It has a cathedral and a university (1957). The country's main industrial center and one of Africa's most important cities, its industries include sugar refining and groundnut-oil production. Population (1992 est): 1,730,000.

Dakota. *See* North Dakota; South Dakota.

Dakota. *See* Sioux.

Daladier, Édouard (1884–1970) French statesman; prime minister (1933, 1934, 1938–40). He signed the *Munich Agreement in 1938 and resigned in March, 1940, because of the unpopularity aroused by his failure to assist Finland against Russia (*see* Russo-Finnish War). Arrested by the Vichy government (1940) after the fall of France, he was imprisoned by the Germans from 1942 until the end of World War II.

Dalai Lama The title of the spiritual and political ruler of Tibet and head of the Gelukpa Buddhist school. The title, originating in the 14th century, signifies the incarnation of Avalokiteshvara, the *Bodhisattva of compassion. Chosen by oracles after the death of the previous incumbent, the Dalai Lama is regarded as infallible. The 14th Dalai Lama went into exile in India at the beginning of Chinese Communist rule in Tibet in 1959. *See also* Panchen Lama.

Dale, Sir Henry Hallett (1875–1968) British physiologist, who, in 1914, isolated the chemical *acetylcholine from the fungus ergot. His findings of the effects of acetylcholine on living organs corresponded with the discovery by Otto *Loewi, in 1921, that acetylcholine is a chemical transmitter released by the nervous system. Dale shared the 1936 Nobel Prize with Loewi.

d'Alembert, Jean le Rond (1717–83) French mathematician. The illegitimate son of an aristocrat, d'Alembert was raised by a glazier and his wife. His works include the study of vibrating strings, during which he derived the general solution to the wave equation, and a theorem in mechanics known as d'Alembert's principle, which is essentially a form of Newton's second law of motion. He also collaborated with *Diderot in editing the *Encyclopédie* (*see* Encyclopedists).

Daley, Richard J(oseph) (1902–76) US politician; mayor of Chicago (1955–76). A Democrat, he served in the Illinois legislature (1936–46) before becoming mayor of Chicago. As mayor he was known for his reorganization of the police department and urban renewal programs. Known for his complete control of the city's apparatus, during the 1968 Democratic convention held in Chicago he had the police break up anti-Vietnam War demonstrations with a violence that was widely criticized.

Dalhousie, James Ramsay, 1st Marquess of (1812–60) British colonial administrator; governor general of India (1847–56). Elected to Parliament in 1837, he became president of the Board of Trade in 1845 under Peel. The youngest ever governor general, he was criticized for his aggressive annexation of Indian territories. Following the second *Sikh War (1848–49) he annexed the Punjab and after the second Burmese War (1852) he annexed Rangoon. His annexation of Oudh (1956) caused unrest that contributed to the outbreak of the *Indian Mutiny after his departure.

Dali, Salvador (1904–89) Spanish surrealist painter. He joined the Paris surrealists (1929) and, inspired by Freudian theories of the unconscious, painted startling dream images with photographic realism during self-induced hallucinatory states. A similar disturbing imagery occurs in *Un Chien Andalou* (1929), a film he made with *Buñuel. While living in New York (1940–55), he turned to religious subjects and became a Roman Catholic. His taste for self-advertisement is evident in his autobiographical writings, such as *Diary of a Genius* (1966).

Dalian. *See* Lüda.

Dallapiccola, Luigi (1904–1975) Italian composer and pianist. His interest in composition was stimulated by his acquaintance with Alban Berg and he evolved a personal use of *serialism. His compositions include the opera *Ulisse* (1968), as well as many vocal and instrumental works.

Dallas 32 47N 96 48W A city in NE Texas, on the Trinity River. Founded in 1841, it developed as a cotton market during the late 19th century. The discovery of oil in E Texas during the 1930s accelerated the city's growth, which was further enhanced by the introduction of the aircraft and electronics industries during World War II. Today Dallas is the state's second largest city and the financial and commercial center of the SW. A notable cultural center, it is the site of several colleges. Pres. John F. Kennedy was assassinated there on Nov 22, 1963. Population (1990): 1,006,877.

Dalmatia A coastal belt mainly in Croatia, bordering on the Adriatic Sea. It is penetrated by a narrow corridor giving Bosnia and Hercegovina access to the sea. Predominantly mountainous with an indented coastline and many offshore islands, its picturesque scenery forms the basis of a thriving tourist industry. Wine production is especially important. The chief towns are Zadar, Split, and Dubrovnik. *History*: Dalmatia formed part of ancient Illyria. Ceded to Yugoslavia in 1920, it was occupied by Italy during World War II before being returned to Yugoslavia from 1947 until Croatia's independence in 1991.

Dalmatian dog A breed named for the Adriatic coastal region of Dalmatia. Dalmatians are strongly built and were formerly used as carriage dogs. The short sleek coat has a pure white background with black or liver (brown) spots. Height: 23–24 in (58–61 cm) (dogs); 22–23 in (56–58 cm) (bitches). □dog.

dalton. *See* atomic mass unit.

Dalton, John (1766–1844) British chemist and originator of the modern *atomic theory of matter. Dalton's earliest researches into gases led to his discovery of *Dalton's law of partial pressures. He believed that gases consist of particles, extending his theory in 1803 to suggest that all matter is particulate, but he did not distinguish between atoms and molecules. His discovery of the law of multiple proportions in the same year strongly supported his atomic theory.

Dalton's law of partial pressures The total pressure exerted by a certain volume of a gaseous mixture is equal to the sum of the pressures (called partial pressures) exerted by each gas, if it alone occupied the same volume. Named for John *Dalton.

dam A barrier across a river. Dams are used for diverting the flow of water; raising the water level for navigation purposes; storing water for irrigation, industrial use, or water control; and providing a high-pressure source of water for *hydroelectric power. Gravity dams depend on the weight of their bulk to provide strength. Usually made of concrete and having a flat vertical face upstream, they are no longer used for the largest dams. Arch dams consist of curved concrete structures presenting their convex faces upstream, so that pressure is transmitted to the sides of the dams. They can thus be much less massive than gravity dams and are therefore cheaper to build. *See also* Aswan High Dam; Grand Coulee Dam; Grande Dixence Dam; Kariba, Lake; Paraná, Rio.

Dam, Carl Peter Henrik (1895–1976) Danish biochemist, who discovered vitamin K. He showed that certain symptoms in chicks, such as a tendency to bleed, were due to deficiency of a vitamin, which he named *Koagulations-Vitamin,* or vitamin K. Later, both he and Edward A. Doisy isolated vitamin K from green leaves. They shared a Nobel Prize (1943).

Daman A region in India, on the Gulf of Cambray. It comprised a district of Portuguese India from 1559 until 1961, after which it became part of what is now the territory of Daman and Diu. Chief town: Daman. *See* Goa, Daman, and Diu.

Damanhur 31 03N 30 28E A city in N Egypt, on the Nile Delta. It has an important cotton trade with cotton-ginning and textile industries. Population (1986 est): 191,000.

Damaraland An area in N Namibia, named for the Damara people, who, however, now live mainly in the S. It is excellent cattle-grazing country.

Damascus (Arabic name: Esh Sham) 33 30N 36 19E The capital of Syria, in the SE of the country close to the Lebanese border. Under Ottoman rule from 1516 until 1918, Damascus was taken by the French (1920) and became capital of independent Syria in 1941. The Great Mosque and the Gate of God are the most notable buildings in the city. The university was founded in 1923. It is now the commercial center of the fertile plain to the E. Population (1992 est): 1,451,000.

damask Originally, a woven silk fabric, reversible and elaborately patterned, manufactured in Damascus. Linen damask was later manufactured in France, Flanders, and Ireland but cotton is now usually used. A firm glossy fabric with interwoven designs, damask is chiefly used as table linen.

damask rose An Asian rose, *Rosa damascena,* about 5 ft (1.5 m) high, with spicy-scented pink and white flowers. It is the main source of attar of roses—the rose oil used as the base of many perfumes. Extraction of rose oil is a major industry in Bulgaria and parts of W Asia.

D'Amboise, Jacques (Jacques Joseph Ahearn; 1934–) US ballet dancer and choreographer. He danced for the New York City Ballet from 1950 and played principal roles in such ballets as *Filling Station, Stars and Stripes,* and *Apollo.* He choreographed his own works for the company, including *The Chase* (1963) and *Irish Fantasy* (1964), and worked in movies and television.

Damien, Father (Joseph de Veuster; 1840–89) Belgian Roman Catholic missionary. He worked in the leper settlement on the Hawaiian Island of Molokai from 1873 until his death from leprosy.

Damietta (Arabic name: Dumyat) 31 26N 31 48E A port in Egypt, on the Nile River. Its industries include the manufacture of cotton and silk. Population (1975 est): 113,200.

dammar A resin used in making varnish, obtained from various trees of SE Asia, especially species of *Shorea* (family *Dipterocarpaceae*) and conifers of the genus *Agathis* (including the New Zealand *Kauri pine).

Damocles Legendary courtier of Dionysius I of Syracuse in the 4th century BC. Dionysius seated him at a banquet beneath a sword suspended by a single hair, thus illustrating the insecurity of human life, irrespective of wealth or power.

Damodar River A river in NE India. Rising in West Bengal, it flows mainly ESE through Bihar to join the Hooghly River SW of Calcutta. Its valley contains India's most important coalfield, an irrigation works, a hydroelectric project, and important heavy industry. Length: 370 mi (595 km).

Dampier, William (c. 1652–1715) English explorer. As a buccaneer he carried out several raids on Spanish possessions on the W coast of South America and West Africa in the 1680s, reaching Australia in 1686. In 1699 he was sent by the government to explore Australia and New Guinea, returning to England in 1701. The Dampier Archipelago, off the NW coast of Australia, was named for him. During his last voyage (1708–11) he rescued Alexander *Selkirk from the South Seas.

damping-off A disease, usually affecting seedlings, in which the stem base becomes softened and the plant falls over. Fungi of the genus *Pythium* are usually responsible. Soil sterilization may be undertaken as a preventive measure.

damselfish A lively and aggressive deep-bodied fish, also called demoiselle, belonging to the family *Pomacentridae*. Up to 6 in (15 cm) long, damselfish are often brightly colored and live mainly among reefs in the tropical regions of the Atlantic, Indian, and Pacific Oceans. They feed on plant and animal material. Order: *Perciformes*.

damselfly A slender delicate insect belonging to the suborder *Zygoptera*, closely related to the *dragonflies. It has similar habits but is smaller and has weaker powers of flight. The wings are held over the body at rest. □insect.

damson The plumlike stone fruit of *Prunus damascena*, a slender twisted tree found across the N hemisphere. It has small white flowers that develop into purple fruits. Damsons may be eaten cooked, used in jam, or pressed into a cake called damson cheese. Family: *Rosaceae*. *See also* plum.

Dan, tribe of One of the 12 *tribes of Israel. It claimed descent from Dan, the son of Jacob by his concubine Bilhah. Its territory lay N of the Sea of Galilee and its city of Dan was situated at the northernmost point of the Hebrew settlement. Some of its people occupied an area NW of Judah, which was gradually absorbed by Judah.

Dana, Richard Henry, Jr. (1815–82) US lawyer and writer. Due to illness he left Harvard University in 1834 and went to sea for two years. After returning and graduating from Harvard in 1837, he wrote *Two Years Before the Mast* (1840), a widely acclaimed novel about life at sea. He practiced law and became active in the movement against slavery, and many of his law cases involved fugitive slaves. He was a founder of the Free-Soil Party (1848).

Danae In Greek legend, the daughter of Acrisius, King of Argos. He imprisoned her because an oracle said he would be killed by her child; Zeus visited her, however, and she gave birth to *Perseus. Acrisius cast mother and son out to sea but Polydectes, King of Seriphos, rescued them.

Da Nang (former name: Tourane) 16 04N 108 14E A port in S central Vietnam, on the South China Sea. It was the site of a major US airbase during the Vietnam War. Textiles are the chief industry. Population (1989): 370,670.

dance A social activity or theatrical art in which the body moves rhythmically, usually to music. In ancient times it was primarily used in religious rituals; such dances still exist today among some primitive tribes. During the Middle Ages the Roman Catholic Church often condemned dancing, particularly when it appeared to be a manifestation of mass hysteria. Dancing as a social activity and as an entertainment largely originated in the European courts. These dances usually developed from peasant dances and among the most popular were the galliard, basse danse, *allemande, and volta. The English country dances, so popular at Elizabeth I's court, eventually spread to the continent in the early 18th century and, together with the minuet, dominated ballrooms until the introduction of the *waltz. From the late 19th century the US led the way in social dancing with the *cakewalk, *foxtrot, and *tango; it also introduced the tap dance and contributed to the development of *modern dance. Many 20th-century dances were influenced by jazz, notably the *Charleston (1920s) and the jitterbug (1940s); others, such as the rumba, samba, and conga, were of Latin-

American origin. Popular dancing from the 1960s to the 1980s, commencing with the twist, has shown a trend toward freer movement, unregulated by a set sequence of steps and without bodily contact between the partners. *See also* ballet; folk dance; choreography.

dance of death In late medieval art, literature, and drama, an allegorical dance or procession in which the dead lead the living to the grave; also known as the *danse macabre*. It reflected man's preoccupation with death during an age of plague and warfare and was a popular subject for wall paintings in churches and monasteries in France, Germany, and England during the 14th and 15th centuries. The most famous pictorial version is the series of woodcuts designed by *Holbein the Younger between 1523 and 1526.

dandelion A weedy perennial herbaceous plant of the worldwide genus *Taraxacum*, with a basal rosette of jagged toothed leaves and a solitary flower head of bright-yellow florets, up to 2 in (6 cm) across, borne on a stalk up to 20 in (50 cm) high. The seeds have parachutes of fine white hairs and are dispersed by wind. The common dandelion (*T. officinale*) is found throughout the N hemisphere. Its young leaves may be eaten raw in salads or cooked. Family: *Compositae*. □fruit.

Dandie Dinmont terrier A dog breed named for a character in Sir Walter Scott's novel *Guy Mannering* (1812), who owned a pack of them. The Dandie Dinmont has a long body, short legs, and long drooping ears. Its long coat is a mixture of hard and soft hairs and can be either silvery gray to blue-black or fawn to reddish brown. Height: 8–11 in (20–28 cm).

Dandolo, Enrico (c. 1108–1205) Venetian statesman; *doge (1192–1205). He was regarded as the founder of Venice's colonial empire. Dandolo commanded the fleet at the capture of Constantinople during the fourth *Crusade (1204) and secured for Venice a substantial portion of the conquered Greek territories. Defeated near Adrianople in 1205, Dandolo, aged and blind, led the remnants of the Latin army safely back to Constantinople.

dandruff Dry scaling of the scalp, which occurs in everybody to some degree. It is presumed to be due to an infection and may sometimes become more serious, extending to the face. If it is excessive it can be treated with salicylic acid.

Danelaw The area of Anglo-Saxon England E of Watling Street from the Tees River to the Thames River within which Danish laws and customs prevailed from the late 9th to the late 11th centuries.

Daniel (6th century BC) An Old Testament prophet and Jewish exile in Babylon. **The Book of Daniel** is credited to him although some believe it to have been written in the 2nd century BC. The first six chapters tell of various mainly supernatural episodes involving Daniel and his companions under Kings Nebuchadnezzar and Belshazzar. The remaining six chapters are mostly apocalyptic visions concerning the future of the Jews.

Daniell, John Frederic (1790–1845) British chemist, whose researches into electrochemistry led him to invent the *Daniell cell, the first long-lasting reliable source of electric current. He also invented the hygrometer.

Daniell cell A voltaic cell whose positive pole consists of copper immersed in a solution of copper sulfate and whose negative pole consists of zinc in a solution of sulfuric acid or zinc sulfate. It has an almost constant emf of 1.08 volts. Named for J. F. Daniell.

danio An omnivorous tropical freshwater fish of the genera *Danio* or *Brachydanio*. They have a narrow elongated body, 1.6–2.0 in (4–5 cm) long, often attractively colored, and live in shoals. Family: *Cyprinidae*; order: *Cypriniformes*. *See also* zebra fish.

Danish The official language of Denmark, spoken by about five million people. It belongs to the East Scandinavian branch of the North Germanic languages. Separation from the other Scandinavian languages, to which it is closely related, began in about 1000 AD. It is the most altered form of the common ancestral tongue, having lost the case system and incorporated many words from Low German.

D'Annunzio, Gabriele (1863–1938) Italian poet, novelist, and dramatist. During the 1890s he wrote several novels strongly influenced by *Nietzsche's philosophy, notably *The Triumph of Death* (1894). The erotic novel *The Flame of Life* (1900) described his stormy relationship with the actress Eleanora *Duse, who inspired some of his best poetry and for whom he wrote *The Daughter of Jorio* (1904) and other plays. A militant nationalist, he fought heroically in the air force in World War I and headed the Italian occupation of the Dalmatian port of Fiume in 1919. He joined the fascist party but spent his later years in peaceful retirement.

Dante Alighieri (1265–1321) Italian poet. Born into a noble Guelf family of Florence (*see* Guelfs and Ghibellines), he became actively involved in the political struggle between the Black Guelfs, supported by the Pope, and the White Guelfs, who favored a democratic commune. After the Black Guelfs gained control of Florence in 1301, he lived in exile in various Italian cities, finally settling in Ravenna about 1318. His major works include *La vita nuova* (c. 1292), an autobiographical work concerning his youthful love for the mysterious Beatrice (probably the Florentine aristocrat Beatrice Portinari, who was married and who died at the age of 24), and two influential treatises on the value of vernacular Italian as a literary language. *The Divine Comedy*, begun about 1307, is Dante's spiritual testament, narrating his journey, guided by *Virgil, through Hell and Purgatory and finally, guided by Beatrice, to Paradise.

Danton, Georges Jacques (1759–94) French revolutionary. A leader of the *Cordeliers in 1789 and 1790, he became minister of justice in the new republic in 1792. A member of the first Committee of *Public Safety, he was not included in the second and began to lose power as the *Reign of Terror developed. He and his followers were arrested in March, 1794, charged with a conspiracy to overthrow the government, and Danton was guillotined.

Danu In Celtic mythology, the mother of the gods. She was particularly associated with the *Tuatha Dé Danann, but she was also worshiped in other countries under different names.

Danube River The second longest river in Europe after the Volga River. Rising in the Black Forest in Germany, it flows mainly ESE across central and SE Europe to enter the Black Sea in Romania. Immensely important commercially, it is linked by the Altmühl River with canals to the Main and Rhine rivers. Major cities along its course include Vienna, Budapest, and Belgrade. Length: 1770 mi (2850 km).

Danzig. *See* Gdánsk.

Daphne (botany) A genus of evergreen and deciduous shrubs (70 species) of the Old World, including many important ornamentals. The leaves, up to 5 in (12 cm) long, are arranged spirally up the stem. The small, often fragrant, flowers occur in clusters near the ends of branches. They have no petals; the calyx (fused sepals) has four spreading lobes. The fruit is a berry. The genus includes the deciduous mezereon (*D. mezereum*), with reddish-purple flowers and red berries, and the evergreen spurge laurel (*D. laureola*), with greenish flowers and black berries. These shrubs are native to Eurasia and grow to a height of 40 in (100 cm); their berries are poisonous. Family: *Thymeleaceae.*

Daphne (Greek mythology) A mountain nymph who rejected Apollo and, to escape him, was transformed by Gaea into a laurel tree. Apollo made the laurel a symbol of honor and victory.

Daphnia. *See* water flea.

Daphnis In Greek legend, a Sicilian shepherd who was punished with blindness for infidelity in love. He consoled himself with songs and was thus revered as the inventor of pastoral poetry and song.

Da Ponte, Lorenzo (1749–1838) Italian author, originally a priest. Banished from Italy in 1779, he settled in Vienna and there wrote the libretti for Mozart's operas *The Marriage of Figaro* (1786), *Don Giovanni* (1787), and *Cosi fan tutte* (1790). In 1805 he went to the US, where he vigorously promoted Italian culture and published four volumes of memoirs (1823–27).

Dardanelles (Turkish name: Çannakale Boğazi; ancient name: Hellespont) A strait separating European and Asian Turkey and connecting the Sea of Marmara with the Aegean Sea. It was the scene of an unsuccessful campaign in *World War I. Length: 37 mi (60 km); width: 1–4 mi (1.5–6.5 km).

Dards A number of peoples of N Pakistan and Kashmir of Aryan origin, who speak Indo-European languages. There are three major subgroups: the Western (*or* Kafir), the Central (*or* Khowar), and the Eastern, including Shina and Kashmiri. The Dards were converted to Islam during the 14th century.

Dar es Salaam 6 48S 39 12E The capital and main port of Tanzania, on the Indian Ocean. Founded in 1862, it was capital of German East Africa (1891–1916) and of Tanganyika (1916–64). The university was established in 1970. It is the terminus of the Tanzam (Tanzania–Zambia) railroad and an important commercial and industrial center. Population (1988 est): 1,360,000.

Darién Scheme (1698–99) An attempt by the Company of Scotland to establish a colony in the Darién region, in the E of the Isthmus of Panama. The Scots hoped to control trade between the Atlantic and Pacific Oceans but were forced by the Spanish to abandon their settlement, suffering considerable loss of life.

Darius I (c. 558–486 BC) King of Persia (521–486) of the *Achaemenid dynasty. He obtained the throne after defeating a usurper and on his accession he was forced to deal with revolts throughout the empire. He crushed a revolt of Ionian Greeks (499–94), which precipitated the *Greek-Persian Wars. His invasion of mainland Greece was halted by the Persian defeat at *Marathon (490). Darius was a noted administrator, dividing the empire into provinces known as satrapies. He also encouraged trade and improved communications and may have established *Zoroastrianism as the religion of Persia.

Darjeeling 27 02N 88 20E A town in India, in West Bengal. A popular tourist resort, it has splendid views of the Himalayas, including Mount Kangchenjunga. It is a major tea-growing center. Population: 42,662.

darkling beetle A black or dark brown flightless beetle, also called nocturnal ground beetle, belonging to a widely distributed family (*Tenebrionidae*; 15,000 species), particularly common in warm regions. Darkling beetles vary from .08–1.4 in (2–35 mm) in length. Nearly all are scavengers, feeding on decaying vegetation, dung, fungi, or stored grains and cereals. Mealworms (larvae of *Tenebrio molitor*) are common pests of flour mills, etc., and are also reared commercially as food for birds and fish.

Darlan, Jean (Louis Xavier) François (1881–1942) French admiral. He became commander in chief of the navy in 1939 and served in the Vichy government as navy minister and then as vice premier (1941). He lost his post under Laval (1942) and was sent to command French forces in N Africa, where he brought French resistance to the Allies to an end. His assumption of the post of head of state in French Africa aroused considerable hostility. He was assassinated by a French antifascist.

Darling River A river in E Australia, rising in the Great Dividing Range and flowing generally SW across New South Wales before joining the Murray River at Wentworth. Length: 1702 mi (2740 km).

Darmstadt 49 52N 8 39E A city in Germany, in Hessen. It has a 16th-century palace, which survived the bombing in World War II, and a technical university (1836). Its manufactures include machinery and chemicals. Population (1991 est): 139,000.

darnel A *grass, *Lolium temulentum,* also known as poison grass, native to temperate Eurasia. It is often infected by a fungus of the genus *Claviceps* (*see* ergot) and is poisonous; it was formerly a serious contaminant of rye bread but modern techniques can separate darnel seeds from rye seeds.

Darnley, Henry Stuart, Lord (1545–67) The second husband of Mary, Queen of Scots, and father of James I of England. He married Mary, his cousin, in 1565 and his unpopularity was intensified by his involvement in the murder of her secretary David *Riccio (1566). Darnley himself was murdered, probably by *Bothwell.

Darrow, Clarence (1857–1938) US lawyer, famous for his defense of union leaders and of people charged with murder. His defense of Eugene Debs in the case arising from the Pullman strike (1894), although unsuccessful, established his reputation. Through his efforts the labor leader William Haywood (1896–1928) was acquitted (1906) from the charge of assassinating the governor of Idaho. He was counsel for the defense in the famous "monkey" trial in Tennessee (1925), in which a science teacher, John Scopes, was tried for teaching Darwin's theory of evolution. He was a passionate opponent of capital punishment.

darter A slender elongated bird belonging to a family (*Anhingidae*; 4 species) occurring in tropical and subtropical inland waters, also called snakebird because of its snakelike neck. Darters are about 34 in (88 cm) long and black or brown with white markings; males have plumes on the head and neck. They have thin pointed bills for catching fish underwater and are excellent fliers. Order: *Pelecaniformes* (gannets, pelicans, etc.).

Dartmoor A moorland area of England, in SW Devon. A national park since 1951, it consists of a rolling granite upland rising to tors, the highest of which is High Willhays at 2039 ft (621 m). Its many historic remains include stone circles and Bronze Age and Iron Age settlements. Used extensively as a military training area, its dramatic scenery, picturesque wooded valleys, and outdoor recreational facilities have also made it a major tourist attraction. Area: 365 sq mi (945 sq km).

Dartmouth 44 40N 63 35W A city and port in E Canada, in Nova Scotia on Halifax Harbor. It is an industrial and naval center. Population (1991): 67,798.

Dartmouth College v. Woodward (1819) US Supreme Court ruling that the state could not interfere with a corporate charter. Daniel *Webster argued for Dartmouth College trustees that the amending of the college charter by the New

Hampshire legislature was unconstitutional because the original wishes of the donors who had given land to the college were altered.

darts An indoor target game, probably deriving from archery, in which players throw weighted metal darts at a round board from a set distance. A standard board is divided into 20 irregularly numbered sectors; outer and inner rings score double and treble respectively and there is a central bull's-eye. Various games are played, but the most common in competitions is 301, in which players score downward from 301 to 0, beginning and ending on a double.

Darwin 12 23S 130 44E A city in Australia, the capital and chief port of the Northern Territory. The harbor, Port Darwin, adjoins Clarence Strait. It was almost completely destroyed by a cyclone in 1974, but was rebuilt on the same site. It is the focus of a pastoral and mining region; exports include uranium ore. Population (1990): 73,300.

CHARLES DARWIN *In 1860 the Oxford University debate on Darwin's evolutionary theories aroused much controversy and speculation about man's origins, typified by this contemporary cartoon from the English magazine* Punch.

Darwin, Charles Robert (1809–1882) British naturalist, who originated the concept that living things evolve by means of natural selection. Following attempts to study medicine and theology, Darwin's interest in natural history led him to sail with HMS *Beagle* on an expedition to South America and the Pacific (1831–36). As ship's naturalist, Darwin made exhaustive observations of the geology and natural history of the region, recording these in a journal, which he later published.

Following the voyage, Darwin set about the task of analyzing his observations and forming them into a coherent view of nature. In 1858 he presented his findings to the Linnaean Society and in 1859 published his famous *Origin of Species by Means of Natural Selection* (*see* Darwinism). His views aroused bitter controversy because they conflicted with the account of the Creation in the Bible. This culminated in the debate at Oxford in 1860 between Darwin's supporters, led by T. H. *Huxley, and Bishop Samuel Wilberforce. Huxley's arguments won the day. In *The Descent of Man* (1871), Darwin applied his theories to mankind, and—slowly—this fundamental principle of biology gained widespread acceptance.

Darwinism The theory of *evolution based on the work of Charles *Darwin. Darwin drew his conclusions from the following observations: (1) in any population the organisms show individual variations; (2) the size of the population remains constant although more offspring are produced than are necessary to maintain it. He concluded that the forces acting on the population—competition, disease, climate, etc.—resulted in the survival of those best fitted to the environment, a process he called **natural selection.** The survivors would breed, thus passing on their inheritable advantageous variations to their offspring. With time—in a gradually changing environment—this process would result in a change in the whole population and ultimately the evolution of new *species.

Darwin's theory has now been reinforced and modified by subsequent discoveries in genetics, which—among other things—have revealed the source of the variation on which it is based (mostly genetic *mutations). The modern version of his theory is known as **neo-Darwinism**.

Darwin's finches A subfamily of *finches (*Geospizinae*; 13 species) restricted to the Galapagos Islands and also called Galapagos finches. They appear to have evolved from a single species and differ in such features as bill shape, feeding behavior, and habitat preference in order to avoid competition for available resources. The study of these finches by Charles *Darwin provided evidence for his theory of evolution.

dasyure A small carnivorous *marsupial mammal belonging to a family (*Dasyuridae*; 45 species) occurring in Australia (including Tasmania) and New Guinea, also called marsupial cat or native cat. Dasyures, which vary from 12–67 in (30–170 cm) in length, are nocturnal and good climbers, hunting prey that ranges from insects to small wallabies. *See also* Tasmanian devil.

data processing The organization, transmission, and storage of information. **Automatic data processing** usually refers to systems using punch-card machines, paper tape, magnetic tape, etc., as opposed to **electronic data processing**, which is based on electronic computers. In batch processing, data is grouped and coded before processing. The alternative is on-line processing in which each user feeds data into the system continuously. Many systems incorporate both of these forms of processing for different types of work. Most large organizations now use data processing techniques extensively and have a separate department to provide this service for the rest of the organization.

date A *palm tree, *Phoenix dactylifera,* native to N Africa and SW Asia and cultivated from Morocco to India for its fruits, which are rich in sugar and form a staple food in the producing countries. Male and female flowers grow on separate trees (which reach a height of 80 ft [25 m]); the female flowers develop into clusters of up to 1000 single-seeded berries. The trunk of the tree yields a timber and the leaves are used for basketry, weaving, etc.

dating. *See* fission-track dating; helium dating; potassium-argon dating; radiocarbon dating; radiometric dating; rubidium-strontium dating; thermoluminescence.

Datura A worldwide genus of shrubs and herbs (about 10 species), with smooth pointed oval leaves and drooping trumpet-shaped flowers, white, pink, orange, or yellow. The commonest species is the *thorn apple. Some species are popular ornamentals: angel's trumpet (*D. suaveolens*), a Mexican shrub up to 16 ft (5 m) high with white musk-scented flowers, is cultivated in greenhouses in temperate regions. Family: *Solanaceae*.

Daubenton, Louis Jean Marie (1716–1800) French naturalist, who made detailed anatomical descriptions of many animal species. His other interests included paleontology, plant physiology, and mineralogy. He became the first director of the Museum of Natural History, Paris (1793).

Daubigny, Charles-François (1817–78) French landscape painter. He was associated with the *Barbizon school but painted chiefly by the banks of the Seine and Oise, specializing in twilight and moonlight scenes, e.g. *Evening Landscape* (Metropolitan Museum). He strongly influenced the impressionists.

Daudet, Alphonse (1840–97) French novelist, born at Nîmes. He wrote a number of naturalistic novels on the social and political life of his day but is best remembered for his sketches on Provençal subjects, which were originally written for *Le Figaro* and later collected as *Lettres de mon moulin* (1868). He also wrote plays, notably *L'Arlésienne* (1872), for which Bizet composed incidental music. His son **Léon Daudet** (1867–1942) was a political journalist and novelist. He was violently right-wing in his views and in 1899 helped to found the influential royalist periodical *L'Action française*. His critical essays were published as *Le Stupide XIXᵉ siècle* (1922) and his memoirs, *Souvenirs* (1914–21), cover the years 1890–1905.

Daugavpils (name from 1893 until 1920: Dvinsk) 55 52N 26 31E A city in Latvia. It is an important rail junction and a commercial and industrial center. Population (1991): 129,000.

Daughters of the American Revolution (DAR) US organization for direct female descendants of participants in the *American Revolution. Founded in 1890 and chartered by the US Congress in 1896, it has a large genealogical library in Washington, DC and promotes history, education, patriotism, and the preservation of historic sites through its almost 3000 chapters and about 190,000 members nationwide.

Daumier, Honoré (1808–79) French caricaturist, painter, and sculptor. As a cartoonist for *La Caricature* in Paris he was imprisoned (1832) for depicting the king as Rabelais' gluttonous giant Gargantua. He produced numerous documentary lithographs, such as *Rue Transnonain*. After 1835 he worked for *Charivari*, satirizing the legal and medical professions and other social and political targets. Although his paintings were largely ignored in his lifetime, *The Washerwoman* (Louvre) and *The Third Class Railroad Carriage* (Ottawa) are admired as forerunners of *impressionism.

dauphin From 1350 until 1830 the title of the heirs to the French crown. It was the personal name, and later became the title, of the rulers of the *Dauphiné, which was purchased by the future Charles V in 1350. After becoming king (1364), he granted the Dauphiné and its accompanying title to his son, thus establishing a precedent that was followed until the abdication of Charles X.

Davao 7 05N 125 38E A port in the SE Philippines, in SE Mindanao. The island's commercial center, it grew rapidly in the 1960s and now covers an extensive area. It has timber and fishing industries and exports hemp and coffee. Population (1990 est): 850,000.

Davenport, Charles Benedict (1866–1944) US zoologist, who introduced the use of statistical techniques into biological research. The need for statistics arose from his studies of population genetics.

Davenport 41 32N 90 41W A city in E central Iowa, on the Mississippi River opposite Rock Island, Ill. It was established as a town in 1838. Aluminum is made here. Machine parts, aircraft parts, and food processing are also important industries. Population (1990): 95,333.

David (d. 962 BC) King of Israel (c. 1000–962). Born in Bethlehem, the son of Jesse, David was anointed by Samuel as the successor of Saul, the first King of Israel. He became a close friend of Saul's son, Jonathan, but his successes against the Philistines, including the slaying of Goliath, aroused Saul's jealousy and he became an outlaw. After the death of Saul and Jonathan, David was proclaimed King of Hebron and then of all Israel. He conquered Jerusalem, making it the nation's political and religious center, finally defeated the Philistines, and united the tribes of Israel. His reign was troubled by the revolt of his son Absalom, who was eventually defeated and killed. David was succeeded by Solomon, his son by Bathsheba. He was the author of some of the psalms. According to the Jewish prophets, the Messiah must be a descendant of David.

David I (1084–1153) King of the Scots (1124–53). The first monarch to recognize Matilda as successor to Henry I of England, he used her cause as an excuse to invade N England (1138) after Stephen had seized the throne. Stephen defeated him in the battle of the Standard (1138), near Northallerton. David founded or refounded over a dozen monasteries.

David II (1324–71) King of the Scots (1329–71), succeeding his father Robert the Bruce. He was forced into exile (1334–41) in France by Edward de *Balliol. He supported France against Edward III of England and was captured and imprisoned (1346–57) by the English.

David, Gerard (c. 1460–1523) Dutch painter, who was born in Oudewater (Holland) but settled in Bruges. Apart from his use of Renaissance detail in *Judgment of Cambyses* (Bruges), he was little influenced by the Italianate style current in Antwerp and continued to paint in the tradition of his predecessors.

David, Jacques Louis (1748–1825) French neoclassical painter, known for his historical paintings and portraits. He trained under Joseph-Marie Vien (1716–1809), before winning the Prix de Rome (1774), which enabled him to study in Italy (1775–80). His mature works depicted heroic scenes from Republican Rome and ancient Greece, e.g. *Oath of the Horatii* (Louvre). During the Revolution he painted some of its martyrs, e.g. *Death of Marat* (Brussels), and actively supported Robespierre; after Robespierre's fall he was imprisoned (1794–95). As court painter to □Napoleon I from 1804, his paintings illustrate imperial successes, e.g. *Napoleon Crowning Josephine* (Louvre). After Napoleon's fall David was exiled and died in Brussels.

David, St (*or* St Dewi; c. 520–600 AD) The patron saint of Wales and first abbot of Menevia (now St David's). He was also a missionary and the founder of many churches in Wales. Feast day: March 1. Emblem: a dove.

David ap Gruffudd (d. 1283) The brother of *Llywelyn ap Gruffudd, after whose death (1282) David claimed the title Prince of Wales. He was executed by Edward I for leading the Welsh in rebellion against him.

Davies, W(illiam) H(enry) (1871–1940) British poet. He lived for many years as a tramp in England and America before publishing the first of many volumes of simple rural poetry in 1905. G. B. Shaw contributed an introduction to his *Autobiography of a Super-Tramp* (1907).

da Vinci, Leonardo. *See* Leonardo da Vinci.

Davis, Benjamin Oliver, Sr. (1877–1970) US Army officer; the first African-American general in the Army. He served in the *Spanish-American War, the Philippines (1901–02), taught at Wilberforce University, Ohio (1905–09), in Liberia (1911–12), and again in the Philippines during World War I. Again teaching military science until 1938, he took over the 369th Harlem Regiment of the New York National Guard and was made a brigadier general in 1940.

Davis, Bette (Ruth Elizabeth D.; 1908–89) US film actress. During the 1930s and 1940s she gave intense and dramatic performances in such films as *Of Human Bondage* (1934), *Jezebel* (1938), *Dark Victory* (1939), *The Little Foxes* (1941) and *All About Eve* (1950). In recent years she has appeared in the roles of elderly eccentric or neurotic women.

Davis, David (1815–86) US politician and Supreme Court associate justice. An active lawyer and judge in Illinois, he was a force behind Abraham *Lincoln's nomination for president in 1860. In turn, he was appointed an associate justice (1862–77) to the US Supreme Court, where he was best known for his decision in *Ex parte Milligan* (1866) that said that military courts are not lawful in nonmilitary areas. He later served in the US Senate as a Democrat from Illinois (1877–83).

Davis, Jefferson (1808–89) US military and political leader; president of the Confederate States of America (1861–65). Born in Todd County, Kentucky, Davis graduated from West Point in 1828 and began his military career with service in the *Black Hawk War in 1832. He later returned to civilian life and was elected to the US House of Representatives from Mississippi in 1845. The following year, Davis resigned from Congress to serve in the *Mexican War. He was later US senator (1847–51) and served as secretary of war in the administration of President Franklin *Pierce. Returning to the US Senate (1857–61), Davis supported slavery and the rights of states against federal interference. With the secession of Mississippi from the Union in 1861, he returned to the South and was elected president of the Confederate government. He held that office until the end of the *Civil War, when he was arrested in Georgia by federal troops. From 1865 to 1867, he was imprisoned and indicted for treason, but all charges against him were eventually dropped. His later years were spent at his home in Mississippi where he wrote *The Rise and Fall of the Confederate Government* (1881).

Davis, John (*or* J. Davys; c. 1550–1605) English navigator, who went on three voyages in search of the *Northwest Passage (1585, 1586, 1587), passing through the strait named for him to Baffin Bay. In 1592, seeking the Magellan Strait, he discovered the Falkland Islands. On his last voyage to the East Indies, he was killed by Japanese pirates near Singapore.

Davis, Miles (1926–91) US jazz trumpeter and composer, one of the originators of *cool jazz. He studied music at the Juilliard School in New York and formed his own band in 1948. He has made a number of influential albums, including *Miles Ahead* and the innovative *Kind of Blue*.

Davis Cup An international tennis competition that was instituted in 1900 for teams of men. The US and Australia have won it most often.

Davis Strait A section of the Atlantic Ocean, between SW Greenland and Baffin Island (Canada). Length: 400 mi (640 km). Width: 200–400 mi (320–640 km).

Davitt, Michael (1846–1906) Irish nationalist. He joined the *Fenians in 1865 and after seven years' imprisonment founded the *Land League (1879). Davitt urged the reconciliation of extreme and constitutional nationalism.

Davos (Romansh name: Tarau) 46 47N 9 50E A mountain resort in E Switzerland. Comprising two villages at a height of about 5100 ft (1555 m), it is a health resort and winter-sports center, with the renowned Parsenn ski run.

Davy, Sir Humphry (1778–1829) British chemist. Davy began his career by discovering the value of nitrous oxide as an anesthetic. For this work he was invited to join the Royal Institution in London, where his most important work was the discovery of many new metallic elements. By passing electricity through molten metallic compounds, he discovered potassium in 1807 and the following year, sodium, calcium, barium, magnesium, and strontium. He also encouraged the young Michael *Faraday, employing him as his assistant.

Dawes, Charles Gates (1865–1951) US financier, political leader, and diplomat. Born in Marietta, Ohio, he served as comptroller of the currency in the administration of Pres. William McKinley and as US budget director of Pres. Warren Harding. He later headed a commission to reconstruct the post-World War I German economy. The report of this commission, known as the Dawes Plan (1924), saved Europe from economic collapse and earned him, jointly with Austen Chamberlain, the Nobel Peace Prize in 1925. From 1925 to 1929, Dawes served as US vice president during the administration of Pres. Calvin Coolidge. Pres. Herbert Hoover named him US ambassador to Great Britain (1929–32).

Dawes Act (1887) US law that prepared for Indian citizenship and terminated the reservation system. Indian reservations were broken up and distributed to individuals for farming. In 1924, when citizenship would be granted to the Indians, these lands could be sold. The act was named for Senator Henry Laurens Dawes (1816–1903), its sponsor.

dawn redwood A deciduous conifer, *Metasequoia glyptostroboides,* thought to be extinct until 1941, when the first specimen of modern times was discovered in SW China. Growing to a height of 113 ft (35 m), dawn redwood has soft needles grouped in two rows and rounded green long-stalked cones. It is quite widely grown for ornament. Family: *Taxodiaceae.*

Dawson 64 04N 139 24W A town in NW Canada, in the Yukon on the *Klondike River. During the gold rush it had over 25,000 inhabitants. Population: 1252.

Dawson Creek 55 45N 120 15W A town in W Canada, in British Columbia at the beginning of the *Alaska Highway. Population: 10,528.

Day, Clarence Shepard (1874–1935) US writer. After working as a stockbroker and serving in the Navy, he wrote *This Simian World* (1920), *The Crow's Nest* (1921), and *Thoughts Without Words* (1928). He is best known for his works about his family: *God and My Father* (1932), *Life with Father* (1935), and *Life with Mother* (published posthumously; 1937). *Life with Father* was adapted for the stage in 1939.

Dayak (*or* Dyak) A people of Borneo and Sarawak, speaking languages of the Indonesian section of the Malayo-Polynesian family. There are many groups including the Bahau of central and E Borneo, the Land Dayak of SW Borneo and the Iban (*or* Sea Dayak) of Sarawak. They are a riverine people, who live in large communal wooden huts (longhouses). They live by rice cultivation, fishing, and hunting with blowpipes. Formerly head hunting was common.

Dayan, Moshe (1915–81) Israeli general. Born in Palestine, during the 1930s he fought with the Haganah (Jewish irregulars) and in World War II in the British Army, losing an eye in battle in 1941. From 1953 until 1958 he was chief of Israel's general staff. He was defense minister in 1967 and from 1973 to 1974, when he resigned after criticism of Israel's unpreparedness in the Arab-Israeli War of 1973–74. In 1977 he became foreign minister but resigned in 1979 as a result of disagreement with Begin's cabinet on policy toward the Arabs.

Day Lewis, C(ecil) (1904–72) British poet and critic. He was a leading left-wing poet of the 1930s but his later verse, as in *The Whispering Roots* (1970), was more purely lyrical. He published translations of Virgil's *Aeneid* (1952) and other works and was appointed poet laureate in 1968. As "Nicholas Blake" he wrote a series of sophisticated detective stories.

Daylight Savings Time A time system in which one hour, usually, is added to local (clock) time, i.e. to Eastern Standard Time, so prolonging useful daylight hours. This system is used in temperate latitudes in spring, summer, and early autumn.

day lily A herbaceous plant of the genus *Hemerocallis*, native to Europe and Asia and cultivated as garden flowers. They have long narrow leaves and long stalks bearing clusters of orange or yellow lily-like flowers, which wither after a short time. *H. lilio-asphodelinus* is grown for its sweet scent, and garden hybrids of *H. flava* bloom for a longer time, producing orange, yellow, pink, and red flowers. Family: *Liliaceae*.

Dayton 39 45N 84 10W A city in Ohio, on the Great Miami River. It was the home of the Wright brothers; the nearby Wright-Patterson Air Force Base is a center for military aviation research. Population (1990): 182,044.

Daytona Beach 29 11N 81 01W A resort in Florida, on the Atlantic coast. Its hard white beach has been used for motor racing since 1902. Population (1990): 61,921.

Dazai Osamu (Tsushima Shuji; 1909–48) Japanese novelist. His fiction exploited the conflict between his wealthy family background and his radical political beliefs. His postwar novels, notably *The Setting Sun* (1947) and *No Longer Human* (1948), expressed the nihilistic mood of a generation bereft of the support of traditional values. He committed suicide in 1948.

D-Day (June 6, 1944) The day on which the Allied invasion of Normandy was launched from Britain during *World War II. It led to the liberation of France from German occupation and the final defeat of Germany.

DDT (dichlorophenyltrichloroethane) An organochlorine compound widely used as a contact *insecticide. It is active against many insects, including mosquitoes, flies, fleas, lice, and bedbugs, specifically affecting the central nervous system. However, many insects have become resistant to DDT, which is a very stable compound and accumulates not only in their tissues but also in the tissues of the animals that prey on them, causing toxic effects. Because the chemical has long-lasting effects, its use is closely regulated.

deadly nightshade (*or* belladonna) A branching perennial herb, *Atropa belladonna*, up to 5 ft (1.5 m) tall and native to Eurasia. It has dull green leaves, up to 8 in (20 cm) long, and solitary purple or greenish bell-shaped flowers. The shiny black berries taste sweet but contain a deadly poison. The plant is a source of a variety of alkaloids, especially hyoscyamine and atropine. Family: *Solanaceae*. See also nightshade.

DEADLY NIGHTSHADE *This notorious plant grows in woodlands, thickets, and scrub. It flowers from June to August and produces its deadly black berries from August to November.*

dead men's fingers A colonial soft *coral, *Alcyonium digitatum,* so called because of its fleshy pink fingerlike appearance when out of water. The individual *polyps have an internal skeleton of separate calcareous spicules, which give the tissues a gelatinous consistency. Colonies, which are white, yellow, pink, or orange, are common on rocky coasts of NW Europe.

Dead Sea A lake in E Israel and W Jordan. It is fed by the Jordan River and, having no outlet, is highly saline and supports no life. Area: 401 sq mi (1050 sq km).

Dead Sea Scrolls A group of Hebrew and Aramaic manuscript scrolls, originally stored in jars, found in 11 caves in the area of Khirbat *Qumran, NW of the Dead Sea. The first were accidentally discovered in 1947; the rest were recovered as late as the 1950s. Altogether there are about 500 different documents, dating from 250 BC to 70 AD, which seem to have formed the library of a Jewish, perhaps *Essene, community that existed from about 125 BC to the Jewish revolt in 66–70 AD, when the scrolls were hidden in the caves for safekeeping. They include texts of many Old Testament books, commentaries, prayers, psalms, and material peculiar to the community, including an apocalyptic prophecy. They are valuable as evidence of the accuracy of previously known Old Testament texts, for the information they provide about a Jewish community contemporaneous with early Christianity, and archeologically as examples of the Hebrew and Aramaic scripts of the period.

Deadwood 44 05N 115 40W A town in W Central South Dakota, in the N Black Hills. A frontier mining town named for the dead wood left from a forest fire, it thrived during the gold rush (1875–1876). Calamity Jane and Wild Bill Hickok lived and are buried here. Western frontier days are recreated in tourist attractions. Population (1990): 1830.

deafness A common condition in which hearing is absent or impaired. Deafness is described as either conductive, in which the mechanism for transmitting sound to the inner ear is defective, or sensorineural, when there is damage to the auditory nerve or the part of the brain concerned with hearing. Conductive deafness may be caused by wax in the outer ear, infection in the middle ear, or—as with Beethoven—otosclerosis (a disease of the small bones in the middle ear). Sensorineural deafness occurs commonly in old people but can also be due to infection, head injury, drugs (such as streptomycin), *Ménière's disease, or exposure to continuous loud noise. Some forms of deafness can be treated by removing wax, curing infection, or by microsurgery; untreatable forms can be alleviated with a *hearing aid.

Deák, Ferenc (1803–76) Hungarian statesman. After the *Hungarian Revolution of 1848, Deák became the country's minister of justice and in 1849, after the fall of the revolutionaries, the leader of the opposition to Austrian dominance. Deák believed in the dynastic union of Austria and Hungary but desired separate constitutions and kingdoms, and he was largely responsible for the establishment in 1867 of *Austria-Hungary.

Deakin, Alfred (1856–1919) Australian statesman, who was three times prime minister (1903–04, 1905–08, 1909–10). He succeeded Sir Edmund *Barton, and like him was a member of the Federal Convention that drafted the constitution for the new Commonwealth of Australia. He was a considerable influence on the early development of the Commonwealth and introduced the "White Australia" policy restricting nonwhite immigration.

Dean, Dizzy (Jay Hanna D.; 1911–74) US baseball pitcher. He played for the St Louis Cardinals (1930, 1932–37) and the Chicago Cubs (1938–41) and achieved 150 career wins before an injury forced his retirement.

Dean, James (James Byron; 1931–55) US film actor. He trained at the Actors' Studio, and became a cult hero for his generation. His films were *East of Eden* (1954), *Rebel Without A Cause* (1955), and *Giant* (1955), released following his death in a car crash.

Deane, Silas (1737–89) US patriot and diplomat. Active in movements leading to American independence, Deane was sent to Paris by the Continental Congress to buy war supplies and negotiate treaties of commerce and alliance with France (1776–78). Accused of embezzlement, he went into exile, settling in London.

Dearborn 42 18N 83 14W A city in Michigan, near Detroit. The birthplace of Henry Ford, it is the headquarters of the Ford Motor Company. Population (1990): 89,286.

death The permanent cessation of all bodily functions in an organism. Until recently a person was medically pronounced dead when his heartbeat and breathing movements ceased, but since the advent of mechanical ventilators the heartbeat may be maintained long after "natural" breathing has stopped as a result of irreversible brain damage. Death is therefore now defined on the basis of brain function: when the parts of the brain that control respiration and other vital reflexes have ceased to function, the patient is said to be brain dead, i.e. truly dead, although his heart may continue to beat for some time with the aid of mechanical life-support systems. With recent advances in transplant surgery, it is important to establish brain death in those patients who could be suitable donors of kidneys and other organs.

death cap A highly poisonous mushroom, *Amanita phalloides*, fairly common in and near deciduous woodlands. Its cap, 2.8–5.0 in (7–12 cm) in diameter, is usually pale greenish yellow but may be olive green or grayish. The stalk is white or greenish white, with a baglike sheath (volva) at its base. Death cap can be fatal, even in small amounts, and symptoms may not appear for up to 24 hours.

death's-head moth A *hawk moth, Acherontia atropos, with a wingspan of 5 in (125 mm), found in Europe, Africa, and Asia, whose thoracic markings resemble a skull and crossbones. These moths emit squeaks when handled and may enter beehives to steal honey.

Death Valley A desert area in SE California. The hottest and driest part of North America, its temperatures exceed 102°F (39°C) during summer. The flora and fauna that survive these harsh conditions are of interest to scientists and many tourists are attracted to the area during winter. In 1933 it was declared a national monument.

deathwatch beetle A widely distributed wood-boring beetle, *Xestobium rufovillosum*, about 28 in (7 mm) long, that can cause immense damage to old buildings and furniture. It lays eggs in small crevices in the wood and the larvae tunnel in, eventually reducing it to powder. The pupae often make knocking sounds by repeatedly striking their heads against the walls of their burrows. Family: *Anobiidae*.

DeBakey, Michael Ellis (1908–) US physician and surgeon. An innovator in the techniques of heart surgery, he was responsible for the invention of the roller pump for blood transfusions (1932). He pioneered a grafting method for aneurysms, performed the first artery bypass operation (1964), and was the first to successfully implant a heart pump in a human (1966).

de Bary, Heinrich Anton (1831–88) German botanist and founder of mycology (the study of fungi). He determined the life cycles of many fungi, including important disease-causing species. In 1866 he showed that lichens each comprise a fungus and an alga living in a mutually beneficial partnership. For this he coined the word symbiosis.

Debré, Michel (1912–) French statesman; prime minister (1959–62). A Gaullist, Debré became prominent as a member of the Saar Economic Mission in 1947. He became a member of the Rassemblement pour la République upon its formation in 1976 by Jacques *Chirac. Debré is the author of many works on politics and economics.

Debrecen 47 30N 21 37E A city in E Hungary. It was a center of Protestantism in E Europe. Lajos Kossuth proclaimed Hungary independent of the Habsburgs in the Great Church of Debrecen in 1849. There are now various industries and a university (1912). Population (1988 est): 217,500.

de Broglie, Louis Victor, 7th Duc (1892–1987) French physicist, who won the 1929 Nobel Prize for his theory that elementary particles have associated waves, known as *de Broglie waves. The theory was confirmed by the subsequent observation of *electron diffraction and forms the basis of the branch of quantum mechanics known as *wave mechanics.

de Broglie wave A wave associated with any moving elementary particle with nonzero mass, since such particles exhibit wave properties under appropriate conditions. For example, they may be diffracted by a crystal lattice. The de Broglie wavelength of a particle mass m and velocity v is h/mv, where h is the *Planck constant. They were first postulated by Louis *de Broglie in 1923.

Debs, Eugene V(ictor) (1855–1926) US labor organizer and political leader. Born in Terre Haute, Indiana, Debs worked as a railroad employee and became active in the Brotherhood of Locomotive Firemen. In 1880 he was named national secretary and treasurer of the Brotherhood and was elected to the Indiana legislature in 1884. An outspoken advocate of organized labor, he helped to establish the American Railway Union in 1893 and was imprisoned for his role in the *Pullman Strike in the following year. Debs established the Social Democratic Party of America in 1898 and ran for president as a socialist candidate five times. In 1905 he helped to found the *Industrial Workers of the World (IWW). Debs was convicted during World War I of violation of the Espionage Act, and his 1920 campaign for president won almost a million votes. He was released by President Harding in 1921 and wrote *Walls and Bars* (1927), an exposé of prison conditions.

Deburau, Jean-Gaspard (1796–1846) French pantomimist, born in Bohemia. He joined a troupe of acrobats in Paris in 1811 and created the standard pantomime character of Pierrot, the pale and melancholy lover.

Debussy, Claude (Achille) (1862–1918) French composer. He spent most of his life in Paris and is regarded as the originator of musical impressionism. He married twice and wrote his *Children's Corner Suite* (1906–08) for his daughter Chou-chou. Debussy developed an individual style that employed whole-tone, pentatonic, and modal scales as well as unusual harmonies and tone colors. His most famous works include *Prélude à l'après-midi d'un faune* (for orchestra; 1892–94), the opera *Pelléas et Mélisande* (1892–1902), *La Mer* (three symphonic sketches; 1903–05), a string quartet, and a sonata for flute, viola, and harp. He also wrote sonatas for cello and for violin; piano music, including two sets of *Images* (1905, 1907) and 24 preludes (1910–13); and songs.

Debye, Peter Joseph Wilhelm (1884–1966) Dutch physicist and chemist, who was awarded the 1936 Nobel Prize for chemistry for his theoretical work on *dipole moments and the behavior of ions in solution. He also extended the technique of *X-ray crystallography so that it could be applied to powders. Most of his work was done in Germany but in 1940 he left Europe for Cornell University, where he remained until his retirement in 1950.

Decadents A group of late-19th-century French symbolist poets and their contemporaries in England. They aimed to create a literature liberated from all moral and social responsibilities. A journal entitled *Le Décadent* was published in France from 1886 to 1889. Poets linked with the movement included *Rimbaud, *Verlaine, and *Mallarmé in France, and Arthur *Symons, Oscar *Wilde, and Ernest *Dowson in England. *See also* Aesthetic movement.

Decapoda A worldwide order of *crustaceans (over 8500 species), with five pairs of thoracic appendages—anterior pincers and four pairs of walking legs. They include the *shrimps and *prawns (suborder: *Natantia,* "swimming forms") and *lobsters, *crayfish, and *crabs (suborder: *Reptantia,* "walking forms").

decathlon An athletic competition for men, consisting of 10 events over two days. On the first are 100 m sprint, long jump, shot put, high jump, and 400 m sprint; on the second are 110 m hurdles, discus throw, pole vault, javelin throw, and 1500 m run. Competitors score for performances in each event, the winner gaining the highest total.

Decatur, Stephen (1779–1820) US naval officer. He established his reputation in the war with the Barbary pirates of Tripoli (1800–05), in which he raided Tripoli harbor and burned the captured US frigate *Philadelphia* (1804). In the *War of 1812 he defeated two British frigates (1812, 1815). He was killed in a duel.

Decatur 39 51N 89 32W A city in central Illinois, on the Sagamon River. Abraham Lincoln practiced law and received his first endorsement for president here in 1860. Decatur manufactures heavy brass items, heavy machinery, electronic parts, and food products. Population (1990): 83,885.

Deccan A region of India, considered either as the entire peninsula or as the arid plateau between the Narmada and Krishna Rivers. Sloping gently from the Western to the Eastern Ghats, it is cut by many rivers flowing E.

December Twelfth month of the year. Derived from *decem* (Latin: ten) when it was the tenth month of the Roman 10-month calendar. It has 31 days, and it is on December 25 that Christmas is observed. The zodiac signs for December are Sagittarius and Capricorn; the flowers are holly and narcissus, and the birthstones are the ruby, turquoise, or zircon.

Decembrists (*or* Dekabrists) Members of an anti-Tsarist revolt in December, 1825, following the death of Alexander I. They were members of various clandestine organizations formed after the Napoleonic Wars by former military officers, who, after being exposed to western liberalism, had become discontented on their return to Russia with the country's reactionary government. The revolt failed, largely because of poor organization. Five leaders were executed and their followers imprisoned or exiled to Siberia.

decibel (dB) A unit used to compare two power levels on a logarithmic scale. It is one-tenth of a bel, but this unit is rarely used. Two power levels P and P_0 differ by n decibels when $n = 10 \log_{10} P/P_0$. The unit is often used to express a sound intensity in which case P_0 is usually taken as the intensity of the lowest audible note of the same frequency as P. *See also* phon.

deciduous plants. *See* evergreen plants.

decimal system The number system in common use, having a base 10 and thus using ten separate numerals. It also involves the use of a decimal point to express numbers less than one, instead of the method of fractions: for example, $\frac{1}{4}$ is expressed as 0.25. The decimal system was invented by the Hindus and adopted by the Arabs in the 9th century (*see also* mathematics). The use of decimal fractions originated in Italy in the 12th century but was first formalized by the mathematician Simon Stévin (1548–1620) in 1585. The use of the decimal point did not occur until the beginning of the 18th century. Decimalization of currency systems was introduced by France after the Revolution and followed by most other European and American countries, except for Britain, which did not decimalize until 1971. *See also* metric system.

Decius, Gaius Messius Quintus Trajanus (c. 201–51 AD) Roman emperor (249–51). Decius attempted to restore Roman traditions, persecuting Christians in the name of Roman state cults. He was defeated and killed by the Goths at Abrittus.

Declaration of Independence The formal document adopted by the 13 colonies on July 4, 1776. After the decision of the Second Continental Congress early in June 1776 to seek independence from Great Britain, a committee consisting of John *Adams, Benjamin *Franklin, Thomas *Jefferson, Robert *Livingstone, and Roger *Sherman was appointed to draft the formal document. Although Adams and Franklin assisted in its formulation, the text of the Declaration was written by Jefferson. Drawing on the principles of the political philosophy of John *Locke and Charles-Louis *Montesquieu, Jefferson enumerated the specific grievances of the American colonies against the British government and asserted the general principles of human rights that he believed justified independence. The Declaration of Independence quickly became one of the most influential proclamations in the western political tradition.

Declaratory Act. *See* Stamp Act.

declination. *See* magnetic declination; right ascension.

decomposition The breakdown of the complex organic molecules of dead plants and animals and animal wastes into their simple components by bacteria and fungi. These microorganisms (**decomposers**) serve as the ultimate link in *food chains: the simple nitrogenous compounds released into the soil by decomposition can be used by plants (the producers) to manufacture their own food. *See also* nitrogen cycle.

decompression sickness (*or* caisson disease) An occupational hazard of pilots and underwater divers caused by too rapid a return to normal atmospheric pressure. At high pressures large amounts of gas can be carried in the blood. A rapid return to normal pressure causes nitrogen (the main component of inhaled air) to form bubbles out in the blood; this interrupts the blood supply to the tissues, producing joint pain (the bends), general discomfort, and respiratory problems (the chokes). Decompression sickness is prevented by a slow return to atmospheric pressure; it is treated by placing the patient in a hyperbaric chamber.

Decorated The style of □gothic architecture predominant in England between 1300 and 1370. In contrast to the geometric restraint of its predecessor, *Early English, Decorated is characterized by complex flowing patterns, especially in window tracery. Roof vaults were intricately ribbed and the ogee or double-curved *arch with elaborate ornamentation became common. The early 14th-century nave of Exeter Cathedral demonstrates the style's profusion of ribs and arches. *Compare* Flamboyant.

decorative arts Arts and crafts the function of which is primarily ornamental. The modern concept of the decorative arts was pioneered by such designers as William *Morris. Despite persistent attempts to demonstrate that mass production need not necessarily compromise design, modern endeavors in the decorative arts tend to center on small workshops producing individually handmade items in such fields as *bookbinding, *enamelwork, *jewelry, *pottery, and wallpaper.

Dedekind, (Julius Wilhelm) Richard (1831–1916) German mathematician, who gave the irrational *numbers the same level of respectability as the rational numbers. He achieved this by means of the Dedekind cut, a method of cutting an infinite line representing the real numbers. He became involved in the controversy between Georg *Cantor and Leopold Kronecker (1823–91), taking Cantor's side against Kronecker's attempt to banish all but the integers from mathematics.

deduction In logic, argument from general principles to particular conclusions. It is thus analytic and certain, in contrast to *induction, the conclusions of which are never more than strong probabilities.

de Duve, Christian (1917–   ) Belgian biochemist, noted for his contributions to cell biology. De Duve discovered lysosomes, components of living cells that are responsible for breaking down substances within the cell. He shared a Nobel Prize (1974) with Albert Claude and George Emil Palade.

Dee River The name of three rivers in the UK. **1.** A river in NE Scotland, flowing E to the North Sea at Aberdeen. Length: 87 mi (140 km). **2.** A river in North Wales and NW England, rising in Gwynedd and flowing E and N through Llangollen and Chester to the Irish Sea. Length: 70 mi (112 km). **3.** A river in S Scotland, flowing S to the Solway Firth. Length: 50 mi (80 km).

deed In law, a document in writing, signed, sealed and delivered, transferring a right over property (title-deed) or creating an obligation on its maker. To be binding it need not fulfill conditions applicable to a *contract. A deed may be between two parties, to establish mutual obligations, or it may involve one party only (deed poll), as, for example, when a person publishes a change of name.

deer A *ruminant mammal of the family *Cervidae* (41 species), occurring mainly in the N hemisphere, although a few are found in South America and N Africa and they have been introduced to SE Asia and Australasia. Nearly all deer have bony antlers that are shed and replaced every year (the *Chinese water deer and the *musk deer are exceptions). Deer range in size from the *elk (up to 7 ft [2 m] high) to the South American pudu, which is only about 16 in (40 cm) high at the shoulder. Most deer live in herds but some, such as the *muntjac, are solitary.

deerhound A long-established British breed of dog, formerly used for hunting deer. It has a deep-chested long body with long legs and a long tapering head with small ears. The wiry coat is usually blue-gray but may be shades of brown or fawn. Height: 30 in (76 cm) (dogs); 28 in (71 cm) (bitches).

deer mouse A North American rodent belonging to the genus *Peromyscus* (60 species), also called white-footed mouse; 5–15 in (12–37 cm) long including the tail (2–8 in [4–20 cm]), these climbing and burrowing animals have large eyes and ears; they are omnivorous and are often used as laboratory animals. Family: *Cricetidae.*

defamation In law, a false and derogatory statement about another person that causes him to be hated, ridiculed, or held in contempt or that tends to injure him in his profession or trade. It is libel if made in a permanent form (e.g. in writing, newspapers, broadcasts, sound films) and slander if made in a transient form, by spoken words or gestures. The remedy for both types of defamation is by civil proceedings, although libel may also be a crime if its publication is calculated to provoke a breach of the peace. Not only the originator of a libel but everyone who has subsequently repeated or published it may be sued by the person libeled. Action for libel cannot be brought against "privileged" proceedings or statements. Judicial and parliamentary proceedings, for example, are "absolutely privileged" and nothing said in them can be the subject of a libel action. A statement judged to be a fair comment on a matter of public interest is also not actionable as defamation.

Defense, Department of US cabinet-level agency that provides military forces for deterrence of war and for the protection of the country. The Secretary of Defense directs the department, which includes the *Army, *Navy, *Air Force, and *Marine Corps. Originally established as the war department (1789), it was reorganized (1947; 1949) and renamed (1949).

defense mechanisms In psychoanalysis, the means by which undesirable and antisocial impulses can be unconsciously avoided or controlled by the subject. *Repression, *sublimation, and *projection are important defenses. Others include reaction formation, in which an impulse is turned into its opposite, as when one displays excessive concern for a person whom one secretly hates; and displacement, in which an impulse is transferred onto a more acceptable subject (e.g. kicking the dog instead of the boss). Defense mechanisms are a part of normal life, but if they become excessively strong they can distort the development of personality and even give rise to symptoms of *neurosis.

deficit financing The fiscal policy of stimulating the economy by government spending in excess of revenue by borrowing to finance the resultant deficit. Deficit financing was advocated by the British economist J. M. *Keynes as a method of countering the *Depression of the 1930s; although Keynes' ideas were not assimilated in time to influence that period, deficit financing became normal practice after World War II (*see* multiplier; national debt).

deflation A government action to slow down the economy, with the aim of easing *inflation or cutting down on imports and thus helping the *balance of payments. Both monetary policy (credit "squeeze") and fiscal policy (increasing taxes, cutting government spending) can be used to deflate the economy. *See also* multiplier.

Defoe, Daniel (1660–1731) British novelist, economist, and journalist. His early career as a merchant ended in bankruptcy in 1692. A Nonconformist, he welcomed the arrival of William of Orange in 1688 and wrote *The True-Born Englishman* (1701) in his defense. He subsequently worked as a journalist. His famous novels were written late in his career, *Robinson Crusoe* in 1719 and *Moll Flanders* and *Colonel Jack* in 1722.

defoliant A chemical applied to foliage in order to cause premature shedding of leaves; examples are ammonium thiocyanate and cacodylic acid. Defoliants are used to aid mechanical harvesting of cotton and for other peaceful uses. They are also employed in *chemical warfare.

De Forest, Lee (1873–1961) US electrical engineer, who invented the triode valve (1906), which became the basic *amplifier in all electronic circuits until superseded by the transistor. In the early 1920s he developed a method of converting sound waves into light of varying intensity, which was used as the basis of recording film soundtracks.

Degas, (Hilaire Germain) Edgar (1834–1917) French painter and sculptor, born in Paris. He trained in the École des Beaux-Arts, where he was influenced by the draftsmanship of *Ingres. His early works were portraits, e.g. *The Bellelli Family* (Louvre), recalling the old masters that he had studied in Italy (1856–60), and history paintings, e.g. *Young Spartans Exercising* (National Gallery, London). From the mid-1860s he turned to painting contemporary scenes, particularly of ballet and racecourses. In these works, characterized by informal poses and unusual angles, Degas was indebted both to Japanese prints and to photography. In 1872 he visited his mother's family in New Orleans and painted the *New Orleans Cotton Office* (Pau, France). His pastels of women at their toilet shocked his contemporaries but are now regarded as being among his finest works. He exhibited frequently with the impressionists but was little influenced by their style.

De Gasperi, Alcide (1881–1954) Italian statesman; prime minister (1945–53). After imprisonment (1930–31) as an antifascist, De Gasperi withdrew to the Vatican City, where he worked in the library and organized the modern Christian Democratic Party during World War II. From 1945 to 1953 he headed coalition cabinets, which included communists until 1947, when De Gasperi expelled them. A Christian Democratic electoral victory in 1948 gave popular sanction to this measure.

de Gaulle, Charles André Joseph Marie (1890–1970) French general and statesman who was an outstanding international figure in the mid-20th century; president (1958–69). An advocate of mechanized warfare during the 1930s, when he wrote his best-known book, *Vers l'armée de métier* (1934), he was promoted early in World War II to general (1940). He entered the cabinet of Paul *Reynaud but opposed the Franco-German armistice, becoming leader of the *Free French in London and a symbol of French patriotism. The Free French contributed heroically to the Allied war effort but de Gaulle resented his dependence on Britain and the US and the antagonism between them was to continue after the war. In 1943 he became head of the newly formed Committee of National Liberation in Algiers and, after the Allied liberation of France (1944), formed a provisional government of which he was president from 1945 until resigning in 1946. In 1947 he formed the unsuccessful Rassemblement du Peuple Français, dissolving it in 1953. In 1958 he was summoned from retirement to deal with the crisis in Algeria, where French settlers, fearing the establishment of Algerian independence, were in revolt. He became president of the new Fifth Republic in 1959 and moved toward the achievement of Algerian independence. Successful by 1962, he subsequently pursued his vision of a Europe of nationally self-conscious states, free of US influence. He thus opposed the postwar multinational organizations, refusing to sign the *Nuclear Test-Ban Treaty (1963) and withdrawing France from the military arm of NATO (1966). He was also passionately opposed to British membership in the European Economic Community. At home his position was greatly weakened by the student and industrial unrest of May 1968 and in the following year he resigned following defeat in a referendum on constitutional reform. His policies, however, have endured in the right-wing Gaullist movement in contemporary French politics.

CHARLES DE GAULLE

degree 1. A unit of plane angle equal to $1/360$th of a complete revolution. It is subdivided into 60 minutes, each of which consists of 60 seconds. **2.** An interval on a temperature scale: 1° on the *Celsius (centigrade) scale is equal to one-hundredth of the difference in temperature between freezing and boiling water. It is also equal in magnitude to 1 *kelvin. 1° on the *Fahrenheit scale is $9/5$ times the Celsius degree.

De Havilland, Sir Geoffrey (1882–1965) British ▢aircraft designer and manufacturer, who produced some of the first jet-propelled aircraft. During both World Wars he designed several military aircraft, including the well-known Mosquito of World War II.

Dehra Dun 30 19N 78 03E A city in India, in Uttar Pradesh. The Indian Military Academy (1932) is situated here. Population (1991): 270,028.

dehydration A potentially serious condition resulting from excessive loss of water from the body. The water that is continuously lost from the body in urine, sweat, expired air, and feces must be replaced by drinking. Dehydration may result from insufficient intake of water in those shipwrecked or too ill to drink or from excessive loss in fever, vomiting, diarrhea, or from the skin in hot climates. It may lead, if not treated, to shock and death. It can be avoided by ensuring that patients receive fluid in the form of drinks or intravenous infusions. Intravenous fluids can be given slowly to treat those seriously dehydrated.

Deirdre The tragic heroine of the Irish legend known as *The Fate of the Sons of Usnech,* of which the earliest surviving account appears in the 12th-century *Book of Leinster.* To escape marrying King Conchobar of Ulster, Deirdre eloped with Noíse, son of Usnech. When they returned, Noíse and his brothers were killed by the king and Deirdre died of grief. The legend has been dramatized by J. M. Synge and W. B. Yeats.

deism A system of belief in God that, in contrast to *theism, discounts revealed religion, especially Christianity, and takes God as the philosophical *first cause. More specifically, deism was a rationalistic anti-Christian movement in England in the late 17th and early 18th centuries that criticized and rebutted the Scriptures after the manner of *Locke's *empiricism and regarded dogmatic religions as corruptions of man's natural relation with God. Leading deists were Lord *Herbert of Cherbury, Matthew Tindal (1655–1733), and the 3rd Earl of *Shaftesbury. Deism, often tending toward *atheism, had more influence on German and French thinkers, including *Voltaire, than in England.

Dekker, Thomas (c. 1572–1632) British dramatist and pamphleteer. His best-known play, *The Shoemaker's Holiday* (1600), expresses his exuberant affection for London life. He often collaborated with *Webster, *Middleton, and other dramatists. His pamphlets, such as *The Seven Deadly Sins of London* (1606) and *The Gull's Hornbook* (1609), are racy blends of fact, wit, and homily.

de Klerk, Frederik Willem (1936–   ) South African political leader; president (1989–   ). A lawyer, he entered Parliament in 1972, representing the ruling National Party. He became known for his moderate approach to South Africa's racial problems and held several cabinet posts before succeeding P. W. Botha as president. As president, de Klerk accelerated racial reforms, including ending discriminatory laws and recognizing the African National Congress, whose leader, Nelson Mandela, was released from prison. De Klerk maneuvered carefully between his own conservative party and black African demands for faster reform. He shared the Nobel Peace Prize with Mandela in 1993.

de Kooning, Willem (1904–   ) US painter of Dutch birth, noted for his figurative subject matter. He also painted abstract compositions, some in black and white, influenced by Arshile *Gorky, *Picasso, and *Miró. His famous but controversial series of *Women* (1950–53), portraying females as grotesque and aggressive creatures, established him as a leading exponent of *action painting.

Delacroix, Eugène (1798–1863) French Romantic painter, born near Paris. He studied with Baron Guérin (1774–1883) but was influenced by *Géricault, *Rubens, and *Constable. His richly colored paintings were often inspired by incidents in Dante, Shakespeare, and Byron, and by contemporary events, e.g. *Massacre at Chios* (1824; Louvre), based on a Turkish atrocity in Greece, and *Liberty Leading the People* (1830; Louvre). The influence of a visit to Morocco (1832) can be seen in some of his exotic later works, e.g. *Women of Algiers* (1834; Louvre). From 1833 he worked on decorations in public buildings, such as the Louvre, Palais-Bourbon, and Saint-Sulpice. He was a friend of *Chopin and George *Sand, both of whom he painted in 1838. His *Journal* contains valuable information on his life and work.

De la Mare, Walter (1873–1956) British poet, novelist, and anthologist, whose work is imbued with an atmosphere of mystery and magic. The verse collection *Songs of Childhood* (1902) and the romance *Henry Brocken* (1906) were written while he was working for an oil company, from which he retired to devote himself to full-time writing. Among his best-known works are the poem "The Listeners" (1912), the fantastic novel *Memoirs of a Midget* (1921), and the anthologies *Come Hither* (1923) and *Love* (1943).

Delaroche, (Hippolyte) Paul (1797–1859) French history and portrait painter. Throughout his life he enjoyed great success with such sentimental history paintings as *The Children of Edward IV in the Tower* (1830; Louvre). He was a professor at the École des Beaux-Arts from 1832, for which he produced the mural of the *Apotheosis of Art* (1837–41).

Delaunay, Robert (1885–1941) The earliest French painter of completely abstract compositions. His first major works represented the Eiffel Tower (1910–11) in cubist style but in his series of *Discs* (1912–13) he pioneered *orphism (which he called *simultaneisme*), a style in which color alone was the subject matter.

Delaware The second smallest state in the US. It shares the Delmarva Peninsula with Maryland and Virginia, with Maryland to the W and S and a small portion of Pennsylvania abutting on the N. The Delaware Bay, the mouth of the Delaware River, and the Atlantic Ocean form its seaboard. New Jersey lies across the mouth of the Delaware River to the E. One of the Middle Atlantic states, it occupies part of the low-lying ground of the Atlantic coastal plain, with higher ground in the NW, where most of the state's population and industry are concentrated. It is one of the most industrialized states; Wilmington contains the administrative centers of several large chemical companies and is nicknamed "the chemical capital of the world." Motor vehicles, synthetic rubber, textiles, and food products are also produced. There is limited mining of sand and gravel. The state's farmers produce poultry, soybeans, milk, corn, and vegetables. There is some fishing of coastal and inland waters. *History*: it was discovered by Henry Hudson, who sailed up the Delaware River in 1609. At the time the region was occupied by Delaware Indians. The Dutch established a settlement (1631) but it was the Swedes who founded the first permanent settlement Fort Christiana (now Wilmington) in 1638. Delaware was subsequently captured by the Dutch (1655) and the English (1664). It became part of Pennsylvania in 1682 and shared a governor with that colony until 1776. It was the first of the original 13 states of the US. Eleuthère DuPont's gunpowder mill, founded in 1802, established the state's industrial base. Delaware fought as part of the Union during the Civil War, but many of its rural inhabitants remained loyal to the South. The division between the urban N and the rural S persists today. Area: 2057 sq mi (5328 sq km). Population (1990): 666,168. Capital: Dover.

Delaware American Algonkian-speaking Indian tribe found in what is now New Jersey, Delaware, and Pennsylvania; also known as Lenni-Lenape. Divided into three groups (Munsee, Unalachtigo, and Unami), they were basically an agricultural people who also crafted baskets, pottery, and leather clothing; their most important ceremony was the Corn Dance. With the coming of white settlers they gradually moved westward. Today, most Delaware live on reservations in Oklahoma and Ontario, Canada.

Delaware River A river that rises in the Catskill Mountains in SE New York and flows S to Delaware Bay, forming the boundaries between New York and Pennsylvania (from Hale Eddy to Port Jervis), New Jersey and Pennsylvania, and New Jersey and Delaware. During the Revolutionary War, George Washington and his troops crossed the river several times to wage battles in New Jersey. It passes Trenton, N.J., Philadelphia, Pa., and Wilmington, Del., and handles great quantities of their commerce. The scenic Delaware Water Gap, a pass through the Appalachians, is in NW New Jersey and E central Pennsylvania. Length: 280 mi (451 km).

Delbrück, Max (1906–81) US biologist and Nobel Prize winner (1969); born in Germany. He came to the US in 1937 to study genetics. His discovery that bacterial viruses reproduce or multiply by the hundred thousands in a short period of time proved his theory of genetic recombination. For this and his other work in molecular biology, he shared the Nobel Prize in 1969.

Delcassé, Théophile (1852–1923) French politician; foreign minister (1898–1905, 1914–15). His conciliatory policy over the *Fashoda incident (1895) and his negotiations leading to the *Entente Cordiale with Britain (1904) paved the way to the *Triple Entente between Britain, France, and Russia. He urged a strong stand against Germany during the 1905–06 Moroccan crisis but, failing to win support, resigned.

Deledda, Grazia (1871–1936) Italian novelist. Most of her novels, such as *Ashes* (1904) and *The Mother* (1920), are realistic treatments of peasant life in her native Sicily. She won the Nobel Prize in 1926.

Delescluze, Louis Charles (1809–71) French journalist and radical republican. Active in the revolutions of 1830 and 1848, he was deeply opposed to the Second Empire of Napoleon III. A member of the *Commune of Paris, he was shot at the barricades.

Delft 52 01N 4 21E A city in the W Netherlands, in South Holland province. William the Silent was murdered here in 1584. Since the late 16th century it has been famous for its pottery and porcelain known as delftware. Population (1981 est): 84,129.

Delian League A confederacy of Greek city states formed in 478 BC during the *Greek-Persian Wars under the leadership of Athens. Members met on the sacred island of Delos, voted on policy, and contributed funds assessed by *Aristides. After the peace between Greece and Persia (c. 450) Athens regarded its allies as subjects. The League treasury was moved to Athens and secession was punished as revolt. The League was disbanded after Athens' defeat (404) in the Peloponnesian War but was revived in defense against Sparta in 378, lasting until the defeat (338) of Athens and Thebes at *Chaeronea.

Delian problem The problem of constructing a cube that has twice the volume of a given cube. Also known as the duplication of the cube, it was first set by the oracle of Delos in the 5th century BC as a condition for ending a plague.

The problem cannot be solved by ruler and compass alone, a fact not recognized until the 19th century.

Delibes, Leo (1836–91) French composer, a pupil of Adolphe Adam. Early in his career he wrote a number of operas and operettas. In 1863 he became accompanist at the Paris Opéra and, later, second chorus master. His best-known works are the ballet *Coppélia* (1870) and *Sylvia* (1876).

deliquescence The process in which some crystalline substances, such as calcium chloride ($CaCl_2$), absorb water from the atmosphere to such an extent that they dissolve; this is extreme hygroscopic (water-attracting) behavior. Deliquescent substances are used in several industries to provide dry atmospheres.

delirium An acute state of mental disturbance in which the patient has hallucinations and delusions and is incoherent, agitated, and restless. It is most commonly associated with a high fever, particularly in children, although it may also be due to a variety of metabolic disorders. It also occurs in association with alcoholic poisoning and with alcohol withdrawal, when it is called **delirium tremens**. It can also be caused by intoxication with other drugs.

Delius, Frederick (1862–1934) British composer of German descent. After an abortive business career, he went to live in Florida and subsequently made his home at Grez-sur-Loing, near Paris. Largely self-taught, he was influenced by Debussy and Grieg. His works include *Paris, the Song of a Great City* (1899), *Appalachia* (for orchestra and chorus; 1902), *On Hearing the First Cuckoo in Spring* (1912), and *North Country Sketches* (1913–14). He also wrote four operas, four concertos, chamber music, choral works, and songs. Delius became blind in 1925 but continued to compose with the help of his aide, Eric Fenby.

Della Robbia, Luca (1400–82) Florentine Renaissance sculptor. Working first in marble, he produced the *Cantoria* (1431–38), his famous relief depicting singers, musicians, and dancers, for the Duomo, Florence. Subsequently he specialized in enameled terracotta sculptures, the glazing process being his own invention. Their production was carried on by his nephew **Andrea della Robbia** (1435–1525) and sons **Giovanni della Robbia** (1469–c. 1529) and **Girolamo della Robbia** (1488–1566).

Delorme, Philibert (?1510–70) French architect of the Renaissance. Influenced by classical architecture, which he studied in Rome in the 1530s, his buildings include the Château d'Anet (c. 1552), designed for Diane de Poitiers, and the palace of the Tuileries (1580). He also wrote two treatises on architecture (1561, 1568).

Delos (Modern Greek name: Dhílos) 37 23N 25 15E A Greek island in the S Aegean Sea, one of the Cyclades. It was of great importance in antiquity (*see* Delian League), and many ancient temples and other buildings, an altar built of the horns of sacrificed animals, and nine marble lions have been excavated here. Area: 1 sq mi (3 sq km).

Delphi A village in central Greece. In antiquity, it was the principal sanctuary and oracle of *Apollo. The sacred enclosure, still an imposing sight, is set in spectacular mountain scenery. It contained Apollo's temple, "treasuries" where the Greek states stored their offerings, a theater, and over 3000 statues. A stadium for the *Pythian Games, a gymnasium, and other shrines stood nearby. The oracle's advice about religion, morality, commerce, and colonial projects, interpreted from the trance utterances of a priestess, was widely sought by individuals and states. As traditional beliefs declined after the 4th century BC the oracle lost influence. It was closed by the Christian emperor Theodosius (390 AD).

Delphinium A genus of annual or perennial herbs (250 species), also called larkspur, up to 7 ft (2 m) high with tall spikes of deep-blue flowers and divided leaves. Delphiniums, native to the N hemisphere, are popular garden plants. Cultivated varieties usually range from 12 to 71 in (30 to 180 cm) high and have single or double flowers in shades of blue, pink, purple, or white. Family: *Ranunculaceae*.

delta A large fan-shaped accumulation of sediment deposited at the mouth of a river, where it discharges into a sea or lake. It forms when the river's flow is slowed down on meeting the comparatively static sea or lake, resulting in a reduction of the river's load-bearing capacity. Clay particles also coagulate on meeting salt water and are deposited. The river is increasingly divided by the deposition into channels. Being fertile, deltas (such as the Nile Delta) are often extensively cultivated but are also prone to flooding.

demand The quantity of goods or services that consumers wish to buy. Demand can be elastic (when a small change in price causes a large change in the demand), inelastic (a large change in price results in a small change in demand), or of unitary elasticity (a change in price leads to a proportional demand). The elasticity of demand influences government policy in deciding on which goods to levy a *sales tax.

Demerara River A river in E Guyana, flowing N to enter the Atlantic Ocean at Georgetown. Length: 215 mi (346 km).

Demeter A Greek corn goddess and mother goddess, sister of *Zeus. She was worshipped at Eleusis, whose people, it was said, had aided her in her search for her daughter *Persephone, abducted to the underworld. In gratitude she instructed them in agriculture and religion (*see* Eleusinian Mysteries). She was identified with the Roman goddess Ceres.

de Mille, Cecil B(lount) (1881–1959) US film producer and director. His best-known films were epic productions involving spectacular crowd scenes and special effects. Many of these were based on biblical themes, notably *The Ten Commandments* (1923; remade 1956), *The King of Kings* (1927), and *Samson and Delilah* (1949). His niece **Agnes de Mille** (1909–93) was a ballet dancer and choreographer. American themes and traditions were a distinctive feature of her ballets, as in *Rodeo* (1942), choreographed for the Ballets Russes in Monte Carlo. She also choreographed for films and musicals, notably *Oklahoma!* (1943), *Carousel* (1945), and *Paint Your Wagon* (1951). Her autobiographical writings include *Dance to the Piper* (1952) and *Speak to Me, Dance with Me* (1973).

democracy A form of government in which people either rule themselves (direct democracy), as in ancient Athens, or elect representatives to rule in their interests (indirect democracy), as in most modern democracies. Elections, to be democratic, must be held regularly, be secret, and provide a choice of candidates; the elected assembly must also be free to legislate and to criticize government policy. Modern democratic ideas stem from 18th-century *utilitarianism and current debate centers on the elitist theory of democracy—that modern democratic government is by a political elite, which although voted into power invites little participation by the electorate.

Democratic Party One of the two major political parties in the US. Originally founded as the *Democratic Republican Party by Thomas *Jefferson in 1792, it opposed the encroachment of the federal government on the rights of the states and individuals. Under the leadership of Jefferson, James *Madison, and James *Monroe, the party effectively destroyed the power of the *Federalists. During the administration of Andrew *Jackson, it became known as the

Democratic Party and began to support the power of the federal government as a means of protecting individual rights and interests. In 1860, just before the *Civil War, the Democrats split over the issue of *slavery into northern and southern factions and the party, dominated by southern Democrats, was eclipsed until regaining northern support in the 1880s. The party gained strength under the administration of Woodrow *Wilson and with the New Deal programs of Franklin *Roosevelt in the 1930s, the Democrats enjoyed the strong support of minorities and organized labor. The policies of Presidents John *Kennedy and Lyndon *Johnson reinforced the party's commitment to civil rights and social legislation.

Democratic Republican Party US political party in the early 1800s. It was the party of Thomas *Jefferson, James *Madison, and James *Monroe and, previously, had been the *Anti-Federalist Party. It opposed a strong federal government and advocated states' rights, strict interpretation of the Constitution, and social reforms at the local level.

Democratic Republicans (Jacksonian) US political party, a faction of the Democratic Republican Party that supported Andrew *Jackson for the presidency. Its members believed in a strong federal government. By Jackson's first term (1829–33) it had become known as the Democratic Party.

Democritus (c. 460–370 BC) Greek philosopher and scientist, born at Abdera (Thrace). He developed the first materialist theory of nature. His *atomism, developed from *Leucippus, considered that all matter consists of minute particles—atoms—the multifarious arrangement of which accounts for different properties of matter apparent to our senses. Democritus wrote also on cosmology, biology, perception, and music. His ethical theory foreshadowed *Epicureanism in valuing spiritual tranquility most highly. Of his works, many fragments, but nothing complete, survives.

demography A branch of the social sciences concerned with the statistical study of the sizes, distribution, and composition of human populations. The subject also includes collecting and analyzing birth, death, and marriage rates for whole populations or groups within them. Demography is primarily a branch of sociology but it also overlaps with such diverse fields as economics, mathematics, geography, and genetics.

demoiselle An elegant *crane, *Anthropoides virgo,* of dry grassy regions of central Europe and Asia. It is smoky gray in color with a black head and neck, long black breast feathers, and long white plumes behind each eye.

De Morgan, Augustus (1806–71) British mathematician and logician. De Morgan was one of the first to recognize that different *algebras may exist other than the one corresponding to the real numbers, which was then taken to be the only algebra. He also encouraged and collaborated with George *Boole in the development of symbolic logic.

Demosthenes (384–322 BC) Athenian orator and statesman. Demosthenes attacked Philip of Macedon's imperial ambitions in Greece in a series of orations called the *Philippics* (351, 344, 341) and promoted an Athenian alliance with Thebes against Philip. This was defeated by Philip at *Chaeronea (338), whereby Macedonian supremacy in Greece was assured. After the death of Philip's son, Alexander the Great (323), Demosthenes again encouraged a Greek revolt. Condemned to death by Alexander's successors, Demosthenes fled Athens and committed suicide. His simple yet impassioned oratory was much admired in antiquity but his politics were anachronistic; the military power of Macedon could not be denied by even Demosthenes' oratory.

demotic script A form of Egyptian hieroglyphic writing. Pictorial hiero-glyphics became less realistic and increasingly cursive from about 2500 BC until in the 7th century BC they developed into the cursive script called demotic. This continued in common use until the 5th century AD. *See also* Rosetta Stone.

Dempsey, Jack (William Harrison D.; 1895–1983) US boxer, who was world heavyweight champion from 1919 to 1926. Renowned for his persistence and ferocious punching, he attracted enormous audiences and gate money. He lost his title to Gene Tunney (1897–1978).

JACK DEMPSEY

dendrite. *See* neuron.

dendrochronology (*or* tree-ring dating) An archeological dating technique based on the *annual rings of trees. Variations in ring widths have been shown to correspond to rainfall and temperature variations and thus very old tree trunks can give a record of past climates. Any construction incorporating timber, for example buildings or ships, can be dated by comparing the timber-ring patterns with a specimen of known age.

dendrology. *See* tree.

Deneb An extremely luminous remote white supergiant star, apparent magni-tude 1.25 and about 1600 light years distant, that is the brightest star in the con-stellation Cygnus.

dengue A tropical disease caused by a virus and characterized by painful joints, fever, and a rash. The virus is transmitted by the bite of a mosquito, and symptoms begin within a week after the bite. Dengue usually lasts for a week and is rarely fatal. There is no specific treatment.

Deng Xiao Ping (*or* Teng Hsiao-p'ing; 1904–   ) Chinese communist states- man; vice premier (1977–80) and vice chairman of the Central Committee of the Chinese Communist Party (1977–82). He held various prominent Party posts after the establishment of the People's Republic of China in 1949 until being dismissed during the *Cultural Revolution. In 1973 he was rehabilitated but was again dismissed three years later. Following his reinstatement in 1977 he exerted considerable influence on Chinese government and in 1978 made a state visit to the UÏ

Denikin, Anton Ivanovich (1872–1947) Russian general. After the Russian revolution (1917), he became commander of the *White Russian army, attempt- ing to hold S Russia against the Bolsheviks. He occupied most of the Ukraine but internal divisions and Bolshevik counterattacks led to eventual defeat (1920). Denikin fled to France.

De Niro, Robert (1943–   ) US actor, noted for his ability to immerse himself in his screen character. After a success in *Bang the Drum Slowly* (1973), about a dying baseball player, he won an Academy Award as best supporting actor in *The Godfather: Part II* (1974). Subsequent major films included *Taxi Driver* (1976), *The Deer Hunter* (1978), *Raging Bull* (1981, Academy Award, best actor), *Cape Fear* (1991), and *This Boy's Life* (1993).

Denis, St (3rd century) The patron saint of France. Of Italian birth, he was sent to Gaul as a missionary and there became the first Bishop of Paris. He was martyred under the Emperor Valerian. His shrine is in the Benedictine abbey at St Denis near Paris. Feast Day: Oct 9.

Denison 33 45N 96 33W A city in NE Texas. Pres. Dwight D. Eisenhower was born here. Food processing is a major industry, and the manufacture of elec- trical equipment and furniture is also important. Population (1990): 21,505.

Denmark, Kingdom of (Danish name: Danmark) A country in N Europe, between the Baltic and the North Seas. It consists of the N section of the Jutland peninsula and about a hundred inhabited islands (chiefly Sjælland (Zealand) Fyn, Lolland, Falster, Langeland, and Bornholm). *Greenland and the *Faeroe Islands are also part of the Danish kingdom. The country is almost entirely flat with some slightly undulating land in the E of the mainland. *Economy*: agricul- ture, organized on a cooperative basis, is important both for the home and export markets, especially dairy produce and bacon. Since World War II, however, in- dustry has dominated the economy, the main areas being engineering, chemi- cals, brewing, fishing, and food processing. Furniture, textiles, porcelain, metal goods, and glass are valued for their high-quality design. Its high volume of ex- ports include meat and meat products, dairy produce, cereals, fish, machinery, and metals. *History*: Viking kingdoms occupied the area from the 8th century to the 10th century, when Denmark became a united Christian monarchy under Harald Bluetooth. His grandson, Canute, ruled over Denmark, Norway, and England, forming the Danish Empire, which was dissolved soon after his death. In 1363 Norway again came under the Danish crown by royal marriage. In 1397 Denmark and Norway joined with Sweden to form the Kalmar Union, which lasted until 1523. The Peace of Copenhagen (1660) concluded a long period of conflict between Denmark and Sweden. At this time it became an absolute monarchy, which continued until 1849, when a more liberal government was formed. Having supported Napoleon in the Napoleonic Wars, Denmark was compelled to cede Norway to Sweden by the Treaty of Kiel (1814). In the middle of the 19th century Denmark lost its S provinces of Schleswig, Holstein, and Lauenburg to Prussia, N Schleswig being returned (by plebiscite) in 1920. During World War II Denmark was occupied by Germany but a resistance movement grew in strength and aided the Allied victory. Iceland, which had previously been united with Denmark, became independent in 1944. A new constitution was formed in 1953, with a single-chamber parliament (elected by proportional representation) and executive power in the hands of the monarch through his ministers. In 1973 Denmark joined the EEC, but in June 1992 voters turned down a treaty to create a federal state among EEC members. The pact was approved in 1993. Head of state: Queen Margrethe II. Prime minister: Poul Rasmussen. Official language: Danish. Official religion: Evangelical Lutheran. Official currency: krone of 100 øre. Area: 16,631 sq mi (43,074 sq km). Population (1990 est): 5,134,000. Capital and main port: Copenhagen.

Dennis v. United States US Supreme Court decision that ruled that the Smith Act (1940), which provided for criminal punishment of anyone teaching, advocating, or encouraging violent overthrow of the government, was constitutional. Members of the US Communist Party appealed their conviction under this law, but the conviction was upheld by the Court, which felt they constituted a "clear and present danger."

density The mass of unit volume of a substance. In *SI units it is measured in kilograms per cubic meter; in these units water has a density of 1000 kg m^{-3}. **Relative density** (formerly called "specific gravity") is the density of a substance divided by the density of water at 4°C. This value is numerically one thousandth of the density. In the c.g.s. system, density (in grams per cubic centimeter) is numerically equal to relative density. The density of a gas (vapor density) is often expressed as the mass of unit volume of the gas divided by the mass of the same volume of hydrogen at standard temperature and pressure.

dentistry The branch of medical science concerned with the care of the teeth, gums, and mouth. Scientific dentistry is a relatively recent development—the first dental school was established in Philadelphia in 1840 and the first European school was the Royal Dental Hospital, founded in London in 1858. Modern dentistry includes a number of specialties. Restorative dentistry is concerned with the repair of teeth damaged by *caries and the replacement of teeth lost through injury or extraction. Orthodontics deals with the correction of badly positioned teeth, usually by means of braces or other appliances but sometimes by surgery on the jaw. Periodontics includes the care of the gums and other structures supporting the teeth and the treatment of the diseases affecting them (*see* periodontal disease). Oral surgery deals not only with the extraction of teeth but also with the surgical repair of fractures or abnormalities of the jaws and facial bones. Preventive dentistry is an important branch, concerned with preventing tooth decay and gum disease by such measures as education in oral hygiene and *fluoridation of the public water supply.

Denver 39 45N 105 00W The capital city of Colorado, on the South Platte River. Founded in 1858 during the Colorado gold rush, Denver is the financial, administrative, and industrial center for a large agricultural area. A US Mint is sited here and it is within easy reach of 12 national parks. Population (1990): 467,610.

deodar A *cedar, *Cedrus deodara,* native to the Himalayas, where it forms vast forests, and widely planted for ornament in temperate regions and for timber in S Europe. Reaching a height of 245 ft (75 m) in the wild, it is distinguished from other cedars by its young branches, which droop down, and by its large barrel-shaped cones, up to 6 in (14 cm) long.

d'Éon, Charles de Beaumont, Chevalier (1728–1810) French secret agent in the service of *Louis XV. His fondness for wearing women's clothes, both as a disguise and in normal life, led to wagers in society about his actual sex. He did nothing to prevent such speculation, which continued until the matter was resolved at the autopsy after his death in London.

deontology A system of *ethics in which duty, rather than rights, virtue, or happiness, is fundamental to morality. It was the title of a book by *Bentham. *Compare* teleology.

deoxyribonucleic acid. *See* DNA.

depreciation The loss in value of capital equipment as a result of wear and tear, obsolescence, etc. For example, a machine that costs $10,000 and is expected to last ten years depreciates at the rate of $1000 a year. To keep its stock of capital equipment, therefore, a firm must set aside a certain sum each year to account for depreciation. The calculation of the depreciation provision is sometimes complicated by the difficulty in judging the life of a machine: changes in taste or technological developments may shorten the useful life of a machine. To encourage firms to maintain their capital equipment, governments usually allow for depreciation when calculating corporation tax.

depression (economics) A period during the *trade cycle in which demand is low compared to industry's capacity to satisfy it. Profits, and therefore confidence and investment, are also correspondingly low (*see* accelerator principle). A depression is also characterized by high unemployment, as occurred in the 1930s (*see* Depression). The influence of the British economist J. M. *Keynes has led governments since World War II to adopt *deficit financing policies to counter depressions, but the advent in the 1970s of the previously unknown combination of depression and *inflation has led to a revival of interest in the rival doctrine of *monetarism. A depression is also called a slump.

depression (meteorology) A *cyclone in the midlatitudes; also called a low or a disturbance. Frequently accompanied by *fronts, depressions move toward the NE in the N hemisphere and toward the SE in the S hemisphere. They are characterized by unsettled weather and are the main source of rainfall in the lowland areas of the midlatitudes.

depression (psychiatry) Severe and persistent misery. It can be a normal reaction to distressing events, such as bereavement (reactive depression). Sometimes, however, it is out of all proportion to the situation or may have no apparent external cause (endogenous depression): it can then be a sign of mental illness. In *manic-depressive psychosis the depression is severe and leads the sufferer to despairing and guilty beliefs and even to delusions of being evil and worthless; sleep, appetite, and concentration can all be disturbed. In depressive neurosis the symptoms are less extreme but may still lead to *suicide. Treatment with *antidepressant drugs is often effective and psychotherapy is helpful. Severe cases may need *electroconvulsive therapy.

Depression, Great The period during the early 1930s when worldwide economic collapse precipitated commercial failure and mass unemployment. Beginning in the US with the stock market crash of October 1929, when share prices fell so disastrously that thousands were made bankrupt and the American banking system was severely shaken, the Depression caused serious economic problems throughout the world. International trade was severely affected, industrial production dropped, and millions were unemployed. In the US, Pres. Herbert *Hoover was criticized for his handling of the economic crisis, and he was defeated by Franklin *Roosevelt in the 1932 election. Roosevelt's *New Deal brought Americans hope of recovery through the use of government funds for public works and social assistance programs. In Europe, however, the Depression caused continuing social unrest and in Germany contributed to the rise of *Hitler's Nazi movement. The Depression was finally ended by the outbreak of World War II and massive military spending by the industrialized nations.

Depretis, Agostino (1813–87) Italian statesman; prime minister (1876–78, 1878–79, 1881–87). At first a supporter of *Mazzini and opponent of *Cavour, Depretis became converted to constitutional monarchism in 1861. He headed several coalitions of moderate Left elements in parliament. His foreign policy contributed to the formation of the 1882 *Triple Alliance of Italy, Austria-Hungary, and Germany.

De Quincey, Thomas (1785–1859) British essayist and critic. In 1802 he ran away from his Manchester business family and then studied at Oxford; there he took opium for toothache and became addicted for life. He lived largely by journalism, writing numerous essays on diverse subjects. Among his friends were *Wordsworth and *Coleridge. His autobiographical *Confessions of an Opium Eater* first appeared in 1822 and was revised in 1856.

Derain, André (1880–1954) French postimpressionist painter. In his bold designs and vibrant colors, particularly in his Thames paintings (1905–06), he was initially a leading exponent of *fauvism, but after 1907 he came under the influence of *Cézanne and painted in a cubist manner. He later reverted to a traditional style after an intensive study of the Old Masters. He produced some notable scenery and costume designs for Diaghilev's *Ballets Russes.

Derby 52 55N 1 30W A city in central England. Its growth as a manufacturing center began in the late 17th century; the first silk mill in England was established here in 1719 and by the 18th century Derby had become a center of porcelain manufacture. Today Derby is an important engineering center (with Rolls-Royce engines). Fine porcelain (*see* Derby ware), electrical equipment, paints, and textiles are also manufactured. Population (1981): 215,736.

Derby, Edward (George Geoffrey Smith) Stanley, 4th Earl of (1799–1869) British statesman; Conservative prime minister (1852, 1858–59, 1866–68). A noted orator, he became leader of the Conservative Party after the defection (1846) of the Peelites over the *Corn Laws. His government's achievements included the Jewish Relief Act (1858) and the *Reform Act (1867).

Derby ware Porcelain first produced by William Duesbury (1725–86) at Derby in the 1750s. Early manufactures resemble * Chelsea porcelain and Duesbury later bought the Chelsea works (1770). Utility products were decorated in bold blue, red, and gilt "Japan" patterns, but important portrait and fictional figures were also made in quantity. Leading artists decorated the fine dessert services with landscapes and specimen flora.

dermatitis Inflammation of the skin (the term eczema is often used synonymously with dermatitis). The patient has an itching red rash that may become scaly. Dermatitis may result from contact with irritant or allergy-provoking substances, infections, drugs, or radiation (particularly sunlight) or it may occur without obvious cause. Treatment is aimed at removing the cause and easing the condition with creams.

dermatology. *See* skin.

Dermot MacMurrough (?1110–71) King of Leinster. After being defeated by rival kings and banished (1166) from Ireland, he obtained aid from the English and with their support regained his kingdom in 1169–70. He has been unpopular with Irish nationalists ever since, for introducing the English into Ireland.

Derris A genus of tropical woody vines (80 species), especially *D. elliptica* of the East Indies, the roots of which contain rotenone, a useful insecticide. Family: *Leguminosae.*

dervishes Members of Sufi religious brotherhoods (*see* Sufism), which hold various esoteric beliefs and have spread throughout Islam since the 12th century AD. Many of them perform ecstatic rituals, such as hypnotic chanting and whirling dancing, at prayer meetings (called *zikrs*). The dervishes of the Mevlevi order, founded in Anatolia (Turkey) in the 13th century, are famous for their dancing and are commonly called "whirling dervishes."

Desai, (Shri) Morarji (Ranchhodji) (1896–) Indian statesman; prime minister from 1977 until his resignation in 1979. As a young man he was a follower of Mahatma *Gandhi. Later, in the Congress Party, he came to oppose Indira Gandhi and during the state of emergency declared during her first administration he was imprisoned. In the 1977 elections he defeated her to become prime minister as leader of the new Janata Party.

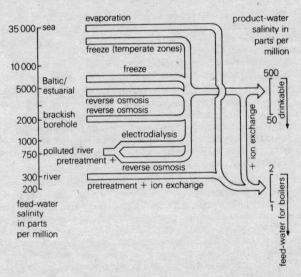

DESALINATION *The initial and final salinities for various desalination techniques and feed-water sources.*

desalination The removal of salt from brine to produce fresh water. Desalination is used to irrigate arid regions in which sea water is available, especially if solar power can be used as an energy source. Several methods are employed, the most common being evaporation of the sea water by heat or by reducing the pressure on it (flash evaporation). The vapor is condensed to form relatively pure water. Freezing is another technique; pure ice forms from brine as it freezes. The method theoretically requires less energy than evaporation but the process is slower and technically more difficult. Reverse *osmosis is another method used. Pure water and salt water are contained on either side of a permeable membrane. The pressure of the salt water is raised above the osmotic pressure, causing water to pass from the brine to the pure side. Because the osmotic pressure required is about 25 atmospheres there are difficulties with large-scale application.

In electrodialysis, the ions are subjected to an electric field instead of increased pressure, the positive and negative ions being filtered off through separate membranes. Another method used for low salinities is ion exchange; in this method the salt ions are chemically removed from the solution.

Descartes, René (1596–1650) French philosopher, one of the most original thinkers of all time. After a Jesuit education he spent nine years in travel and military service before turning to study. After 1628 he settled in Holland, where he lived until 1649, when Queen Christina invited him to Sweden. Here the cold climate and predawn tutorials with the queen caused a fatal attack of pneumonia.

Descartes' *Discourse on Method* (1637) introduced his technique of methodical doubt, which he developed in his greatest work the *Meditations* (1641). Asking "How and what do I know?" he arrived by a process of reduction at his famous statement "Cogito ergo sum" ("I think, therefore I am"). From this core of certainty he proceeded to prove to his own satisfaction God's existence (he was a sincere and lifelong Roman Catholic) and hence the existence of everything else. The importance of this approach lies not in what he proves or discards but in making *epistemology the gateway to knowledge. Equally influential was his dualism: he considered that the world was composed of two different kinds of substance—mind (*res cogitans*), which is the essence of human beings, and matter (*res extensa*). Descartes never satisfactorily answered the problem he thus set of how mind and matter can interact—nor has anyone else.

A distinguished mathematician and scientist, Descartes also contributed to the foundations of geometry (*see* coordinate systems) and optics. He held that mathematics was the supreme science in that the whole phenomenal world could be interpreted in terms of mathematical laws. He avoided confrontation with the Church by separating the realm of mathematics from that of theology and by cautiously suppressing his acceptance of the correctness of the Copernican system (*see* Copernicus).

descent The social recognition of biological relationship to a common ancestor. All societies limit the extent to which such relationships are traced but to differing degrees and in different ways. In many primitive societies the descent system is the basis of group membership, property and other rights, and social status. Unilineal systems count descent in one line only and are termed patrilineal or agnatic when this is through males and matrilineal or uxorial when through females. Double unilineal systems count both lines but for distinct purposes. Cognatic systems, usually found in more advanced societies, count descent in either line.

desensitization In immunology, a method of treating some *allergies, such as hay fever. Small amounts of the substance (allergen) that provokes the symptoms of the allergy are injected at intervals. This stimulates the production of *antibodies in the blood that will combine with the allergen during subsequent exposure and prevent it from reacting with a different set of antibodies, attached to certain cells, to cause the allergic symptoms.

desert A virtually barren area of land where precipitation is minimal and sporadic, limiting vegetation growth. The mean annual rainfall is usually taken as being below 10 in (250 mm) for desert conditions to exist. Deserts may occur in areas of high atmospheric pressure, such as the *Sahara, or near the W coast of continents cooled by cold ocean currents (e.g. the *Atacama and *Kalahari Deserts). They are also found in continental interiors where mountain barriers restrict precipitation, such as the *Gobi Desert. Many deserts are characterized by stony scrublands with occasional resistant rock uplands and some areas of shifting sand dunes. The wind is an important agent of erosion and the rain, falling as violent downpours, is capable of moving large amounts of debris.

Desert cultures A group of Stone Age North American cultures in Nevada, Utah, Arizona, and New Mexico dating from the period 8000–2000 BC. Adapted to arid or semiarid conditions, they were based upon hunting small game and gathering wild plant foods in small nomadic groups. Baskets, milling stones, bone tools, and chipped stone weapon points were made.

desert rat. *See* jerboa.

De Sica, Vittorio (1901–74) Italian film director. He started his career as an actor and began directing in 1940. His postwar films, in which he treated contemporary social themes with compassion and political awareness, included *Shoeshine* (1946), *Bicycle Thieves* (1948), and *Umberto D* (1952). His later films treated less controversial themes and included several romantic comedies.

Desiderio da Settignano (c. 1430–64) Italian Renaissance sculptor. Working chiefly in Florence, he specialized in marble portrait busts. His tomb for the humanist Carlo Marsuppini (Sta Croce, Florence) is renowned.

desman A small aquatic insectivorous mammal belonging to the family *Talpidae* (moles). The Russian desman (*Desmana moschata*) is about 8 in (20 cm) long; the Pyrenean desman (*Galemys pyrenaicus*) is smaller. They have webbed hind feet and partly webbed forefeet, live in burrows in river banks, and feed on invertebrates and fish.

Des Moines 41 35N 93 35W The capital city of Iowa. Founded in 1843, it has developed into an important industrial and commercial center situated in the heart of the Corn Belt. Many insurance companies have their headquarters here. Population (1990): 193,187.

Desmond, Gerald Fitzgerald, 15th Earl of (d. 1583) Anglo-Irish magnate, who opposed the increasing imposition of English authority on Ireland. Periodically imprisoned in the 1560s and 1570s, his 1579 rebellion led to his being outlawed. He was captured and killed.

Desmoulins, Camille (1760–94) French revolutionary and journalist. His fiery oratory contributed to the storming of the *Bastille (July 14, 1789), and in 1792 he became an unremitting critic of the Girondins. Subsequently counseling moderation, he was arrested with the followers of *Danton in 1794 and guillotined. His best-known work is his *Histoire des Brissotins* (1793).

De Soto, Hernando (c. 1496–1542) Spanish explorer. Setting out from Spain in 1539 to conquer territory for the empire of *Charles V, De Soto landed with 600 men on the W coast of Florida at Tampa Bay and began extensive and destructive explorations in search of gold. Unsuccessful in finding the riches that he sought, in 1541 De Soto led his men up the Mississippi, becoming the first Europeans to explore the river. After progressing as far as the Arkansas River and exploring the region of modern Oklahoma, he died on the return journey.

des Prez, Josquin. *See* Josquin des Prez.

Dessalines, Jean Jacques (c. 1758–1806) Emperor of Haiti (1804–06). He rose to military pre-eminence in the slave revolt led by *Toussaint-L'Ouverture. When Toussaint was captured by the French in 1802 Dessalines assumed the leadership of the Haitians and with British help defeated the French (1803). His habitual cruelty as emperor provoked a palace revolution, during which he was assassinated.

Dessau 51 41N 12 14E A city in eastern Germany, on the Mulde River near its confluence with the Elbe River. Dessau was the former capital of Anhalt state. Many of its historic buildings were destroyed during World War II. Production of armaments, vehicles, and machinery are the main industries. Population (1990): 120,000.

destroyer A fast heavily armed naval vessel that is smaller than a *cruiser, has a displacement of about 3000 tons, and is 330–450 ft (110–150 m) long. Destroyers are not armored. Because of their speed, armament, and versatility, they are employed in antisubmarine warfare, in convoy work, and in "hunter-killer" attack groups consisting of one carrier and five or six destroyers.

destroyer escort A smaller lighter somewhat more maneuverable version of the *destroyer, developed during World War II mainly as protection for convoys.

Destutt, Antoine Louis Claude, Comte de Tracy (1754–1836) French philosopher and politician. He narrowly escaped the guillotine during the French Revolution. In prison he planned his *Eléments d'idéologie* (1801–15), in which, inspired by *Locke and *Condillac, he derives all thought from sensory "ideas" and their combinations.

detached retina A condition in which the retina—a layer of specialized light-sensitive cells at the back of the eye—becomes separated from the layer beneath it (the choroid). It happens slowly and painlessly and the patient loses part of his vision. It is caused by injury to the eye or inflammation in the eye and is most common in very nearsighted people. Detached retina is treated surgically, sometimes using a laser beam to weld the retina back into position.

DETECTIVE STORY *Sherlock Holmes, the famous English detective, with his companion Dr. John H. Watson (left).*

detective story A genre of popular fiction in which a mystery, often a murder, is solved by logic and intuition, usually by an individual detective. Ancient

Chinese literature had a rich detective tradition, but in the modern West the first true detective story is probably *Poe's "Murders in the Rue Morgue" (1841). The form was popularized in England by Wilkie *Collins's *The Moonstone* (1868) and the appearance of Sir Arthur Conan *Doyle's detective Sherlock Holmes. The English tradition is typified by Agatha *Christie and Dorothy L. *Sayers, whose first books appeared in the 1920s. In the 1930s the tersely realistic "thrillers" of the US writers Dashiell *Hammett and Raymond *Chandler began a different trend. Among the best writers of the genre are John Dickson Carr, Ellery Queen, Rex Stout, Josephine Tey, Michael Innes, and R. van Gulik. G. K. *Chesterton, "Nicholas Blake" (C. *Day Lewis), Nicholas Freeling, Georges *Simenon, Eric Ambler, Ross McDonald, Ian Fleming, and John Le Carré, among others, have raised it far above a merely popular level.

detergents Chemicals used for cleaning. Although the term includes *soaps it is usually applied in a more restricted sense to synthetic *surfactants. Such detergents have large molecules, typically composed of a hydrocarbon oil-soluble part and a water-soluble part. Alkyl sulfonates are common examples. These compounds are thus able to promote the solution of oil, grease, etc., in water.

determinant. *See* matrix.

determinism The philosophical theory that every event has a cause and that all events are determined by causal physical laws. One view holds that determinism means that every event could be causally explained and could be predicted if the conditions are not too complex for analysis. A stronger view is that a specific event could not have failed to happen, or was predetermined. Applied to human actions, determinism appears to conflict with the concept of *free will. If even desires, intentions, and motives are determined or conditioned (as some psychologists believe) and if actions are, in principle, predictable, this contradicts the idea that actions are freely chosen, and hence the concept of moral responsibility. However, some philosophers believe that determinism and free will are compatible and that a person acts freely if his desires are the cause of his actions. *See also* predestination.

Detmold 51 56N 8 52E A city in NW Germany, in North Rhine-Westphalia. The capital of the former state of Lippe, it has two palaces. German tribes defeated the Romans here in 9 AD. It has furniture and metallurgical industries. Population (1981 est): 65,000.

detonator A sensitive primary explosive used to ignite a less sensitive high explosive. Detonators may be initiated by percussion, flash, or electrical current. The less sensitive and safer the high explosive is to handle, the stronger the detonator required. Some high explosives require two-stage detonation. A common detonator is mercury fulminate.

Detroit 42 23N 83 05W A city in Michigan, on the Detroit River. Founded in 1701, it was largely rebuilt following a fire in 1805. The fifth largest city in the US, it is dominated by the motor-vehicle industry, with General Motors, Ford, and Chrysler factories comprising 7100 industrial plants. A major port (serving the Great Lakes) and rail center, its other industries include chemicals, steel, and oil refining. It is the home of the University of Detroit (1911) and Wayne State University (1933). Population (1990): 1,027,974.

Deucalion In Greek legend, the son of Prometheus and father of Hellen, the ancestor of the Greek race. Warned of the flood sent by Zeus to destroy mankind, he and his wife Pyrrha survived on a boat and repopulated the earth.

deus ex machina (Latin: god from the machinery) A sudden and improbable resolution of an involved situation. The term refers to the convention in ancient Greek drama in which a god was lowered by a crane to conclude a plot.

deuterium (D; *or* heavy hydrogen ^{2}H) An *isotope of *hydrogen having a nucleus consisting of one proton and one neutron. It occurs naturally in hydrogen to an extent of about 0.0156%. It can be separated from the more common isotope by electrolysis of water. It is used as a radioactive tracer. Heavy water (deuterium oxide; D_2O) is used in *nuclear reactors as a moderator. *See also* thermonuclear reactor. At no 1; at wt 2.014.

Deuteronomy The fifth book of the Old Testament, attributed to Moses, although this is widely disputed; it may have been compiled in the 7th century BC. It is a series of addresses by Moses to the Israelites immediately before the occupation of the Promised Land of Canaan (Palestine). After repeating the *Ten Commandments, he exhorts the people to live differently from the surrounding nations, gives a code of religious and civil laws to be observed in Canaan, blesses those who keep the *convenant and curses those who disobey the Law, appoints Joshua as his successor, and gives custody of the book of the Law to the *Levites. The book closes with the song of Moses, his blessing of the people, and an appendix recording his death.

De Valera, Eamon (1882–1975) Irish statesman; prime minister (1932–48, 1951–54, 1957–59) and president (1959–73). A commandant in the 1916 *Easter Rising, he nevertheless escaped execution and in 1917 was elected to the British parliament and became the president of *Sinn Féin. From 1919 to 1922 he was president of the newly declared Irish Republic but rejected the terms of the Anglo-Irish treaty of 1921 (*see* Home Rule). In 1926 he founded *Fianna Fáil.

devaluation A downward change in the value of one country's currency in terms of other currencies. A country that devalues makes its exports cheaper and its imports more expensive; thus devaluation should help correct a *balance-of-payments deficit by increasing the volume of exports and decreasing the volume of imports. The measure is not always effective, however, because the increased import bill may be larger than the increase in receipts from exports: this is likely if the *demand for the country's exports is elastic, while demand for the imports is inelastic. Under the Bretton Woods fixed-rate system (*see* Bretton Woods Conference) devaluations only occurred occasionally but were large and destabilizing. In the floating-rate system that replaced it, the value of a currency in terms of others is determined by supply and demand with a minimum of government interference; as a consequence devaluations are gradual.

Devanagari An alphabetic *writing system used for *Sanskrit, *Hindi, and other languages of India. It has 48 letters and is written from left to right. Vowels are frequently omitted in Devanagari, a short *a* being understood after each consonant unless a different vowel is specified. It was developed from the ancient Brahmi script, which was probably derived from Aramaic in the 7th or 8th century BC. It is therefore historically related to the Hebrew, Arabic, Greek, and Roman alphabets.

developing countries Countries that do not have sophisticated industries and consequently have a low per capita income. They include almost all the countries in Africa, Asia, and South America. The economies of these so-called Third World countries are characterized by abundant cheap unskilled labor and a scarcity of capital for investment. Some observers consider the marked difference in incomes between the industrial and the developing nations (the "north–south split") to be politically as important as the division between *communism and *capitalism (the "east–west split"). Some 70% of the world's population lives in developing countries in largely agricultural economies from which poverty, hunger, disease, and illiteracy have not been eliminated, despite the efforts of various UN agencies. Many of these economies rely shakily on one main crop, which in years of crop failure, poor world demand, or low market prices can cause severe hardship.

Deventer 52 16N 6 10E A city in the E central Netherlands, in Overijssel province on the IJssel River. During the middle ages it was a major educational center; Erasmus and Thomas à Kempis studied here. Population (1981 est): 64,824.

Devil. *See* Lucifer.

devil ray. *See* manta ray.

devil's coach horse A large carnivorous beetle, *Staphylinus olens*, also called a cock-tail. It is about 1 in (25 mm) long and occurs commonly in gardens of W Europe. If threatened it curls its flexible abdomen upward and forward and releases an offensive odor. Family: *Staphylinidae* (*see* rove beetle).

Devil's Island (French name: Île du Diable) 5 16N 52 34W One of the three Îles du Salut, off the coast of French Guiana in the S Caribbean Sea. It contained a convicts' leper colony before becoming a French penal settlement (1895–1938). Area: less than 1 sq mi (2 sq km).

devolution The delegation of political powers from a central government to regional governments. For example, in the UK the establishment of a parliament in Northern Ireland was the first important act of devolution.

Devolution, War of (1667–68) The conflict between France and Spain for possession of the Spanish Netherlands, which *Louis XIV of France claimed had devolved (descended) to him through his wife Maria Theresa, daughter of Philip IV of Spain (1605–65; reigned 1621–65). Louis' troops, under *Turenne and *Vauban, invaded the Netherlands but were withdrawn when an alliance between England, the United Provinces of the Netherlands, and Sweden threatened to intervene against the French. Peace was made at Aix-la-Chapelle.

Devon A county of SW England, bordering on the Atlantic Ocean in the N and the English Channel in the S. The chief rivers are the Dart, Exe, and Tamar. Agricultural activities include dairy farming and sheep farming. Industry is concentrated around Exeter and Plymouth, a major naval base. There is a thriving tourist industry centered on the coastal resorts. Area: 2591 sq mi (6715 sq km). Population (1991): 998,200. Administrative center: Exeter.

Devonian period A geological period of the Upper Paleozoic era, between the Silurian and Carboniferous periods. It lasted from about 415 to 370 million years ago. It is divided into seven stages, based on invertebrate fossil remains, such as corals, brachiopods, ammonoids, and crinoids. The rocks containing these fossils were marine deposits but the Devonian period also shows extensive continental deposits (Old Red Sandstone). Fossils from these rocks include fish, land plants, and freshwater mollusks.

De Voto, Bernard (Augustine) (1897–1955) US writer, teacher, and historian. After teaching at Northwestern University (1922–27) and Harvard University (1929–36), he was an editor for the *Saturday Review of Literature* (1936–38) and wrote (1935–55) for *Harpers* magazine. He edited *Mark Twain in Eruption* (1940) and *The Journals of Lewis and Clark* (1953) and wrote *Mark Twain's America* (1932), *Mark Twain at Work* (1942), *Across the Wide Missouri* (1947; Pulitzer Prize, 1948), and *The Course of Empire* (1952). He was also a novelist; his novels include *The Crooked Mile* (1924), *The Chariot of Fire* (1926), *The House of Sun-Goes-Down* (1928), *We Accept with Pleasure* (1934), and *Mountain Time* (1947). He wrote thrillers under the pseudonym "John August."

de Vries, Hugo Marie (1848–1935) Dutch botanist, who first recognized the importance of *mutation. De Vries observed how, occasionally, a new variety would arise from his plant-breeding experiments. He realized that this sudden variation, which he termed mutation, could play an important part in the evolution of living things. De Vries worked out his own laws of inheritance only to discover, in 1900, *Mendel's original work, which had previously been ignored.

dew The condensation of moisture, which forms on the ground or on objects near the ground, especially at night. It occurs when the cool air near the ground falls to a temperature, called the **dew point,** at which it becomes saturated and the water vapor present condenses into water droplets. The ideal conditions for dew formation are calm weather with a clear sky.

dewberry A straggling Eurasian shrub, *Rubus caesius*, very similar to the *blackberry but with weaker creeping stems and fewer prickles. The fruit has fewer berries per head and a purplish bloom. The name is also applied to many North American *Rubus* species that trail along the ground. Family: *Rosaceae*.

de Wet, Christian Rudolf (1854–1922) Afrikaner politician and soldier. De Wet commanded the Orange Free State forces in the second *Boer War, organizing the guerrilla tactics that were initially so successful. He was later minister of agriculture in the Orange Free State (1907–10). In 1914 he led a revolt against Botha's plan to conquer German South West Africa and was imprisoned for treason.

Dewey, George (1837–1917) US naval officer. He first saw active duty in various naval engagements during the *Civil War. He was promoted to the rank of commodore in 1896. At the time of the outbreak of the *Spanish-American War, Dewey was dispatched to the Philippines in command of the American fleet. His decisive victory over the Spanish fleet in Manila Bay won his national acclaim as one of the heroes of the war. In 1899 he was named Admiral of the Navy, a rank never before attained by an American officer.

Dewey, John (1859–1952) US philosopher and educator. Born in Burlington, Vt. and educated at the University of Vermont and Johns Hopkins University, Dewey became one of the most prominent advocates of philosophical *pragmatism. As chairman of the philosophy department of the University of Chicago and director of its School of Education (1894–1904), he was among the first to experiment with modern teaching methods. He later became a professor at Columbia University (1904–30), where he developed the theory of "instrumentalism," by which he believed that education must equip students to deal with the practical problems they would confront in later life. In works such as *Reconstruction in Philosophy* (1920), *Experience and Nature* (1925), and *Experience and Education* (1938), Dewey held that philosophy must constantly confront changing conditions and produce appropriate new solutions and beliefs.

Dewey, Melvil (1851–1931) US librarian, creator of the Dewey Decimal System for classification of books. He worked as a librarian at Amherst College, his alma mater, from 1874, and it is here that he first introduced his system of classification. Librarian (1883–88) at Columbia University, he initiated a school for librarians and brought it to Albany, N.Y., when he became director of the New York State Library (1888–1906). He was a founder of the American Library Association (1876) and helped to establish *Library Journal*.

Dewey, Thomas E(dmund) (1902–71) US lawyer and politician; governor of New York (1943–55). After graduating from Columbia University Law School in 1925, he worked as an assistant US attorney in New York (1931–33) before becoming a US attorney himself. By 1935 he had been appointed a special prosecutor and launched a campaign to destroy the crime syndicate in New York; his successful prosecutions led to his election as New York City's district attorney (1937). He served as the Republican governor of New York (1943–55), working to develop and expand the highway and welfare systems and to eliminate discriminatory practices in employment and housing. He ran unsuccessfully for president in 1944 and 1948.

Dewey Decimal Classification An international system for classifying and arranging the books in a library, originated in 1873 by Melvil *Dewey for the Amherst College Library. Books are divided according to subject matter into ten groups, each group having a hundred numbers; principle subdivisions within each group are divided by ten, and with the use of decimal numbers further subdivisions can be generated without limit (e.g. 300: Social Sciences; 370: Education; 372: Elementary Education; 372.3: Elementary Education, Science and Health). The system is being constantly revised and is now in its 18th edition. *See also* Universal Decimal Classification.

dextrose. *See* glucose.

Dhahran 26 18N 50 05E A new town in E Saudi Arabia, on the Persian Gulf coast opposite Bahrain. It ships out oil brought by pipeline from the Abqaiq area just inland.

Dhaka. *See* Dacca.

dharma A Sanskrit term with various religious and philosophical meanings. In Buddhism it signifies the truth, the teaching of the Buddha in whole or in part. It also denotes the law regarding the ultimate nature of things. In Hinduism, it refers to social law or caste duty.

Dharmashastra Traditional Indian lawbooks, still in force. Written in Sanskrit, they comprise some 5000 works, compilations of maxims, treatises, and commentaries. Their composition extended from the 8th century BC to the 19th century AD and is said to be based on the *Vedas. Their emphasis is on outlining the ethical behavior proper to one's caste in any given situation, rather than pronouncing definitive legislation; when properly applied, however, they did act as a valid legal system. British influence hardened and regularized the application of the law and introduced the concept of legal precedent. Since 1955 conventional legislation has been introduced to modify the dharmashastra law as applied by the courts and its importance is diminishing.

Dhaulagiri, Mount 28 39N 83 28E A mountain in NW central Nepal, in the Himalayas. It was first climbed in 1960 by a Swiss team. Height: 26,810 ft (8172 m).

dhole A wild *dog, *Cuon alpinus*, of SE Asia, Sumatra, and Java. Dholes are reddish brown, about 4.5 ft (1.4 m) long including the tail (16 in [40 cm]); they hunt in packs of 5–40 individuals, attacking mainly deer and antelope but occasionally even tigers.

diabase (*or* dolerite) A dark-colored hypabyssal igneous rock, the medium-grained equivalent of gabbros, occurring mainly as dykes, sills, and plugs. It contains calcic plagioclase feldspar and augite, and sometimes olivine, hypersthene, quartz, or feldspathoids.

diabetes One of several diseases with a common symptom—the production of large quantities of urine. The term usually refers to **diabetes mellitus** (*or* sugar diabetes), in which the body is unable to utilize sugars to produce energy due to a deficiency of the pancreatic hormone *insulin. Symptoms include thirst, weight loss, and a high level of glucose in the urine and in the blood (hyperglycemia), which—if untreated—leads to coma. Possible long-term complications of diabetes include damage to the arteries, especially in the eyes (which can affect vision). There appears to be a certain tendency to inherit diabetes, which is often triggered by such factors as physical stress. In children the disease appears more suddenly and is usually more severe than in older people. Treatment is based on a carefully controlled diet, often with insulin injections or pills to reduce the amount of sugar in the blood.

Diabetes insipidus is a rare disease due to a deficiency of the pituitary hormone vasopressin, which regulates water balance in the body. The patient produces large quantities of watery urine and is always thirsty. It is treated with doses of the hormone.

Diaghilev, Sergei (Pavlovich) (1872–1929) Russian ballet impresario. He began his career in the imperial theaters in St Petersburg in 1899 and between 1904 and 1908 organized several art exhibitions there and in Paris. His first theatrical production, the opera *Boris Godunov*, staged at the Paris Opéra (1908), was followed by his season of Russian ballet (1909). Its outstanding success resulted in the organization of a permanent company (1911), the *Ballets Russes, which Diaghilev directed until his death. □Cocteau, Jean.

dialect The language of a particular district or group of people. The distinction between language and dialect is not clear cut. As a general rule any two dialects of a language may be expected to be mutually comprehensible. But, for example, the various "dialects" of Chinese are quite separate, being held together only by a common ideographic writing system, while Dutch, Flemish, and Afrikaans are called separate languages for political reasons, although there is a considerable degree of mutual comprehensibility and they might therefore reasonably be regarded as different dialects of the same language. Dialects develop as a result of geographical separation: slightly differing versions of one original language develop in different places within a generation or so of the time of separation. Social factors also affect dialect development. In English, for example, the medieval dialect of London has developed into a socially prestigious class dialect spoken in most parts of Britain (*see* received pronunciation). *See also* idiolect.

dialectical materialism The official philosophy of *Marxism. Materialism, as opposed to *idealism, Marx and Engels derived from contemporary (1850) science; dialectic, or argument from thesis and antithesis to synthesis, they borrowed from Hegel's idealism. Engles even proposed a dialectical theory of evolution. As philosophy, not surprisingly, dialectical materialism is obscure and apparently unrelated to Marxist political theory. However, **historical materialism,** expounded in the *Communist Manifesto*, is a coherent account of history on an economic basis: for every system of production there is an appropriate organization of class and property. While economic forces continually develop production systems, the class and property structure remains unchanged, causing tension between economic forces and social relations, which continues until the ultimate rational socialist society evolves.

dialysis A process, discovered by Thomas Graham (1804–69), for separating mixtures of fluids by diffusion through a semipermeable membrane. Different substances in a solution diffuse at different rates. The passage of large particles, such as *colloids, is almost completely blocked by a semipermeable membrane, whereas salt solutions pass through easily. The technique of dialysis is used in artificial kidney machines, or dialyzers, which take over the function of diseased kidneys by filtering waste material from the blood but leaving behind proteins, blood cells, and other large particles.

diamagnetism A form of magnetism occurring in materials that when placed in a *magnetic field, have an internal field proportional to but less than that outside. Such substances tend to orientate themselves at right angles to the direction of the *flux and tend to move from the stronger part of a field to the weaker part. Diamagnetism is caused by the motion of atomic electrons, which, since they are charged, constitute a current. This current tends to oppose the magnetic field in accordance with *Lenz's law.

diamond The hardest known mineral, comprising a cubic variety of crystalline *carbon, formed under intense heat and pressure. Diamonds are found in ancient volcanic pipes, mainly in S Africa and Siberia, and in deposits off the coast of Namibia. Over 80% of diamonds mined are used industrially, mainly for cutting and grinding tools; the others are used as gems. The largest diamond yet discovered is the *Cullinan diamond (3106 carats), found in 1905 at Pretoria. Many industrial diamonds are produced synthetically from graphite subjected to very high temperatures and pressures (above 1697°F [3000°C] and 100,000 atmospheres). Birthstone for April.

diamondback The largest and most dangerous *rattlesnake. The eastern diamondback (*Crotalus adamanteus*) and the western diamondback (*C. atrox*) may reach lengths of 6 ft (2.5 m).

diamondbird An Australasian *flowerpecker of the genus *Pardalotus* (7–8 species), about 3 in (8 cm) long with a short tail and a white-spotted plumage. Unlike other flowerpeckers, diamondbirds feed on insects and nest in tree holes and rock crevices.

Diamond Head 21 16N 157 49W An extinct volcanic crater on the S tip of the island of Oahu in NW Hawaii. Rising 761 ft (232 m) above the Pacific Ocean, it overlooks Waikiki Beach.

Diana The Roman goddess identified with the Greek Artemis, associated with women and childbirth and with the moon. She is usually represented as a virgin huntress armed with bow and arrows. The position of priest at her shrine of Ariccia (Italy) was customarily held by a runaway slave, who murdered his predecessor.

Diane de Poitiers, Duchesse de Valentinois (1499–1566) The mistress of *Henry II of France, who was 20 years her junior. She dominated court life until her death in 1559, when she was forced by Henry's wife *Catherine de' Medici to retire to Chaumont.

Dianthus A genus of annual and perennial herbs (300 species), mainly from Europe and Asia, having flower stems (often branched) with swollen joints and showy white, pink, or red flowers. Common species include *D. barbatus* (*see* sweet william), *D. caryophyllus* (*see* carnation), and *D. plumarius* (*see* pink). Family: *Caryophyllaceae*.

diaphragm 1. In anatomy, a dome-shaped sheet of muscle that separates the thorax (chest cavity) from the abdomen. The diaphragm is attached to the spine, lower ribs, and breastbone and contains a large opening through which the esophagus (gullet) passes. It plays an important role in producing breathing movements (*see* respiration). **2.** *See* contraception.

diarrhea The frequent passing of liquid stools, usually more than three a day. It is a symptom, not a disease; causes include anxiety, allergy, infection or inflammation of the intestines, impaired absorption of food, and side effects of drugs. It can be eased by the use of drugs but proper treatment must aim at eliminating the cause.

Dias, Bartolomeu (c. 1450–c. 1500) Portuguese navigator. In 1486, given command of three ships by John II, he set out to explore the coast of Africa. Blown by a storm around the Cape of Good Hope (which he himself named the Cape of Storms) he reached present-day Algoa Bay on the E coast of Africa but was forced by his unwilling crew to return. He was drowned near the Cape while accompanying *Cabral on the expedition that discovered Brazil.

diaspora (Greek: dispersion) The collective term for Jewish communities outside the land of Israel. Beginning with the *Babylonian exile (6th century BC),

Jews spread to most parts of the world, while continuing to regard Israel as their homeland. The resulting tension between Israel and the diaspora has continued to the present day, the dispersion being viewed sometimes negatively, as exile, and sometimes positively. The most important centers of the diaspora were, in antiquity, Babylonia and Egypt; in the middle ages, Spain and France; and in early modern times, E Europe. In the late 19th century there was a massive exodus of Jews from Russia and Poland, and the Nazi *holocaust destroyed many old European communities. The main center is now the US, with some six million Jews.

diastole. *See* blood pressure; heart.

diastrophism The large-scale deformation of the earth's crust resulting in the major structural features of the earth's surface, such as the continents, ocean basins, mountain ranges, fault-lines, etc. It is now widely believed that *sea-floor spreading and the consequent movement of the rigid plates that form the earth's crust (*see* plate tectonics) are responsible for diastrophism.

diathermy The production of heat in the body's tissues by means of a high-frequency electric current passing between two electrodes applied to the patient's skin. It has been used to relieve deep-seated pain in rheumatic conditions. The principle has also been utilized in surgery, one electrode, in the form of a knife, snare, or needle, being used to coagulate blood and therefore seal off blood vessels during incisions or to destroy unwanted tissue.

diatoms Microscopic *yellow-green algae of the class *Bacillariophyceae* (about 16,000 species), occurring abundantly as single cells or colonies in fresh water and oceans (forming an important constituent of *plankton) and also in soil. They have silicon-rich cell walls (called frustules), often beautifully sculptured, composed of two halves that fit together like a pill box. Fossilized frustules form a porous rock called diatomaceous earth (*or* kieselguhr), used in filters, insulators, abrasives, etc.

Díaz, Porfirio (1830–1915) Mexican soldier, who became president (1876–1911) following a coup. He ruled dictatorially, supported by conservative landowners and foreign capitalists. His promotion of economic development benefited only a small elite and no attention was paid to the needs of the Indians. He fled the country in 1911 in the face of a revolution led by Francisco Madero (1873–1913).

diazepam. *See* benzodiazepines.

Dicentra A genus of annual and perennial herbaceous plants (about 300 species) from North America and E Asia, up to 35 in (90 cm) high. They have divided compound leaves and sprays of hanging flowers that are flattened sideways, with the outer petals pouched and the inner ones joined at the tips. Many species are ornamentals (*see* bleeding heart; Dutchman's breeches). Family: *Fumariaceae.*

Dickens, Charles (1812–70) British novelist. Son of a naval clerk, he worked in a factory when his father was imprisoned for debt and later as a solicitor's clerk and court reporter. He began his writing career by contributing to popular magazines, achieving sudden fame with *The Pickwick Papers* (1837), which he followed with *Oliver Twist* (1838) and *Nicholas Nickleby* (1839) and the very successful *Old Curiosity Shop* (1840–41); like all his novels, these first appeared in monthly installments. In the 1840s he traveled abroad, visiting the US in 1842. After 1843, with *The Christmas Carol*, he published many Christmas stories. *David Copperfield* (1849–50) was a strongly autobiographical work, portraying Dickens' father as the feckless Mr Micawber. His later novels, from *Bleak House* (1853) to the incomplete *Edwin Drood* (1870), were increasingly pessimistic in tone; *Great Expectations* (1860–61) and *Our Mutual Friend* (1864–65), in their depiction of the destructive powers of money and ambition, develop most fully Dickens' radical view of society. Although Dickens' marriage was an unhappy one, it produced ten children. In 1856 he and his wife agreed to separate. He formed a relationship with Ellen Ternan, a young actress. In 1858 he began his famous public readings from his work, the strain of which hastened his death.

CHARLES DICKENS *The author with his daughters.*

Dickey, James (1923–   ) US poet and novelist. A pilot during World War II, he wrote of his experiences in his poetry. His poems are collected in *Into the Stone and Other Poems* (1960), *Drowning with Others* (1962), *Helmuts* (1964), *Buckdancer's Choice* (1965; National Book Award, 1966), *The Zodiac* (1976), *The Strength of Fields* (1979), and *Puella* (1982). He also wrote a novel, *Deliverance* (1969), which was made into a movie (1972). He was elected to the American Academy of Arts and Letters in 1987.

Dickinson, Emily (1830–86) US poet. Daughter of a Calvinist lawyer, she lived a largely secluded life after the age of 30, with her family at Amherst, Mass. She wrote numerous letters and over 1700 poems, mostly brief intense lyrics on themes of love, death, and nature; only seven were published during her lifetime.

dicotyledons The larger of the two main groups of flowering plants, which includes hardwood trees, shrubs, and many herbaceous plants (*compare* monocotyledons). Dicots are characterized by having two seed leaves (cotyledons) in the embryo. Typically the flower parts are arranged in fours or fives (or multiples of these) and the leaves have a netlike pattern of veins. *See also* angiosperms.

dictionaries. *See* lexicography.

Dicynodon A large herbivorous *therapsid (mammal-like) reptile that lived in the late Permian period, which ended 240 million years ago. It occurred worldwide in large numbers and had a long high-domed skull with a horny beaklike jaw and a single upper pair of teeth.

Diderot, Denis (1713–84) French philosopher and writer. With *Voltaire, Diderot helped create the *Enlightenment, mainly through the *Encyclopédie*, which he edited after 1750 (*see* Encyclopedists). Fascinated by science, he developed a form of *pantheism. His writings, notably *Lettre sur les aveugles* (1749), were materialistic and anti-Christian in tenor.

didgeridoo An aboriginal musical instrument, consisting of a wooden tube three to four feet long, sounded by blowing across one of the open ends. The other rests against a hole in the ground to increase resonance. It plays two notes: the fundamental, used to set up a basic rhythm, and a harmonic, used in counter-rhythm against it.

Dido In Greek legend, the daughter of a king of Tyre, who fled to Africa when her husband was murdered; there she founded *Carthage. According to legend she burned herself to death on a funeral pyre to avoid marriage to Iarvas of Numidia; in *Virgil's *Aeneid* she killed herself after being abandoned by her lover *Aeneas.

Diefenbaker, John G(eorge) (1895–1979) Canadian statesman; Progressive Conservative prime minister (1957–63). His party's victory in 1957 broke 22 years of Liberal government and in 1958 the Conservatives gained an overwhelming majority (208 out of 256 seats). He lost the 1963 election following opposition to proposals to build nuclear weapons in Canada and resigned the party leadership in 1967.

dielectric A substance that acts as an electrical *insulator and can sustain an electric field. When a voltage is applied across a perfect dielectric there is no energy loss and the electric field strength changes simultaneously with voltage. In the real dielectrics, such as air, ceramics, or wax, which are used in *capacitors, there is always a small energy loss.

dielectric constant. *See* permittivity.

Diels, Otto Paul Hermann (1876–1954) German chemist, who shared the 1950 Nobel Prize with Kurt Alder (1902–58) for their discovery of the **Diels-Alder reaction**, by which linear organic molecules are converted into cyclic molecules. The reaction is now widely used in the synthesis of alkaloids, polymers, etc.

Dieman, Anthony van (1593–1645) Dutch colonial administrator. As governor general of Batavia from 1636, he was responsible for the conquest of Malacca (1641) and parts of Ceylon (1644) important to the spice trade. He also commissioned *Tasman to explore the S Pacific in the interest of trade (1642, 1644), expeditions that discovered Van Dieman's Land (now Tasmania).

Dien Bien Phu, Battle of (March–May 1954) The decisive battle of the Indochina war, in NE Vietnam, in which Vietnamese forces defeated the French. The collapse of the French fortress coincided with the Geneva Conference, which ended French control of Indochina.

Dieppe 49 55N 1 05E A port and resort in N France, in the Seine-Maritime department on the English Channel. Occupied by the English (1420–35), it became a Huguenot stronghold but declined in importance after the revocation of the Edict of Nantes. It was the scene of heavy fighting during World War II. Population (1983 est.): 39,500.

Diesel engine. *See* internal-combustion engine.

dietetics The study of the principles of nutrition and their application to the selection of appropriate diets both to maintain health and as part of the treatment of certain diseases. A balanced diet should contain foods with adequate amounts of all the nutrients—carbohydrates, fats, proteins, minerals, and vitamins—as well as foods with a high content of dietary *fiber. An important aspect of the work of dieticians is to work out the special diets that are required for various diseases. Diabetes mellitus, for instance, requires a diet low in carbohydrate, whereas some liver diseases respond well to a low-protein diet. Obesity can be managed with a low-calorie diet.

Dietrich, Marlene (Maria Magdalene von Losch; 1901–92) German film actress and singer. Her image of sultry beauty was developed by Josef von *Sternberg in such films as *The Blue Angel* (1930). In 1930 she went to Hollywood, where she made numerous films of varying quality, including *Shanghai Express* (1932), *Blonde Venus* (1932), *Destry Rides Again* (1939), and *Judgment at Nuremburg* (1961). In her later career she gave many cabaret performances.

MARLENE DIETRICH *In* The Garden of Allah *(1936), with Sir C. Aubrey Smith (left) and Charles Boyer (right).*

diffraction The spreading or bending of light waves as they pass the edge of an object or pass through an aperture. The diffracted waves subsequently interfere with each other producing regions of alternately high and low intensity. This phenomenon, first discovered in 1665 by Francesco Grimaldi (1618–63), can be observed in the irregular boundary of a shadow of an object cast on a screen by a small light source. A similar effect occurs with sound waves. *See also* interference.

diffusion 1. The mixing of different fluids, or the distribution of a substance from a region of high concentration to one of lower concentration, by means of the random thermal motion of its constituents. In gases, according to Graham's law (named for Thomas Graham; 1805–69), the rates at which gases diffuse are inversely proportional to their densities. Mixing of fluids is complete after a certain time unless one set of particles is sufficiently heavy for sedimentation to occur. Diffusion also occurs between certain solids; for example gold will slowly diffuse into lead. **2.** The scattering of a beam of radiation on reflection from a rough surface or on transmission through certain media. When diffusion occurs the laws of reflection and refraction are not obeyed.

diffusionism A theory claiming that all civilization and culture were transmitted from certain circumscribed areas of the ancient world and disregarding the possibility of independent invention and discovery. In its most extreme form it held that this original center was Egypt. Other schools believed that certain other centers were also important. Their ideas dominated *ethnology between 1910 and 1925 but are now mainly discredited.

Digby, Sir Kenelm (1603–65) English courtier and scientist. He entered James I's service in 1623 and led a privateering expedition against French ships in the Mediterranean Sea in 1627–28. A Roman Catholic, he was forced to leave England during the Civil War. He finally returned to England in 1654. A founding member of the Royal Society (1663), he discovered that plants need oxygen.

digestion The process by which food is converted into substances that can be absorbed by the *intestine. The process begins in the mouth, where the food is chewed and mixed with saliva, and continues with the action of digestive enzymes secreted by the *stomach, duodenum, and *pancreas. Rhythmic contractions of the muscular layer of the intestinal wall (called peristalsis) ensures a constant mixing of enzymes and food and the propulsion of food along the intestine. The products of digestion include amino acids, various sugars (such as lactose, maltose, and glucose), and fat molecules; these are absorbed by the intestine and conveyed to the bloodstream.

Diggers An English sect that flourished under the *Commonwealth, so called because of their attempts to dig common land. Led by Gerrard *Winstanley, the Diggers believed in the economic and social equality of men. In April 1649, they established a community where they attempted to put into practice their beliefs in agrarian communism. The support they attracted alarmed the government and they were dispersed in March 1650. *See also* Levellers.

digger wasp A solitary *wasp of the families *Sphercidae* or *Pompilidae* (*see* spider wasp). Digger wasps are black with yellow or orange markings. They burrow into wood, plant stems, or the ground to build nests, which they stock with insects, such as caterpillars, grasshoppers, and flies; these have been paralyzed to provide food for the developing larvae.

digital computer. *See* computer.

digitalis A crude drug prepared from the dried leaves of foxglove plants. Digitalis is purified to digoxin, digitoxin, and lanatoside C. These drugs are used to improve the action of a failing or inefficient heart and to reduce a dangerously fast heart rate. Side effects of digitalis compounds include nausea, vomiting, and pulse irregularities.

digital recording. *See* recording of sound.

Dijon 47 20N 5 02E A city in France, the capital of the Côte-d'Or department on the Burgundy Canal. The former capital of Burgundy, it is the site of the palace of the Dukes of Burgundy and has a cathedral (13th–14th centuries). An important railroad center, it has varied industries and is famous for its mustard. Population (1990): 151,636.

dik-dik A small African antelope belonging to the genus *Madoqua* (7 species), found in the undergrowth of forested areas. 12–16 in (30–40 cm) high at the shoulder, dik-diks are generally solitary and only the males have horns. When disturbed, they take flight in a series of erratic leaps.

dike A wall-like body of igneous rock that is intruded (usually vertically) into the surrounding rock in such a way that it cuts across the stratification (layering) of this rock. *Compare* sill.

dilatation and curettage (D and C) An operation in which the neck (cervix) of the womb is dilatated (widened) and the lining of the womb is scraped out. D and C may be performed for a variety of reasons, including the removal of any residual membranes after a miscarriage, removal of cysts or tumors, removal of a specimen of tissue for examination in the diagnosis of various gynecological disorders, and for termination of a pregnancy (*see* abortion).

dill A widely cultivated annual or biennial European herb, *Anethum graveolens*, 24 in (60 cm) high. The smooth stem bears feathery leaves and umbrella-like clusters of small yellow flowers, which produce small hard flat fruits. The young leaves and fruits are used to flavor soups, cakes, salads, fish, and pickled cucumber. Family: **Umbelliferae*.

Dillinger, John (1903–34) US criminal and bank robber. After a crime-filled youth, he began robbing banks, was captured and escaped twice, and finally was shot and killed by Federal Bureau of Investigation agents outside a movie theater in Chicago. Because of his daring and notorious escapades he was dubbed "public enemy number one."

Dilthey, Wilhelm (1833–1911) German pioneer of biographical historiography. In contrast to Hegelian reliance on the cosmic spirit and metaphysical inquiry, Dilthey sought to conduct empirical inquiry, using historical facts, biographies, and the surviving records of great personalities. An early sociologist, he studied documents of cultural, religious, and social traditions.

DiMaggio, Joe (Joseph Paul D.; 1914–   ) US baseball player. An outfielder, he played for the New York Yankees (1936–42; 1946–51). Nicknamed the "Yankee Clipper," he had a career batting average of .325 and hit in 56 consecutive games (1941). He was elected to the Baseball Hall of Fame (1955). He was briefly the second husband (1953–54) of Marilyn Monroe.

dimensional analysis A method of testing or deriving a physical equation in which each term is expressed in the dimensions of mass, length, time, and (if electric or magnetic quantities are present) either charge or current. Each term must have the same dimensional formula if the equation is true. Dimensional analysis is also useful in predicting the behavior of a full-scale system from a model.

diminishing returns, law of The law that as more of a variable factor of production, such as labor, is applied to a fixed quantity of another factor, such as capital (machinery), the returns to each additional unit of the variable factor will eventually decrease. For example, in a small factory, employing one laborer may increase production by freeing machine operators from some tasks, but employing a second laborer will not increase production by as much again.

Dimitrii Donskoi (1350–89) Prince of Moscow (1359–89) and Grand Prince of Vladimir (1362–89). His defeat of Khan Mamai at the battle of Kulikovo on the Don River in 1380 began the liberation of Russia from the *Golden Horde.

Dimitrov, Georgi (1882–1949) Bulgarian statesman. Dimitrov became a member of the executive committee of the *Comintern in 1921. Exiled in 1923, he moved in 1929 to Berlin, where in 1933 he was accused with others of setting fire to the Reichstag. Acquitted, he became a citizen of the Soviet Union and secretary general of the Comintern. In 1944 he returned to Bulgaria and became prime minister (1946). He died in Moscow.

Dinant 50 16N 4 55E A town in S Belgium, on the Meuse River. It was famous for its artistic metalwork (*dinanderie*) in the Middle Ages. A popular tourist center, it is overlooked by an 11th-century citadel situated on a cliff above the river. Population (1971 est): 9862.

Dinaric Alps (Serbo-Croat name: Dinara Planina) A mountain range in SE Europe from Croatia to N Albania, extending some 435 mi (700 km) NW–SE between the Alps and the Balkan Mountains and rising to 8274 ft (2522 m).

D'Indy, Vincent (1851–1931) French composer, the pupil and biographer of Franck and the cofounder of the Paris Schola Cantorum (1894). He was greatly influenced by Wagner and wrote a number of large-scale orchestral compositions, as well as operas and chamber music. His most famous work is the *Symphony on a French Mountaineer's Song* (for piano and orchestra; 1886).

Dinesen, Isak (Karen Blixen, Baroness Blixen-Finecke; 1885–1962) Danish author, who took up writing after 20 years spent managing a coffee plantation in Kenya. She is best known for two collections of stories in the gothic style: *Seven Gothic Tales* (1934) and *Winter's Tales* (1942).

dingo An Australian wild *dog, *Canis familiaris* (formerly *C. dingo*), introduced about 3000 years ago from Asia. It is about 48 in (120 cm) long, including the tail (12 in [30 cm]), and has a smooth tan-colored coat. It is nocturnal and generally solitary.

Dinka A Nilotic people of the Nile basin region of the Sudan. Warlike and independent, the Dinka move with their cattle from dry-season pastures by the rivers to wet-season settlements, where they grow millet. There are many independent tribes of varying size each with numerous levels of segmentation into smaller clans and patrilineal kinship units. Age-set organization is important for men, who attain adulthood by undergoing the ordeals of initiation ceremonial. Ritual life emphasizes sacrificing to ancestral spirits and the god Nhial.

dinoflagellates A group of mostly marine unicellular organisms that form part of the *plankton. Usually measuring 0.0008–0.0039 in (0.02–0.1 mm), many have cellulose cell walls. They move by beating two hairlike structures (flagella). Some species contain the green pigment chlorophyll and can manufacture their own food (by photosynthesis); others can engulf food particles. Since they have characteristics of both plants and animals, dinoflagellates can be classified as algae or protozoans.

dinosaur An extinct reptile that was the dominant terrestrial animal during the Jurassic and Cretaceous periods (200–65 million years ago). Dinosaurs first appeared about 210 million years ago and included many varied forms, ranging in size from about 24 in (60 cm) to such mighty creatures as *Diplodocus*, which reached 87 ft (27 m) in length. There were two orders: the *Saurischia, which were mostly carnivores and included the bipedal *Allosaurus and *Tyrannosaurus*; and the *Ornithischia, which were all herbivores and included the bipedal *Iguanodon*, the horned *Triceratops*, and *Stegosaurus*. Why both orders died out at the end of the Cretaceous period along with other reptiles, such as *ichthyosaurs, *pterosaurs, and *plesiosaurs, is still not certain. Dinosaurs had large bodies with heavy bones and protective armor and were probably unable to adapt to climatic changes and the effects of a rise in the sea level, which flooded their coastal habitats and led to changes in vegetation.

Dio Cassius (c. 150–235 AD) Roman historian, who was twice elected consul and was appointed governor of Africa and Dalmatia. In 80 books, written in Greek, he recorded the history of Rome from the arrival of Aeneas to his own time.

Dio Chrysostom (2nd century AD) Greek philosopher and orator. A friend of the Emperor Trajan, he admired the Roman state, from his family estates in Bithynia (Asia Minor), and eulogized its compound of monarchy, aristocracy, and democracy.

Diocletian(us), Gaius Aurelius Valerius (245–313 AD) Roman emperor (284–305). He was born in Dalmatia and rose to prominence in the army, to which he owed his accession. In 293 he established the tetrarchy to govern the Empire more effectively in a time of civil strife: the Empire was divided into East and West, with each ruled by an emperor and his associate. Diocletian ruled in the East with *Galerius, who was probably responsible for the persecution of Christians begun in 303. In 305 Diocletian retired to Salona (now Split, Croatia), where his palace can still be seen.

diode. *See* semiconductor diode; thermionic valve.

Diodorus Siculus (1st century BC) Greek historian, born in Sicily. His *Bibliotheca historica* is a history of the Mediterranean countries from their legendary origins up to his own time; of its 40 volumes, only 15 survive.

Diogenes Laertius (3rd century AD) Greek compiler of the opinions and biographical details of classical philosophers, including the *Presocratics. The historical authenticity of his biographical material, for example about the life of *Epicurus, is doubtful.

Diogenes of Sinope (412–322 BC) The founder of the philosophical sect of the *Cynics. Influenced by *Antisthenes, Diogenes claimed, in contrast to almost all Greek thinkers, total freedom and self-sufficiency for the individual. Unlike modern anarchists, he saw no need for violent rebellion to assert his independence, which he thought he already had. His ostentatious disregard for social conventions made him the subject of many stories. He is reported to have lived in a large tub in Athens. According to another story, he went about in daylight with a lamp, saying that he was searching for an honest man.

Diomedes A legendary Greek hero of the Trojan War who commanded 80 ships from Argos. He wounded *Ares and *Aphrodite, took the place of the absent *Achilles in an attack on Troy, and captured the Palladium, the sacred image of *Athena.

Dionysius of Halicarnassus (1st century BC) Greek historian who taught at Rome after 30 BC. He compiled a history of Rome from its origins to the first Punic War in 20 books, of which 10 survive. He also wrote literary criticism and treatises on rhetoric.

Dionysius the Areopagite, St (1st century AD) Greek churchman. He was converted to Christianity by St Paul and was traditionally the first Bishop of Athens. In the middle ages he was thought to be the author of several theological treatises in Greek. These are now attributed to *Pseudo-Dionysius the Areopagite. Feast day: Oct 9.

Dionysius (I) the Elder (c. 430–367 BC) Tyrant of Syracuse (405–367), who fought the Carthaginians in a series of wars, which were ultimately unsuccessful, for control of Sicily and the Greek cities of S Italy. His son **Dionysius (II) the Younger**, who succeeded him as tyrant (367–356, 347–344), was a patron of writers and philosophers and was taught briefly by Plato.

Dionysus (*or* Bacchus) The Greek god of wine, originally a vegetation god. He was the son of *Semele by Zeus, who saved him at her death; he was reared by the nymphs of Nysa. A common theme of many legends concerning him is a people's refusal to accept his divinity and his subsequent retribution: thus Pentheus, King of Thebes, was torn to death by the god's ecstatic female followers, the maenads. Athens held five festivals in Dionysus' honor.

Diophantus of Alexandria (mid-3rd century AD) Greek mathematician; one of the few Greeks to study algebra rather than geometry. He discovered the method of solving problems by means of algebraic equations. His work was preserved by Arabic mathematicians and, in the 16th century, was translated into Latin after which it inspired many advances in algebra. Diophantine equations are named for him.

diopter A unit used to measure the power of a lens equal to the reciprocal of its focal length in meters. The power of a converging lens is taken to be positive and that of a diverging lens as negative.

Dior, Christian (1905–57) French fashion designer, who first became known with his 1947 collection, which introduced the New Look, characterized by fitted bodices and long full skirts. His later designs, which included the H-line and the A-line, aspired to a similar ideal of femininity.

CHRISTIAN DIOR *The French fashion designer at the opening of a 1950 fashion show. His seven mannequins are all modeling New Look evening dresses.*

diorite A coarse-grained plutonic igneous rock of intermediate composition. It consists mainly of plagioclase feldspar and ferromagnesian minerals (often hornblende, biotite, or pyroxene). It usually occurs in small intrusive masses or in parts of *batholiths.

Dioscorides Pedanius (c. 40–c. 90 AD) Greek physician, who compiled the first pharmacopoeia. He traveled widely as a surgeon in the Roman army and in his work *De materia medica* (c. 77 AD) he described nearly 600 plants and their medicinal properties.

Dioscuri. *See* Castor and Pollux.

dip circle. *See* magnetic dip.

diphtheria An acute bacterial infection primarly affecting the nose, throat, or larynx. It has been virtually eliminated from most western nations as a result of extensive immunization, although it formerly caused the death of many children. It is still found in Africa and India. Diphtheria produces a membrane across the throat that chokes the child. Alternatively death may be caused by poisons damaging the heart. The disease can be cured using penicillin and antitoxin.

Diplodocus A huge amphibious dinosaur of the Jurassic period (200–136 million years ago) that was the largest terrestrial vertebrate ever to exist, reaching a length of 87 ft (27 m). It had a narrow body with massive pillar-like legs, a long neck with a tiny head, and a long tail. It fed on soft vegetation found in swamps and shallow lakes and had very few teeth. Order: *Saurischia.

dipole, electric and magnetic A pair of equal and opposite electric charges or *magnetic poles. The dipole moment is defined as the magnitude of one of the charges or poles multiplied by the distance separating them. Some molecules have an electric dipole moment due to the preferential attraction of the bonding electrons for one of the atoms. In the case of hydrogen chloride, for example, the chlorine atom gains a slight negative charge and the hydrogen atom a slight positive charge. Measurement of dipole moments often provides evidence regarding the shapes of molecules.

dipper An aquatic songbird of the family *Cinclidae* (4 species), also called water ouzel, of Eurasia and America. Dippers are found near fast-flowing mountain streams, diving into the water to search for insects and small fish. The Eurasian white-breasted dipper (*Cinclus cinclus*) is about 7 in (17 cm) long and has a dense dark-brown plumage with a white breast.

Diprotodon An extinct Australian giant *wombat that was about the size of a rhinoceros. It lived during the Pleistocene epoch, about a million years ago.

Diptera An order of insects comprising the two-winged, or true, flies. *See* fly.

Dirac, Paul Adrien Maurice (1902–84) British physicist, who made two fundamental contributions to the development of the quantum theory. In 1928 he introduced a new notation for handling quantum equations that combined *Schrödinger's use of *differential equations with *Heisenberg's approach using *matrices. Two years later he incorporated *relativity into quantum theory and produced an equation that predicted the existence of antiparticles. For his work he shared the 1933 Nobel Prize with Schrödinger.

direction finder Equipment for locating the source of a radio signal, such as a ship at sea. It consists of one or more directive *aerials (usually in the form of a loop), designed to detect signals from a specific direction, and a receiver. Frequencies normally used are between 0.1 and 2 megahertz. The process can be automatic, often using a rotating aerial with a *cathode-ray tube to display signal strength and direction. Reflections from mountains or tall buildings can cause errors in a land-based direction-finding system. *Radar is a form of direction finding based on picking up reflections of a transmitted signal.

Directory (1795–99) The government of the First Republic of France, comprising five directors who were elected by a Council of Ancients (men over 40

years old) and a Council of Five Hundred. The Directory, which marked a retreat from the extremity of the early years of the *French Revolution, has been
criticized for its corruption and administrative incompetence but it achieved successes in the Revolutionary Wars. It was overthrown by a coup d'état on behalf
of *Napoleon.

Dire Dawa 9 40N 41 47E A city in central Ethiopia. It is in a hot dry region
with little cultivation. Local industries include manufacturing cotton goods and
cement. Population (1978 est): 72,202.

Dirichlet's theorem A theorem in *number theory stating that there are an
infinite number of *prime numbers contained in the set of all numbers of the
form $(a \times n) + b$, where a and b are themselves prime and n is a natural number, i.e. 1, 2, 3, ... The theorem was first suggested by *Gauss and proved by
the French mathematician Peter Gustav Lejeune Dirichlet (1805–59).

dirigibles Balloons that obtain their thrust from a propeller. The first airship to
fly was a French steam-powered machine, designed in 1852 by H. Giffard; however, the first practical airship was the electrically powered *La France* (1884),
built by Renard and Krebs. By 1900 the initiative in airships had passed to Germany, with the machines of Count Ferdinand von Zeppelin (1838–1917) leading
the field. Between 1910 and 1914 Zeppelins were in extensive passenger service, carrying some 35,000 passengers, without mishap. In World War I these
machines were used by the Germans to bomb England—the first effective use of
aerial bombardment. From then onward the history of airships is one of disaster
followed by disaster. The British *R101* caught fire at Beauvais in 1930, the US
Shenandoah and the *Akron* were lost in 1933, and the German *Hindenberg* was
destroyed in 1937. These disasters with hydrogen-filled airships cost many lives
and gave them a reputation from which they have never recovered. However, the
availability of the nonflammable gas helium created a mild revival of interest in
the 1970s, especially in the Soviet Union.

disaccharide A carbohydrate comprising two linked *monosaccharide sugar
units. *Lactose, maltose, and *sucrose are important disaccharides.

disarmament The reduction of the fighting capability of a nation. Limited
disarmament treaties were made under the auspices of the *League of Nations in
the 1930s, in an attempt to avoid a repetition of the disastrous loss of life in
World War I. But German rearmament under the Nazis and Japanese expansion-
ism in Asia thwarted these attempts. After World War II the main concern was to
contain the spread of nuclear weapons. An attempt was made by the UN to limit
both conventional arms and nuclear weapons, especially of the defeated countries, but during the Cold War both the Soviet Union and the western powers assisted in the rearmament of their former enemies. In 1963, however, the Soviet
Union, the US, and the UK signed a *Nuclear Test-Ban Treaty. In 1967 the same
countries signed a treaty banning the use of nuclear weapons in outer space; in
the same year 59 countries signed a nuclear nonproliferation treaty. As a result
of an initiative by President Johnson, talks between the Soviet Union and US
were started in 1969 to limit and reduce strategic nuclear arms; known as SALT
(Strategic Arms Limitation Talks) they reached limited agreements in 1974
(SALT I) and again in 1979 (SALT II). *See also* Geneva Conferences; Hague
Peace Conferences.

Disciples of Christ (*or* Campbellites) A Christian denomination originating
within Presbyterianism in the 19th century but founded as a separate denomination in Philadelphia in 1827 by Alexander Campbell (1788–1866). They preach
a simple biblical creed, are congregational in organization, and celebrate weekly
communion as the central act of worship.

discriminant A mathematical expression derived from the coefficients of a polynomial that gives information about the roots of the polynomial. An example occurs in the general quadratic equation $ax^2 + bx + c = 0$. This equation has just one solution if its discriminant $b^2 - 4ac$ is zero.

discus throw A field event in athletics. The circular discus is made of wood and metal, the men's weighing 4.4 lb (2 kg) and the women's 2.2 lb (1 kg). It is thrown as far as possible with one hand from within a circle 8.2 ft (2.5 m) in diameter.

disinfectant A substance or process that kills germs or prevents their multiplying. Carbolic acid (phenol) was introduced for this purpose in medicine in the 1870s by Joseph *Lister. It is still used, as are many of its derivatives, in cleaning materials and, in weaker solutions, in skin disinfectants. Chlorine and such compounds as sodium hypochlorite kill bacteria and also some viruses. Chlorinated phenols, such as hexachlorophane, are also widely used in pharmaceutical products. Many other chemicals, including hydrogen peroxide (H_2O_2), iodine (I_2), formaldehyde (HCHO), and other aldehydes, are also used as disinfectants. Dry heating to 110°F (40°C) for about three hours will kill all disease-causing germs. Boiling water and ultraviolet light are also effective disinfectants.

dislocation Displacement of a bone at a joint, producing severe pain, difficulty in moving the joint, and usually obvious deformity. Shoulders, elbows, hips, vertebrae, and fingers are all commonly dislocated in injuries. Often one of the bones in the joint will be broken, and for this reason it is unwise to attempt to put the joint back before an X-ray film has been taken.

Disney, Walt (1901–66) US film producer and animator. His most famous cartoon character, Mickey Mouse, was designed in 1928. His films include full-length cartoon features, such as *Snow White and the Seven Dwarfs* (1938), *Pinocchio* (1939), and *Bambi* (1943), nature documentaries, and adventure films, such as *Treasure Island* (1950) and *Mary Poppins* (1964), all made for family audiences. His *Fantasia* (1940) used colorful visual images and cartoons to accompany several pieces of classical music played by an orchestra under *Stokowski. He opened Disneyland, an amusement park, in California in 1955. Walt Disney World was later opened (1971) near Orlando, Fla.

display In zoology, a specialized means by which animals communicate with each other. Displays can be vocal (such as birdsong), visual (by posture or colorful plumage), chemical (by means of *pheromones), or tactile (for instance bees communicate in a dark hive largely by touch). Displays ensure social integration and cohesion of populations by communicating the whereabouts and identity of individuals. They are used to establish social rank, maintain territory, synchronize breeding, and give warning of danger.

Disraeli, Benjamin, 1st Earl of Beaconsfield (1804–81) British statesman; Conservative prime minister (1868, 1874–80). Of Italian-Jewish descent, Disraeli was baptized a Christian in 1817. He became a member of Parliament in 1837. Disraeli was critical of Peel's Conservative Government (1841–46) and opposed the repeal of the *Corn Laws. He was three times chancellor of the exchequer (1852, 1858–59, 1866–68): in 1858 he introduced an unsuccessful parliamentary reform bill but was largely responsible for the 1867 *Reform Act. He became prime minister in February, 1868, but lost office following the autumn election, which was won by the Liberals under Gladstone. His second ministry carried important social legislation. In 1875 he bought Britain a major stake in the Suez Canal and in 1876 secured passage of a bill that conferred the title Empress of India on Queen Victoria. He successfully pursued British interests at the Congress of *Berlin (1878). Under Disraeli's leadership the Conservative Party came to be clearly identified with policies that upheld the monarchy, Empire, and Church of England, while sponsoring social reform. A flamboyant and witty parliamentarian, he earned the respect and friendship of the queen. Also a writer, Disraeli's novels include *Vivien Grey* (1826), *Coningsby, or the New Generation* (1844), and *Sybil, or the Two Nations* (1845).

DISRAELI *A contemporary cartoon, entitled, "A Bad Example," shows the prime minister (right) and Gladstone, his political opponent, throwing mud at one another.*

dissonance A combination of two or more musical notes that sounds harsh to the ear. This harshness is caused by the *beats that are produced when two notes (or their overtones) of similar pitch are sounded together. For example C and F-sharp are dissonant because the second overtone of C is G, which beats with F-sharp. A common type of dissonance in diatonic music consists of chords that sound incomplete in themselves and need to resolve onto a consonance. All diatonic music relies on the contrast between dissonances and consonances, without which such music would sound predictable and uninteresting. The use of *chromaticism in the late 19th century increased the amount of dissonance in music; in the 20th century such composers as Bartok and Stravinsky deliberately cultivated the use of unresolved dissonances.

distemper (veterinary science) A highly contagious virus disease affecting dogs, foxes, ferrets, badgers, etc. Canine distemper occurs mainly at 3–12 months; symptoms include fever, loss of appetite, and a discharge from the eyes and nose. Complications may include conjunctivitis, bronchitis, pneumonia, and gastroenteritis. The disease can be prevented by vaccination at about 11 weeks with a booster dose at two years.

distillation A method of purifying or separating the components of a liquid by boiling or evaporating the liquid and condensing the vapor. It is used for separating either liquids from solids or a mixture of liquids whose components have different boiling points. The latter is known as fractional distillation. Distillation is employed in petroleum refineries to separate the various *hydrocarbons, in the production of alcoholic spirits, and in extracting pure water from sea water.

distribution function A mathematical function that gives the probability of finding a system in a particular state or within a range of states. For example, the probability of one of the molecules of a gas having velocity between v and $v + dv$ in a given direction is Fdv, where F is the distribution function.

distributive law A law concerning the combination of mathematical operations. In arithmetic, for example, multiplication is said to obey the distributive law, or to be distributive, with respect to addition because $a(b + c) = ab + ac$.

District of Columbia A federal district of the E US, coextensive with the federal capital, *Washington. Area: 69 sq mi (178 sq km).

dithyramb An ancient Greek hymn to the god *Dionysus. Originally sung extempore, it developed into a literary form—traditionally originated by the poet Arion—around the 6th and 7th centuries BC. Its best-known authors include *Bacchylides and *Pindar. Aristotle believed that Greek drama developed out of this form.

dittany A perennial European herbaceous plant, *Dictamnus albus*, also known as the gas plant or burning bush. A strong-scented gland-covered plant, it gives off so much aromatic oil that it is said to burst into flames when ignited. Dittany produces a drooping spike of white or pink flowers. Family: *Rutaceae*. The name is also applied to several other plants. Crete dittany (*Origanum dictamnus*) is a herb closely related to marjoram, with thick woolly leaves and pinkish flower clusters. Family: *Labiatae*.

Diu. *See* Goa, Daman, and Diu.

diuretics A large class of drugs that increase the excretion of urine by the kidneys. Diuretics are used in the treatment of diseases in which fluid accumulates in the tissues. These illnesses include heart failure, kidney failure, and some liver diseases (such as cirrhosis). Some diuretics (e.g. frusemide) cause loss of potassium from the body and are prescribed with a potassium supplement. Diuretics may also be used in the treatment of high blood pressure.

diurnal motion The apparent daily motion of astronomical bodies from E to W across the sky, in circles parallel to the celestial equator (*see* celestial sphere). It is caused by the earth's W-to-E rotation.

diver A large aquatic bird belonging to a family (*Gaviidae*; 3 species) occurring in the N hemisphere, also called loon. Divers breed on lakes and ponds and spend the winter in temperate coastal waters. They have small pointed wings and black and white plumage and they dive deeply, feeding on fish, frogs, and aquatic insects. Order: *Gaviiformes*.

divide. *See* watershed.

dividend A share in the profits of a company paid to stockholders. The rate of dividend is generally declared at the company's annual general meeting and will reflect the preceding year's profit. The dividend **yield** of the share is the income it produces expressed as a percentage of its current value.

divine right of kings A political doctrine claiming that monarchs are responsible only to God and that their subjects owe them unquestioning obedience. The theory originated in the middle ages and was most fully developed in the 16th and 17th centuries, especially in England, where it was associated particularly with the Stuart kings, and in France, where its leading exponent was Louis XIV.

diving beetle An aquatic beetle—a true *water beetle—belonging to a family (*Dytiscidae*; about 4000 species), occurring worldwide but particularly common in Europe and Asia. Diving beetles have dark streamlined bodies and vary in length from 0.08–1.5 in (2–38 mm): the largest genera are *Cybister* and *Dytiscus*. The adults and larvae (water tigers) are voracious carnivores.

diving duck A *duck that dives to the bottom of lakes or rivers to feed, aided by a dense high-domed skull. Diving ducks, which include the *goldeneye, *pochard, and *scaup, usually have a drab plumage, thick neck, narrow wings, and large feet; the legs are set far back and they walk awkwardly on land. *Compare* dabbling duck.

division of labor The separation of tasks in an industrial process, with the allocation of one worker to each specific task in the manufacture of an object. The term was first introduced by Adam *Smith in his *Wealth of Nations* (1776). The object is to increase output; however, extreme division of labor, as in a car factory, can lead to intense boredom for the worker, who is confined to repeating one operation continuously.

divorce The legal process by which a marriage is ended. Grounds for divorce vary widely among the states, but the trend has been toward easier grounds, such as "irreconcilable differences."

Diwali An important Hindu religious festival. Held over the New Year according to the Vikrama calendar (October–November), it is celebrated especially among the merchant classes and honors *Lakshmi, the goddess of wealth (or in Bengal, Kali). There is feasting, gambling, and lighting of lamps in honor of *Rama. Jains commemorate at this time the death of their saint *Mahavira.

Dix, Dorothea (Lynde) (1802–87) US reformer and crusader for improved conditions in the treatment of the mentally ill. After teaching in Worcester, Mass., she established her own school for girls (1821–35) in Boston. It was while teaching a Sunday school class at the Cambridge jail in 1841 that she was deeply affected by the poor treatment of the mentally ill. After this experience she spent the rest of her life improving conditions for the mentally ill throughout the US and, eventually, in Europe. Legislation, as a result of her efforts, provided for improved conditions in mental institutions.

Dixieland A type of jazz played in imitation of the traditional *New Orleans style, named for the Original Dixieland Jazz Band (founded 1912). It is usually played by small bands. It emerged in the early years of the 20th century but declined during the *swing and bebop eras. Among the most outstanding Dixieland musicians were King Oliver, Jelly Roll Morton, Sidney Bechet, and Louis *Armstrong.

Diyarbakır 37 55N 40 14E A town in SE Turkey, on the Tigris River. It was taken by the Turks in 1515 and has 4th-century walls. Gold and silver filigree work is produced here; wool and grain are traded. It has a university (1966). Population (1990): 381,144.

Djajapura. *See* Jajapura.

DIWALI *The final day of the five-day festival is dedicated to the tie between brothers and sisters, who exchange special gifts. The bracelet on the boy's wrist, given to him by his sister, symbolizes the bond between them.*

Djakarta. *See* Jakarta.

Djambi. *See* Jambi.

Djerba Island 33 45N 11 00E A Tunisian island in the Mediterranean Sea, linked to the mainland by a causeway. Area: 197 sq mi (510 sq km).

Djibouti, Republic of (name until 1977: the French Territory of the Afars and the Issas) A small country in NE Africa, on the Gulf of Aden at its entrance to the Red Sea. It consists chiefly of an arid rocky coastal plain rising to a plateau inland. The main population groups are Somalis (chiefly Issas) and Afars, with Arabic and European minorities. *Economy*: the port of Djibouti (a free port since 1949) is the country's economic focus handling an important transshipment trade but it was adversely affected by the closure of the Suez Canal (1967–75). The port is linked by rail to Ethiopia and handles about half of that country's trade. Exports include hides, skins, sugar, and Ethiopian coffee. Inland the predominantly nomadic population tends goats, sheep, and camels. *History*: French involvement, centered on the port, began in the mid-19th century. It was made a French colony known as French Somaliland in 1896 and proclaimed an overseas territory in 1967. It became independent in 1977 as Djibouti with Hassan Gouled Aptidon as its first president. The country suffered from the war between Ethiopia and Somalia through the disruption of trade. The sustained drought in East Africa in the early 1980s worsened already distressing conditions in Djibouti, where poverty is pervasive. The problem of Ethiopian refugees and the influx of foreigners from war-torn South Yemen in 1986 placed an even greater economic burden on the country's weak economy. Djibouti is entirely dependent on foreign aid for its survival, relying heavily on French support. In 1992 a new constitution was approved. Official languages: Hamitic languages of Somali. Official currency: Djibouti franc of 100 centimes. Area: 8409 sq mi (21,783 sq km). Population (1990 est): 337,000. Capital and chief port: Djibouti.

Djilas, Milovan (1911–   ) Yugoslav politician and writer. A member of
*Tito's resistance group in World War II, Djilas became a prominent figure in
the postwar communist government. His criticism of the regime led to his demo-
tion (1954) and he was twice imprisoned (1956–61, 1962–66) for publishing
critical material abroad. His books include *New Class* (1957), *Land Without Justice* (1958), and *Conversations with Stalin* (1962).

Djoser (*or* Zoser) King of Egypt (c. 2980–c. 2950 BC) of the 3rd dynasty, famous for his pyramid at *Saqqarah, near Memphis.

DNA (*or* deoxyribonucleic acid) A nucleic acid that is the chief constituent of
the *chromosomes, carrying genetic information, in the form of *genes, necessary for the organization and functioning of living cells.

The molecular structure of DNA was first proposed by J. D. *Watson and F. H.
*Crick in 1953. It consists of a double helix of two strands coiled around each
other. Each strand is made up of alternating pentose sugar (deoxyribose) and
phosphate groups, with an organic base attached to each pentose group. There are
four possible bases: adenine (A), guanine (G), cytosine (C), and thymine (T).
The bases on each strand are joined by hydrogen bonds and are always paired in
the same way: A always binds with T and G with C. During replication, the
strands of the helix separate and each provides a template for the synthesis of a
new complementary strand, thus producing two identical copies of the original
helix. This special property for accurate self-replication enables DNA to dupli-
cate the genes of an organism during the cell divisions of growth (*see* mitosis)
and the production of germ cells for the next generation (*see* meiosis).

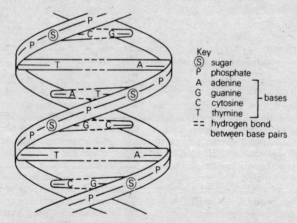

DNA *The structure of a DNA molecule takes the form of a
double helix. The sequence of base pairs constitutes the genetic code, which controls the inheritance of characteristics.*

Dnepr River (*or* Dnieper R.) A river in Russia. Rising in the Valdai Hills, NE
of Smolensk, it flows mainly SE through Russia, Belarus, and Ukraine to enter
the Black Sea. It is the third longest river in Europe. Length: 1420 mi (2286 km).

Dneprodzerzhinsk (name until 1936: Kamenskoye) 48 30N 34 37E A port
in Ukraine, on the Dnepr River. A major industrial center, it produces iron and
steel, machine tools, and chemicals. Population (1991 est): 284,000.

Dnepropetrovsk (name from 1787 until 1796 and from 1802 until 1826: Ekterinoslav) 48 29N 35 00E A city in Ukraine on the Dnepr River. It is one of the country's largest industrial cities, producing especially iron and steel, and it is also a transportation center. Population (1991 est): 1,189,000.

Dnestr River (*or* Dniester R.) A river flowing mainly SE from the Carpathian Mountains, through Ukraine and Moldova to the Black Sea near Odessa. Length: 877 mi (1411 km).

Doberman pinscher A breed of dog developed by Louis Dobermann in Germany in the late 19th century. It has a powerful streamlined body with a very short tail and a long muzzle. The short smooth coat is black, brown, or blue-gray with tan markings. Dobermans are widely used as police, guard, and guide dogs. Height: 28 in (70 cm) (dogs); 26 in (64 cm) (bitches).

Dobruja (Bulgarian name: Dobrudzha; Romanian name: Dobrogea) An area in E central Europe, in SE Romania and NE Bulgaria. It consists of a low-lying alluvial plain between the Danube River and the Black Sea.

dobsonfly A winged insect belonging to the family *Corydalidae*, occurring in all continents except Europe. Male dobsonflies have enormously exaggerated jaws, sometimes over 1 in (25 mm) long. Eggs are laid near fresh water and the larvae (hellgrammites) are aquatic, using their biting jaws to feed on insects and small invertebrates. They migrate to the soil to pupate. Order: *Neuroptera*.

Dobzhansky, Theodosius (1900–75) US geneticist, born is Russia. His studies of wild populations of fruit flies revealed the extent of genetic differences between individuals and how, through natural selection, this enabled the populations to adapt rapidly to changing conditions. Dobzhansky also studied the formation of new species and has written influential articles on evolution and philosophy.

dock A plant (usually perennial) of the genus *Rumex*, of temperate regions. 4–80 in (10–200 cm) tall, it has a deep stout root and large lance-shaped leaves. The small greenish flowers are borne in small clusters on branched flower stems. They produce small nutlets, often surrounded by the reddish papery remains of the petals. Dock leaves are the traditional antidote to nettle stings. Family: *Polygonaceae. See also* sorrel.

docks Structures designed to enable ships to load and unload cargo or passengers or to undergo repairs. A **wet dock** is situated on a tidal river or on the coast and has gates to maintain the water level irrespective of the tide. Ships can only enter or leave such a dock when the tide brings the water level outside it to the level inside. Where the range of the tide is small (less than 13 ft [4 m]) a **tidal dock** can be used. In this the dock is open to the harbor and ships in dock rise and fall with the tide. In **dry docks** the water enters at one end only and gates enable all the water to be pumped out, so that repairs can be made to a ship's hull. **Floating docks** have the advantage of being movable, but they have a relatively short life. Floating docks also have watertight compartments from which the water can be pumped out and they can be used for repair work. *See also* dredger.

Doctorow, E(dgar) L(awrence) (1931–   ) US novelist. Known for blending real people with imaginary characters, he wrote *Welcome to Hard Times* (1960), *Big as Life* (1966), *The Book of Daniel* (1971), *Ragtime* (1975), *Loon Lake* (1980), *Lives of the Poets* (1984), *World's Fair* (1985), and *Billy Bathgate* (1989).

documentary film A film that portrays and interprets factual reality, often for educational purposes. The term was coined by John Grierson, leader of a school of British documentary film directors in the 1930s, to describe one of the most influential early documentaries, Robert *Flaherty's *Nanook of the North* (1920). The propaganda films produced in Nazi Germany, notably Leni Reifenstahl's *Triumph of the Will* (1934), were an exception to the generally left-wing political sympathies of documentary films. Many documentary films have been produced for television.

dodder A twining parasitic plant of the widely distributed genus *Cuscuta* (150 species), which absorbs food by inserting rootlike organs into the stems of other plants. Dodder has no chlorophyll (green pigment): it consists simply of a yellow or pinkish cordlike stem bearing round clusters of tiny yellow or white bell-shaped flowers. The leaves are reduced to scales and there are no roots. Family: *Cuscutaceae*.

Dodecanese (Modern Greek name: Dhodhekánisos) A group of Greek islands in the SE Aegean Sea. Although known as the 12 Islands, it in fact consists of some 20 islands and islets, which include Cos, *Rhodes (the largest), and Pátmos. They were taken from Turkey by Italy in 1912 and passed to Greece in 1947. Total area: 1050 sq mi (2719 sq km). Capital: Rhodes.

Dodge City 37 45N 100 01W A city in SW Kansas, on the Arkansas River. An important stop for westward travelers on the Santa Fe Trail in the 1880s. It became a major cattle-shipping center with the coming of the Santa Fe Railroad. Meat packing is still carried on, and tourism is important. Population (1990): 21,129.

dodo A large clumsy flightless bird, *Raphus cucullatus*, that lived on Mauritius but was extinct by 1681. Weighing about 51 lb (23 kg), it had a gray-blue wispy plumage, stout yellow legs, tiny wings, a tuft of curly white tail feathers, and a large head with a massive hooked bill; it probably fed on fruit or roots. Family: *Raphidae*; order: *Columbiformes* (pigeons, etc.)

Dodoma 6 10S 35 40E A city in E central Tanzania. It has been designated as the future capital to replace Dar es Salaam, and some government operations began to move there in 1983. Population (1988): 203,000.

dog A carnivorous mammal belonging to the family *Canidae. Ancestors of the modern domestic dog (*Canis familiaris*), probably derived from wolves or jackals, were first domesticated over 10,000 years ago. Wild dogs generally live and hunt in packs, relying on speed and cooperation to secure their prey. They are specialized hunters with long legs, sharp teeth, strong jaws, and acute hearing and smell.

The intelligence and social nature of dogs have led to their selective breeding by man for a variety of purposes, principally as sporting dogs, working dogs, and ornamental breeds for household pets. There are up to 400 modern breeds and standards for over 100 recognized US breeds have been established.

dogbane A perennial herb of the genus *Apocynum* (about 7 species), found mostly in the tropics and subtropics, especially the American species *A. androsaemifolium*. Up to 5 ft (1.5 m) high, dogbane has simple leaves and small white or pink bell-shaped flowers clustered at the tips of the shoots. The juice contains alkaloids and has been used in arrow poisons. Family: *Apocynaceae*. *See also* Indian hemp.

doge The title of the chief magistrate of Venice from about 697 AD to the fall of the Venetian Empire in 1797. The doge was elected for life and wielded considerable power until 1172 when his authority was restricted by the creation of a supreme Great Council of 480 members. Further constitutional checks made the doge little more than a figurehead. The first **Doge's Palace** was built in 814 and destroyed by an uprising in 976. Subsequent structures were destroyed by fire, and the present richly decorated gothic palace originated in the early 14th century, with later additions.

Dogen (1200–53) Japanese Buddhist monk, who introduced the *Soto school of Zen Buddhism to Japan. An orphan of noble birth, he became a monk at 13 and studied the Buddhist scriptures before visiting several Chinese monasteries (1223–27), where he studied Zen. After returning to Japan, he devoted himself to teaching the form of Zen practice that emphasizes quiet meditation. His teaching is embodied in his chief work, *Shobogenzo* (*Knowledge concerning the Dharma*).

dogfish A small *shark belonging to one of a number of families. *Scyliorhinus stellaris*, up to 40 in (1 m) long, and *S. canicula*, up to 30 in (75 cm) long, are brown-spotted dogfish commonly found in Mediterranean and British coastal waters. They are edible and purchased as "rock salmon." Chief families: *Triakidae* (smooth dogfish or smooth hounds); *Squalidae* (spiny dogfish); *Scyliorhinidae* (spotted dogfish).

Dogger Bank A vast sandbank in the central North Sea, 55–120 ft (17–36 m) below water. Several naval battles have taken place on the bank, notably the battle of Dogger Bank (January 24, 1915) between British and German forces. It is a major fishing ground.

doggerel A crude, naive, form of poetry, often irregular in rhythm and meter. Early examples are John *Skelton's *Colin Clout* (1519) and Samuel *Butler's *Hudibras* (1663–78). It is much used in comic verse, as in the work of the poet Ogden *Nash. The word can be used perjoratively.

dog rose A shrubby *rose, *Rosa canina*, 40 in–16 ft (1–5 m) high. It grows in woods, hedges, and roadsides of Europe, North Africa, and SW Asia. The arching stems have strong curved prickles and bear clusters of scentless white or pink flowers on long stalks.

dog's tooth violet A spring-blooming plant of the genus *Erythronium* (20 species), also known as adder's tongue, native to Eurasia and North America. They have white, yellow, or purple nodding flowers with two leaves at the base; the fruit is a pod. Several species are grown as rock-garden ornamentals. A European species is *E. dens-canis*, with purple flowers. Family: *Liliaceae*.

dogwood A shrub or small tree of the genus *Cornus* (about 45 species), mostly of the N hemisphere. It has oval pointed leaves with prominent curved veins and dense clusters of four-petaled flowers. The fruit is a berry. The common European dogwood (*C. sanguinea*) has white flowers, blood-red shoots and autumn leaves, and black berries; Cornelian cherry (*C. mas*), of central and SE Europe, has small yellow flowers and attractive red berries. The American flowering dogwood (*C. florida*) has showy pinkish blossoms and red berries. Family: *Cornaceae*.

Doha 25 15N 51 36E The capital of Qatar, on the E coast. Its modern development (including an international seaport and airport) has been funded by oil revenues. Population (1986 est): 217,000.

Dohnányi, Ernö (Ernst von D.; 1877–1960) Hungarian composer and pianist. He spent his last years in the US. He was greatly influenced by Brahms, who praised his early works. Unlike his contemporaries, Bartók and Kodály, Dohnányi remained uninfluenced by Hungarian folk song. His best-known composition is the *Variations on a Nursery Theme* (for piano and orchestra; 1913), based on the tune "Baa Baa Black Sheep."

Dolby system An electronic device for reducing the hiss in sound reproduction, particularly in *tape recorders. It was invented by Ray Dolby (1933–   ),
who set up a company to make Dolby noise-reduction units. These are now built
into high-quality tape recorders and are increasingly used in film sound tracks
and prerecorded cassettes. The Dolby system selectively boosts the higher frequencies in the sound signal before recording it, to drown out the constant hiss
produced by the tape, and attenuates them when playing back. Its unique feature
is that it operates only when the music is quiet enough for the hiss to be heard.
This avoids both distortion that occurs if lower frequencies are boosted to the
same level and distortion from boosting already loud higher frequencies.

dolce stil nuovo (Italian: sweet new style) A style of love poetry founded by
the Bolognese poet Guido Guinizelli (c. 1240–76) and perfected by the Florentine poets *Cavalcanti and *Dante. It is characterized by a spiritualization of
*courtly love, the use of the vernacular, and the sonnet, ballad, and canzone
verse forms. Among its best-known examples are Dante's lyrics to Beatrice. The
style influenced *Petrarch, *Bembo, Dante Gabriel *Rossetti, and Ezra *Pound.

doldrums The equatorial belt within which the trade-wind zones converge.
Winds are light and variable but the strong upward movement of air caused by
the meeting of the trade winds produces frequent thunderstorms, heavy rains,
and squalls. Navigation by sailing ships was difficult in these areas; ships often
became becalmed for several days.

Dole, Sanford (Ballard) (1844–1926) US lawyer and jurist; president
(1894–98) and governor (1900–03) of Hawaii. Born of missionary parents in
Honolulu, he was educated in the US and returned to Hawaii to practice law. He
was an associate justice of the Hawaiian Supreme Court (1887–93) and became
president after Queen Liliuokalani was deposed (1893) and Hawaii was proclaimed a republic. Hawaii was annexed by the US in 1898, and he became territorial governor two years later. From 1903–15 he was a district judge.

dolerite. *See* diabase.

Dollfuss, Engelbert (1892–1934) Austrian statesman; chancellor (1932–34).
He became prominent as leader of the Lower Austrian Farmers' League. Ruling
by decree from 1933, his chancellorship was increasingly strained by his inability to control the Austrian Nazis or to cooperate with the Social Democrats. He
suppressed the Social Democratic revolt in February, 1934, and was assassinated in July during an abortive attempt by the Nazis to seize power.

dolmen (Breton: table stone) A prehistoric tomb made of huge stone slabs set
upright and supporting a stone roof. Widely distributed in *Neolithic Europe,
dolmens were often covered by a *barrow.

dolomite A mineral consisting of calcium magnesium carbonate,
$CaMg(CO_3)_2$, colorless, white or gray in color. Rocks containing over 15% magnesium carbonate are called dolomites, those containing less are magnesian
limestones, and those containing both dolomite and calcite are dolomitic limestones. Dolomite occurs as a primary sediment, in metalliferous veins and in
limestones altered by the process of dolomitization, by which the calcium carbonate is wholly or partly converted to dolomite by magnesium-rich sea water,
or by magnesium-rich solutions permeating joints in the rock.

Dolomites (Italian name: Alpi Dolomitiche) A section of the Alps in NE Italy.
Composed of dolomitic limestone, they are characterized by their steep-sided
rocky peaks, the highest of which is Marmolada at 10,956 ft (3342 m).

dolphin 1. A toothed *whale of the family *Delphinidae* (about 50 species).
Agile and streamlined and up to 15 ft (4.5 m) long, dolphins live in large groups,

or schools, and feed mainly on fish; they often accompany ships. They are intelligent creatures with well-developed abilities for social communication and *echolocation. The common dolphin (*Delphinus delphus*), which grows to 7 ft (2.1 m), is blue-black with a white belly and striped body. *See also* bottlenose; porpoise.
2. A fast-moving fish of the family *Coryphaenidae* (2 species). The common dolphin (*Coryphaena hippuras*) has a bluish tapering body, up to 7 ft (2 m) long, with a large blunt head, a forked tail, and a long dorsal fin. It occurs in tropical and temperate seas and feeds on fish and invertebrates. Order: *Perciformes*.

Domagk, Gerhard (1895–1964) German biochemist, who (in 1932) noticed the powerful effects of a dye, Prontosil, in combating bacterial infection. From this dye was isolated the first of the *sulfonamide drugs (sulfanilamide) which paved the way for the treatment of a wide range of bacterial diseases. Domagk received the 1939 Nobel Prize but was prevented from accepting it until 1947, after the fall of Hitler.

dome A roof or ceiling that is hemispherical in section. In classical architecture it was generally supported by a circular drum and topped by a lantern. The Romans developed the technique of building a dome in cast concrete while the Byzantines introduced the use of four pendentives to build a dome over a square section. Another method was invented in the 15th century by *Brunelleschi, using a strong brick cone to bear the weight and a lighter outer shell for visual effect. The Pantheon and St Peter's in Rome, Hagia Sophia, Istanbul, and St Paul's, London, all have famous domes.

Domenichino (Domenico Zampieri; 1581–1641) Italian painter, born in Bologna. He trained under Ludovico *Carracci. In Rome (1602–31) he painted frescoes of the *Life of St Cecilia* (1615–17; S Luigi dei Francesi) and *Last Communion of St Jerome* (Vatican Museum). His landscapes influenced *Poussin and *Claude.

Domenico Veneziano (active c. 1438–1461) Italian painter of the early Renaissance, probably born in Venice. He settled in Florence, where he painted his famous *St Lucy Altarpiece* (central panel; Uffizi).

Dome of the Rock The great mosque in Jerusalem, built in 691 AD by the *Umayyad caliph, 'Abd al-Malik. It is named for the rock (sacred also to the Jews) over which it was built and stands within the enclosure of the destroyed Jewish *Temple of Jerusalem. It is the third most holy place of Islam, after *Mecca and *Medina. The edifice, also erroneously called the Mosque of Omar by Europeans, is an impressive example of early Islamic architecture.

Domesday Book (1086) The survey of England ordered by William I to assess the extent of his own possessions and the value for taxation purposes of the estates of his tenants in chief. Royal commissioners collected, shire by shire, details about each *manor, naming its present owner and its owner under Edward the Confessor, changes in its size since Edward's reign, and many other details. Only a few areas of England were omitted, so the book is a key source for the history of early medieval England.

dominance In genetics, the condition in which one of the *alleles of a gene predominates in the function of that gene. Gregor *Mendel, in his famous experiments, crossed pea plants from a line producing yellow seeds with plants from a line producing green seeds. The resulting offspring all produced yellow seeds, i.e. the dominant allele of the gene determining seed color was that carried by the yellow-seeded plants; the allele carried by the green-seeded plants was recessive.

Domingo, Placido (1941–) Spanish tenor, educated in Mexico. He made his debut at the Metropolitan Opera, New York, in 1968. A leading tenor, he sings a wide range of roles but specializes in Verdi and Puccini.

Dominic, St (Domingo de Guzmán; c. 1170–1221) Spanish churchman, who founded the *Dominicans. One of the canons regular attached to the cathedral at Osma, Castile, and later its prior, he became one of the first successful missionaries to the heretical *Albigenses in the south of France. In 1216 with papal encouragement he founded a religious order devoted to preaching. From his headquarters in Rome he sent out his preachers to establish houses in many major cities. Feast Day: Aug 4. Emblems: a star and a dog holding a torch in its mouth.

Dominica, Commonwealth of An island country in the West Indies, the largest of the Windward Islands. It is of volcanic origin and very mountainous. The population is mainly of African descent. *Economy*: chiefly agricultural; exports include bananas, limes, and lime oil. *History:* discovered by Columbus in 1493, it changed hands several times between the French and the British during the 18th century before finally becoming British in 1783. It became internally self-governing in 1967 and an independent republic within the British Commonwealth in November, 1978. Prime Minister Eugenia Charles, as head of the Organization of Eastern Caribbean States, issued the invitation to the US government to intervene in Grenada in 1983. President: Aurelius Marie. Prime minister: Eugenia Charles. Official language: English. Official currency: East Caribbean dollar of 100 cents. Area: 289 sq mi (728 sq km). Population (1990 est): 94,200. Capital: Roseau.

Dominican Republic A country in the Caribbean Sea, occupying the E two thirds of the island of Hispaniola (Haiti occupies the W third). It is largely mountainous, rising to over 10,000 ft (3000 m). It is subject to hurricanes. The population is mainly of mixed African and European descent. *Economy*: chiefly agricultural, the principal cash crop is sugar. Other cash crops include coffee, cocoa, and bananas. Mining and light industry are being developed in an attempt to diversify the economy. The principal mineral export is ferro-nickel and gold and silver mining began in 1975. Oil and hydroelectricity are being exploited. There is a growing tourist industry. *History*: the island was discovered in 1492 by Columbus, who named it Hispaniola. The E became a Spanish colony, while the French established themselves in the W, in what became Haiti. The Spanish colony was ceded to the French in 1795 and soon fell to the Haitian *Toussaint L'Ouverture, who proclaimed himself ruler of all Hispaniola. The Spanish were restored in the E in 1809 and in 1821 the colony gained independence. It was held by Haiti from 1822 until 1844, when the Dominican Republic was founded. Political and economic instability led to US occupation (1916–22) and the establishment (1930) of Trujillo's 30-year dictatorship. Following his assassination Juan Bosch was elected (1962) president only to be deposed (1963) in a military coup. An attempt by constitutionalists to reinstate Bosch was thwarted by the US in 1965. Joaquin Balaguer, a puppet president under Trujillo, was elected to the presidency in 1966 and was reelected in 1970 and 1974. Silvestre Antonio Guzman was elected in 1978. In 1983 Salvador Jorge Blanco was elected president in a landslide victory, promising to create in the Dominican Republic a democratic socialist state based on the Swedish model. A serious economic crisis, the worst in two decades, forced him to impose even more severe economic austerity measures on the populace, dampening their enthusiasm for him and hopes for prosperity in the country. Balaguer was elected again in 1986 and 1990, but he announced in 1991 that he would not run again in 1994. Official language: Spanish. Official currency: Dominican Republic peso of 100 centavos. Area: 18,700 sq mi (48,442 sq km). Population (1989 est): 7,307,000. Captial and main port: Santo Domingo.

Dominicans (Latin *Ordo Praedicatorum*: Order of Preachers) A Roman Catholic order of friars, also known as Black Friars, Friar Preachers, or (in

France) Jacobins, founded by St *Dominic and formally organized at Bologna in 1220–21. Their purpose was preaching and teaching, the individual friars leading mendicant lives much of the time. Among their great scholars was St Thomas *Aquinas. They were prominent defenders of orthodoxy in the *Inquisition and leading missionaries to the New World, although the Jesuits superseded them in this role during the Counter-Reformation. There are also two orders of Dominican nuns.

Domino, Fats (Antoine D.; 1928–   ) US jazz singer, pianist, and songwriter, who became famous in the rock and roll era. His songs, which contain blues elements, include "Blueberry Hill" and "Jambalaya."

dominoes A game played with rectangular pieces marked at each end with a group of dots or a blank space. In a set of 28 pieces, each group adds up to a number from 1 to 6. Dominoes were used in China in ancient times but not in Europe until the 18th century. There are many games, but in the basic game each player first draws seven pieces. The player with the double six places it face up on the table. The next player places next to it a six on the end of another domino; if this domino has, for instance, a two on the other end the third player must match either the two or the remaining six. Doubles are placed crosswise, the others end to end. A player who cannot make a match misses his turn or in some games takes another domino. The first to get rid of all his pieces wins.

Domitian(us), Titus Flavius (51–96 AD) Roman emperor (81–96). His frustrating inactivity under his father *Vespasian and his brother *Titus made him a harsh ruler. His government became increasingly absolute and from about 84, as censor for life, he controlled the Senate. His suspicion of treachery culminated in a reign of terror, which precipitated his own murder.

Don River A river in Russia, flowing mainly S to the Sea of Azov. A canal links it to the Volga River. Length: 1224 mi (1981 km).

Donatello (Donato de Nicolo di Betti Bardi; c. 1386–1466) Florentine sculptor. A pioneer of the Renaissance style, Donatello first broke with tradition in his marble sculptures of *St Mark* and *St George* (1415) for the exterior of Orsanmichele. These and his prophets for the campanile of the Duomo are modeled as lifelike rather than idealized figures. Simultaneously he developed a new form of relief sculpture, in which he created perspective by incising the surface of the marble rather than modeling it in depth. Working also in bronze from the early 1420s, he produced *David* (c. 1430–35; Bargello, Florence), the influential equestrian monument in Padua known as the *Gattamelata* (1447–53), and the high altar for S Antonio, Padua (1446–50). His late works include the expressive painted wooden sculpture of *Mary Magdalen* (1454–55; Baptistry, Florence).

Donatists Members of a schismatic North African Christian group of the 4th and 5th centuries AD, named for Donatus, one of their bishops. They held that the validity of the sacraments depended on the personal holiness of the minister. St *Augustine's repudiation of their views in the early 5th century crystallized Catholic teaching on these matters. He argued that since the true minister is Christ, the personal worthiness of the priest could not affect the validity of the sacraments.

Donatus, Aelius (4th century AD) Roman grammarian and rhetorician. Donatus was the tutor of St Jerome, and his Latin grammar, *Ars Grammatica*, became a universally accepted textbook in the middle ages.

Doncaster 53 32N 1 07W An industrial city in N England, in South Yorkshire, with railroad workshops and coalmining. Population (1981): 81,610.

Donegal (Irish name: Dún Na Ngall) A county in the N Republic of Ireland, in Ulster bordering on the Atlantic Ocean. Chiefly mountainous, it has a rugged indented coastline. Agricultural products include barley, oats, and potatoes; cattle and sheep are reared. Linen and tweed are manufactured. Area 1865 sq mi (4830 sq km). Population (1986): 130,000. County town: Lifford.

Donets Basin (or Donbass) An industrial region in Ukraine. It is the oldest center of coal production in the country and still its major coal-producing and steel-manufacturing area. Area: about 10,000 sq mi (25,900 sq km).

Donetsk (name until 1924: Yuzovka; name from 1924 until 1961: Stalino) 48 22N 40 02E A city in Ukraine on the Kalmius River. The major city of the *Donets Basin, it has important coalmining and metallurgical industries. Population (1991 est): 1,121,000.

Dongola (or Dunqulah) 19 10N 30 27E A small town in the N Sudan, on the Nile River. It was the capital of the Christian kingdom of Nubia (6th–14th centuries).

Dongting, Lake (or Lake Tung-t'ing) A lake in SE China. Seasonally fed or drained by the Yangtze River, it regulates the river's flooding. Area: (winter) 1500 sq mi (3900 sq km); (summer) about 4000 sq mi (10,000 sq km).

Dönitz, Karl (1891–1980) German admiral. He made his name as a U-boat commander in World War I and in the first three years of World War II he developed the "pack" system of submarine attack. In 1943 he became grand admiral and then commander in chief of the German navy. He was appointed chancellor after Hitler's death and was imprisoned from 1946 to 1956 for war crimes.

Donizetti, Gaetano (1797–1848) Italian composer of operas. He became paralyzed and mentally ill toward the end of his life. He wrote with great facility and his 75 stage works rely more on *coloratura display, the popular characteristic of his age, than on intrinsic dramatic effect. Revivals of such operas as *Lucia di Lammermoor* (1835) and *Daughter of the Regiment* (1840) have been successful with such singers as Joan Sutherland or Maria Callas in the title roles.

Don Juan The great aristocratic libertine of European literature. His probable first appearance was in Tirso de Molina's play *El burlador de Sevilla* (1630), in which he kills the father of his latest victim; he mockingly invites the old man's statue to dinner, and it drags him off to hell. This plot is retained in subsequent versions, most notably *Molière's *Don Juan* (1665) and *Mozart's *Don Giovanni* (1787). In satirical treatments by *Byron (*Don Juan*, 1819–24) and G. B. *Shaw (*Man and Superman*, 1903) Juan is more hunted than hunter.

donkey A domesticated *ass. Donkeys are more commonly used for pack and draft work than for riding: being stronger in the hindquarters than the forequarters, they must bear the load over the pelvis, which is a less comfortable position for a rider. *See also* hinny; mule.

Donleavy, J(ames) P(atrick) (1926–) Irish-American novelist. His successful first novel, *The Ginger Man* (1956), was followed by further comic picaresque novels including *The Saddest Summer of Samuel S.* (1967), *The Onion Eaters* (1971), *The Destinies of Darcy Dancer, Gentleman* (1977), and *Schultz* (1979).

Donne, John (1572–1631) English poet, greatest of the Metaphysical school. He received a Roman Catholic education, studied at Oxford and Lincoln's Inn, and took part in naval raids on Spain. In 1601 he secretly married the niece of his patron, Sir Thomas Egerton, and was briefly imprisoned. Failing to gain secular advancement, despite having several influential patrons, he became an Anglican priest in 1615 and was appointed Dean of St Paul's in 1621. His poetry is rich, involved, and often obscure; it combines passionate feeling for God, woman, and humanity with brilliant intellectual wit. Almost all of it, even religious works, such as *La Corona* (1607) and the Holy Sonnets, was written before 1615.

JOHN DONNE *A miniature portrait (1616) by Isaac Oliver.*

Donner Party (1846–47) A group of US pioneers en route to California that became trapped by snow in the wilderness. Led by George Donner, a wagon train party of 87 left Illinois but, using a new route around the southern end of the Great Salt Lake, became trapped by mountain snow when they reached a pass through the mountains. Forced to camp for 4 months, the 47 survivors eventually resorted to cannibalism to ward off starvation.

Doolittle, Hilda (1886–1961) US poet, who wrote under the initials H. D. Born in Pennsylvania, she went to England in 1911 and married Richard *Aldington. A leading exponent of Imagism, her books include *Sea Garden* (1916), *Hymen* (1921), *The Walls Do Not Fall* (1944), and *Helen in Egypt* (1961).

Doppler, Christian Johann (1803–53) Austrian physicist, who explained and derived, in 1842, an expression for the change in frequency of a wave when the source is moving relative to an observer (*see* Doppler effect). He attempted to apply this principle to the coloration of stars; although the effect is too small to be observed visually, it is now widely used spectroscopically in astronomy.

Doppler effect The apparent change in the frequency of a wave caused by relative motion between the source and the observer. When the source and the observer are approaching each other, the apparent frequency of the wave increases; when one is traveling away from the other, the apparent frequency decreases. An example of the Doppler effect is the change in pitch of a train whistle as the train passes through a station. The effect can also be observed as a shifting of the wavelength of light from a receding star toward the red end of the spectrum. In this case the effect is known as the *redshift. Named for Christian *Doppler.

dor beetle A large shiny black convex beetle, with broad digging legs, belonging to a family (*Geotrupidae*; about 300 species) of dung feeders. Dor beetles burrow into the soil beneath dung and lay their eggs on plugs of dung hauled down for use as a food source.

Dorcas gazelle A small *gazelle, *Gazella dorcas*, of N Africa and S Asia, also called afri. A desert animal, it is light red with a pale flank stripe and distinctive face stripes.

Dorchester 50 43N 2 26W A market town in S England, the administrative center for Dorset on the Frome River. It has several Roman remains and is associated with Thomas Hardy, featuring as Casterbridge in his novels. Population (1981): 14,049.

Dordogne River A river in SW France. Rising in the Auvergne Mountains, it flows SW and W to enter the Gironde estuary NNE of Bordeaux. It is important for hydroelectric power and has famous vineyards along its lower course. Length: 293 mi (472 km).

Dordrecht (*or* Dort) 51 48N 4 40E A port in the SW Netherlands, in South Holland province. It has a thriving timber trade and metallurgical, shipbuilding, and chemical industries. Population (1991 est): 110,500.

Doré, (Paul) Gustave (Louis Christophe) (1832–83) French illustrator, painter, and sculptor, born in Strasbourg. He established his wide and lasting popularity in the 1850s with his illustrations of Rabelais' books and Balzac's *Contes drôlatiques*. These were followed by illustrations to Dante, Cervantes, Tennyson, etc., showing his taste for the grotesque and dramatic. His realistic scenes of poverty in *London* influenced Van Gogh. □Camelot.

Dorgon (1612–50) Prince of Manchuria, who controlled China as regent for a child emperor from 1643 to 1650. Continuing the expansionist policy of his father *Nurhachi, Dorgon helped to lay the foundations of the *Qing dynasty in China, basing its power on centralized government instead of the clan system.

Doria A family that was prominent in Genoa from the 12th to 18th centuries. The most notable member of the family was **Andrea Doria** (1466–1560). An admiral and condottiere, he served the French against Emperor Charles V, ousted imperial troops from Genoa, and then transferred his allegiance to Charles and expelled the French in return for the emperor's recognition of Genoese liberty (1528). He then became the ruler of Genoa, initiating the period of aristocratic rule (1528–1797) during which the Doria family contributed six doges of Genoa.

Dorians Iron Age Greek conquerors (c. 1100–1000 BC) of the S Aegean region. Moving southward from Epirus and SW Macedonia, they displaced the *Achaeans and brought about the final collapse of the Bronze age *Mycenaean civilization. They settled in the S and E Peloponnese, near the isthmus of Corinth, in the S Aegean islands, the Dodecanese, and SW Anatolia. There were three major tribes: the Hylleis, Pamphyloi, and Dymanes. The Doric dialects they spoke belonged to the Western Greek group.

Doric order. *See* orders of architecture.

dormancy A period of reduced metabolic activity during which a plant or animal or a reproductive body (e.g. seeds or spores) can survive unfavorable environmental conditions. The onset of dormancy may be triggered by a number of factors, including changes in temperature, daylength (*see* photoperiodism), and availability of water, oxygen, and carbon dioxide. The dormant phase of a life cycle is represented as spores in bacteria and fungi, cysts in protozoans and some invertebrates, and seeds, buds, and bulbs or similar organs in plants. *See also* hibernation.

dormouse A climbing *rodent belonging to the family *Gliridae* (about 10 species) of Eurasia and Africa. The common dormouse (*Muscardinus avellanarius*) is reddish, about 2.4 in (6 cm) long with a 2 in (5 cm) bushy tail. It sleeps in a nest above ground level during the day, feeding at night on nuts, berries, and seeds. During winter it hibernates beneath debris or tree stumps, occasionally waking to feed on stored food.

Dornier, Claudius (1884–1969) German aircraft designer and manufacturer, who constructed the first all-metal aircraft (1911). At his works in Friedrichshafen he manufactured both civil and military planes.

Dorr's Rebellion (1841–42) A US rebellion in Rhode Island, led by Thomas W. Dorr (1805–54), that protested the lack of reforms in the state constitution. Because of restrictions in the constitution regarding landowners' voting rights and representation in the legislature, Dorr, a legislative member, and his followers attacked the state house and proclaimed Dorr governor under their own constitution. Rioting followed, and Dorr was arrested and spent a year in jail. By 1843 a new constitution, incorporating many of the reforms advocated by Dorr, was put into effect.

Dorset A county of SW England, bordering on the English Channel. The chief rivers are the Frome and the Stour. Agriculture is predominant, especially livestock farming. Tourism is important, notably in Bournemouth and Weymouth. Many towns are associated with the writings of Thomas *Hardy, who included Dorset within his fictitious region of Wessex. Area: 1017 sq mi (2634 sq km). Population (1991): 645,200. Administrative center: Dorchester.

Dort. *See* Dordrecht.

Dortmund 51 32N 7 27E A city in western Germany, in North Rhine-Westphalia in the *Ruhr. A port on the Dortmund–Ems Canal and a major industrial center, it produces steel, furniture, textiles, coal, and beer. Its university was established in 1966. Population (1991 est): 599,000.

Dortmund–Ems Canal A major canal in Germany. Opened in 1899, it links the Ruhr industrial area with the North Sea near Emden. Length: about 168 mi (270 km).

Dos Passos, John (1896–1970) US novelist. Born in Chicago, Dos Passos served as an ambulance driver in World War I and returned from that experience to publish his first novel, *Three Soldiers*, in 1921. He later served as foreign correspondent in Spain, Mexico, and the Near East. His greatest work was the trilogy *U.S.A.*, in which he experimented with stream-of-consciousness style and the use of historical personalities as characters to produce a radical interpretation of American history from 1900 until the Depression. It comprises the novels *The Forty-Second Parallel* (1930), *1919* (1932), and *The Big Money* (1936).

Dostoievski, Fedor Mikhailovich (1821–81) Russian novelist. Son of a landowner murdered by his serfs, he graduated as a military engineer in 1843, but resigned his commission and began writing. In 1849 he was sentenced to four years hard labor in Siberia, followed by army service, for printing socialist propaganda. In 1864 his wife and brother died, and he incurred heavy gambling debts. He lived in W Europe from 1867 to 1871 with his new wife, his secretary Anna Snitkina, plagued by his epilepsy and compulsive gambling. He returned to Russia in 1871 and became relatively prosperous, stable, and conservative. His major novels, in which he explored moral and political themes with merciless psychological realism, are *Crime and Punishment* (1866), *The Idiot* (1868–69), *The Possessed* (1869–72), and *The Brothers Karamazov* (1879–80).

dotterel A small Eurasian *plover, *Eudromias morinellus*, that nests in tundra regions and migrates to the Mediterranean and SW Asia for the winter. It is 8 in (20 cm) long and mottled brown above with a broad white eye stripe and a gray breast separated by a narrow white band from its russet belly.

Dou, Gerrit (1613–75) Dutch painter of domestic interiors and portraits, born in Leyden. He studied under *Rembrandt (1628–31), who influenced his early portrait *Rembrandt's Mother* (c. 1630; Rijksmuseum, Amsterdam). *The Poulterer's Shop* (National Gallery, London), showing his interest in still life, is a more typical work.

Douai 50 22N 3 05E A city in N France, in the Nord department. It became a center for English Roman Catholics following the establishment of a college by William Allen in 1568 and it was here that the *Douai Bible was published. Douai is the coal mining center of N France and has iron and steel industries. Population (1975): 47,570.

Douai Bible The Roman Catholic version of the Bible in English, translated from the *Vulgate by Roman Catholic scholars from Oxford, who had fled to Europe during the reign of Elizabeth I and who were members of the English College at Douai. The New Testament was published at Reims in 1582 and the Old Testament at Douai in 1609–10. Although it retained a number of difficult technical expressions foreign to colloquial English, its language influenced the translators of the *King James Version.

Douala 4 04N 9 43E The largest city in Cameroon, on the Wouri River estuary. A deepwater port and the chief export point of the country, it is also a major West African industrial center with brewing, food-processing, textiles, and timber industries. Population (1987 est): 810,000.

double bass The lowest-pitched □musical instrument of the violin family. The flat back and sloping shoulders of some double basses are derived from the *viol family. Unlike the violin, viola, and cello, its four strings are tuned in fourths (E, A, D, G). It has a range of over three octaves, from the E an octave below the bass stave. The double bass is a member of the symphony orchestra; it is also played in jazz and dance bands, usually by plucking the strings. Music for the double bass is written an octave higher than it sounds.

Doubleday, Abner (1819–93) US Union general and sportsman. A graduate of West Point, he served in the *Mexican War and, from 1861, in the *Civil War, serving as a general in the battles of Bull Run, South Mountain, Antietam, Fredericksburg, and Gettysburg. He is incorrectly credited with inventing baseball in 1839 in Cooperstown, N.Y.

double vision The condition in which a person sees two images of a single object. Known medically as diplopia, it is caused by lack of coordination between the muscles that move the eyes. Temporary double vision may occur after taking drugs or alcohol; alternatively it may be due to damage or disease of one of the nerves that supply the eye muscles.

Doubs River A river in E France. Rising in the Jura Mountains and flowing SW to join the Saône River, it forms part of the Swiss-French border. Length: 267 mi (430 km).

Douglas, Stephen Arnold (1813–61) US politician, lawyer, and orator. He practiced law in Illinois and served in the state legislature before serving in the US House of Representatives (1843–47) and as a Democrat senator from Illinois (1847–61). He worked for the passage of the *Compromise of 1850, advocated popular sovereignty in the territories (the right of territorial settlers to decide for themselves the question of slavery), and originated the *Kansas-Nebraska Act of 1854. In 1858 his opponent for the Senate seat was Republican Abraham *Lincoln. From this election campaign evolved the *Lincoln-Douglas Debates, a series of debates on the slavery question. Barely 5 ft (1.5 m) tall, he was often called the "Little Giant."

STEPHEN A. DOUGLAS *"The Little Giant," whose doctrine of "popular sovereignty" was the main issue of the Lincoln-Douglas debates.*

Douglas, William O(rville) (1898–1980) US jurist, conservationist, and writer; Supreme Court associate justice (1939–75). Born in Minnesota, he practiced law in New York City and Washington and taught at Yale University (1928–36). While a member of the Securities and Exchange Commission (1936–39; its chairman from 1937), he advocated reform of the New York Stock Exchange practices. Pres. Franklin D. *Roosevelt appointed him to the US Supreme Court in 1939. He was known as a liberal who championed civil rights and opposed censorship. Upon retirement in 1975 he had the longest tenure of any judge on the court. An avid conservationist, he wrote *Of Men and Mountains* (1950), *Beyond the High Himalayas* (1952), and *A Wilderness Bill of Rights* (1965).

Douglas fir A conifer, *Pseudotsuga menziesii*, native to W North America and cultivated widely both for ornament and for its high-quality timber, used for construction, poles, masts, etc. 198–295 ft (60–90 m) high, it has flexible blunt-tipped needles and cylindrical cones, about 3 in (8 cm) long, with three-pronged bracts protruding from the scales. Family: *Pinaceae*.

Douglas-Home, Sir Alec (Alexander Frederick D.-H., Baron Home of the Hirsel; 1903–   ) British statesman; Conservative prime minister (1963–64). He was a Member of Parliament (1931–45, 1950–51) before becoming 14th Earl of Home. He was foreign secretary (1960–63) and then, to widespread surprise, succeeded Macmillan as prime minister, renouncing his peerages. Following the Conservative electoral defeat (1964) he resigned the party leadership (1965). He received a life peerage in 1974.

Douglass, Frederick (1817–95) US abolitionist and reformer. An escaped slave (1838), he delivered anti-slavery lectures in New England until forced to flee to England in 1845. He was able to return to the US when his freedom was purchased in 1847, and he started publication of *North Star* (1847–63), an abolitionist newspaper. He worked to aid fugitive slaves, for women's rights, and then, during the Civil War, for the emancipation of slaves. He was later minister to Haiti (1889–91).

Doukhobors (Russian: fighters against the spirit) Russian nonconformist Christian sect founded in the 18th century. Because of their anarchistic doctrines (denial of the state's right to levy tax, etc.) and heterodox religious views (belief in reincarnation, denial of Christ's divinity), they were for a long time persecuted. With the help of *Tolstoy and English Quakers, they emigrated from Georgia to Canada in 1898, where they subsequently came into conflict with the government over such matters as sending their children to state schools. In 1958 some members of the sect were permitted to return to the Soviet Union. About 13,000 remained in Canada.

Doulton English pottery works, originally at Lambeth (London), specializing in salt-glazed stoneware. Brown stoneware vessels with relief molded portrait and landscape ornament were typical of the period to 1850. From 1856 Sir Henry Doulton (1820–97) encouraged artist potters to produce unique studio pottery in colored glazes, using wood-fixed kilns. These were exhibited at the 1867 Paris Exhibition.

Douro River (Spanish name: Duero) A river in SW Europe. Flowing W from N central Spain, it forms part of the border between Spain and Portugal before entering the Atlantic Ocean at Oporto. Length: 556 mi (895 km).

douroucouli A nocturnal *monkey, *Aotus trivirgatus*, of Central and South America, also called night monkey or owl monkey. It is 22–30 in (55–75 cm) long including the tail (12–16 in [30–40 cm]) and moves through trees stalking small animals. It also eats fruit and leaves. Family: *Cebidae*.

dove. *See* pigeon.

Dover 51 08N 1 19E A port in SE England, in Kent on the Strait of Dover. An ancient Cinque Port, it is the UK's chief ferry and Hovercraft port for the Continent. Population (1981): 32,843.

Dover 39 10N 75 32W The capital city of Delaware, near Delaware Bay. Founded in 1683, it has many 18th- and 19th-century buildings. Population (1990): 27,630.

Dover, Strait of (French name: Pas de Calais) A channel separating England from NW France comprising the narrowest part of the *English Channel. Minimum width: 21 mi (34 km).

Dow-Jones Index A weighted average of the prices on the New York Stock Exchange of 30 industrial shares, computed each working day by Dow Jones and Co. The first index was devised in 1897 using only 12 shares. It is the principal indicator of movements in share prices in the US.

Down A historic county in E Northern Ireland, bordering on the Irish Sea. It consists of lowlands in the E rising to the Mourne Mountains in the SW. Agriculture is the chief occupation; dairy farming is especially important. Area: 952 sq mi (2466 sq km).

Downing Street A street in the Greater London borough of the City of Westminister, adjoining Whitehall. No 10 is the official residence of the prime minister; the chancellor of the exchequer resides at No 11. It was named for the English statesman Sir George Downing (1623–84).

Downs, North and South Two roughly parallel ranges of chalk hills in SE England, separated by the *Weald. The North Downs extend W–E between Guildford, in Surrey, and Dover, in Kent. The South Downs extend generally SE from Winchester, in Hampshire, to Beachy Head. The Downs have traditionally been sheep-farming areas.

Down's syndrome A chromosomal abnormality, formerly called mongolism, in which a baby has one extra chromosome; it is named for the English physician J. L. H. Down (1828–96). In spite of mental and motor-skill handicaps, these children can, with special education, live relatively normal lives in a family. Down's syndrome is more commonly seen in babies of mothers over 40; it can be detected during pregnancy (*see* amniocentesis).

dowsing The use of divining- or dowsing-rods to discover subterranean minerals or water. From the 16th century divining-rods were employed by miners and treasure hunters, a function now largely usurped by metal detectors. Dowsing of water is still of practical value; skilled dowsers can estimate the depth and flow of underground streams. The rod is traditionally a Y-shaped stick which, when its two prongs are grasped, twists in the hands of the dowser as he walks over the relevant place. An alternative means are metal rods, held parallel and a few inches apart, which swing across each other. The nature of the stimuli causing these reactions is still unexplained.

Doyle, Sir Arthur Conan (1859–1930) British author, creator of the archetypal detective Sherlock Holmes. Born in Edinburgh, Conan Doyle graduated from medical school there but soon turned to writing. Holmes, inspired by the diagnostic methods of an Edinburgh lecturer, brought Conan Doyle great success. Holmes first appeared in the novel *A Study in Scarlet* (1887), narrated, as are nearly all the short stories and novels about him, by his dogged but unimaginative friend Dr John H. Watson, almost a self-caricature by the author. Conan Doyle also created the coarsely brilliant Professor Challenger in *The Lost World* (1912) but he valued most highly his historical novels, such as *The White Company* (1890). Knighted in 1902 for his service, and subsequent defense of British involvement, in the second Boer War, Conan Doyle became a champion of *spiritualism after the death of his son in World War I.

D'Oyly Carte, Richard (1844–1901) British theater impresario and manager. He produced most of the comic operas of Gilbert and Sullivan. The Savoy Theatre, which he opened in 1881 to house these productions, was the first London theater to have electric lighting.

Drabble, Margaret (1939–   ) British novelist. Most of her novels concern the moral and emotional problems of women in contemporary society. They include *The Millstone* (1965), *The Needle's Eye* (1972), *The Ice Age* (1977), *The Middle Ground* (1980), *The Radiant Way* (1987), and *A Natural Curiosity* (1989). She has also written a study of Arnold Bennett (1974).

Draco (7th century BC) Athenian lawgiver. His legal system is reputedly the first comprehensive code of laws drawn up in Athens. It was so harshly punitive that "draconian" has since been used to describe any rigorous or cruel law. Draco's code prescribed the death penalty by the state for most offenses, taking retribution out of the hands of private citizens. *Solon abolished Draco's code in 590 BC, retaining only his homicide laws.

Dracula, Count The central character of Bram *Stoker's gothic novel *Dracula* (1897) and of many horror films, a Transylvanian *vampire. The name, meaning "demon," was applied to Vlad IV the Impaler, a 15th-century Walachian prince who was the prototype of the fictional character.

Draft Riots (1862–63) Outbreaks of violence in both the North and the South US protesting against conscription methods during the Civil War. The worst riot took place in New York City in 1863. Workers, angry over their inability to buy their way out of the draft, as the wealthy could, rioted in the streets; over 1000 deaths and $1,500,000 of damage occurred.

dragonet A small spiny-rayed fish, of the family *Callionymidae*, that has a smooth slender body, 4–8 in (10–20 cm) long, flattened anteriorly and often brightly colored. The pelvic fins are located in front of the pectoral fins. Dragonets live on the bottom in temperate and tropical seas and feed on invertebrates. Order: *Perciformes*.

dragonfish A small *bony fish belonging to an order (*Pegasiformes*; about 5 species) found in warm waters of the Indian and Pacific Oceans. They have an elongated body, up to 6 in (16 cm) long, with bony armor, a long snout, and large horizontal winglike pectoral fins.

dragonfly A strong agile brightly colored insect belonging to the widely distributed suborder *Anisoptera* (about 4500 species). It has a long body, large eyes, and transparent veined wings (spanning up to 7 in [180 mm]), which are held horizontally at rest. Both the adults and freshwater nymphs (naiads) are active carnivores and control many insect pests, such as mosquitoes, flies, and gnats. Order: *Odonata*.

dragonroot A perennial North American herbaceous plant, *Arisaema dracontium*, also called green dragon or dragon arum. The flower comprises a central column of sexual organs surmounted by a long tapering cylindrical structure (the spadix) and surrounded by a much shorter pointed green sheath (the spathe). The tuberous roots were formerly used in medicine. Family: *Araceae*.

dragon's blood A red gum that exudes from the fruit of some palms. It was once used in Europe as a medicine because of its astringent and healing properties. It is used as a varnish for violins and in photoengraving.

dragon tree A treelike plant, *Dracaena draco*, native to the Canary Islands. Growing 59 ft (18 m) tall and 20 ft (6 m) wide, it has large sword-shaped leaves at the tips of the branches and clusters of greenish-white flowers followed by orange berries. The dragon tree is sometimes grown as a pot plant for its foliage. The trunk was formerly used as a source of a red gum resin, *dragon's blood. Family: *Agavaceae*.

drag racing 1. A form of *automobile racing that originated in the US. It is held in heats of two cars on a straight strip a quarter of a mile (402 m) long. Using a standing start, races depend heavily on acceleration with the "elapsed time" (from start to finish) and "terminal velocity" of each vehicle measured electronically. Speeds have reached 250 mph (403 kph) in specially constructed light powerful vehicles (slingshots *or* rails), although races are also held for modified production models. **2.** A form of motorcycle racing organized in the same way.

DRAGON TREE *This plant is unusual in that—like broadleaved trees—it produces true wood. The most famous of these trees was one in Tenerife, which was said to be 6000 years old.*

Drake, Sir Francis (1540–96) English navigator and admiral. Drake's first important voyages were trading expeditions to Guinea and the West Indies and in 1567 he accompanied Sir John *Hawkins (a relative) to the Gulf of Mexico. In 1572 he embarked on a plundering expedition, destroying towns on the Isthmus of Panama and capturing considerable quantities of booty. In 1578 he became the first Englishman to navigate the Straits of Magellan intending, with Elizabeth I's consent, to raid the Pacific coast. Alone out of five ships, his *Golden Hind* sailed N but unable to find a way back to the Atlantic Ocean crossed the Pacific Ocean, returning home via the Cape of Good Hope. He landed at Plymouth in 1580 and was knighted by Elizabeth on board the *Hind* in

1581. Drake crowned his career by helping to defeat the Spanish *Armada at Gravelines (1588). He died on an expedition to the West Indies.

Drakensberg Mountains (*or* Quathlamba) The chief mountain range in S Africa, extending from Cape Province (South Africa) along the E border of Lesotho to Swaziland, reaching 11,425 ft (3482 m) at Thaba Ntlenyana.

Drammen 59 45N 10 15E A seaport in S Norway, at the mouth of the Drammen River. It exports timber, wood pulp, and paper. Population (1981 est): 49,523.

Drapeau, Jean (1916–) Canadian lawyer and politician; mayor of Montreal (1954–86). He formed the Montreal Civic Party (1960) and was reelected as mayor on a platform for city beautification and development. During his terms in office the subway system and Expo '67 were built, and the 1976 Summer Olympics were held in Montreal. After his retirement in 1986, he was appointed Canada's representative to the UN Educational, Scientific, and Cultural Organization in Paris.

Drava River (*or* R. Drave) A river in E central Europe, flowing E from N Italy through Austria, then SE forming part of the Yugoslav-Hungarian border to join the Danube River. Length: 450 mi (725 km).

Dravidian languages A large language family of up to 20 languages spoken mainly in S India. The major languages of the family are *Tamil, which has a literary tradition dating back 2000 years, *Kanarese (*or* Kannada), Telugu, *Malayalam, and Tulu. These are all spoken in a contiguous area in India, and Tamil is also spoken in Sri Lanka. There is one Dravidian language, Brahui, that is separated from the main bloc by almost a thousand miles and is spoken in Pakistan. The Dravidian languages are all agglutinative (*see* languages, classification of) and this is strong evidence for separating them from the other major language bloc of the subcontinent, the *Indo-European group.

dreams Ideas and images experienced during *sleep. Dreams may take place at any stage of sleep, but they are particularly associated with the paradoxical phase, in which the eyes move rapidly about. Dreams in this stage of sleep are the most vivid in their imagery and the farthest removed from waking thoughts. Everyone has dreams: most people have paradoxical sleep about four or five times a night, for about 20 minutes at a time; whether or not the dream is remembered depends on how quickly after it the sleeper wakes up.

If a person is repeatedly deprived of the chance to dream (by being woken when a dream starts) he becomes irritable, inefficient, and eventually suffers *hallucinations. After such deprivation, he dreams more frequently when he is again allowed to. The new combinations of ideas produced in dreams can be creative and valuable. *Psychoanalysis gives much weight to the content of dreams as an approach to understanding the unconscious mind. Experimental studies indicate that the content of dreams is affected by the dreamer's mood and by stimuli that occur while he sleeps. *See also* nightmares.

Dred Scott v. Sanford (of Sandford; 1857) A Supreme Court ruling that declared the *Missouri Compromise unconstitutional. Dred Scott, a slave, had been brought from Missouri, a slave state, to Illinois, a free state, and then to Wisconsin, a free territory. Upon his return to Missouri, he filed suit against his owner, John Sanford, maintaining that he was a free man because he had been a resident of a free state and a free territory. Although a step backward in the fight against slavery, the 13th and 14th amendments (1865–1868) rendered this court decision invalid.

dredger A vessel designed to deepen underwater channels in rivers, docks, canals, etc., by removing material from the bottom. The types used include the suction dredger, which sucks up mud through a rubber pipe from the bottom and either deposits it in barges or in its own tanks; the bucket-ladder dredger, which carries an endless chain of buckets supported on a frame; and the grab dredger, which operates much like a power shovel.

Dreiser, Theodore (1871–1945) American novelist. Born in Terre Haute, Ind., son of a poor German immigrant, Dreiser worked as a reporter on various newspapers throughout the Midwest. In 1894 he settled in New York City where he published his first novel, *Sister Carrie*, in 1900. This work, in its disturbing portrayal of the hypocrisy of contemporary sexual mores, was initially attacked by critics and withdrawn by the publisher, but was later recognized as an important work of social realism. Dreiser's most famous novel, *An American Tragedy* (1925), based on an actual murder case, brought him both critical and financial success. Later in his career, Dreiser became increasingly committed to the cause of socialism and published several nonfiction works including *Tragic America* (1932) and *America is Worth Saving* (1941).

Drenthe (*or* Drente) A low-lying province in the E Netherlands, bordering on Germany. Parts of its extensive bogs and heaths have been reclaimed for agriculture; produce includes potatoes, rye, and dairy products. Oil is extracted around Shoonebeek. Area: 1037 sq mi (2685 sq km). Population (1988): 437,000. Captial: Assen.

Dresden 51 5N 13 41E A city in SE Germany, on the *Elbe River, the capital of Saxony. One of the world's most beautiful cities prior to its devastation by bombs in 1945, it has since been rebuilt. Dresden is a center of culture, light industry, and market gardening. The china industry moved to Meissen in 1710. It is the site of a music college and a technical university. Population (1990): 520,000.

Dresden, Battle of (August 26–27, 1813) A battle fought near the capital of Saxony between 120,000 French troops led by Napoleon and an Austrian, Prussian, and Russian force of 170,000. Napoleon inflicted a crushing defeat on the allies, who lost 38,000 men.

Dresden porcelain. *See* Meissen porcelain.

dressage The training of a riding (*or* carriage) horse to make it calm, supple, and responsive to its rider (*or* driver). It was originally a training for military charges; the present, more humane, methods only developed in the 18th century. The most advanced stage is *haute école* equitation in which a horse is taught to perform intricate leaps and movements. This classical art is practiced by the *Spanish Riding School in Vienna and the Cadre Noir of the French Cavalry School at Saumur. Dressage competitions consist of a sequence of complex prescribed movements. *See also* equestrianism.

Drew, Daniel (1797–1879) US financier and stockbroker. He entered the brokerage business in 1844 after having run a steamboat company since 1834. He speculated in stock in the Erie Railroad and successfully, although unscrupulously, fought Cornelius Vanderbilt for control of the line (1866–68). He was forced to declare bankruptcy (1876) after the panic of 1873. Drew Theological Seminary (1866) in Madison, N.J., was founded by him.

Dreyer, Carl Theodor (1889–1968) Danish film director. He began his career in films as a scriptwriter in 1912. His major films concern spiritual and supernatural themes and are distinguished by their atmospheric concentration and intensity. They include *La Passion de Jeanne d'Arc* (1928) and *Ordet* (1955).

Dreyer, Johan Ludvig Emil (1852–1926) Danish astronomer, who compiled the *New General Catalogue of Nebulae and Clusters of Stars* (1888). This work is still a standard reference catalogue for nonstellar objects, which are referred to by their catalogue number, e.g. the galaxy NGC 175.

Dreyfus, Alfred (1859–1935) French Jewish army officer. Unjustly accused of revealing state secrets to the German military attaché in Paris, in 1894 Dreyfus, the victim of *antisemitism, was deported for life to *Devil's Island. His case was reopened in 1898, largely owing to the championship of Zola and Clemenceau, becoming a cause célèbre and the focus of conflict between royalist, nationalist, and militarist elements on the one hand and socialist, republican, and anticlerical factions on the other. Following a retrial in 1899, Dreyfus was pardoned but not completely cleared until 1906, when he received the Legion of Honor.

Driesch, Hans Adolf Eduard (1867–1941) German zoologist, whose work gave impetus to modern embryology. His interpretation of studies on developing sea urchin embryos led him to become a lifelong advocate of *vitalism.

drift 1. The debris, including boulders, sand, clay, and gravel, deposited by glaciers or by glacial meltwater. 2. The superficial deposits occurring above the solid underlying rock on the earth's surface. Geological maps are published in both drift and solid editions to distinguish between them.

drill An *Old World monkey, *Mandrillus leucophaeus*, of central West Africa, smaller than the closely related *mandrill. Drills inhabit inland forests, moving about on the ground in small groups and eating leaves, fruit, and worms.

driver ant An African *ant of the genus *Dorylus* or related genera, which has a lifestyle similar to the New World *army ant. Subfamily: *Dorylinae*.

Drogheda (Irish name: Droichead Átha) 53 43N 6 21W A port in the Republic of Ireland, in Co Louth on the River Boyne. Its garrison was massacred by Cromwell in 1649. Drogheda exports cattle and has brewing, linen and cotton, and engineering industries. Population: 19,762.

dromedary. *See* camel.

drone. *See* bee.

drongo A songbird belonging to a family (*Dicruridae*; 20 species) occurring in Old World tropical forests. About 9–14 in (22–35 cm) long, drongos are usually black, often with long tail plumes, and have a harsh song. They have stout sharp-hooked bills and feed on large insects, which are often caught in flight. These birds are noted for fiercely defending their territories against intruders.

dropsy. *See* edema.

dropwort A perennial herb, *Filipendula vulgaris*, of grasslands and clearings in Eurasia and N Africa. Up to 28 in (70 cm) high, it has compound leaves with 8–20 divided toothed leaflets. The flowers, which occur in flat-topped terminal clusters, have 5–6 red-tinged white petals and long prominent stamens. The tuberous roots may be eaten. Family: *Rosaceae*.

Drosera. *See* sundew.

Drosophila A genus of small *fruit flies (about 1000 species), also called vinegar flies. Most species feed on fermenting materials, such as rotting or damaged fruit, but a few are predatory or parasitic. Some species, especially *D. melanogaster*, have been used extensively in laboratory studies of heredity and evolution because of the large chromosomes in their salivary glands and their short life cycle. Family: *Drosophilidae*.

drought An extended period of dry weather with a virtual absence of precipitation, causing a lack of moisture in the soil. Droughts in densely populated areas reliant on agriculture, such as India and China, can have disastrous effects.

drowning Suffocation due to water in the air passages. Death occurs much more rapidly in fresh water than sea water. This is because fresh water flows through the lungs into the blood, causing the red blood cells to burst and release potassium, which causes the heart to stop. Salt water mechanically prevents the oxygen reaching the lungs. It can take up to ten minutes to drown, and anybody rescued should immediately be given *artificial respiration.

drug dependence The condition resulting from regular use of a drug such that its withdrawal causes emotional distress (psychological dependence) or physical illness (physical dependence). Drugs causing psychological dependence include cannabis, LSD, and the nicotine in tobacco. Physical dependence is associated with such drugs as morphine, heroin, barbiturates, and alcohol. Withdrawal of these drugs causes unpleasant symptoms (withdrawal symptoms) that disappear on taking further doses. Overdosage of such drugs is common and can be fatal. Physical dependence is invariably associated with severe psychological dependence and requires specialist treatment. *See also* alcoholism.

drugs Compounds that alter the physiological state of living organisms (including man). Medicinal drugs are widely used for the treatment, prevention, and diagnosis of disease. The wide range of drugs available for this purpose includes the anesthetics (*see* anesthesia), *analgesics, *antibiotics, *cytotoxic drugs, *diuretics, hormonal drugs, and *tranquilizers.

Some drugs are taken solely for the pleasurable effects they produce. Many such drugs are addictive (*see* narcotics) and—despite rigorous controls to restrict their use—illegal trade in them continues. The most widely used illicit drugs include *opium and its derivatives and synthetic substitutes, stimulants such as cocaine and amphetamine, hallucinogens such as LSD, marijuana, and some sedatives. *See also* drug dependence.

Druids Ancient Celtic priests who were also revered as teachers and judges. Information about them is largely derived from Julius Caesar's hostile account in his *Gallic Wars*. They worshiped nature gods, believed in the immortality of the soul and *reincarnation, and also taught astronomy. Their central religious rite involved the sacred oak tree, from which they cut mistletoe with a golden knife. They sacrificed humans, usually criminals, on behalf of those near to death. In Gaul and Britain they were wiped out by the Romans, their last stand being in Anglesey (61 AD), but in Ireland they survived until the arrival of Christian missionaries. They had no proven association with *Stonehenge, despite the use of the site by the revived 20th-century Druidic Order.

drumfish A carnivorous fish, also called croaker, belonging to the family *Sciaenidae* (about 160 species), that occurs mainly along warm seashores. They have two dorsal fins and are usually silvery in color. Most species produce sounds by amplifying muscle movements through the swim bladder. Order: *Perciformes*.

drumlin A small streamlined hill, formed through glaciation and composed of glacial till or drift, sometimes with a rock core. Drumlins usually occur in groups or swarms (sometimes called basket-of-eggs topography), their long axes parallel to the direction of ice flow. They are common features in Co Down, Northern Ireland.

drums Musical instruments of ancient origin, in which a pitched or unpitched sound is produced by striking a tight skin stretched over a frame or resonating chamber. Drums are played either with sticks of various kinds or with the hands. The family includes the orchestral *timpani, the bass drum, snare drum, and tambourine. *Compare* percussion instruments; stringed instruments; wind instruments.

drupe A stone fruit, such as a cherry, plum, or peach. The fruit wall (pericarp) develops into three layers: an outer skin (epicarp), succulent flesh (mesocarp), and a stone (endocarp) containing the seed.

Drury Lane Theatre The oldest theater in London, first opened in 1663. The present building dates from 1813. It has housed every form of dramatic production. Its early managers included actor David *Garrick, and playwright R. B. Sheridan, whose *School for Scandal* had its first performance there.

Druses (*or* Druzes) Adherents of the Druse religion, a sect probably named for one of its founders, al-Darazi, who preached the divinity of the Fatimid caliph al-Hakim (996–1021 AD). After his death they won some support in S Syria and developed extreme heterodox ideas. Druses are not generally accepted as Muslims. Their scriptures are based on the Bible, the Koran, and on Sufi writings. Today they live mainly in Syria, Lebanon, and Israel.

dryad In Greek mythology, a type of *nymph inhabiting trees, especially oak trees. A dryad was believed to die when the tree died.

dry cleaning Cleaning fabrics using a solvent other than water. Its main advantage over washing is that it rarely affects the shape or color of the article. Commercial dry cleaning plants are mainly automatic and the most common solvent is perchloroethylene. Like washing, the solvent, which may contain a detergent, loosens and flushes away dirt particles. Drying is by spinning and warm air. The solvent is recycled.

Dryden, John (1631–1700) British poet and critic. He welcomed the Restoration of the monarchy with two panegyrics to Charles II and was appointed poet laureate in 1668. He wrote several successful plays for the recently reopened theaters, for example *Marriage à la Mode* (1673) and *All for Love* (1677). He also wrote brilliant verse satires, notably *Absalom and Achitophel* (1681) and *MacFlecknoe* (1682). He became a Catholic in 1685 and lost the laureateship on the accession of the Protestant William of Orange in 1688. His last major work was a translation of Virgil (1697).

dry farming Crop production in regions receiving less than 20 in (50 cm) of rainfall per annum. This involves special farming techniques, especially planting quick-growing drought-resistant crops to make the best use of limited rainfall. Traditionally, winter wheat is grown in alternation with a fallow year, in which moisture and nutrient levels are allowed to recover. Appropriate husbandry, such as leaving a protective layer of crop residue, contour plowing, and the use of fertilizers, all help to maximize yields under difficult conditions.

Dryopithecus A genus of extinct apes, also called oak apes, with teeth and jaws similar to those of chimpanzees and gorillas. Most *Dryopithecus* remains come from India dating from the late Tertiary period (between 19 and 1 million years ago).

Dryopteris A genus of *ferns (about 150 species), known as buckler ferns, found mainly in N temperate regions. They have firm feathery branched fronds, often growing in crowns, 6–60 in (15–150 cm) high, from short stout scaly rhizomes. Large clusters of spore capsules (sori) occur in two rows on the underside of the leaflets. A common species is the male fern (*D. filix-mas*). Family: *Aspidiaceae*.

795 **DuBois, W(illiam) E(dward) B(urghardt)**

drypoint A technique of engraving. The finished print is characterized by a shadowy effect produced by the ridges thrown up by the incision on the copperplate. Early masters of drypoint include *Durer and *Rembrandt.

dry rot The decay of timber caused by cellulose-digesting fungi, especially *Serpula lacrymans*. Spores are liable to germinate in timber having a moisture content of over 20% and the fungus appears as a whitish mass on the surface. The timber becomes cracked and crumbly and the infection may spread to adjoining dry timbers. Treatment is by removal of infected timbers and application of fungicide to the remaining parts. *Compare* wet rot.

Drysdale, Sir (George) Russell (1912–81) Australian painter, born in England. After training in Melbourne, London, and Paris, he specialized in scenes of the Australian outback.

dualism Any philosophical theory asserting either that the universe is made up of two irreducible and independent substances or that it is based on two fundamental principles (for example, good and evil). It is thus distinguished from monism—the belief in just one substance (or principle)—and pluralism, which holds that there are many. One of the most pervasive dualistic theories in philosophy since *Descartes is the view that the world is constituted of mental substance (mind or consciousness) and physical substance (body or matter).

Dubai. *See* United Arab Emirates.

Du Barry, Marie Jeanne Bécu, Comtesse (?1743–93) The last mistress of *Louis XV of France from 1768 until his death (1774), when she was banished from court. She was guillotined during the French Revolution.

Dubček, Alexander (1921–92) Czechoslovak statesman. Dubček participated in the resistance to the Nazi occupation and after World War II rose to become secretary of the Czechoslovak Communist Party in 1968. As leader, he granted Czechoslovakia many liberal reforms, which were opposed by the Soviet Union and led to the Soviet invasion of Czechoslovakia in August, 1968. Dubček was taken to Moscow, where he agreed to cooperate with Soviet demands but in April, 1969, he lost his post and was ousted from the Party in 1970.

Dublin (Irish name: Baile Átha Cliath) 53 20N 6 15W The capital of the Republic of Ireland, on Dublin Bay. An important commercial and cultural center, it is also the largest manufacturing center and the largest port in the Republic. Its industries include whiskey, distilling, brewing (it has the largest brewery in the world), clothing, glass, and food processing. It is noted for its wide streets (notably O'Connell Street) and its 18th-century Georgian squares. It has the University of Dublin (founded 1592) and the National University of Ireland (founded 1909); Dublin also contains the famous Abbey Theatre. Literary names associated with the city include W. B. Yeats and J. M. Synge. *History*: during the 18th century Dublin prospered as the second largest city of the British Empire but declined during the 19th century. The Easter Rising of 1916 took place here. Population (1991): 477,675.

Dublin (Irish name: Baile Átha Cliath) A county in the E Republic of Ireland, in Leinster bordering on the Irish Sea. Chiefly low lying, it rises in the S to the Wicklow Mountains and is drained by the River Liffey. The county is dominated by the city of Dublin. Agricultural produce includes barley, wheat, and potatoes, and cattle are reared. Area: 356 sq mi (922 sq km). Population (1991): 1,024,429. County town: Dublin.

DuBois, W(illiam) E(dward) B(urghardt) (1868–1963) US educator, writer, and reformer. He taught at Atlanta University (1897–1910) after being educated at Fisk, Howard, and Harvard universities. In 1905 he founded the Niagara Movement, which evolved into and merged with the *National Association for the Advancement of Colored People (NAACP) in 1909, and edited *Crisis*, the organization's journal, until 1932. An advocate of African colonial independence, he played leadership roles in the Pan African conferences (1900, 1919, 1921, 1923, 1927) and chaired the conference in 1945. He joined the American Communist Party in 1961, a result of his interest in socialism, and left the US to live in Ghana. His works include *The Philadelphia Negro* (1899) and *Souls of Black Folk* (1903).

DUBLIN *The public viewing the damage in the center of the city following the Easter Rising (1916).*

Dubrovnik (Italian name: Ragusa) 42 40N 18 07E A port in Croatia on the Adriatic coast. It flourished as a city state until the early 19th century, and now, with its picturesque setting and medieval walls, is popular among tourists. The town was damaged by two earthquakes in April 1979. During Croatia's struggle for independence in 1991, the city was severely damaged during fighting. Population (1985): 35,000.

Dubuffet, Jean (Phillipe Arthur) (1901–85) French painter and sculptor, who achieved notoriety in 1946 with his "junk" pictures. Using plaster, sand, straw, etc., he produced extremely distorted and flattened images, influenced by graffiti on walls and the art of children and the insane. He showed his own collection of works and those of children and psychiatric patients in a Paris exhibition entitled *l'Art brut* (brutal art) in 1949.

Du Cange, Charles du Fresne, Sieur (1610–88) French historian. An outstandingly prolific writer, Du Cange wrote glossaries of the middle ages that were a significant and original contribution to historical research. He also wrote widely on the Byzantine Empire and edited the works of the medieval chroniclers Villehardouin and Joinville.

Duccio di Buoninsegna (c. 1255–c. 1318) Italian painter, founder of the Sienese school. His major works are the *Rucellai Madonna* (Uffizi) for Sta Maria Novella, Florence, and the *Maestà* (1308–11), an altarpiece of Siena Cathedral, which contemporaries hailed as a masterpiece and carried in procession through the city. A fusion of *Byzantine and *gothic styles, it illustrates his gift for narrative painting.

W. E. B. DUBOIS *A pioneer spokesman in the movement for African-American equality and an advocate of world socialism.*

Duchamp, Marcel (1887–1968) French artist. His first success was *Nude Descending a Staircase* (1912; Philadelphia), influenced by *cubism and *futurism. This was followed by his controversial *ready-made objects, for example a urinal, first exhibited in New York. He lived in New York after 1915 and became leader of its *dada art movement. His best-known work is the glass and wire picture of *The Bride Stripped Bare by Her Bachelors, Even* (1915–23; Philadelphia).

duck A small short-necked waterbird belonging to the family *Anatidae* (ducks, geese, and swans), occurring in salt and fresh waters throughout the world except Antarctica. Ducks are adapted for swimming and diving, having a dense waterproofed outer plumage with a thick underlayer of down. The blunt spatulate bill is covered with a sensitive membrane and has internal horny plates for sifting food from water. The 200 species of duck are mostly gregarious; many are migratory and strong fliers. Ducks feed either at the surface of the water (*see* dabbling duck) or dive to forage in deeper water (*see* diving duck). Order: *Anseriformes* (ducks and geese).

duck-billed platypus An aquatic *monotreme mammal, *Ornithorhynchus anatinus*, of Australia and Tasmania. Platypuses grow to 22 in (55 cm) long and have webbed feet. They use their broad flat toothless beak for sieving invertebrates from stream bottoms. The female lays two eggs in a grass-lined burrow constructed in a river bank, incubates them for two weeks, then suckles the tiny young (about 0.7 in [17 mm] long). Family: *Ornithorhynchidae.*

duckweed A small floating aquatic plant of the genus *Lemna* (about 10 species), forming dense carpets on or just below the surface of ponds, streams, etc. The plants have no distinct stems and leaves, consisting of a group of small round leaflike structures (thalli) that continuously reproduce by budding. Minute petalless flowers are enclosed in a sheath on the margin of the thallus. *L. minor, L. gibba,* and *L. polyrhiza* have roots; *L. triscula* is rootless. Duckweeds are the simplest and smallest of flowering plants. Family: *Lemnaceae.*

Duero River. *See* Douro River.

Dufay, Guillaume (c. 1400–74) Burgundian composer and priest (*see* Burgundian school), associated with Cambrai Cathedral for much of his life. An outstanding composer of the middle ages, he wrote masses, motets, magnificats, and French and Italian chansons. He was also a famous teacher.

Du Fu (*or* Tu Fu; 712–70 AD) Chinese poet of the Tang dynasty. Du Fu's failure to become a high official forced him to lead a life of poverty and traveling to escape famines and rebellions. The major themes of his poetry are thus the social injustices of his time and the effects of civil strife on Chinese life.

Dufy, Raoul (1877–1953) French painter, born in Le Havre. His early influences were *impressionism and then *fauvism. He later developed an individual style in lively and often witty racecourse and regatta scenes, notable for the way forms are drawn sketchily over areas of thinly applied color.

dugong A marine herbivorous mammal, *Dugong dugon,* of the Indo-Pacific region. Up to 10 ft (3 m) long, dugongs—also known as sea cows—have blue-gray rough skin and a bristly snout; the males have short tusks. Their forelimbs are flippers and they lack hind limbs, having a flukelike tail for swimming. Dugongs feed on sea grass on the sea bed and, together with *manatees, are a threatened species. Family: *Dugongidae*; order: *Sirenia.*

Duhamel, Georges (1884–1966) French novelist. Trained as a doctor, he worked as an army surgeon during World War I. His major works are his two novel cycles, *Salavin* (1920–32), exploring the theme of human aspirations in a materialistic age, and *The Pasquier Chronicles* (1933–44).

duiker A small nocturnal African antelope belonging to the subfamily *Cephalophine* (17 species), inhabiting bush or forest. 14–30 in (35–75 cm) high at the shoulder, both sexes usually have smooth backward-pointing horns and often a distinct stripe along the back. They plunge into cover when disturbed, hence their name, which in Afrikaans means "diver."

Duisburg 51 26N 6 45E A city in western Germany, in North Rhine-Westphalia at the confluence of the Rhine and Ruhr Rivers. Heavily bombed in World War II for its armaments industry, it is the largest European inland port and a steel-producing center. Its university was established in 1972. Population (1991 est): 576,000.

Dukakis, Michael (Stanley) (1933–   ) US politician. The governor of Massachusetts (1975–81; 1983–91), he was the unsuccessful Democratic presidential candidate in 1988. A decline in his popularity followed, causing him not to seek reelection as governor.

Dukas, Paul (1865–1935) French composer, teacher, and critic. He is best known for his orchestral scherzo *The Sorcerer's Apprentice* (1897). His works also include the opera *Ariane et Barbe-Bleue* (1907) and the ballet *La Péri* (1912). A perfectionist, he destroyed many of his works shortly before his death.

Dukhobors. *See* Doukhobors.

dulcimer A musical instrument consisting of a shallow resonating box with strings stretched over two movable bridges. It is played with two small hammers. Descended from the Persian *santir* and much used in European and Asian folk music, it is particularly popular in Hungarian gypsy music under the name *cimbalom.

Dulles, John Foster (1888–1959) US statesman and diplomat. He began his career as an international attorney. He held various diplomatic positions in the State Department during World War I and served as counsel to the American Peace Commission at the *Versailles Conference. After World War II, Dulles was named delegate to the *San Francisco Conference and was instrumental in the creation of the *United Nations, to which he was US ambassador (1945–49). Dulles was named Secretary of State in the Eisenhower administration (1953–59). Throughout the *Cold War, he espoused a policy of active opposition to the expansion of communism. He developed a strategy of "brinkmanship" to contain the People's Republic of China, and he supported a hard line against the Soviet Union. Dulles also helped to formulate the Eisenhower Doctrine, which created a temporary balance of power in the Middle East. His brother, **Allen Welch Dulles** (1893–1969) was also a statesman and diplomat. After serving in several government posts abroad, he was part of the American peace commission in 1918 and the US Department of State's Near Eastern Affairs chief (1922–26). During World War II he served with the Office of Strategic Services (OSS) and then, after working on the establishment of the Central Intelligence Agency (CIA) (1947), went on to become its deputy director (1951–53) and director (1953–61).

Dulong and Petit's law The product of the mass of 1 mole of a solid element and its specific heat capacity is constant and equal to 25 joules per kelvin. The law is only true for simple substances and at normal temperatures. Named for the French physicists P. Dulong (1785–1838) and A. Petit (1791–1820).

dulse An edible purplish-red *seaweed, *Rhodymenia palmata*, found growing on rocks, shellfish, and other seaweeds on N Atlantic coasts. A red alga, it has flat leathery lobed fronds about 5–16 in (12–40 cm) long, which are often eaten as a salty confection of the same name.

Duluth 46 45N 92 10W A city in Minnesota, at the W end of Lake Superior opposite Superior, Wis. It is the commerical and industrial center of N Minnesota and large quantities of iron ore and grain are shipped from its port. Population (1990): 85,493.

Duma The Russian parliament from 1906 to 1917. The Duma, which was established in response to the *Revolution of 1905, transformed Russia into a constitutional monarchy. It was composed of an upper chamber, the state council, and a lower chamber. Half the members of the state council were appointed by the monarch and the remainder of the deputies in both chambers were elected. Owing to their radicalism, the first two Dumas (1906, 1907) were quickly dissolved by Emperor Nicholas II but the third (1907–12) and fourth (1912–17) more conservative Dumas lasted their legal five-year terms. At the beginning of the Russian Revolution the Duma established the provisional government that enforced Nicholas' abdication.

Dumas, Alexandre (1802–70) French novelist and dramatist, often called Dumas *père*. His father was a soldier, the son of a marquis and a black woman, and he became a general in the French Revolutionary armies. Brought up in poverty and largely self-educated, Alexandre began writing melodramatic historical plays in 1829. After 1839 he began writing his famous historical romances, including *The Count of Monte Cristo* (1844–45), *The Three Muske-teers* (1844), and *The Black Tulip* (1850). His works were hugely successful but the uninhibited extravagance of his private life kept him continually in debt.

His illegitimate son **Alexandre Dumas** (1824–95), a dramatist, was often called Dumas *fils*. His best-known work is the novel *La Dame aux camélias* (1848), the basis of a play and Verdi's opera *La Traviata*. His other plays, which include *Le Demi-monde* (1855) and *Le Fils naturel* (1858), were mostly moralistic treat-ments of such themes as adultery and prostitution.

Du Maurier, George (Louis Palmella Busson) (1834–96) British carica-turist and novelist. Born in Paris, he moved to London in 1860 and contributed caricatures to *Punch* and other magazines. His novel *Trilby* (1894), remembered for its sinister hypnotist Svengali, is based on his life as an art student in Paris. The best-known works of his granddaughter **Daphne Du Maurier** (1907–89) are romances, usually set in her home county of Cornwall. They include *Rebecca* (1938) and *The Flight of the Falcon* (1965).

Dumbarton Oaks Conference (1944) A conference called by the Allies, in Washington, D.C., that led to the formation of the *United Nations. The Soviet Union, the UK, and the US met first and China, the UK, and the US met during the last week of the conference. From these meetings evolved a proposal for an international organization for the promotion of peace and security. The four par-ticipants in these meetings were to be permanently represented on the Security Council.

Du Mont, Allen Balcom (1901–65) US engineer, who developed the *cathode-ray tube (CRT). He set up a company to manufacture allied electronic devices in 1931 and invented the oscilloscope (*see* cathode-ray oscilloscope), which incorporated his new durable CRTs. He also utilized them in television receivers, which he began manufacturing in 1937.

Dumont d'Urville, Jules Sébastien César (1790–1842) French navigator. He went on two surveying expeditions to the South Seas (1822–25, 1826–29) and on the second circumnavigated the world in the *Astrolabe*, returning with specimens of plants and rocks. In repeating this exploit (1837–40), he discov-ered the Adélie (his wife's name) coast of Antarctica.

Dumoriez, Charles François du Périer (1739–1823) French general. Dur-ing the French Revolution he became commander of a division in Nantes (1791). In 1792 he became minister of foreign affairs but resigned to command the northern army against Austria and Prussia. He won victories at Valmy and Jemappes (1792) but after defeat in early 1793 conspired to overthrow France's revolutionary government. Deserted by his troops he went over to the Austrians, eventually settling in England.

Dunant, (Jean-) Henri (1828–1910) Swiss philanthropist, who inspired the foundation (1864) of the International *Red Cross. In 1859 he organized relief for the wounded at the Battle of Solferino, an experience that led him to propose the establishment of an international relief agency. He won the first Nobel Peace Prize in 1901.

Dunbar, Paul Laurence (1872–1906) US poet and novelist. The son of for-mer slaves, he was known for his poetry and stories written in dialect. His poetry is collected in *Lyrics of Love and Laughter* (1903) and *Lyrics of Sunshine and Shadow* (1905). Short story volumes include *The Heart of Happy Hollow* (1904). One novel, *The Sport of the Gods* (1902), is about African-Americans, while *The Uncalled* (1898), *The Love of Landry* (1900), and *The Fanatics* (1901) are about the world of whites.

Dunbar 56 00N 2 31W A resort and fishing village in E central Scotland, on the Lothian coast, scene of *Cromwell's victory over the Scots (1650).

Duncan I (d. 1040) King of the Scots (1034–40). His claim to the throne was challenged by Macbeth, by whom he was murdered.

Duncan, Isadora (1878–1927) US dancer. She lived mostly in Europe, where she gained a reputation for both her innovative modern interpretive dancing and her flamboyant lifestyle. Her accidental death was caused by her scarf being caught in the wheel of the car in which she was traveling.

Dundalk (Irish name: Dún Dealgan) 54 01N 6 25W A port in the Republic of Ireland, the county town of Co Louth. Its chief industries are engineering, brewing, printing, and linen manufacturing, and its main exports are beef and cattle. Population: 21,672.

Dundee 56 28N 3 00W A city in E Scotland, the administrative center of Tayside Region on the Firth of Tay. It is a port and university town, known chiefly for the manufacture of jute goods. Dundee also provides supplies and services for the North Sea oil industry and has engineering and shipbuilding industries. Population (1981): 174,746.

Dundee, John Graham of Claverhouse, 1st Viscount (c. 1649–89) Scottish soldier, who led a *Jacobite rebellion (1689) in support of the deposed James VII of Scotland (James II of England). He won an outstanding victory against loyalist forces at Killiecrankie but was mortally wounded.

Dunedin 45 52S 170 30E A port in New Zealand, in SE South Island at the head of Otago Harbor. Founded by Scottish Presbyterians in 1848, it has two cathedrals (Anglican and Roman Catholic) and the University of Otago (the oldest in the country, founded in 1869). Industries include the manufacture of woolen goods, agricultural machinery, and footwear. Population (1974 est): 83,900.

Dunfermline 56 04N 3 29W A city in E Scotland, in Fife Region on the Firth of Forth. Several Scottish kings, including *Robert the Bruce, are buried in the 11th-century abbey. Dunfermline produces silk, synthetic fiber, and rubber products and there are rich coal deposits nearby. It is the birthplace of Andrew *Carnegie. Population (1981): 52,057.

dung beetle A *scarab beetle, also called a tumblebug, that has the habit of rolling dung into balls, which serve as a food source for both the adults and larvae. Dung beetles are usually dark and small, varying between 0.2 and 1.2 in (5 and 30 mm) in length.

Another group of dung-eating beetles belong to the family *Geotrupidae* (*see* dor beetle).

Dunkirk (French name: Dunkerque) 51 02N 2 23E A port in N France, in the Nord department on the Strait of Dover. Sacked by the English (1388), it was ceded to Cromwell in 1658 but was later sold (1662) by Charles II to Louis XIV. During *World War II British and other Allied troops were successfully evacuated from its beaches (1940) following the fall of France. Dunkirk is a rapidly growing industrial center and has an oil refinery and naval shipbuilding yards. Population (1975): 83,759.

dunlin A common *sandpiper, *Calidris alpina*, that breeds in far northern regions, ranging south to N Britain. 8 in (20 cm) long, it has a bill with a curved tip and a black and russet plumage that changes to gray in winter.

Dunlop, John Boyd (1840–1921) Scottish inventor, who is credited with inventing the pneumatic tire (1887). Dunlop began to produce his tires commercially in 1890. Initially for bicycles, they later contributed greatly to the development of motor cars.

DUNG BEETLE *Using its head and paddle-like antennae, this beetle constructs balls of dung, which it buries and feeds on. The females lay eggs in dung balls, which provide food for the larvae.*

dunnock A shy inconspicuous songbird, *Prunella modularis*, also called hedge sparrow (although it is an *accentor and not a sparrow). About 6 in (14 cm) long, the dunnock has a dull-brown plumage with a grayish throat and breast. It has a fine sharp bill and feeds on insects. Cuckoos often lay their eggs in dunnocks' nests.

Dunois, Jean d'Orléans, Comte de (1403–68) French general in the Hundred Years' War. He defeated the English in 1427, then brilliantly held Orléans until relieved by Joan of Arc (1429). Further victories led to his triumphal entry into Paris (1436). After the renewal of war, he drove the English out of N France.

Dunsinane A hill in E Scotland in the Sidlaw Hills. The ruined fort on its summit is said to be Macbeth's castle and is referred to in Shakespeare's play *Macbeth*. Height: 1012 ft (303 m).

Duns Scotus, John (c. 1260–1308) Scottish-born Franciscan philosopher, who, with Roger *Bacon and *William of Ockham, carried on controversy against *Aquinas. Contradicting Aquinas, Duns Scotus held that what makes one thing distinct from another is its form, or essence, that is its essential properties rather than its accidental properties, as the latter may be removed or change without altering its identity. Although nicknamed the Subtle Doctor by contemporaries, Duns Scotus suffered Renaissance ridicule, so that his name has given rise to the derisive label "dunce."

Dunstan, St (924–88 AD) English churchman and monastic reformer, born near Glastonbury. Of noble birth, he lived as a hermit until appointed Abbot of Glastonbury in 943. He rebuilt its monastery and initiated a revival of English monasticism. The chief minister under Kings Eadred and Edgar, he also became

Bishop of Worcester (957), Bishop of London (959), and Archbishop of Canterbury (960). He lost favor under Ethelred II. Feast day: May 19. Emblem: a pair of tongs.

duodecimal system A system of numbers that has a base of 12 as opposed to the base 10 of the normal *decimal system. For example, the number 31 in the decimal system becomes 27 in the duodecimal system since $31 = (2 \times 12) + 7$.

duodenal ulcer. *See* peptic ulcer.

duodenum. *See* intestine.

DuPont de Nemours, Eleuthère Irénée (1771–1834) US industrialist; born in France. With his father, Pierre Samuel (1739–1817), he founded E. I. DuPont de Nemours & Company in 1802. He had come from France to the US with his father in 1799 and saw a need for a better quality gunpowder in America. By 1802 he had established a gunpowder mill near Wilmington, Del and soon prospered, especially during the War of 1812. The company grew rapidly under his descendants to become one of the giants of US industry.

du Pré, Jacqueline (1945–87) British cellist. She studied with Paul Tortelier and Mstislav Rostropovich, making her debut in 1961 in Elgar's cello concerto, a work with which she became particularly associated. In 1967 she married the pianist Daniel *Barenboim, with whom she gave recitals. Multiple sclerosis put an end to her performing career in 1973, but she was subsequently active as a cello teacher.

Duralumin An aluminum *alloy containing 3.5% copper and 0.5% magnesium. It becomes harder in the few days after heating and quenching and retains this hardness as long as its temperature remains below 115°F (150°C). It is used in aircraft manufacture.

Durance River A river in S France, flowing mainly SSW to the Rhône River near Avignon. It provides Marseilles with water. Length: 189 mi (304 km).

Durand, Asher Brown (1796–1886) US artist and engraver. In the early years of his career he was a partner in several engraving firms. His engraving of artist John Trumbull's (1756–1843) *Signing of the Declaration of Independence* (1820) brought him fame and he later did work for the Federal Bureau of Printing and Engraving. His paintings, done mostly after 1835, concentrated on natural landscapes and were scenes of upper New York and New England. He was a member of the Hudson River School of painting. He served as president of the National Academy of Design (1845–61), which he helped to establish in 1826.

Durango 24 01N 104 40W A city in N Mexico. It lies S of Cerro del Mercado, a hill famous for its iron-ore mines. Industries include iron founding, sugar refining, and textiles. Population (1980): 321,150.

Durante, Jimmy (James Francis D.; 1893–1980) US entertainer. Known as "Schnozzola," because of his large nose, he was in vaudeville from the age of 17 and by 1919 was part of a team with Eddie Jackson and Lou Clayton. Several songs became his trademarks, among them "Inka, Dinka, Doo" and "September Song." He appeared in such stage shows as *Show Girl* (1929) and *Jumbo* (1935) and the films, *Ziegfeld Follies* (1946) and *It's a Mad, Mad, Mad, Mad World* (1963), as well as on radio and television.

Durazzo. *See* Durrës.

Durban 29 53S 31 00E The main seaport in South Africa and the largest city in Natal, on the Indian Ocean. Founded in 1835, it has a diversified manufacturing industry, including car assembly and sugar refining, and it is an important tourist center. It contains part of the University of Natal. Population (1991): 634,301.

Dürer, Albrecht (1471–1528) German *Renaissance painter, engraver, draftsman, and woodcut designer. The son of a goldsmith, he was born in Nuremberg, where he trained under the woodcut designer and altarpiece painter Michael Wohlgemuth (1434–1519). His first Italian visit (1494–95) resulted in a series of watercolors of the Alps. He was influenced by Italian artists, particularly *Mantegna and Antonio *Pollaiuolo, but his woodcuts of the *Apocalypse* (1498) are still *gothic in style. In about 1500, he became preoccupied with the study of human proportions. Paintings of this period include the *Self-Portrait* as Christ (1500; Alte Pinakothek, Munich) and *Adoration of the Magi* (1504; Uffizi). On his second Italian visit (1505–07) he painted *The Feast of the Rose Garlands* (Prague) for the church of the German community in Venice. He worked for Emperor Maximilian I from 1512 to 1519. In this period he executed his most famous engravings, including *Knight, Death, and the Devil* (British Museum, London). His last important work was *The Four Apostles* (Alte Pinakothek, Munich). He was also a friend of Luther and sympathized with the Reformation.

ALBRECHT DÜRER *A self-portrait (detail) painted in 1498, when the artist was 26 years old (Albertina, Vienna).*

Durham 35 59N 78 54W A city in N central North Carolina, NW of Raleigh. The American Tobacco Company, started in 1881 by the Duke family, was instrumental in the growth of Durham and today is its largest industry. Duke University (1924; 1851 as Trinity College) is here, as is the Duke Medical Center. Other products manufactured include chemicals, machinery, textiles, lumber, and processed foods. Population (1990): 136,611.

Durham, John George Lambton, 1st Earl of (1792–1840) British colonial administrator, governor general of Canada (1838–39). As Lord Privy Seal he helped to draft the 1832 parliamentary *Reform Act and was sent to Canada after serving (1835–37) as ambassador to Russia. In Canada he was criticized for giving amnesty to rebellious French-Canadians and resigned. His *Report on the Affairs of British North America* (1839) greatly influenced subsequent British colonial policy (*see* British Empire).

durian A tree, *Durio zebethinus*, of SE Asia, up to 98 ft (30 m) tall with oblong tapering leaves and large creamy white flowers. The spherical spiny-coated fruit, 6–8 in (15–20 cm) in diameter, is notorious for its noxious smell, but the custardlike pulp is eaten in large amounts by local people and animals. The seeds are roasted. Family: *Bombacaceae*.

Durkheim, Emile (1858–1917) French sociologist and one of the founding fathers of modern *sociology. In opposition to attempts to explain human conduct solely in terms of psychology, he developed an account of stability and change in whole societies in *The Division of Labor in Society* (1893); in *The Rules of Sociological Method* (1895) he set out a methodology for a science of society. His *Suicide* (1897) was a pioneering study in social statistics. Another major work, produced during the latter part of his life, was *The Elementary Forms of Religious Life* (1912), in which he examined the social foundations of religion.

durmast An Eurasian *oak, *Quercus petraea*, up to 130 ft (40 m) tall. It has long-stalked oval leaves with rounded lobes and hairy undersides and unstalked conical acorns (hence its other name—sessile oak). Its durable wood is used for furniture, construction work, and boat building, and the bark for tanning.

durra An economically important variety of *sorghum *S. vulgare* var. *durra*, also called millet, native to the Nile valley. Its grain is used chiefly for livestock feed.

Durrell, Lawrence George (1912–90) British novelist and poet. Born in India, he lived mostly in the Mediterranean countries. His best-known work is *The Alexandria Quartet*, comprising *Justine* (1957), *Balthazar* (1958), *Mountolive* (1958), and *Clea* (1960), an elaborate exploration of the nature of modern love. His work includes poetry (*Collected Poems*, 1968), humorous sketches (*Esprit de Corps*, 1959), and several travel books on the Greek islands. Other novels are *The Black Book* (1938), *Numquam* (1970), and *Monsieur* (1975). His brother **Gerald Malcolm Durrell** (1925–   ) is a naturalist and popular writer, noted for the autobiographical *My Family and Other Animals* (1956) and *The Stationary Ark* (1976), about his zoo and wildlife conservation trust on the isle of Jersey.

Dürrenmatt, Friedrich (1921–90) Swiss dramatist and novelist. His plays are often experimental in form and usually satirical in intention, mocking hypocritically conventional values. The best known are *The Old Lady's Visit* (1956) and *The Physicists* (1962). He also wrote short stories and detective novels.

Dürres (Italian name: Durazzo) 41 18N 19 28E A port in W central Albania, on the Adriatic Sea. It was founded by Green in the 7th century BC and is now Albania's major commercial town and principal port. Products include flour, salt, and bricks. Population (1989 est.): 82,000.

Duse, Eleonora (1858–1924) Italian actress. She acted in plays by contemporary French dramatists and is especially associated with plays by Gabriele D'Annunzio, her lover, and by Ibsen. Her international reputation as a tragic and romantic actress rivaled that of Sarah Bernhardt.

Dushanbe (name until 1929: Dyushambe; name from 1929 until 1961: Stalinabad) 38 38N 68 51E The capital city of Tajikistan, on the Dushanbinka River. It has food and textile industries and is a cultural and educational center. Population (1991 est): 582,000.

Düsseldorf 51 13N 6 47E A city in Germany, captial of North Rhine-Westphalia on the Rhine River. The birthplace of Heinrich Heine, it is noted for its art academy (1767). A port and major commercial and industrial center of the *Ruhr, its main industry is iron and steel. Population (1991 est): 576,000.

Dust Bowl, the An area extending across W Kansas, Oklahoma, and Texas, and into Colorado and New Mexico. During the 1930s droughts and overfarming resulted in severe erosion of the topsoil. As many as half the residents left. The plight of the farmers was illustrated by the photography of Dorothea Lange (1895–1965) and Steinbeck's novel *The Grapes of Wrath* (1939).

Dutch The national language of the Netherlands, belonging to the Germanic language group. In Belgium it is one of the two official languages and is known as Flemish (*or* Vlaams). It is derived from Low Franconian, the speech of the Salic Franks, who settled in this area, and has numerous local variants.

Dutch East Indies. *See* Indonesia.

Dutch elm disease A serious disease, first described in the Netherlands in 1919, that reached epidemic proportions in the US and Britain, killing millions of elm trees. The fungus responsible, *Ceratocystus ulmi*, blocks the vessels that carry water to the leaves, which wilt and eventually die. The disease is carried by *bark beetles. Protective measures can be taken but are too expensive for widespread use.

Dutch Guiana. *See* Suriname.

Dutchman's breeches An ornamental perennial herb, *Dicentra cucullaria*, from North American woodlands. Its arching stems bear cream or pale-yellow drooping flowers with saclike spurs. The gray-green fernlike leaves arise from underground tubers. Family: *Fumariaceae* (fumitory family). *See also* Dicentra.

Dutchman's pipe An ornamental climbing vine, *Aristolochia durior* (or *A. sipho*), from the American Midwest. Up to 30 ft (9 m) long, it has large kidney-shaped or heart-shaped leaves. The brown-and-black patterned tubular flowers are attached to swollen greenish-yellow tubes, bent to resemble a pipe, and are pollinated by carrion flies. Family: *Aristolochiaceae*.

Dutch metal A highly ductile gold-colored type of brass that contains between 85% and 88% of copper. It is used for bronzing and imitation gold leaf.

Dutch Republic. *See* United Provinces of the Netherlands.

Dutch Wars **1.** (1652–54) The war between England and the Netherlands precipitated by commercial rivalry, which had been aggravated by Oliver Cromwell's *Navigation Act (1651). The English were victorious. **2.** (1665–67) The war between England and the Netherlands (supported by France from 1666). Caused by commercial and colonial rivalry, the English defeated the Dutch off Lowestoft (1665) but in 1667 the Dutch entered the Thames and the Medway, bombarding Chatham. The Treaty of Breda concluded the war. **3.** (1672–78) The war brought about by the invasion of the Netherlands by Louis XIV of France (supported at sea by England). The English were defeated by the Dutch (1672–73) and concluded the Treaty of Westminster (1674). By late 1673 France had been forced to withdraw from the Netherlands but entered the Spanish Netherlands and defeated the alliance of Spain, Austria, and the Dutch. The war was concluded by the Treaties of *Nijmegen. **4.** (1780–84) The war between Britain and the Netherlands caused by Dutch support for the American colonies during the *American Revolution. The Dutch were defeated.

Duvalier, François (1907–71) Haitian politician, known as Papa Doc; president (1957–71). He used his secret police, the Tonton Macoutes, to eliminate all opposition and exploited black nationalism and voodoo practices to maintain popular sympathy. In 1964 he became president for life, a post in which his son **Jean-Claude Duvalier** (1951–) succeeded him in 1971. Known as Baby Doc,

Jean-Claude slightly moderated his father's policies but was forced to flee in 1986 amid economic and political chaos.

DUTCH ELM DISEASE *The elm bark beetle lays its eggs in burrows beneath the bark of elm trees, where they hatch into larvae (above). The characteristic tunnels seen in affected trees (below) are caused by the burrowing larvae.*

Duvall, Robert (1931–) US actor, known for his strong characterizations in both leading and supporting roles. He first achieved fame in *The Godfather* (1972), and *The Godfather: Part II* (1974) and went on to star in such films as *Apocalypse Now* (1979), *The Great Santini* (1980), *Tender Mercies* (1982, Academy Award, best actor), and *Falling Down* (1993). He also played the lead in the acclaimed television miniseries *Lonesome Dove*.

Dvina River 1. (Northern *or* Severnaya) A river in NW Russia, formed by the confluence of the Sukhona and Yug rivers and flowing generally NW to the White Sea. Length: 466 mi (750 km). **2.** (Western *or* Dangava) A river in N Europe, in Russia, Belarus, and Latvia, flowing SW and NW from the Valdai Hills to the Gulf of Riga. Length: 634 mi (1021 km).

Dvinsk. *See* Daugavpils.

Dvořák, Antonín (1841–1904) Czech composer. He was a friend of Brahms and director of the Prague conservatoire (1901–04). From 1892 to 1895 he was director of the National Conservatory in New York, during which time he wrote his famous ninth symphony, entitled "From the New World." Besides the symphonies he wrote concertos for piano, violin, and cello, orchestral tone poems, chamber music, piano music, and songs. His Czech nationalism is particularly evident in his famous *Slavonic Dances* for piano duet (1878–86).

dwarfism Abnormal smallness. The commonest cause is lack of food, and growth can be accelerated if enough food is given. Dwarfism can also occur in children with disease of the pituitary gland, in which insuffient *growth hormone is produced. This can be cured by administration of the growth hormone. Other chronic diseases, such as heart or kidney disease, can cause dwarfism. Children who are emotionally deprived may also fail to grow. The dwarfs seen in circuses are called achondroplastic dwarfs; their small size is due to faulty bone development.

dybbuk (Hebrew: adhesion) In Jewish folklore, an evil spirit, specifically the soul of a sinful person, which, after death, possessed the body of a living person. The dybbuk could be exorcised by invocation of the divine name. Possession by such a spirit is the subject of a famous play, *The Dybbuk*, by the Russian author Solomon Anski (1862–1920).

dyeing The process of permanently changing the color of a material. Natural dyes, such as *madder and *indigo, have been known since 3000 BC. Mauveine, the first synthetic dye, was discovered in 1856 by W. H. *Perkin. Most modern commercial dyes are made from *aromatic hydrocarbons extracted from coal tar or oil. To dye fibers or textiles, the material is immersed in a solution containing the dye, so that the dye molecules adhere to the surface of the fibers. The solvent is usually water but occasionally other solvents are used. An inorganic chemical (such as a salt of chromium), known as a mordant, may be added to make the dye less soluble once it has adhered to the fiber. Dyes used without a mordant are called **direct dyes**. **Vat dyes** are insoluble in water, but are applied in reduced soluble form and then reoxidized. These are used particularly in cellulosic fibers. *See also* pigments.

dyer's broom A stout biennial or perennial plant, *Isatis tinctoria*, also called dyer's greenweed or dyer's furze. 20–48 in (50–120 cm) high, it has arrow-shaped leaves and dense clusters of bright-yellow flowers that produce winged fruits. Native to Eurasia but naturalized elsewhere, its leaves ferment to a distinctive blue dye (*see* woad). Family: *Cruciferae*.

dyer's rocket A biennial herb, *Reseda luteola*, also called weld. It is widespread on waste ground throughout most of the N hemisphere. Up to 28 in (70 cm) high, it has lance-shaped leaves with wavy margins and long slender spikes of pale-yellow flowers, 0.16–0.20 in (4–5 mm) across, formerly used to make a yellow dye. Family: *Resedaceae*.

Dylan, Bob (Robert Allen Zimmerman; 1941–) US singer and songwriter. An outstanding lyricist, he spoke for the protest movement of the 1960s with such folk albums as *The Times They Are A-changin'* (1964). In *Highway 61 Revisited* (1965), he introduced electronic instruments and rock rhythms. *John Wesley Harding* (1968), following a two-year retirement, and *Blood on the Tracks* (1975) confirmed his inventiveness.

dynamics. *See* mechanics; Newtonian mechanics.

dynamite An explosive plastic solid consisting of 75% nitroglycerine and 25% kieselguhr, a porous form of silicon dioxide (SiO_2). It was invented in 1864 by *Nobel. Nitroglycerine alone is very sensitive to shock. The kieselguhr makes it safe to handle. Dynamite is used for blasting, particularly under water.

BOB DYLAN *In concert in 1969.*

dynamo. *See* electric generator.

dyne The unit of force in the *c.g.s. system equal to the force that will impart to a mass of one gram an acceleration of one centimeter per second per second.

dysentery An infection of the large bowel causing painful diarrhea that often contains blood and mucus. It may be caused either by bacteria of the genus *Shigella* or by amebae. It can occur wherever there is poor sanitation, but amebic dysentery is much more common in tropical countries. Treatment for bacillary dysentery is usually by administration of fluids to prevent dehydration, but for amebic dysentery drugs to kill the amebae are also given.

dyslexia Difficulty in learning to write, spell, and read. It is commonly discovered at school when a child cannot read as well as would be expected. Dyslexic children are usually of normal intelligence and with special teaching can improve greatly, although some never manage to deal well with the written word.

dysmenorrhea Painful menstrual periods. In most cases the cause is not known. Treatment is usually with pain killers, but starting a course of oral contraceptive pills will also stop the pain. If the pain starts after years of pain-free periods there may be disease of the reproductive organs.

dysprosium (Dy) A lanthanide element discovered in 1886. It forms the oxide (Dy_2O_3) and halides (for example DyF_3) and can be separated from the other lanthanides by ion-exchange techniques. At no 66; at wt 162.50; mp 816°F (1412°C); bp 1328°F (2335°C).

Dzerzhinsk (name until 1919: Chernorech; name from 1919 until 1929: Rastyapino) 56 15N 43 30E A port in central Russia on the Oka River. It supports chemical, textiles, and cable industries. Population (1991 est): 287,000.

Dzhambul (name until 1939: Auliye-Ata) 42 50N 71 25E A city in S Kazakhstan on the Talas River. Its industries include phosphates, metal, leather, and food processing. Population (1991 est): 312,000.

Dzungarian Basin. *See* Junggar Pendi.

E

Ea (*or* Enki) The ancient Mesopotamian god of water and the sea, with Anu and Enlil one of the supreme triad. He created the Tigris and Euphrates rivers. A guardian against demons and patron of the arts and sciences, including magic, his main attribute was wisdom.

Eadred (d. 955) King of England (946–55), who reconquered Northumbria by expelling Eric Bloodaxe (954), its Norwegian king. Eadred bequeathed a sum of money to relieve the poor in Northumbria and to aid defense against Viking raids.

Eads, John Buchanan (1820–87) US civil engineer, best known for his design and construction of the steel triple-arched Eads Bridge, which spans the Mississippi River at St Louis, Missouri. Opened in 1874, it is now considered a landmark in the history of civil engineering.

Eadwig (*or* Edwy; d. 959) King of England from 955 to 957, when he lost Mercia and Northumbria. He forced St *Dunstan into exile.

eagle A large, broad-winged bird of prey occurring throughout the world, mostly in remote mountainous regions. Eagles have a large, hooked bill and strong feet with curved talons and are typically dull brown but may be a combination of black, gray, white, or chestnut; the head is often crested. With a wingspan of 4.3–7.8 ft (1.3–2.4 m), they can soar for long periods searching for food—generally live prey, such as mammals or reptiles. Family: *Accipitridae* (hawks and eagles), *See also* bald eagle; golden eagle; harpy eagle; Philippine eagle; sea eagle.

eagle owl A large Eurasian *owl of the genus *Bubo*, ranging from cold northern forests to hot southern deserts. It reaches 28 in (70 cm) in length, is tawny with brown mottling, and has orange eyes and large ear tufts.

eaglewood (*or* aloes wood) The resinous heartwood of a tree of the genus *Aquilaria* (especially *A. agallocha*), of SE Asia. Under certain conditions it becomes resinous and fragrant and is used in religious ceremonies and perfumery. Family: *Thymelaeaceae*.

Eakins, Thomas (1844–1916) US painter of portraits and everyday life, particularly sports scenes. He lived mainly in Philadelphia, except for visits to Paris (1866–69) and Spain (1870), where he was influenced by the realism of Velázquez. His teaching methods, particularly his use of live nude models, were controversial, as were some of his paintings, such as *Gross Clinic* (1875), showing a surgeon operating. Other works include *Max Schmitt in a Single Scull* (1871), *The Chess Players* (1876), and *Walt Whitman* (1888).

ealdorman The chief royal official of the Anglo-Saxon shire. Almost always of noble rank, he presided over the shire court, sharing one third of its profits, executed royal orders, and raised the shire military levy. Ealdormen later became the hereditary earls, and the sheriffs succeeded to their duties.

Eames, Charles (1907–78) US designer and architect. He taught at the Cranbrook Academy of Art (1939–41) and there designed, with Eero *Saarinen, an award-winning molded plywood chair for which he became famous. He also designed movie sets, museum and industrial exhibits, and made documentary movies.

ear The organ of hearing and balance in vertebrate animals (including man). The human ear is divided into external, middle, and inner parts. Sound waves are transmitted through the auditory meatus and cause the eardrum (tympanic membrane) to vibrate. These vibrations are transmitted through the three small bones (ossicles) of the middle ear to the fenestra ovalis, which leads to the inner ear. A duct (the Eustachian tube) connects the middle ear to the back of the throat (pharynx), enabling the release of pressure that builds up in the middle ear. The cochlea—a spiral organ of the inner ear—contains special cells that convert the sound vibrations into nerve impulses, which are transmitted to the hearing centers of the brain via the cochlear nerve. The inner ear also contains the organs of balance: three semicircular canals, each of which registers movement in a different plane. The semicircular canals and cochlea are filled with fluid and are known together as the labyrinth of the ear.

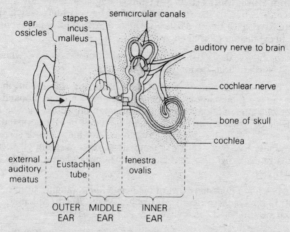

EAR *A vertical section through the human ear shows its internal structure; the middle and inner ears are embedded in the bone of the skull. The arrow indicates the direction of sound waves entering the ear.*

Earhart, Amelia (1898–1937) US aviatrix, who was the first woman to fly solo across the Atlantic (1932) and from Hawaii to California across the Pacific (1935). Her plane was lost over the Pacific between New Guinea and Howland Island, on an attempted flight around the world with F. J. Noonan.

Early, Jubal (Anderson) (1816–94) US Confederate general. A graduate of the US Military Academy at West Point in 1837, he soon resigned his commission and settled in his native Virginia to practice law. He joined the Confederate Army at the beginning of the Civil War in 1861 and, as a colonel, was instrumental in the Confederate victory at the 1st Battle of *Bull Run. Promoted to general, he served in the major battles in Virginia and was in command of the troops that made an unsuccessful drive toward Washington, D.C., in 1864.

Early English The style of □Gothic architecture predominant in England in the 13th century. It is characterized by narrow, pointed windows and arches, in contrast to the rounded features of the preceding period (*see* Norman architecture). These lancet windows are often grouped in threes or fives (e.g. the Five Sisters window in York Minster). Dog-tooth carving, heavily undercut crockets (stylized foliage) on capitals, and columns with detached shafts in black Purbeck marble are typical decorative elements. Salisbury Cathedral (begun 1220) and the nave of Lincoln Cathedral (begun 1192) show the style at its best.

AMELIA EARHART *A photograph taken in 1932.*

earth The third planet from the sun, at an average distance of 93 million mi (149.6 million km) from it. Its diameter at the equator is 7926 mi (12,756 km), slightly less at the Poles; its shape is therefore a flattened sphere (a geoid). It completes an orbit of the sun in 365 days, 6 hours, 8 minutes and makes one rotation on its axis every 23 hours 56 minutes.

The earth is believed to be about 4600 million years old, the oldest rocks so far discovered being 3800 million years old. Geologists divide this time into eras, periods, and epochs (*see* geological time scale). The earth consists of an inner core of solid iron, surrounded by an outer core of molten iron. Surrounding this is the solid mantle, inner and outer, which is separated from the crust by the *Mohorovičić Discontinuity. The crust consists of basaltic oceanic crust surmounted by less dense granitic continental crust, which forms the continents. The crust varies in thickness from 3.1 mi (5 km) under the oceans to 37.2 mi (60 km) under mountain ranges. The composition of the crust is approximately 47% oxygen, 28% silicon, 8% aluminum, 4.5% iron, 3.5% calcium, 2.5% each sodium and potassium, and 2.2% magnesium. All other elements are present to an extent of less than 1% each.

70.8% of the earth's surface is ocean. The greatest ocean depth is over 36,000 ft (11,000 m), in the Marianas Trench; the greatest height of land is 29,028 ft (8848 m), at Mount Everest.

earthnut A slender perennial herb, *Conopodium majus*, of European woods and meadows. Up to 40 in (1 m) high, it is also called pignut or hognut, as its tubers are eaten by livestock. It has finely divided leaves and clusters of pinkish white flowers. Family: *Umbelliferae*.

The name is also sometimes applied to the *groundnut.

earthquake A series of shocks felt at the earth's surface, ranging from mild tremblings to violent oscillations, resulting from the fracturing of brittle rocks within the earth's crust and upper mantle. The magnitude of an earthquake depends on the amount of energy liberated when the overstrained rocks fracture. The *Richter scale is used for comparing earthquake magnitudes. The point of origin of the *seismic waves produced is the focus and the point on the earth's surface directly above this is the epicenter. The majority of earthquakes occur in certain well-defined seismic zones, corresponding with the junction of lithospheric plates (*see* plate tectonics); these include the circum-Pacific belt, the Alpine-Himalayan belt, and the midocean ridges.

earthstar A fungus of the genus *Geastrum*, with a starlike, inedible fruiting body. Initially globular, the outer layer peels back in segments to form the "rays" of the star, surrounding a thin papery inner globe. Spores are released through a pore in the top. The collared earthstar (*G. triplex*), occurring in woodland, is 2–4 in (6–10 cm) across, pale brown, and has five or more rays. Class: *Basidiomycetes*.

Earth Summit An informal name for the United Nations Conference on Environment and Development, a world environmental meeting held in Rio de Janeiro in June 1992. Attended by 178 nations from around the globe, the summit sought to protect, through treaties, the planet's biological resources and to stabilize the atmospheric levels of heat-trapping gases such as carbon dioxide and methane. The US, while supporting the summit's overall goals, opposed specific parts of the treaties.

earthworm A terrestrial *annelid worm belonging to a class (*Oligochaeta*) found all over the world. Earthworms feed on rotting vegetation, pulling the dead leaves down into their burrows and improving the fertility of the soil. The body consists of about 100 segments, each with four pairs of bristles for gripping the surface as the worm moves. The largest earthworm is *Megascolides australis*, which reaches a length of about 11 ft (3.3 m).

earwig A nocturnal ☐insect belonging to an order (*Dermaptera*; about 1100 species) found in Europe and warm regions. It has a dark slender body, 0.2–2.0 in (5–50 mm) long, and a pair of pincers (cerci) at the end of the abdomen. At rest, the membranous semicircular hindwings are covered by short, leathery forewings. Most earwigs are herbivorous, sometimes becoming pests in farms and gardens. The females lay eggs in the soil and care for them throughout development.

East China Sea (Chinese name: Dong Hai) A shallow section of the W Pacific Ocean, between China, South Korea, the Ryukyu Islands, and Taiwan. A monsoon area, it is rich in fish.

Easter The feast of the resurrection of Christ, the major feast of the Christian calendar. Associated by the early Church with the Jewish *Passover, the date of celebrating Easter was a matter of controversy from earliest times. At the Council of *Nicaea in 325 AD, it was agreed that it would be linked to the full moon on or following the vernal equinox and might thus fall on any Sunday between Mar 22 and Apr 25 (*see also* Orthodox Church). The keeping of a vigil on the night of Easter Saturday is a traditional part of the observance. *See also* Good Friday; Lent.

Easter Island (*or* Rapanui) 27 05S 109 20W A Chilean island of volcanic origin in the S Pacific Ocean. It is famed for its stone sculptures 10–40 ft (3–12 m) high, of unknown origin. The population is of Polynesian stock. Fruit and vegetables are grown and wool is exported. Area: 64 sq mi (166 sq km).

EASTER ISLAND *The vast stone statues, of which there are over 600 on the island, occupy stone terraces.*

Easter Rising (1916) An armed insurrection in □Dublin against the British Government. Patrick Pearse, a leader of the Irish Republican Brotherhood, and James Connolly with his Citizen Army, a total of 2000 men, occupied strategic positions in the city and proclaimed the establishment of the Irish Republic. Serious street fighting ensued with the government employing artillery. Hopes of German arms and munitions were frustrated and the insurgents surrendered unconditionally. The rising was largely confined to Dublin and minor disturbances in Wexford and Galway. Some 15 of the leaders were subsequently executed.

East Germany. *See* Germany.

East India Company 1. (British) A commercial company that was incorporated in 1600 to trade in East Indian spices and came to wield considerable political power in British India. Its dominance in India was established at the expense of the French *East India Company by Robert *Clive's victories in the Seven Years' War (1756–63). For the next decade the Company controlled government, its powers then being restricted by a series of *Government of India Acts. Supreme political power was vested in a Board of Control, responsible to the British parliament, while the Company retained administrative and commercial powers. In the 19th century these were gradually limited and the Company ceased to exist in 1873. **2.** (Dutch) A commercial company founded in 1602 to foster Dutch trade in the East Indies. By the late 17th century, it concentrated almost exclusively on the administration of *Java. **3.** (French; Compagnie des Indes orientales) A trading company founded by *Colbert in 1664 to administer French commerce and colonialism in India. An unsuccessful rival of the British East India Company, it ceased to exist in 1789.

East Indies A term now usually referring to the *Malay Archipelago but sometimes to Indonesia (formerly called the Dutch East Indies). It may also include SE Asia and India.

East London (former name: Port Rex) 33 00S 27 54E A port in South Africa, in SE Cape Province on the Indian Ocean. It is the gateway to the Transkei and Ciskei Bantu Homelands and an important tourist center. Population (1980): 160,582.

Eastman, George (1854–1932) US inventor of the Kodak camera (1888). In 1884 he patented a photographic film consisting of a paper base on which the necessary chemicals were fixed rather than being applied to photographic plates when required. The Kodak camera, containing wind-on film, was improved in 1889, when Eastman replaced the paper-based film with celluloid. He founded (1892) the Eastman Kodak Company. In 1928 he developed a process for color photography. He was also a philanthropist, donating large sums to promote education.

East Pakistan. *See* Bangladesh.

East Riding. *See* Yorkshire.

East River A river in the E US, a tidal strait and navigable waterway flowing through New York City and connecting New York Harbor with Long Island Sound. Length: 16 mi (26 km).

Eastwood, Clint (1930–   ) US movie actor and director, noted for his strong characterizations. His first film successes came with *A Fistful of Dollars* (1964) and other "spaghetti Westerns." He achieved further fame with five movies in which he played San Francisco police detective "Dirty" Harry Callahan. In his later career he often directed, as in *Unforgiven* (1992), for which he received an Academy Award as best director, and *A Perfect World* (1993). Other films included *The Outlaw Josey Wales* (1976) and *In The Line of Fire* (1993).

Eaton Affair (1831) A social conflict in Washington, D.C., that led to the reorganization of Pres. Andrew *Jackson's cabinet. Secretary of War John Henry Eaton (1790–1856) married for a second time in 1829. His wife, Margaret O'Neill (1796–1879), was not accepted socially by the other cabinet wives, especially Mrs. John Calhoun, the vice president's wife. Although she was defended by President Jackson and others, Eaton felt forced to resign from the cabinet.

Ebert, Friedrich (1871–1925) German statesman; first president of the German *Weimar Republic (1919–25). A trade union leader, he later became a deputy in the Reichstag and from 1913 led the Social Democrats. Although a constitutional monarchist, he accepted the republican presidency when the German Empire collapsed in 1918. As president he suppressed extremists of the Right and Left.

Ebla An ancient city (modern Tell Mardikh) S of Aleppo (Syria). It was conquered by *Sargon of Akkad and an archive of over 15,000 Akkadian cuneiform tablets containing trade and other records from this period (c. 2300 BC) was discovered here in 1975.

ebony The valuable heartwood of several tropical evergreen trees of the genus *Diospyros*. Ebony is very hard, heavy, usually deep black, and able to take a high polish. It is used for cabinetwork, inlaying, knife handles, piano keys, and turned articles. The trees have oval leathery leaves, small, creamy-white flowers, and round berries. The most important species are *D. ebenum* (up to 49 ft [15 m] high) from India and Sri Lanka and *D. reticulata* from Mauritius. Family: *Ebenaceae*.

Eboracum (*or* Eburacum). *See* York.

Ebro River (Latin name: Iberus) The second longest river in Spain. Rising in the Cantabrian Mountains, it flows generally SE to the Mediterranean Sea. It is an important source of hydroelectricity and irrigation and its delta is canalized. Length: 565 mi (910 km).

Eccles, Sir John Carew (1903–) Australian physiologist, who (in the 1950s) showed how the different nerve endings (synapses) could either allow the transmission of nervous impulses to other nerves (excitatory) or could prevent their passage (inhibitory). He was awarded the 1963 Nobel Prize together with A. L. *Hodgkin and A. F. *Huxley.

Ecclesiastes (Greek: the preacher) An Old Testament book, traditionally ascribed to Solomon (10th century BC) but in fact one of the later books to be accepted as part of the Hebrew Bible. It is pessimistic in tone, consisting of poetic reflections on the futility of human life.

Ecclesiasticus A book of the *Apocrypha, also known as the Wisdom of Jesus the son of Sirach. It was written about 180 BC in Palestine by Joshua (*or* Jesus) ben-Sira. It stresses the need to fear and obey God, gives practical advice for daily living, and underlines the value of having a good name.

Ecevit, Bülent (1925–) Turkish statesman; prime minister (1974, 1977, 1978–79). He represented the Republican People's Party in the Grand National Assembly (1957–60) and was a member of the Constituent Assembly of 1961. From 1961 to 1965 he was minister of labor. In 1974 he ordered the Turkish invasion of Cyprus and in 1978, following violent civil unrest, imposed martial law on Turkey.

Echegaray y Eizaguirre, José (1832–1916) Spanish dramatist. A mathematician and economist, he was appointed minister of finance in 1874. His plays include *Madman or Saint* (1877) and *The Son of Don Juan* (1895), influenced by *Ibsen. He won the Nobel Prize in 1904.

echidna A *monotreme mammal belonging to the family *Tachyglossidae* (5 species), of Australia, Tasmania, and New Guinea. The Australian echidna (*Tachyglossus aculeatus*), or spiny anteater, is about 18 in (45 cm) long, with very long spines among its fur, and digs for ants, picking them up with its long sticky tongue; it has no teeth. Echidnas lay a single egg, which is incubated in a pouch on the female's belly. The young echidna is suckled at a teat in the pouch.

Echidna In Greek legend, a monster, half woman and half serpent. By the monster *Typhon she gave birth to many other legendary monsters, including Chimera, Cerberus, Orthus, Scylla, the Sphinx, and the dragons of the Hesperides and of Colchis.

echinoderm A marine invertebrate animal of the phylum *Echinodermata* (over 6000 species), including *starfish, *sea urchins, *crinoids, *sea cucumbers, *brittle stars, etc. Echinoderms usually have a skin-covered skeleton of calcareous plates, often bearing spines. They use hydrostatic pressure created by a water vascular system to extend numerous small saclike organs (tube feet) used in locomotion, respiration, feeding, etc. Echinoderms generally occur on the sea floor and are found at all depths, usually feeding on other animals or detritus. The sexes are generally separate and sex cells are fertilized in the sea. The larvae are mostly free-swimming.

Echinoidea A class of marine invertebrate animals (900 species) belonging to the phylum *Echinodermata* (*see* echinoderm), in which the body is covered by a rigid skeleton of calcareous plates bearing movable spines. The class includes the *sea urchins, *heart urchins, and *sand dollars.

Echo In Greek legend, a nymph deprived of speech by Hera and able to repeat only the final words of others. Her hopeless love for *Narcissus caused her to fade away until only her voice remained.

echolocation A method by which certain animals can sense and locate surrounding objects by emitting sounds and detecting the echo. Insectivorous bats emit high-frequency sound pulses (12–150 kHz) and, detecting the echo by means of large ears or folds of the nostril, are able to locate their prey when hunting on the wing. Toothed whales and porpoises emit brief intense clicks, enabling them to discriminate objects as small as fine wires. Some shrews and certain cave-dwelling swiftlets also use echolocation as a means of orientation.

echo sounding The use of sound waves to measure the depth of the sea below a vessel or to detect other vessels or obstacles. The device used consists of a source of ultrasonic pulses (about 30 kHz frequency, usually at 1 pulse per second) and an electronic circuit to measure the time taken for the pulse to reach the sea bed or the other vessel and its echo to return to the transducer. This may be displayed on a *cathode-ray tube, paper chart, or neon light. The device was developed originally by the Allied Submarine Detection Investigation Committee (ASDIC) in 1920 and was formerly known by this acronym. The name was changed to sonar (*so*und *na*vigation and *r*anging) in 1963. Echo-sounding, depth-measuring devices are now fitted to most ships.

Eck, Johann Maier von (1486–1543) German Roman Catholic theologian. He was a leading defender of Roman Catholicism during the early years of the Reformation. He publicly disputed with *Luther at Leipzig (1519) and with *Melanchthon at Worms (1541).

Eckermann, Johann Peter (1792–1854) German writer. His early work impressed *Goethe, whose unpaid assistant he became in 1823. His *Conversations with Goethe* (1836–48) is a brilliant literary account of the poet's last years.

Eckert, John Presper (1919–   ) US electronics engineer, who with John W. Mauchly built the first electronic computer (1946). Known as ENIAC (*E*lectronic *N*umerical *I*ntegrator *and* *C*omputer), it was commissioned by the US Government and used by the army. Eckert and Mauchly also produced Binac (*Bin*ary *A*utomatic *C*omputer) and Univac I (*Univ*ersal *A*utomatic *C*omputer).

Eckhart, Meister (Johannes E.; c. 1260–c. 1327) German Dominican theologian and mystic. Joining the Dominicans in 1275, he studied in Cologne and Paris and became provincial of his order in Saxony in 1303. During his professorship at Cologne University (1320–27) he was charged with heresy and in 1329 his writings were condemned by the pope. They have influenced a number of Protestant theologians and Romantic and existentialist writers.

eclipse The passage of all or part of an astronomical body into the shadow of another. A **lunar eclipse** occurs when the moon can enter the earth's shadow at full moon. The gradual obscuration of the moon's surface is seen wherever the moon is above the horizon. A **solar eclipse**, which is strictly an *occultation, occurs at new moon, but only when the moon passes directly in front of the sun. The moon's shadow falls on and moves rapidly across the earth. Observers in the outer shadow region (the penumbra) will see a **partial eclipse**, with only part of the sun hidden. Observers in the dark inner (umbral) region of the shadow will see a **total eclipse**, in which the sun's disk is completely, but briefly, obscured; the *corona can, however, be seen. If the moon is too far away totally to cover the sun, an **annular eclipse** is observed, in which a rim of light is visible around the eclipsed sun.

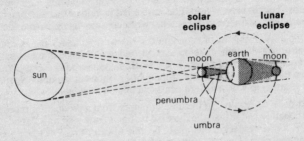

ECLIPSE

ecliptic The great circle in which the plane of the earth's orbit around the sun meets the □celestial sphere. As a result of the earth's orbital motion, the ecliptic marks the apparent path of the sun across the celestial sphere, relative to the background stars, over the course of a year.

eclogue A short dramatic poem, originally pastoral in theme and setting. Originated by *Theocritus in the 3rd century BC, the form was used by Virgil and revived during the Renaissance by Dante and other Italian poets. English writers of eclogues include Spenser, Marvell, and Swift. In the 20th century, Louis MacNeice and W. H. Auden have made ironic use of the form.

ecology The scientific study of organisms in their natural environment. Modern ecology, dating from the work of such scientists as Charles *Elton in the 1930s, is concerned with the relationships of different species with each other and with the environment (habitat) in which they live. A *community of organisms and their habitat is called an *ecosystem. Ecologists can calculate the productivity of various ecosystems in terms of energy, with important applications in agriculture. In addition, the effects of man's intervention on natural ecosystems can be predicted, enabling the effective conservation of wildlife and management of game and fish. Ecologists have also introduced biological methods of pest control in certain cases, so avoiding pollution by pesticides.

econometrics The application of statistical techniques to *economics. Econometrics is used in the testing of the validity of economic theories and in forecasting future trends. The usual process is to develop a mathematical model of a specific theory; the model is then tested against observations of the real world and, if the theory is not refuted as a result, the model can then be used to make forecasts.

economic growth An expansion in the output of a nation's economy, measured by an increase in the *gross national product (GNP). Economic growth is generally regarded as desirable because it is the best way of raising the *standard of living; however, it can have drawbacks, such as increased pollution, which do not show up in the GNP. The level of *investment in the economy is an important factor in the rate of growth, but the reasons for faster growth in some countries than in others are not at all certain. It is also necessary to distinguish between growth and growth per capita. In a developing country the rate of growth may be high, but the rate of growth per capita may be low because of a large increase in the population.

economics A social science concerned with the production of goods and services, their distribution, exchange, and consumption. **Microeconomics** is concerned with the problems facing individuals and firms, while **macroeconomics** is concerned with the economy of a country and regulation of the economy by governments. The division is useful because what is rational for the individual firm or household is not necessarily rational when considering the whole economy.

Contemporary problems in economics in the western democracies center upon the control of *inflation, *unemployment, and the *balance of payments, as well as the encouragement of *economic growth. Economics is beset by controversy between the conflicting schools of thought of *monetarism and *Keynesianism as to the extent to which governments can influence economies.

economies of scale An increase in output from a production process that is proportionately larger than the increase in inputs (raw materials, labor, etc.). For instance, a double-decker bus might be able to carry twice as many passengers as a single-decker, using the same number of crew and requiring only 40% more fuel. Such economies of scale are common in the manufacturing industry and are an inducement to use fewer but larger factories.

ecosystem A *community of living organisms together with the nonliving habitat that they occupy. Some ecosystems are clearly defined (for example, a pond or lake); others have no definite boundaries, merging with neighboring ecosystems. An ecosystem receives inputs of solar energy, nutrients, water, and gases and discharges heat, oxygen, carbon dioxide, and organic compounds. The organisms typically comprise producers (plants, manufacturing organic material from inorganic compounds); consumers (animals, feeding on plants and each other); and decomposers (microorganisms bringing about decay). Together they form an interdependent *food chain or food web.

ectopic pregnancy Pregnancy occurring elsewhere than in the womb. The commonest site of an ectopic pregnancy is in a Fallopian tube, but it may also occur in the cervix of the womb or very rarely inside the abdomen. It may lead to abortion or, more seriously, to rupture of the tube, with pain, bleeding, and shock. The usual treatment of an ectopic pregnancy is surgical removal of the fetus and tube. Since the patient has a second tube there is usually no reason why she should not subsequently have a normal pregnancy.

Ecuador, Republic of A country in NW South America, lying on the Equator, from which it takes its name. It includes the *Galápagos Islands 600 mi (1000 km) out in the Pacific. It consists chiefly of a coastal plain in the W, separated from the tropical jungles and rivers of the Amazon basin (Oriente) by ranges and plateaus of the Andes (containing several active volcanoes, including *Cotopaxi). There are frequent earthquakes, which are often disastrous. The population is largely of Indian and mixed race, with minorities of European and African descent. *Economy*: mainly agricultural, with livestock, cereals, and vegetables in the upland valleys and tropical farming in the lower coastal areas, where the main cash crops (bananas, coffee, and cocoa) are grown. Much of the country is forested and valuable hardwoods are produced, although a great deal remains to be exploited. Ecuador is the world's leading producer of balsawood.

Fishing is important, especially shrimps, and fishing limits have recently been extended to 200 mi (320 km), in spite of opposition from the US. There are some mineral resources; the most important is oil, several new oilfields having been discovered in the Oriente in recent years. In 1972 the construction of the Andean pipeline, which brings oil from the E to the coast, was completed and Ecuador is now South America's second largest oil producer (Venezuela being the first). Industry is being developed, especially the petrochemical, pharmaceutical, cement, and steel industries. Main exports include oil, bananas, cocoa, and coffee. *History*: the Andean kingdom of Quito had already been conquered by the Incas when the Spanish established a colony in 1532. It became part of the viceroyalty of Peru and later of New Granada. It gained independence in 1821 after revolts under Marshal Sucre, and in 1822 joined Gran Colombia under Bolívar. In 1830 it became the independent republic of Ecuador. In 1961 the president, Velasco Ibarra, was overthrown in a left-wing military coup and exiled. After several years of unsettled government he was again elected president. In 1970 he assumed dictatorial powers and in 1972 was deposed by a military regime. This regime was replaced by a three-man junta in 1976. In 1979 a new constitution, providing for a president limited to one four-year term and a single-chamber legislature, was put into effect. In 1981 a border dispute with Peru was settled by international arbitration. In the early 1980s the government found itself in a precarious political position, reflected in a number of cabinet reshufflings. Distressing economic and social conditions resulted in ongoing labor strikes, high inflation, and a devalued sucre. Ecuador was forced to borrow heavily from the International Monetary Fund and foreign lenders. In the early 1990s, Ecuador faced a weak economy, a large national debt, labor strikes, guerrilla insurgents, and the threat of an Indian separatist movement. The country pulled out of OPEC, in an attempt to increase oil revenues, in 1992, an election year in which rightists triumphed. Head of state: president. Official language: Spanish; the main Indian language is Quechua. Official currency: sucre of 100 centavos. Area: 104,505 sq mi (270,670 sq km). Population (1989 est): 10,490,000. Capital: Quito. Main port: Guayaquil.

ecumenical movement A movement among Christian Churches to reestablish unity. The first major schism within Christianity was caused by the rupture between the Eastern and Western Churches in the 11th century; the second occurred within the Western Church at the *Reformation. It was only with the growth of missionary activity in the 19th century that the need for reunion became pressing. Historical divisions meant nothing to the new converts in countries outside the traditional sphere of Christianity. In 1910 the Edinburgh Missionary Conference opened negotiations among the Churches of the Reformation, a process that ultimately led to the foundation of the *World Council of Churches in 1948. The Orthodox Churches gradually came to take a more active role in this body, and further encouragement to the movement came with Pope *John XXIII's invitation to other Churches to send observers to the second *Vatican Council, the results of which clearly indicated Roman Catholic support for ecumenism. Since then the most obvious progress has occurred on the local level, where interdenominational cooperation is now widespread.

eczema. *See* dermatitis.

Edam 52 30N 5 02E A city in the NW Netherlands, in North Holland province on the IJsselmeer. It is famous for its round, red-skinned cheeses. Population (1987): 24,200.

Eddas Two Old Norse compilations made in Iceland in the early 13th century. Together they comprise the major store of pagan Scandinavian mythology. The **Poetic** (*or* Elder) **Edda** (c. 1200) contains poems on the gods, heroic legends, and traditional charms and proverbs. The **Prose** (*or* Younger) **Edda** (1223) was the work of Snorri *Sturluson, who planned it as a textbook for writers of *skaldic poetry, prefaced by a section on the Norse cosmogony, pantheon, and myths.

Eddington, Sir Arthur Stanley (1882–1944) British theoretical astronomer, who correctly calculated that the temperature of the sun's interior must be millions of degrees Celsius or it would collapse under gravitational forces. He also showed that the luminosity of a star increases with its mass (the mass-luminosity law). Eddington was a talented popularizer of science: his *Expanding Universe* (1933) contained the novel idea that the galaxies are flying apart.

Eddy, Mary Baker (1821–1910) US religious leader, founder of *Christian Science. Brought up as a Congregationalist and frequently ill as a young woman, Mrs Eddy was much influenced by the faith healer Phineas Parkhurst Quimby (1802–66). She published her beliefs in *Science and Health* (1875) and in 1879 founded the Church of Christ, Scientist, in Boston. The *Christian Science Monitor*, an influential daily newspaper, first appeared in 1908.

eddy current An electric current induced in a conductor that experiences a changing magnetic field. In *electric generators, motors, and transformers, energy is lost by unwanted eddy currents, either producing heat or opposing motion. In these devices eddy currents are reduced by laminating the iron cores to increase their resistance. Eddy currents are useful in some applications, such as eddy-current heating, mechanical damping and eddy-current brakes, and electricity meters.

Ede 52 03N 5 40E A city in the central Netherlands, in Gelderland province. Its museum contains a fine collection of Van Gogh paintings. Population (1981 est): 83,738.

edelweiss A common perennial alpine plant, *Leontopodium alpinum*, from Europe and South America, often grown in rock gardens. About 6 in (15 cm) high, it has woolly leaves arranged like a star and clustered heads of tiny yellow flowers surrounded by whitish, felted bracts. Family: *Compositae* (daisy family).

edema The accumulation of fluid in body tissues, leading to swelling, popularly known as dropsy. There are many causes of edema, including heart failure, kidney failure, liver failure, and malnutrition. Fluid in the lungs (pulmonary edema) will cause breathlessness. *Diuretic drugs can usually resolve edema by causing the patient to pass more urine. Swelling of the ankles occurs quite commonly: for example, in hot weather and in women before menstruation. It is usually relieved by resting with the legs raised.

Eden, (Robert) Anthony, 1st Earl of Avon (1897–1977) British statesman; Conservative prime minister (1955–57). Foreign secretary from 1935 to 1938. During World War II he was secretary for war and then (1940–45) foreign secretary. From 1951 to 1955 he was again foreign secretary, playing an important part in the 1954 *Geneva Conference and in the establishment of the *European Defense Community. He succeeded Churchill as prime minister and in 1956, following Nasser's nationalization of the *Suez Canal and an Israeli attack on Egypt, joined France in an offensive against Egypt. Egypt retained control of Suez and, despite Eden's claim that the Anglo-French initiative had ended the war between Egypt and Israel, he was greatly criticized and resigned shortly afterward. He became Earl of Avon in 1961.

Eden, Garden of In the Old Testament, the location of Paradise, in which Adam and Eve were created and lived until expelled because of disobedience (Genesis 2–3). Although the narrative may allude to a place in the fertile part of Mesopotamia, the geographical elements are probably mythological.

Edgar (c. 943–75) The first king of a united England (959–75). He allowed his Danish subjects to retain Danish laws. Edgar promoted a monastic revival and encouraged trade by reforming the currency. He improved defense by organizing coastal naval patrols and a system for manning warships.

Edgar (c. 1075–1107) King of the Scots (1097–1107); a vassal of William Rufus of England. In 1098 he lost the Hebrides to Norway.

Edgar the Aetheling (c. 1050–c. 1130) The grandson of Edmund II Ironside, his title Aetheling means royal prince. His claim to the English throne was rejected in 1066 owing to his minority and ill health. Although he initially submitted to William I, in 1068 and 1069 he led revolts against the king but came to terms with him in 1074.

Edgeworth, Maria (1767–1849) Anglo-Irish writer chiefly famous for her novels of Irish regional life, including *Castle Rackrent* (1800), *Patronage* (1814), and *Ormond* (1817), which influenced Sir Walter *Scott. She also wrote imaginative but moralizing children's stories.

Edinburgh 55 57N 3 13W The capital of Scotland, situated in the E center of the country on the S shore of the Firth of Forth. The financial, legal, and cultural center of Scotland, employment depends largely on service occupations. Food, drink, and printing are the primary manufacturing industries; the city's port is at Leith. Edinburgh is distinguished by its spacious layout and attractive buildings. In the old town, atop cliffs that rise above the city, stands the castle. The Royal Mile extends E from the castle rock to the Palace of Holyrood House (begun c. 1500). The other famous thoroughfare in the city is Princes Street, flanked by the picturesque Princes Street Gardens. The university (1583) is famous for its medical faculty among other notable faculties. The Royal Scottish Academy, the Royal Scottish Museum, and other national institutions are situated in Edinburgh. St Giles Cathedral dates from the 12th century. *History*: strategically important in medieval times in the wars between England and Scotland, Edinburgh emerged as the national capital in the 15th century. After James VI of Scotland (James I of England) moved his court to London in 1605 Edinburgh suffered a decline. It entered a golden age in the mid 18th century as a center of learning. The fame of the city as a cultural center was revived in 1947 with the foundation of the annual Edinburgh International Festival. Population (1991 est): 435,000.

Edirne (former name: Adrianople) 41 40N 26 34E A city in European Turkey, at the confluence of the Tunca and Maritsa Rivers. Round the main square are three mosques, one of which, the Selimiye Mosque, has 19 domes. Population (1970): 53,806.

Edison, Thomas Alva (1847–1931) US inventor, one of the most prolific of all time, eventually registering more than 1000 patents in his own name. Self-educated, Edison invented an automatic vote recorder at age 22. His improved stockticker, invented in 1871, earned him enough money to establish his own manufacturing plant in Newark, N.J. In 1876 he moved his laboratory to Menlo Park, N.J., where he developed some of his most important inventions. The most famous of these, the electric light bulb, took over a year to perfect, but he finally constructed a long-lasting filament bulb in 1879. He also constructed a complete system of electric power distribution for potential customers. Among the other inventions developed at the Menlo Park laboratory were an improved telephone transmitter and the phonograph. He also discovered thermionic emission, called the Edison effect, which later provided the scientific basis for the electron tube. In 1887, Edison moved his laboratory to West Orange, NJ., where he produced, among other inventions, the first motion picture camera, the mimeograph machine, the fluoroscope, and an improved electric battery. His Edison Electric Light Company, established in 1889, later became the General Electric Company.

Edmonton 53 34N 113 25W A city in W Canada, the capital of Alberta on the North Saskatchewan River. A 19th-century trading post, it became an agricultural settlement and grew into a city with the arrival of the railroad (1891). The discovery of oil (1947) stimulated an economy already prosperous from distribution, transportation, manufacturing, and agricultural industries. Edmonton is the site of the University of Alberta (1906) and numerous cultural institutions. Population (1991): 616,741.

Edmund I (921–46) King of England (939–46), who expelled the Norse king Olaf from Northumbria (944). He supported *Dunstan in the reintroduction of the monastic rule of St Benedict. An outlaw stabbed him to death at Pucklechurch.

Edmund II Ironside (c. 981–1016) The son of Ethelred II of England, his struggle with Canute for the vacant throne ended in Edmund's defeat at Ashingdon (1016). However, Canute agreed on the partition of England with Edmund, but after Edmund's sudden death Canute acquired the whole kingdom.

Edmund, St (Edmund Rich; c. 1175–1240) English churchman; Archbishop of Canterbury. After an academic life at Oxford and Paris he was made archbishop in 1234. Supported by the barons he successfully opposed Henry III's policies until his power was diminished by the arrival of the papal legate, Cardinal Otho, in 1237. Feast day: Nov 16.

Edo A people of S Nigeria living to the W of the Niger River. Their language belongs to the *Kwa subgroup of the Niger-Congo family. They live in villages and grow yams, corn, and the cash crops of rubber and cocoa. Their sacred king (or oba) formerly held political, economic, and ritual authority, but most Edo are now Christians or Muslims.

Edom The mountainous and barren land SW of the Dead Sea, which was traversed in antiquity by important caravan routes. The Edomites, according to the Old Testament, were descendants of Esau and may have been subjected by the Israelites under King David. They were converted to Judaism in the late 2nd century BC after being defeated by the *Maccabees. They later migrated to S Judea.

education The process of learning. Highly developed systems of learning emerged early in Asia, especially in China. Institutionalized education could also be found in various forms in ancient Greece and Rome, which later influenced the development of formal education in medieval Europe, although the latter owes a great debt to early Arabic and Hebrew scholarship. Medieval European monastic schools originally established for those intending to enter the monasteries gradually admitted other pupils and extended the curriculum to include grammar, logic, rhetoric, geometry, arithmetic, music, and astronomy. A basic education was also provided in some areas for the children of the poor, usually by the local parish priest. Humanist education based upon the classics emerged during the Renaissance; the Gymnasien, which was established at Strasbourg, provided the model for the academic schools of Protestant Europe, although its influence was slow in reaching England. European schools experienced a decline in standards during the 17th and 18th centuries. Widespread education could be said to stem from the introduction of compulsory attendance at primary schools (see primary education), first established successfully in Prussia in 1763. In the US education patterns originally followed European models. The country developed its own distinctive approaches to education in the 19th century under the impetus of innovators such as Horace Mann and as the college and university network grew. Today, education varies from state to state. Secondary education, however, is nonselective and provides both academic and vocational courses. Approximately 80% of children stay on beyond the compulsory school-attendance age of 16 and about 40% enter higher education. *See also* adult education; special education.

Education, Department of US cabinet-level executive branch department. It establishes policy for, administers, and coordinates most federal assistance to education. Headed by the secretary of education, the department was created in 1979; previously, it was part of the Department of *Health, Education, and Welfare.

Edward I (1239–1307) King of England (1272–1307), succeeding his father Henry III. He married (1254) *Eleanor of Castile. In the *Barons' War (1264–67) he defeated the barons at Evesham (1265). As king, he is noted for encouraging parliamentary institutions at the expense of feudalism and for subduing Wales, on which he imposed the English system of administration. He later tried to assert his authority over Scotland and died while on his way to fight Robert Bruce (*see* Robert I).

Edward II (1284–1327) King of England (1307–27), succeeding his father Edward I. He was born in Caernarvon and became the first English Prince of Wales (1301). He married *Isabella of France (1308). His reign was troubled by his extravagance, his military disasters in Scotland, notably at Bannockburn (1314), and the unpopularity of his favorites, Piers Gaveston (d. 1312) and Hugh le Despenser (1262–1326). Isabella and her lover, Roger de *Mortimer, murdered him.

Edward III (1312–77) King of England (1327–77), succeeding his father Edward II. He married (1328) Philippa of Hainault. Edward assumed effective power in 1330 after imprisoning his mother *Isabella of France and executing her lover Roger de *Mortimer. Thereafter his reign was dominated by military adventures, his victories in Scotland, especially at *Halidon Hill (1333), encouraging him to plan (1363) the union of England and Scotland. Through his mother he claimed the French throne, thus starting (1337) the *Hundred Years' War. His son *John of Gaunt dominated the government during his last years.

Edward IV (1442–83) King of England (1461–70, 1471–83) during the Wars of the *Roses. He married (1464) Elizabeth Woodville. The Yorkist leader, he was crowned after defeating the Lancastrians at Mortimer's Cross and Towton (1461). He was forced from the throne (1470) by the Earl of *Warwick but regained it after defeating the Lancastrians at *Tewkesbury (1471).

Edward V (1470–1483?) King of England (1483), succeeding his father Edward IV. His uncle, the Duke of Gloucester, imprisoned Edward and his brother Richard in the Tower of London, deposed Edward after a reign of only three months, and had himself crowned as Richard III. The two boys, known as the Princes in the Tower, were probably murdered in 1483.

Edward VI (1537–53) King of England (1547–53) and the son of Henry VIII, whom he succeeded, and Jane *Seymour. Effective power was held by the protector, the Duke of *Somerset, until 1550, when the Duke of *Northumberland seized power. Edward became a fervent Protestant and during his reign the *Reformation in England made substantial progress.

Edward VII (1841–1910) King of the United Kingdom (1901–10), succeeding his mother Queen Victoria. He married (1863) *Alexandra of Denmark. As Prince of Wales his indiscretions caused Victoria to exclude him from all affairs of state. A popular king, he ably represented Britain abroad.

Edward VIII (1894–1972) King of the United Kingdom (1936), succeeding his father George V. While both Prince of Wales and king, he expressed sympathy for victims of the Depression. He abdicated on Dec 11, 1936, because of objections to his liaison with the twice-divorced Mrs. Wallis Simpson (1896–1986), whom he married in France in 1937. He became Duke of Windsor and was appointed governor of the Bahamas during World War II. He subsequently lived in France, where he remained until his death.

Edward, Lake (name 1976–79: Lake Idi Amin Dada) 0 20S 29 35E A lake in Zaïre and Uganda. Its only outlet, the Semliki River, eventually flows into the Nile River. Area: about 820 sq mi (2124 sq km).

Edward, the Black Prince (1330–76) Prince of Wales and the eldest son of Edward III. His nickname is probably posthumous and may refer to the black armor he was said to have worn at Crécy (1346). He won victories against France in the *Hundred Years' War and ruled Aquitaine from 1360 until ousted (1371) by a revolt, during which he was responsible for the massacre of Limoges (1370).

Edwards, Jonathan (1703–58) US theologian and philosopher. As minister of the Congregational Church at Northampton, Mass. (1727–50), his strongly Calvinistic preaching led to the revival movement known as the *Great Awakening. Dismissed because of his overzealous orthodoxy, he continued to preach and in the year of his death became president of the College of Princeton, N.J. His best-known theological work, *Freedom of the Will* (1754), is a discussion of determinism.

Edward the Confessor (c. 1003–66) King of England (1042–66), nicknamed for his piety and his foundation of a new Westminster Abbey (consecrated 1065). He lived in Normandy (1016–41) and his early reign was dominated by rivalry between his Norman favorites and his father-in-law Earl *Godwin. After 1053 the Godwins were in the ascendant. Edward's childlessness led, ultimately, to the Norman conquest. He was canonized in 1161.

Edward the Elder (d. 924) King of England (899–924), succeeding his father Alfred the Great. He defeated the Danes (918), taking East Anglia, and also conquered Mercia (918) and Northumbria (920).

Edward the Martyr (c. 963–78) King of England (975–78), succeeding his father Edgar. He was murdered at Corfe Castle, reputedly by his stepmother, Elfthryth. He was canonized in 1001.

Edwin (c. 585–633) King of Northumbria (616–33), who became overlord of all English kingdoms S of the Humber, except for Kent. His marriage to Ethelburh, a Christian, led to his conversion and that of his people to Christianity (627). He was killed in battle against Penda of Mercia.

Edwy. *See* Eadwig.

EEC. *See* European Community.

eel A snakelike *bony fish of the worldwide order *Anguilliformes* (or *Apodes*; over 500 species) having, usually, a scaleless body, no pelvic fins, and long dorsal and anal fins continuous with the tail fin. Most species are marine, occurring mainly in shallow waters and feeding on other fish and invertebrates. The freshwater eels (family *Anguillidae*) migrate to the sea to breed—the *Sargasso Sea in the case of European and American species. The transparent, leaflike larvae (leptocephali) develop into young eels (elvers) and return to rivers and streams. ◻fish. *See also* electric eel.

eelgrass A perennial herbaceous marine plant of the genus *Zostera*, especially *Z. marina*, which grows in muddy, intertidal flats and estuaries on the coasts of Europe and North America and is one of the few flowering plants to tolerate sea water. It has creeping, underground stems (rhizomes), which help to stabilize mudbanks, and broad, dark-green, grasslike leaves. Family: *Zosteraceae*.

eelpout A thick-lipped, eel-like fish of the family *Zoarcidae* (about 60 species) that lives on the bottom in cold, oceanic waters and feeds on small fish and invertebrates. Up to 18 in (45 cm) long, eelpouts have small pelvic fins located near the gills. Many produce live young, for example the European *Zoarces viviparus*. Order: *Perciformes*.

eelworm A very small *nematode worm parasitic on plants, causing damage to agricultural crops. Adult eelworms measure up to 0.05 in (1.5 mm) long. The larvae, on hatching, penetrate plant roots, which may react by forming root galls around them. Chief genera: *Anguina, Ditylenchus, Heterodera*.

Efik A people of Calibar province in Nigeria. Their language, Efik-Ibibio, belongs to the *Kwa subgroup of the Niger-Congo family. Their territory became a major trading center, exporting slaves and, later, palm oil. Most Efik live in forest villages where they farm manioc and yams and there is still a flourishing network of markets. Political and economic power was vested in the Ekpe or Leopard Society, a graded secret society based upon propitiation of forest spirits.

EFTA. *See* European Free Trade Association.

Egbert (d. 839) King of Wessex (802–39), who laid the foundations for the supremacy of Wessex over a united England. He faced the first Danish raiders from 835.

Eger 47 53N 20 22E A city in NE Hungary. It was occupied by the Turks from 1596 to 1687 and has a minaret, 115 ft (35 m) high. Wine is produced in the surrounding area. Population (1980): 60,000.

Egeria A Roman goddess associated with fountains; she also presided over childbirth. According to legend she gave advice to Numa Pompilius (the successor of Romulus as king of Rome), who met her nightly at her sacred fountain near Rome.

egg (*or* ovum) The female reproductive cell (*see* gamete), which—when fertilized by a male gamete (sperm)—develops into a new individual of the same species. Animal eggs are surrounded by nutritive material (yolk) and—usually—one or more protective membranes, for example a jelly coat in amphibian eggs, the shell and other layers in birds' eggs. The amount of yolk varies, being greater in the eggs of egg-laying animals since the developing embryo depends on the yolk for nourishment: in mammals the egg is nourished from the maternal circulation and thus has little yolk. *See also* ovary.

eggplant. *See* aubergine.

eglantine. *See* sweet briar.

Egmont, Lamoraal, Graaf van (*or* Egmond; 1522–68) Flemish statesman and soldier, who opposed Philip II of Spain's religious policies in the Netherlands. After distinguished service in the victories against the French, he was appointed stadholder (chief magistrate) of Flanders. With William the Silent and other magnates Egmont left the state council in 1565 in protest against the continuing persecution of Protestants by Philip II. He subsequently pledged his loyalty to Philip, but was executed as a traitor by the Duke of *Alba in 1568. *See also* Revolt of the Netherlands.

Egmont, Mount 39 18S 174 05E A volcanic mountain in New Zealand, in W North Island. It forms an almost perfect cone and is encircled by a fertile ring plain. Height: 8260 ft (2478 m). *See also* Taranaki.

ego In *psychoanalysis, the part of the mind that is closely in touch with the demands of external reality and operates rationally. It includes some motives (such as hunger and ambition), the individual's learned responses, and his (or her) conscious thought. It has to reconcile the conflicting demands of the *id, the *superego, and the outside world.

egoism A philosophical theory of *ethics claiming that morality should be based on the self-interest of the individual. Egoism also claims that self-interest both explains and provides a motivating force for a general adherence to a set of moral principles. The argument is that a system of morality ensures a stable society and that an individual is better off in a stable society. Egoism is the opposite of altruism, which claims that morality has to be based on concern for the welfare of others. Altruists claim that while egoism may provide the motivation for others to obey moral rules, it does not provide such a motivation for the self. This can only arise from a concern for the welfare of others.

egret A white bird belonging to the *heron subfamily. The great white egret (*Egretta alba*) has long, silky, ornamental plumes in the breeding season that were formerly used for decorating hats. The smaller cattle egret (*Aroleola ibis*) is 20 in (50 cm) long and follows large grazing animals, feeding on insects disturbed by their hoofs.

Egypt, Arab Republic of (Arabic name: Misr) A country in NE Africa, extending into SW Asia. Most of the country consists of desert—the *Sinai Peninsula, the Eastern Desert (a vast upland area), and the Western Desert (an extensive low plateau), while most of the population is concentrated along the fertile Nile Valley. *Economy*: despite limited resources of water and cultivable land, the introduction of modern irrigation schemes, such as the *Aswan High Dam, has led to an increase in the production of cotton, the chief cash crop, as well as a more diversified agricultural sector (rice, millet, maize, sugar cane, and fruit and vegetables). Nevertheless Egypt is still far from being self-sufficient in food production. Restriction of land ownership under the Agrarian Reform Law (1952) led to increased private investment in industry but the considerable expansion of the industrial sector since the 1950s, especially heavy industries, such as iron and steel, chemicals, and electricity, has been mainly the result of government planning, utilizing aid from communist countries. More recently, however, there has been an increase in private industrial activity. Oil was discovered in 1909 and in recent years production has greatly increased. Natural gas is also being exploited and other minerals include phosphate, iron ore, and salt. Egypt's many historical and archeological remains make tourism an important source of revenue. The chief exports are cotton and cotton goods and oil. *History*: ancient Egyptian history is traditionally divided into 30 dynasties, beginning in about 3100 BC with the union of Upper and Lower Egypt by Menes and ending in 343 BC with the death of the last Egyptian king, or *pharaoh, Nectanebo II. The so-called Old Kingdom (3rd–6th dynasties; c. 2686–c. 2160) reached its peak in the reigns of Khufu and his son Khafre, which saw remarkable building achievements, notably the *pyramids at Giza. The 6th dynasty witnessed a decentralization of government and the consequent rise in power of provincial officials, which resulted in the disunity that characterized the First Intermediate Period (7th–11th dynasties; c. 2160–c. 2040). Egypt was reunited by Mentuhotep II (reigned c. 2060–2010), the founder of the Middle Kingdom (12th dynasty; c. 2040–c. 1786), of which the outstanding kings were Sesostris III and Amenemhet III. In the Second Intermediate Period (13th–17th dynasties; c. 1786–c. 1567) Egypt came largely under the control of the invading Asiatic tribes (the Hyksos), which were finally expelled by Ahmose I, founder of the New Kingdom (18th–20th dynasties; c. 1570–1085). During the New Kingdom Thutmose III extended Egypt's frontiers and acquired new territories in Asia and Amenhotep III sponsored buildings at *Karnak and *Luxor. His own son was the heretic king *Akhenaten, but orthodoxy was restored under *Tutankhamen. The reign of Ramses II was troubled by the *Hittites and that of Ramses III, by the Sea Peoples, and the 20th dynasty also saw the priests' power rise at the kings' expense. The outcome of Egypt's decline under the 21st–25th dynasties (1085–664) was the Assyrian invasion under Esarhaddon (671) and the 26th dynasty (664–525) was brought to an end by the Persian Acheamenians. Acheamenian rule was interrupted by the native 28th, 29th, and 30th dynasties (404–343) and was finally ended by Alexander the Great of Macedon, who obtained Egypt in 332.

On Alexander's death Egypt was acquired by the Macedonian Ptolemy I Soter. The Ptolemies ruled until the suicide of *Cleopatra VII in 30 BC, when Egypt passed under Roman rule. In 395 AD, Egypt became part of the Byzantine (Eastern Roman) Empire. The Arabs conquered Egypt in 642 and it was then governed by representatives of the caliphate of Baghdad, under whom Islam was introduced. After 868 it gained virtual autonomy under a series of ruling dynasties. The last of these, the Fatimids, were overthrown by *Saladin, who restored Egypt to the caliphate in 1171. It was ruled by the Mamelukes from 1250 until 1517, when it was conquered by the Ottoman Turks. The Turks governed Egypt through a viceroy but by the early 18th century power was largely in the hands of the Mameluke elite.

In 1798 Napoleon established a French protectorate over Egypt, which in 1801 was overthrown by the British and Ottomans. A mutiny among Albanian soldiers in the Ottoman army in Egypt brought Mehemet 'Ali to power as viceroy (1805) and in 1840 he was recognized by the Ottomans as hereditary ruler. British and French interests in Egypt intensified in the mid 19th century and in 1869 the opening of the Suez Canal enhanced Egypt's international significance. An Arab nationalist revolt was suppressed in 1882 by the British, who thereafter dominated Egyptian government, in spite of nominal Ottoman suzerainty. In 1914, on the outbreak of World War I, Egypt became a British protectorate until independence under King Fu'ad I was granted in 1922. In 1936 his son, Farouk, signed a treaty of alliance with Britain, which retained rights in the Suez Canal zone, and in World War II Egypt joined the Allies. The immediate postwar period saw the first Arab-Israeli War (1948–49) and a military coup (1952) that overthrew the monarchy (1953) and brought *Nasser to power (1954). Nasser's nationalization of the Suez Canal in 1956 precipitated an invasion by Israeli and Anglo-French forces, which were compelled by the UN to withdraw. Conflict with Israel erupted again in 1967, when in the third Arab-Israeli War (the Six Day War) Egypt lost territories that included the Sinai peninsula, partly regained in the fourth war (1973). In 1970 Nasser was succeeded by Anwar el-Sadat, who in 1972 ended Egypt's close relationship with the Soviet Union. In 1979, under US influence, Egypt and Israel signed a momentous peace treaty. Increasing opposition to Sadat's policies culminated in his assassination by Islamic extremists in 1981. He was succeeded as president by Hasni Mubarak. Under Mubarak, the staged transfer of Sinai territory from Israel to Egypt, in accordance with the 1979 peace treaty, was completed. But when Israel invaded Lebanon in 1982, Mubarak recalled his ambassador from Israel. Mubarak held a summit meeting with Israel's Prime Minister Peres in 1986. He was reelected in 1987. In 1990, when Iraq invaded Kuwait, Mubarak worked to mediate a peaceful settlement. When war was imminent in early 1991, he fully backed the US and sent troops to participate in the UN allied force that defeated Iraq in the Persian Gulf War. In late 1991, Mubarak was instrumental in arranging and mediating the Madrid Middle East peace conference. The growing militancy of Muslim fundamentalists was a great concern to the government during the early 1990s. Official language: Arabic. Official religion: Islam. Official currency: Egyptian pound of 100 piastres. Area: 386,198 sq mi (1,000,000 sq km). Population (1991 est): 54,500,000. Capital: Cairo. Main port: Alexandria.

Ehrenberg, Iliya Grigorievich (1891–1967) Soviet author. From 1908 to 1917 he lived in Paris, where he published some poetry; he returned to Russia in 1920 and immediately went back to Paris as a correspondent. He remained in W Europe until 1940. He was a mildly controversial figure under Stalinism but wrote virulent anti-Western propaganda. His novel *The Thaw* (1954) and his memoirs, *Men, Years, Life* (1960–64), were among the earliest open criticisms of Stalin.

Ehrlich, Paul (1854–1915) German bacteriologist. Ehrlich did much to develop the understanding of acquired immunity to disease in animals and, with *Behring, he prepared a serum against diphtheria. In 1910 he announced the discovery of an arsenical compound (Salvarsan) effective in treating syphilis. Ehrlich shared a Nobel Prize (1908) with *Metchnikov.

Eichendorff, Josef, Freiherr von (1788–1857) German Romantic writer. He studied at Heidelberg and Berlin, where he became involved in the Romantic movement, and rose high in the Prussian civil service. His lyrical nature poems were set by many composers. His best-known novel is *Memoirs of a Good-for-Nothing* (1826).

Eichler, August Wilhelm (1839–87) German botanist, who proposed the system on which modern plant classification is based. Eichler divided the plant kingdom into four divisions: Thallophyta (algae and fungi), Bryophyta (liverworts and mosses), Pteridophyta (ferns), and Spermatophyta (seed plants).

Eichmann, Adolf (1906–62) German Nazi politician, prominent in the extermination of Jews during World War II. After the war he went into hiding in Argentina; traced and captured by the Israelis in 1960, he was then tried and hanged for his war crimes.

eider A large sea *duck, *Somateria mollissima*, of far northern sea coasts. About 22 in (55 cm) long, males are mostly white with a black crown, belly, and tail; females are mottled dark brown. The soft, fluffy feathers plucked by the female from her breast to line her nest are the source of eiderdown.

Eiffel Tower A metal tower in □Paris, built for the 1889 Centennial Exposition. The most famous work of the French engineer Alexandre-Gustave Eiffel (1832–1923), the 984 ft (300 m) tower was the highest building in the world until 1930. Although an outstanding engineering achievement, it was originally much disliked, but has become one of the great Parisian landmarks.

Eiger 46 34N 8 01E A mountain in central S Switzerland, in the Bernese Oberland. Its N face, possibly the most difficult climb in the Alps, was not conquered until 1938. Height: 12,697 ft (3970 m).

Eightfold Path (*or* The Noble Eightfold Path) In Buddhism the fourth of the *Four Noble Truths, which summarizes the eight ways that lead the Buddhist to enlightenment. They are: right understanding, right resolve, right speech, right action, right livelihood, right effort, right mindfulness, and right meditation. The Path, which is not a series of successive steps, but an integrated spiritual attitude, was described in the Buddha's first discourse at Benares.

Eijkman, Christiaan (1858–1930) Dutch physician, who originated the concept of dietary deficiency disease. As a doctor in the East Indies, Eijkman noticed that chickens fed on polished rice developed symptoms resembling beriberi. By including rice hulls in their diet, the disease was cured—an effect he attributed to a dietary factor (later shown to be thiamine, or vitamin B_1). Eijkman received the 1929 Nobel Prize with Sir Frederick *Hopkins.

Eilat (Elat *or* Elath) 29 33N 34 57E A city in extreme S Israel, on the Gulf of Aqaba. Ancient Eilat declined in the 12th century and the modern city was founded in 1949 as Israel's only port S of the Suez Canal. There is also an oil-refining industry here. Population: 15,900.

Eindhoven 51 26N 5 30E A city in the S Netherlands, in North Brabant province. It is a manufacturing center specializing in electronics and producing light bulbs, radios, and televisions. Population (1991 est): 193,000.

Einhard (*or* Eginhard; c. 770–840) Frankish historian, a courtier of *Charlemagne. His *Vital Caroli magni*, based on intimate knowledge of the emperor's character and government, is one of the major medieval biographies and a probable source of the 12th-century poem *Chanson de Roland*.

EINSTEIN *A photograph taken in 1932.*

Einstein, Albert (1879–1955) German physicist. Born in Ulm, Einstein was an undistinguished scholar, being interested only in theoretical physics. In 1901 he obtained a post at the Patent Office in Berne, Switzerland, and became a Swiss citizen. While working there, he continued his research and in 1905 published four highly original papers. One gave a mathematical explanation of the *Brownian movement in molecular terms, the second explained the *photoelectric effect in terms of *photons, the third announced his special theory of *relativity, and the fourth related mass to energy. These papers were so revolutionary that their importance was not immediately recognized, and Einstein only secured a university post four years later. In 1915 he extended the theory of relativity to the general case, and, when its predictions had been verified in 1917, he became world-famous, receiving the 1921 Nobel Prize for Physics. In 1930, while Einstein was lecturing in California, Hitler came to power; being Jewish, Einstein decided to remain in the US. He spent the rest of his life at the Institute for Advanced Study in Princeton, unsuccessfully seeking a *unified field theory. He became a US citizen in 1940. Originally a pacifist, Einstein was persuaded in 1939 to write to President Roosevelt warning him that an atom bomb could now be made and that Germany might make one first. Although he took no part in its manufacture, he was an active postwar advocate of nuclear disarmament, aware that without his theory of relativity the nuclear age could not have dawned.

einsteinium (Es) An artificial transuranic element discovered by Ghiorso and others in 1952 in fall-out from the first large hydrogen-bomb explosion. It was named for Albert Einstein. Einsteinium behaves chemically as a trivalent actinide. Its 11 isotopes are all radioactive, the longest-lived having a half-life of 276 days. At no 99; at wt 254.

Einthoven, Willem (1860–1927) Dutch physiologist and pioneer of *electrocardiography. In 1903 Einthoven devised a sensitive galvanometer to detect the electrical rhythms of the heart. He developed his recording technique until he was able to correlate abnormalities in electrical activity with various heart disorders. He was awarded the 1924 Nobel Prize.

Éire. *See* Ireland, Republic of.

Eisenach 50 59N 10 21E A city and resort in south-central Germany, on the NW slopes of the Thuringian Forest. Among its many notable buildings is Wartburg Castle, where Martin Luther completed his translation of the Bible into German. It is the birthplace of J. S. Bach. Its manufactures include motor vehicles and chemicals. Population (1981): 50,700.

DWIGHT D. EISENHOWER *US president (1953–61) and Allied Commander in Europe during World War II.*

Eisenhower, Dwight David (1890–1969) US military leader and statesman; 34th President of the United States (1953–61). Born in Denison, Tex., Eisenhower graduated from West Point in 1915 and supervised the training of armored forces during World War I. In 1933, Eisenhower was named special assistant to Gen. Douglas *MacArthur and served as assistant military adviser in the Philippines (1935–39). After the outbreak of World War II, he was assigned to the office of chief of staff, where he headed the War Plans Division. In 1942 he was placed in command of US forces in Europe and led the Allied invasion of North Africa in the same year. Eisenhower became the supreme commander of the Allied Expeditionary Force in western Europe in 1944, and in that capacity he supervised the *D-Day invasion of Normandy. He was promoted to the rank of General of the Army in December, 1944. With the German surrender in 1945,

Eisenhower was named commander of the US occupation zone in Germany and he later succeeded General George C. *Marshall as US chief of staff. Eisenhower resigned from the army temporarily to become president of Columbia University (1948–51), but he returned to active duty to accept an appointment by President Truman as supreme commander of the Allied powers in Europe (1951–52).

In 1952, Eisenhower entered politics, gaining the Republican nomination for president and defeating Adlai *Stevenson, the Democratic candidate, in the general election. Eisenhower served two terms in the presidency, defeating Stevenson again in 1956. A popular president, "Ike" initiated important social welfare programs and used federal forces to enforce racial integration in the Little Rock, Ark, public schools. In foreign affairs, the Eisenhower administration, through Secretary of State John Foster *Dulles, pursued a policy of confrontation with the Soviet Union in Europe and direct involvement in the Middle East. During Eisenhower's administration, Alaska and Hawaii were admitted to the Union as the 49th and 50th states, and the American space program was established.

Eisenstein, Sergei (1898–1948) Russian film director. His films are characterized by their use of montage, an editing technique in which isolated images are used to emphasize intellectual points. His experimental theories, developed during his early work in the theater, brought him into frequent conflict with the Soviet authorities. His films include *Battleship Potemkin* (1925), *Alexander Nevsky* (1938), and *Ivan the Terrible* (1942–46).

eisteddfod A Welsh assembly in which bards and minstrels compete for prizes in literature, music, and drama. The main literary prizes are a carved oak chair for the best poem in strict Welsh meter and a silver crown for a poem in free meter. Originating in medieval times, the tradition declined after the 16th century but was revived as the chief national cultural festival during the 19th century.

Ekaterinburg. *See* Sverdlovsk.

Ekaterinodar. *See* Krasnodar.

Ekaterinoslav. *See* Dnepropetrovsk.

El Aaiún 27 00N 13 00W A city in West Africa, the chief city of Western Sahara. Phosphate deposits about 60 mi (100 km) to the SE are exported from here. Population (1982): 93,875.

El Alamein, Battle of. *See* World War II.

Elam An ancient country in SW Iran, roughly corresponding to the present-day province of Khuzistan. The Elamite language, related to no other known tongue, appears in pictographic inscriptions before 3000 BC. Elam's capital was *Susa and it was closely linked culturally and politically with *Sumer and *Babylonia (both of which it temporarily overran in the 2nd millennium BC), before absorption into the Persian *Achaemenian Empire (6th century BC). The Elamites were believed to be descended from Shem, the son of Noah, and were thus related to the Hebrews.

eland An antelope belonging to the genus *Taurotragus* (2 species), of African plains. Up to 71 in (180 cm) high at the shoulder, both sexes have horns. The common eland (*T. oryx*) is light brown with thin, vertical white stripes toward the shoulders. The Derby eland (*T. derbianus*) has a black neck with a white band at the base. Both species have a black-tufted tail and dewlap. Elands live in small herds and have been tamed and used as draft animals.

elasticity In physics, the ability of a body to return to its original shape after being deformed. The deforming force is known as a *stress, the resulting deformation is the *strain (*see* elastic modulus). A body is elastic only below a certain stress. Above this point, known as the *elastic limit*, the body is permanently deformed. A substance that is permanently deformed by any stress is said to be plastic. *See also* plasticity.

elastic modulus The ratio of the *stress on a body obeying *Hooke's law to the *strain produced. The strain may be a change in length (Young's Modulus) or a change in volume (bulk modulus).

elastomer A polymer with elastic properties, i.e. one that can be deformed and will revert to its original shape. *Rubber, a natural elastomer, still has many applications, especially for heavy-duty tires. However, synthetic elastomers of styrene-butadiene, polybutadiene, polyisoprene, *silicones, etc., are now far more widely used, not only in car tires, but also in belting for machines, sponge rubber, footwear, and many other products.

Elat (*or* Elath). *See* Eilat.

Elba An Italian island in the Tyrrhenian Sea. It became famous as the place of exile (1814–15) of Napoleon I of France, following his abdication. Area: 86 sq mi (223 sq km).

Elbe River (Czech name: Labe) A river in central Europe, flowing mainly NW from N Czech Republic, through Germany to the North Sea at Hamburg. It is connected by various canal systems to the Weser and Rhine Rivers as well as to the Oder River. Length: 724 mi (1165 km).

Elberfeld. *See* Wuppertal.

Elbert, Mount A mountain in Colorado. It is the highest peak in the *Rocky Mountains. Height: 14,431 ft (4399 m).

Elbląg (German name: Elbing) 54 10N 19 25E A port in N Poland, on the Elbląg River. Founded in the 13th century, it became a member of the Hanseatic League and an important port for trade with England. Its chief industries include engineering and ship building. Population (1992 est): 126,000.

Elbrus, Mount (*or* Mt Elbruz) 43 21N 42 29E A mountain in Georgia, the highest in the Caucasus Mountains. It is an extinct volcano, with two peaks only 101 ft (38 m) vertically apart, and is a tourist and climbing center. Height: 18,481 ft (5633 m).

Elburz Mountains A mountain range in central N Iran, extending 373 mi (600 km) in an arc parallel with the S shore of the Caspian Sea and rising to 18,386 ft (5604 m) at Mount Demavend.

Elche 38 16N 0 41W A city in SE Spain, in Valencia. Local archeological finds include a 5th-century Iberian statue, known as *La Dama de Elche*. It produces dates, pomegranates, and figs. Population (1991): 181,658.

El Cid (Rodrigo Diáz de Vivar; c. 1040–99) Spanish warrior, also known as el Campeador (the Champion), who was immortalized in the epic poem *Cantar del mio Cid*. A vassal of Alfonso VI of Castile, he was exiled by the king in 1079 and began a long career as a soldier of fortune, fighting for both Spaniard and Moor. Always loyal to his king, he was returned to favor and became protector and then ruler of Valencia.

elder A shrub or tree (up to 65 ft [20 m] tall) of the genus *Sambucus* (40 species), found in temperate and subtropical areas. The compound leaves have toothed leaflets and the tiny, cream-colored flowers, grouped into flat-topped clusters, can be used in tea or wine. The red or black berries, rich in vitamin C, are used in wine, jams, and jellies. The common European elder is *S. nigra*. Family: *Caprifoliaceae*.

Eldorado (Spanish: the golden one) An Indian ruler in Colombia who, according to legend, ritually coated himself in gold dust before bathing in a lake. The name was later applied to a region of fabulous wealth the existence of which this legend suggested. The conquest of South America in the 16th century was hastened by expeditions seeking Eldorado, notably those of Francisco *Pizarro (1539) and Jiménez de Quesada (1569–72).

Eleanor of Aquitaine (c. 1122–1204) The wife (1137–52) of Louis VII of France and, after the annulment of their marriage, the wife (1154–89) of Henry II of England. Henry imprisoned her (1174–89) for complicity in their sons' rebellion against him. After Henry's death she helped to secure their peaceful accession as Richard I (1189) and John (1199).

Eleanor of Castile (1246–90) The wife (from 1254) of Edward I of England. A devoted wife, she accompanied Edward on a Crusade (1270–73). He erected the **Eleanor Crosses** wherever her body rested on its way from Nottinghamshire, where she died, to her funeral in London.

Eleatics Greek speculative philosophers, active in the 5th century BC, whose leader was *Parmenides of Elea. Their central doctrine was that reality is timeless, motionless, changeless, and indivisible and that any belief to the contrary was illusion occasioned by the frailty of human senses. The early Pythagoreans (*see* Pythagoreanism) were their major opponents. *See also* Zeno of Elea.

Electoral College The method of election of the president, as provided in the US Constitution (Article II, section I). During a national election citizens vote for a slate of electors in each state that will vote for the president and vice president. The number of each state's electors equals the number of representatives and senators from that state. After a national election, the electors are obliged to vote for that candidate who won the plurality in the state. Discrepancies are settled in the House of Representatives.

electors (1257–1806) The German rulers who elected the Holy Roman Emperor. In 1338 the Archbishops of Mainz, Cologne, and Trier and the dynastic princes of the Palatinate, Saxony, and Brandenburg monopolized the right of election, which was confirmed in 1356. Other electors were the rulers of Bohemia (before 1400 and after 1708), Bavaria (after 1623), and Hanover (after 1708).

Electra In Greek legend, the daughter of Agamemnon and Clytemnestra. She helped her brother, Orestes, escape after the murder of Agamemnon and later helped him to kill Clytemnestra and her lover Aegisthus. She is the subject of plays by Aeschylus, Sophocles, and Euripides. Electra is also the name of one of the Pleiades, of a daughter of Oceanus, and of the mother of the Harpies.

Electra complex. *See* Oedipus complex.

electrical engineering The branch of engineering concerned with the generation, transmission, distribution, and use of electricity. Its two main branches are power engineering and *electronics (including telecommunications) although the latter is now often regarded as a separate discipline. Electrical engineering emerged in the late 19th century with the mathematical formulation of the basic laws of electricity by James Clerk *Maxwell, followed by the development of such practical applications as the Bell telephone, Edison's incandescent lamp, and the first central generating plants. Electrical power engineers design generators, *power stations, and *electricity supply systems as well as *electric motors and transport and traction systems. Electronics engineers are concerned with all forms of electronic communications and *computers. Electrical engineering is an applied science involving advanced mathematical skills and a profound knowledge of physics, in addition to the basic engineering subjects.

electric-arc furnace A type of furnace used in making high-grade *steels, usually from scrap steel, in which the heat source is an electric arc. Electric furnaces provide clean working conditions and accurate temperature control. They avoid the contamination that occurs when fuel is burned in the furnace. Arc furnaces are gradually replacing the *open-hearth process.

electric automobile An automobile driven by one or more electric motors, which are powered by batteries. Because of diminishing oil reserves and the pollution problems associated with the *internal-combusion engine, the search for an effective electric car has been intensified in recent years. Electric cars are not new; the *Columbia* electric car was in use in the US around 1900, and electric delivery vans have been widely used in the UK for short journeys in towns since the 1930s. The basic problem is that some seven tons of conventional lead batteries are required to provide an energy store equivalent to five gallons of gasoline. Even allowing that electric motors are several times more efficient than gasoline engines, no electric car has yet been produced to compete with a conventional car. Two lines of research are being pursued: improving batteries and making workable *fuel cells. Several experimental commuter cars using special lead batteries have been produced, with top speeds around 50 mph (80 km per hour) and a range of 30–50 mi (48–80 km). The hybrid electric car carries its own gasoline-engine-driven charging generator for use outside towns.

electric charge A property of certain elementary particles (*see* particle physics) that causes them to undergo *electromagnetic interactions. The magnitude of the charge is always the same and is equal to 1.6021×10^{-19} coulombs (although quarks, if they exist, would have a fractional charge). Charge is of two kinds, arbitrarily called positive and negative. Like charges repel each other and unlike charges attract each other. The force between them can be regarded as being generated by an exchange of virtual photons between the two particles (*see* virtual particles). On a large scale, charge is always due to an excess or deficiency of *electrons compared to the number of protons in the nuclei of a substance.

electric constant (ϵ_0) A constant that appears in *Coulomb's law when expressed in SI units. Its value is 8.854×10^{-12} farad per meter. It is also known as the absolute *permittivity of free space. *Compare* magnetic constant.

electric eel An eel-like, freshwater fish, *Electrophorus electricus*, that occurs in NE South America. Up to 10 ft (3 m) long, it swims by undulating its long anal fin and has *electric organs—modified muscle tissue—in the tail, which produce electric shocks capable of killing fish and other prey and of stunning a man. Family: *Electrophoridae*; order: *Cypriniformes*.

electric field The pattern of the lines of force that surround an electric charge. The field strength at any point is inversely proportional to the square of the distance of that point from the charge (*see* Coulomb's law). Any other charge placed in this field experiences a force proportional to the field strength and to the magnitude of the introduced charge. The force is attractive if the charges are opposite and repulsive if they are alike.

electric generator A device for converting mechanical energy into electricity, usually by *electromagnetic induction. A simple electromagnetic generator, or dynamo, consists of a conducting coil rotated in a magnetic field. Current induced in this coil is fed to an external circuit by slip rings in an alternating-current generator or by a commutator, which rectifies the current, in a direct-current generator.

Most of the electricity from *power stations is produced by generators as three-phase alternating current, i.e. there are three windings on each generator, which can have an output of hundreds of megawatts, producing three separate output voltages. For transmission there are three live conductor wires with a common neutral wire. This three-phase system optimizes generator design and minimizes transmission losses, if the three loads are balanced. Generally, all three phases are supplied to large factories, but the supply is split to single phase for homes, shops, and offices.

Small generators driven by Diesel engines are used for emergency supplies in factories, hospitals, etc. From the 1970s interest has grown in generators using renewable energy sources, such as hydroelectricity and solar, wave, and wind power (*see* alternative energy).

electricity The phenomena that arise as a result of *electric charge. Electricity has two forms: *static electricity, which depends on stationary charges, and current electricity, which consists of a flow of charges, specifically *electrons.

Static electricity, in the form of an attractive force between rubbed amber and pieces of straw, etc., was known to the ancient Greeks but the word electricity was coined in the 16th century by William *Gilbert (from the Greek *elektron*, amber). The distinction between positive and negative electricity was made at the beginning of the 18th century, but did not acquire a theoretical basis until the discovery of the electron in 1897 by J. J. Thomson.

Current electricity was first demonstrated by *Volta in 1800 and investigated by *Ampère during the next 25 years. *Oersted's discovery (1820) that a magnetic needle was deflected by an electric current inspired *Faraday to a deep investigation of the relationship between electricity and magnetism, which led him to the discovery of *electromagnetic induction, the *electric generator, and the *electric motor. The theory of electromagnetism was elucidated by Clerk *Maxwell in the mid 1850s.

The use of electricity as a source of energy, available in homes and factories for heating, lighting, and motive power, is essentially a characteristic of the 20th century. Our dependence upon it is now taken so much for granted that life seems almost unimaginable without it.

electricity supply The system that generates (*see* power station), transmits, and distributes the electric power in an industrialized society. Power stations are interconnected by transmission lines to form a grid. Grid-control centers continuously monitor the load from factories, offices, homes, etc., and match it with the best combination of available generating capacity, maintaining the supply at a constant voltage and frequency. Base-load stations run continuously. These are usually the larger or cheaper-to-run stations. Less economic or smaller stations that are easier to start up and shut down are brought in to supply the peak demand. The grid voltage is reduced at substations for area distribution and further reduced at local substations to the US domestic supply voltage of 110 volts.

electric motor A device that converts electrical energy into mechanical energy usually for driving machinery. Electric motors, which are clean, quiet, and efficient (75–95%), range from tiny models in instrument-control systems using less than a watt to those using several megawatts to drive large pumps.

Electric motors depend on the principle that a current-carrying conductor in a magnetic field experiences a force and that when two electromagnets are placed close together the two magnetic fields force them apart. The simplest type of motor uses this principle to turn a single coil of wire (the armature or rotor) between the poles of a permanent magnet. Practical motors use a stationary winding (stator) in place of a permanent magnet. Most motors work on an alternating-current (ac) supply. In the induction motor, current is fed to the stator, which induces a current in the rotor; interaction between the magnetic field of the stator and the induced rotor current causes the rotor to rotate. In the synchronous ac motor, current is also fed to the rotor (through slip rings) and the rate of rotation

ELECTRICITY

There are two main methods of making electrons flow to generate a current.

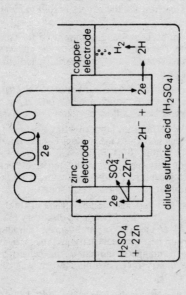

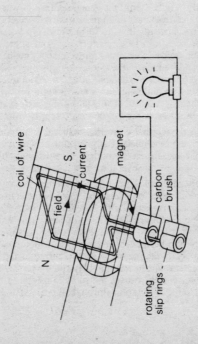

One method is to subject them to a changing magnetic field—this is the principle of the dynamo. If a coil of wire is rotated between the poles of a magnet, the electrons are forced round the coil. This is the power-station method; coal or oil is burned to raise steam to drive a turbine, which rotates the coils.

The other way is to make use of a chemical reaction in an electric cell to dissociate the electrons from their atoms and molecules. The separated charges then flow in opposite directions as a result of the forces between them. This is how a battery works. The sulfuric acid dissolves the zinc electrode producing 2 electrons, a sulfate ion (SO_4^{2-}), 2 zinc ions (Zn^+), and 2 hydrogen ions (H^-).

ELECTRICITY

Modern life depends on electricity in so many ways, yet it is not known exactly what it is.

carbon atom

Atoms consist of electrons, protons, and neutrons. the electrons cluster round the central nucleus of protons and neutrons.

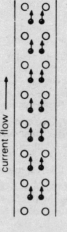

−ve electron   +ve proton

Electrons have a negative electric charge—protons are positively charged. The charges are equal but opposite.

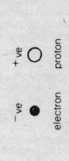

Similar charges repel each other, oppostie charges attract each other. These are the forces harnessed to make electricity.

helium atom

An electrical current consists of a flow of electrons in one direction. But in many atoms, such as helium, they are tightly bound to the nucleus. To flow as a current electrons have to be free.

In a metal wire some of the electrons are free to move about between the metal ions (atoms that have lost an electron). Normally they move about at random and no current flows.

current flow

When the majority of electrons flow in one direction this is an electric current. 1 ampere is equivalent to a flow of 10^{18} electrons per second.

is proportional to the supply frequency. In direct-current (dc) motors, current is also fed to both rotor and stator with the two either in series (series wound) or in parallel (shunt wound). In a dc motor, current is fed to the rotor through a commutator. *See also* linear motor.

electric organ In zoology, a group of modified muscle cells in certain fish that are capable of generating electric shocks. These can be used to stun prey, as in the *electric eel and *electric ray. Other species, such as the elephant-snout fishes, generate an electric field for the detection of objects (including prey and predators) and for navigation in dark or cloudy waters.

electric ray A fish, also called torpedo ray, numbfish, or crampfish, belonging to a family (*Torpedinidae*) found mainly in shallow waters of warm and temperate regions. 12–80 in (30–200 cm) long, rays have *electric organs—modified muscle tissue—on each side of the disklike head to produce electric shocks used in defense and food capture. Order: *Batoidea* (*see* ray).

electrocardiography Examination of the electrical activity of the heart. Impulses generated by the contraction of the heart muscle are transmitted through electrodes attached to the skin to a recording apparatus (electrocardiograph). The recording itself, called an electrocardiogram (ECG), indicates the rhythm of the heart and aids in the diagnosis of heart disease, which may produce characteristic changes in heart rhythm.

electroconvulsive therapy (ECT) A treatment for mental disorders in which an electric current is passed through the brain in order to cause a convulsion. The convulsion is greatly reduced by giving an anesthetic and drugs to relax the muscles. ECT is used as a treatment for severe cases of endogenous *depression.

electroencephalography The measurement of the electrical activity of the brain and the recording of the brain waves in the form of a tracing—an electroencephalogram (EEG). Brain waves were first recorded from electrodes on the scalp by Hans Berger (1873–1941) in 1926. Electroencephalography is now used widely to diagnose diseases of the brain and to study brain function. The frequency of the electrical waves and the way they change with stimuli are related to alertness, responsiveness, and expectation.

electroforming A method of manufacturing metallic articles. A metal-coated plastic mold is used as the cathode in *electrolysis and the metal is deposited onto the mold. The method is used for making thin, intricately shaped articles.

electroluminescence. *See* luminescence.

electrolysis The chemical decomposition of a substance by passing an electric current through it. If a voltage is applied across two electrodes placed in a liquid (electrolyte) containing ions, the positive ions will drift toward the negative electrode (cathode), and the negative ions toward the positive electrode (anode). At the electrodes, the ions may give up their charge and form molecules; for example, hydrogen gas is released at the cathode when water is electrolyzed. Alternatively, the atoms of the electrode may ionize and pass into solution. Electrolysis is used to electroplate metals and in the manufacture of a number of chemicals, such as sodium and chlorine. It is also a way of separating *isotopes. Deuterium (D *or* ^{2}H), for example, is slower than ordinary hydrogen (^{1}H) to pick up electrons at the cathode, and so electrolyzed water gradually becomes enriched with heavy water (D_2O).

electromagnet. *See* magnets.

electromagnetic field A concept describing electric and magnetic forces that, like gravitational forces, act without physical contact (action at a distance). Although both electricity and magnetism have been observed separately for thousands of years, it was not until the 19th century that their interaction was investigated experimentally by Oersted, Faraday, and others. Faraday explained the electromagnetic interaction in terms of magnetic lines of force, forming a field of force, which is distorted by the presence of a current-carrying conductor or by another magnet. James Clerk *Maxwell developed the mathematical theory that electricity and magnetism are different manifestations of the same phenomenon (the electromagnetic field), magnetism being the result of relative motion of *electric fields.

electromagnetic induction The production of voltage in an electrical conductor when it is in a changing magnetic field or if it moves in relation to a steady magnetic field. The direction of the induced *electromotive force opposes the change or motion causing it. Since a current-carrying conductor itself induces a magnetic field, if the current changes, **self-inductance** occurs, opposing the current change. **Mutual inductance** occurs between two adjacent conductors that carry changing currents.

electromagnetic interaction An interaction that occurs between those elementary particles that possess an electric charge. The interaction can be visualized as the exchange of virtual photons (*see* virtual particles) between the interacting particles. The electromagnetic interaction is 200 times weaker than the *strong interaction but 10^{10} times stronger than the *weak interaction. *See also* particle physics.

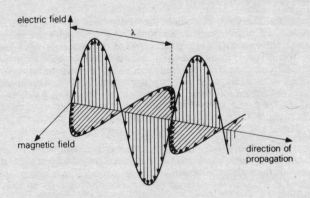

electric field

λ

magnetic field

direction of propagation

ELECTROMAGNETIC RADIATION

electromagnetic radiation Transverse waves consisting of electric and magnetic fields vibrating perpendicularly to each other and to the direction of propagation. In free space the waves are propagated at a velocity of 2.9979×10^{8} meters per second, known as the velocity of light (symbol: c). Their *wavelengths, λ, and *frequency, f, are related by the equation $\lambda f = c$. Those with the highest frequencies are known as *gamma radiation; then in descending order of frequency the **electromagnetic spectrum** includes X-rays, *ultraviolet radiation, visible *light, *infrared radiation, *microwaves, and *radio waves. Electromagnetic radiation exhibits typical wave properties, such as *refraction, *diffraction, *interference, and polarization. However, it can also be regarded as a stream of massless elementary particles called *photons. This dual nature of radiation is analogous to the dual nature of massive elementary particles and *de Broglie waves.

electromagnetic units (emu) A *c.g.s. system of electrical units based on the unit magnet pole, which repels a similar pole one centimeter away with a force of one dyne. Electromagnetic units have the prefix ab- attached to the practical unit (e.g., abvolt).

electromotive force (emf) The electrical potential difference or voltage between two points in an electric circuit. It causes the movement of charge that constitutes an electric current, providing a limited analogy to mechanical force and motion.

electron A stable, negatively charged, elementary particle with mass 9.109,56 $\times$ 10^{-31} kilogram and spin $\frac{1}{2}$. Electrons are responsible for almost all commonly observed electrical and magnetic effects and, since they orbit the nucleus in atoms, are also responsible for most chemical processes. A **free electron** is one that has become detached from an atom. An electric current passing through a metal or low-pressure gas consists of a flow of free electrons; a current of 1 ampere is equivalent to a flow of 6×10^{18} electrons per second.

electron diffraction The *diffraction of a beam of electrons as it passes through spaces, the widths of which are comparable to the wavelength of the electrons. Electrons can be diffracted, for example, by the spacing between particles in a crystal lattice, an effect governed by *Bragg's law. Electron diffraction demonstrates the wave aspect of electrons (see de Broglie wave) since diffraction is specifically a wave effect. The effect is used to investigate the structure of surfaces, films, etc.

electronics The study of devices that control and utilize the movement of *electrons and other charged particles. Originating with the invention of thermionic valves and their use in radios and record players, it expanded rapidly during World War II to include radar, missile guidance systems, and the first electronic *computers. The replacement of bulky *thermionic valves by *semiconductor components, such as *transistors, made possible high-speed digital computers and the miniaturized communications and control systems used in spacecraft. The *integrated circuit was a further step toward more compact and reliable equipment. The latest development is the use of computers to produce tiny wafers of silicon functioning as microprocessors.

The social impact of electronics has been immense, with the development of television, communications satellites, the computerization of office and factory systems, and the widespread use of pocket calculators. The emergence of microprocessors is expected to have even greater impact in replacing human labor by automation.

electron microscope A type of microscope in which a beam of electrons is focused by means of magnetic and electrostatic lenses onto a specimen and scattered by it to produce an image. The *de Broglie wavelength of high-energy electrons is very much less than that of light. Therefore, both the *resolving power and the magnification of an electron microscope are much greater than can be obtained with an optical microscope. Typically an electron microscope can resolve two points, 10^{-9} meter apart, and produce magnifications of up to a million. In the **transmission electron microscope** only very thin specimens can be used: the image appears two-dimensional but a high resolution can be obtained. In the **scanning electron microscope** the specimen, which can be of any thickness, is scanned by the beam producing an apparently three-dimensional image but with lower resolution.

electron probe microanalysis A method of analyzing a very small quantity (10^{-16} kg) of a substance by bombarding it with a fine electron beam (about

1 micrometer in diameter) and examining the X-ray spectrum produced for characteristic lines of the elements. The method can also be used quantitatively.

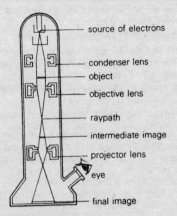

source of electrons

condenser lens
object
objective lens

raypath

intermediate image

projector lens

eye

final image

ELECTRON MICROSCOPE *The beam of electrons in the transmission electron microscope is focused in a similar way to light in an ordinary microscope.*

electron spin resonance The resonance of an unpaired electron in a paramagnetic substance when placed in a magnetic field and exposed to microwaves. Since the electron is unpaired it acts as a small magnet and may either align itself with the field or oppose it. If the energy of the microwave *photons is equal to the energy difference between the two states then the electron resonates. The effect is used to study chemical bonding and structure. *See also* nuclear magnetic resonance.

electronvolt (eV) A unit of energy, widely used in nuclear physics, equal to the increase in the energy of an electron when it passes through a rise in potential of one volt. 1 eV = 1.6×10^{-19} joule.

electroplating The process of depositing a layer of one metal on another by making the object to be plated the cathode in an electrolytic bath (*see* electrolysis). Metals used for electroplating include silver (*see* silverplate), gold, chromium, cadmium, copper, zinc, and nickel; they usually form the anode in the bath. The form of the plated layer varies depending on the composition and temperature of the electrolyte, the use of addition agents, and the current density. Some metals do not adhere well to others; for example, chromium does not adhere to steel and it is usual to plate the steel with copper and then nickel before plating with chromium.

electroscope An electrostatic instrument that detects electric charge or radiation. In a gold-leaf electroscope, the deflection of two suspended gold leaves increases with charge. The quartz-fiber electroscope (QFE), which has a quartz fiber instead of gold leaves, is commonly used to detect radiation. The presence of a radioactive source ionizes the air and causes charge to leak away from the initially charged fiber.

electrostatic generators Machines that use mechanical or other energy to separate electric charge, creating an electric potential. They are used to create strong electrostatic fields, particularly in high energy nuclear physics for acclerating charged particles to bombard atomic nuclei. *See also* Van de Graaff generator.

electrostatics. *See* static electricity.

electrostatic separation The use of a strong electric field to separate substances with different electrical properties. The method is used, for example, in separating out iron ores from a mixture of minerals, and to clean air in chimneys by precipitating charged smoke particles.

electrostatic unit (e.s.u.) A *c.g.s. system of electrical units based on the unit of electrical charge, defined as the charge that repels a similar charge one centimeter away with a force of one dyne. Electrostatic units have the prefix stat- attached to the practical unit (e.g. the unit of charged defined above is the statcoulomb).

elementary particles. *See* particle physics.

elements Substances that cannot be broken down into simpler fragments by chemical means. A sample of an element contains atoms that are chemically virtually identical, since they have the same *atomic number and thus the same number of electrons around the nucleus. Samples of a given element may consist of a mixture of *isotopes. Over 100 elements are known, of which about 90 occur naturally, the rest having been synthesized in nuclear reactions. Elements are often classified as *metals, *metalloids, or nonmetals. *See also* periodic table.

elephant A mammal of the order *Proboscidea*: the African elephant (*Loxodonta africana*) or the Indian elephant (*Elephas maximus*). (The extinct *mammoths also belonged to this order.) Elephants have a tough, brownish-gray skin and a muscular, prehensile proboscis (trunk)—an extension of the nose and upper lip used to convey food (leaves, branches, and other vegetation) and water to the mouth. The upper incisor teeth are continually-growing ivory tusks, for which these animals were formerly extensively hunted. Elephants live in herds; they have a gestation period of 21–22 months and a lifespan of 60–70 years.

The African elephant is the largest land mammal, standing 10–13 ft (3–4 m) high at the shoulder and weighing 5–7.5 tons. The smaller Indian elephant—intelligent and readily trained—is used for transport and heavy work in India, Myanmar, Thailand, and Malaysia.

elephant birds. *See* Aepyornis.

elephant grass A stout, coarse *reedmace, *Typha elephanta*, commonly found in marshes and wet habitats from S Europe to the East Indies. It has long, tapering leaves, which have been used to make baskets. The name is sometimes also applied to the tropical napier grass (*Pennisetum purpureum*), which resembles sugar cane.

elephantiasis A condition caused by chronic infection with certain nematode worms, called *filariae. It is, therefore, a form of filariasis. The worms block the lymphatic channels and cause gross swelling of the legs and scrotum (or vulva). Elephantiasis occurs only in the tropics.

elephant seal A large seal belonging to the genus *Mirounga* (2 species). The male Antarctic elephant seal (*M. leonina*) grows to over 20 ft (6 m); females are about half that size. The slightly smaller northern elephant seal (*M. angustirostris*) lives off the W coast of North America. Elephant seals feed on fish, crustaceans, octopus, and squid. Family: *Phocidae*.

elephant's ear. *See* taro.

Eleusinian mysteries An esoteric religious cult (*see* mysteries) in ancient Greece, with its center at Eleusis. It originated before 600 BC in an agrarian fertility cult, and the main deities worshiped were *Demeter and *Persephone. The myth of Persephone's abduction to the underworld and return was interpreted not only in terms of the dormant seed and the springing corn but also as a symbol of death and resurrection and was probably re-enacted in a darkened room to which only initiates were admitted.

African elephant

Indian elephant

ELEPHANT *The African elephant can be distinguished from the smaller Indian species by its larger ears, flatter forehead, smooth skin, and concave back.*

Elgar, Sir Edward (1857–1934) British composer. He was taught largely by his father, the organist at a Roman Catholic church in Worcester. A professional violinist, Elgar became involved as a conductor with the Three Choirs Festival, where many of his important choral works received their first performance. He also wrote two symphonies and concertos for violin and cello; at the end of his life he wrote three important chamber-music works. His most famous works are the *Dream of Gerontius* (for soloists, chorus, and orchestra; 1900), the *Enigma*

Variations (for orchestra; 1899), and the *Pomp and Circumstance* marches (1901–30).

Elgin Marbles Ancient Greek marble sculptures from the *Parthenon, sold to the British Museum in 1816 by Lord Elgin. He had acquired them from the Turks occupying Athens, who were using the Parthenon for target practice.

Elgon, Mount 1 07N 34 35E An extinct volcano in E Africa, on the Uganda–Kenya border. Its crater is about 5 mi (8 km) in diameter and coffee and bananas are grown on the lower slopes. Height: 14,178 ft (4321 m).

El Greco (Domenikos Theotokopoulos; 1541–1614) Painter of Greek parentage, born in Crete, who worked mainly in Spain. He trained in Venice under Titian in the 1560s and greatly admired the work of Michelangelo, which he saw during a visit to Rome just before he moved to Spain (1577), where he sought the patronage of Philip II. El Greco submitted his *Martyrdom of St Maurice* (1580–82; El Escorial) to Philip but the king rejected it; El Greco then moved to Toledo, where he spent most of the remainder of his life, becoming friendly with leading churchmen and scholars. His early Spanish works, such as the *Assumption of the Virgin* (1527; Chicago), were Venetian in inspiration, but his later paintings of saints and his masterpiece, *The Burial of Count Orgaz* (1586–88; Santo Tomé), are characterized by strident colors and dramatically elongated figures. He also painted three stormy landscapes and a number of portraits.

Elijah An Old Testament prophet, who appears to have lived in the 9th century BC. He attacked the cult of Baal among the Israelites (1 Kings 18) and successfully maintained the monotheistic worship of Jehovah. He was considered the greatest of the Hebrew prophets. He was taken into heaven without dying (2 Kings 2.1–18), and it was believed that he would return before the final restoration of Israel to the people.

Eliot, Charles W(illiam) (1834–1926) US scientist, educator, reformer, and editor. Educated at Harvard University, he taught chemistry at Massachusetts Institute of Technology (MIT) before returning to Harvard to serve as its president in 1869. While there he was instrumental in the rapid growth and raised standards enjoyed by the university. He was also responsible for reshaping US secondary education, believing in adapting schooling to each individual. When he retired in 1909, he started editing the Harvard Classics.

Eliot, George (Mary Ann Evans; 1819–80) British woman novelist. She was influenced by evangelical Christianity as a girl, but rejected her early religious fervor in 1842. She went to London in 1851, worked on the *Westminster Review*, and lived with the journalist George Henry Lewes, who was married but separated from his wife. After publishing stories based on her childhood she wrote the novels *Adam Bede* (1859), *The Mill on the Floss* (1860), and *Silas Marner* (1861). The pioneering and infuential novel *Middlemarch* (1871–72) is a deep and comprehensive depiction of English provincial society. *Daniel Deronda* (1876) contrasts a Jewish family's genuine values with the false ones of society. Lewes died in 1878, and she married a banker, J. W. Cross, six months before her death.

Eliot, T(homas) S(tearns) (1888–1965) British-American poet, critic, and playwright. Eliot was educated at Harvard and traveled extensively in Europe, where he became a close acquaintance of Ezra *Pound. Settling in London, he worked briefly as a bank clerk before the publication of his first volume of poetry, *Prufrock and Other Observations*, in 1917. Although *The Waste Land* (1922) is his best-known work, *Four Quartets* (1935–41) is considered to be his most important poetic achievement. In 1927, Eliot became a British subject and converted to Anglo-Catholicism. From 1922 to 1939 he edited *The Criterion* and became recognized as an influential literary critic. His verse dramas include

Murder in the Cathedral (1935), *The Cocktail Party* (1949), and *The Elder Statesman* (1958). Eliot was awarded the Nobel Prize in literature in 1948.

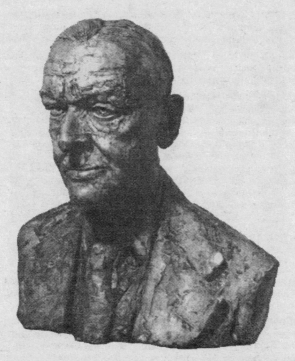

T. S. ELIOT *A bronze bust by British sculptor Jacob Epstein.*

Elizabeth 40 40N 74 13W A city and port in the E US, in New Jersey on Newark Bay. Part of the New York conurbation, its industries include sewing machines, aircraft, and chemicals. Population (1990): 110,002.

Elizabeth (1709–62) Empress of Russia (1741–62); the daughter of Peter the Great. Elizabeth came to power in a coup, which ousted the infant Ivan VI (1740–64). She depended on her advisers, such as *Bestuzhev-Riumin, in government and her reign witnessed no reforms and few territorial acquisitions.

Elizabeth I (1533–1603) Queen of England and Ireland (1558–1603), daughter of Henry VIII and Anne *Boleyn. Her mother's execution and Elizabeth's imprisonment by Mary I made her cautious and suspicious, but her devotion to England made her one of its greatest monarchs. Her religious compromise (1559–63) established Protestantism in England (*see* Reformation). Several plots to place her Roman Catholic cousin, *Mary, Queen of Scots, on the throne led to Mary's execution (1587). England won a great naval victory in 1588 by destroying the Spanish *Armada. Elizabeth never married and was called the Virgin Queen, although her relationships with, among others, the Earl of Leicester and the 2nd Earl of Essex caused considerable speculation.

Elizabeth II (1926–   ) Queen of the United Kingdom (1952–   ), noted for her scrupulous fulfillment of the roles of constitutional monarch and head of the

Commonwealth. She married Prince *Philip in 1947; their four children are Prince *Charles, Princess *Anne, Prince Andrew, and Prince Edward.

ELIZABETH II *The Queen's Silver Jubilee (1977) not only enhanced the prestige of the Crown, but boosted the morale of the country.*

Elizabeth the Queen Mother (1900–) The wife of George VI of the United Kingdom. Formerly Lady Elizabeth Bowes-Lyon, she married in 1923 and had two children, *Elizabeth II and Princess *Margaret.

Elizabethville. *See* Lubumbashi.

elk The largest deer, *Alces alces,* found in forests of N Eurasia and also in N North America. Up to 7 ft (2 m) high at the shoulder, elks have a broad, curved muzzle and a short neck with a heavy dewlap. The coat is gray-brown and males grow antlers spanning up to 71 in (180 cm). They feed on leaves and water plants and form herds in winter. □mammal.

elkhound An ancient breed of working dog originating in Norway and used for tracking and hunting game animals, especially elk. It has a short compact body with the tail curled over the back and a broad head with pricked ears. The thick coat is gray tipped with black. Height: 20.4 in (51 cm) (dogs); 19.3 in (49 cm) (bitches).

Elkins v. United States (1960) US Supreme Court ruling that banned the use of illegally obtained evidence in federal cases.

Ellesmere Island A Canadian Arctic island W of Greenland, the northernmost part of North America. Mostly rugged plateau with large glaciers, it shelters a few weather stations, police posts, and the remnants of Eskimo settlements. Area: 82,119 sq mi (212,688 sq km).

Ellice Islands. *See* Tuvalu.

Ellington, Duke (Edward Kennedy E.; 1899–1974) US jazz composer, band leader, and pianist. After leading bands in Washington, D.C., Ellington went to New York, where he established a group of musicians that remained the core of his band for 30 years. The worldwide success of "Mood Indigo" in 1930 led to European tours and annual concerts in Carnegie Hall. Ellington concentrated on composing large-scale works for jazz orchestra, writing the suite *Black, Brown, and Beige* in 1943 and the "religious jazz" work *In the Beginning God* in 1966.